Odhams Knitting Encyclopaedia

ODHAMS BOOKS

Published by

The Hamlyn Publishing Group Limited
London · New York · Sydney · Toronto
Hamlyn House, Feltham, Middlesex, England
© The Hamlyn Publishing Group Limited 1968
3rd Impression 1973
ISBN 0 600 72123 X
Printed in Hong Kong

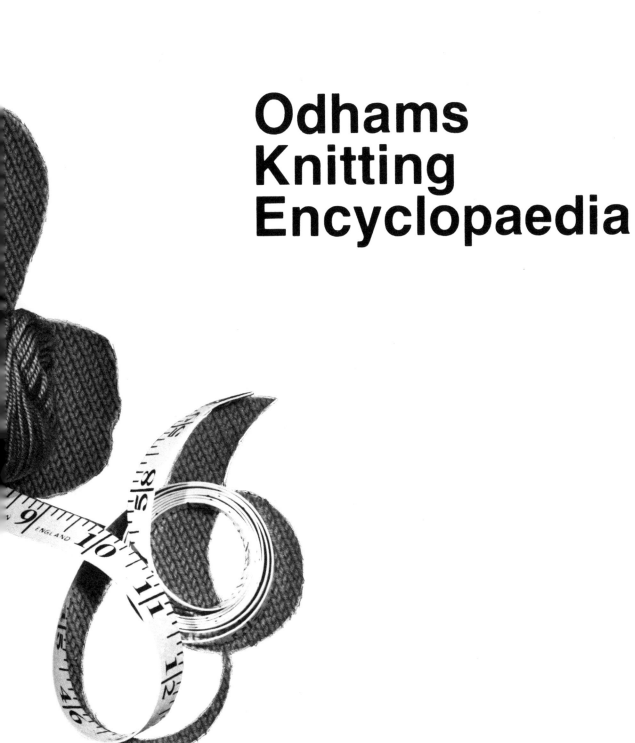

Odhams
Knitting
Encyclopaedia

Introduction

KNITTING is perhaps the most popular of all the creative crafts, for it is easy to learn and needs a minimum of equipment. With mastery of the two basic stitches – knit and purl – a pair of needles and a ball of wool, even a beginner can make simple articles. As skill increases, so does the desire to learn more complicated stitches and produce unusual patterns and individual colour schemes.

This book is planned for *every* knitter – for the beginners and those who teach them, for the experienced knitters who want to experiment with lace or traditional patterns and for the more ambitious who want to design their own garments.

The first section contains, in alphabetical order, full instructions and diagrams for all knitting stitches as well as methods of following instructions, charts for designers and fascinating historical details.

Do you know how to knit a cable or a beaded fabric . . . follow a chart . . . pick up a dropped stitch . . . make exquisite lace borders? The A-Z section explains everything you need to know clearly and concisely.

The second half of the book contains instructions for 50 designs, all beautifully illustrated. These are patterns which you will want to knit again and again. They range from simple bazaar items, toys and dolls' clothes, and classic designs for all the family, to the intricacies of Shetland lace, Aran sweaters and colour-knitting from many countries.

Knitting is a happy craft – we hope this book will increase your enjoyment and your knowledge.

Andrée Mayfield

Contents

part one

THE A B C OF KNITTING
an easy-to-follow guide to stitches, designs etc.

part two

SUPPLEMENT OF GARMENTS TO MAKE

Pullover with coloured borders and girl's cardigan —instructions—pages **124** and **188** respectively

part one
THE A B C OF KNITTING

a

ABBREVIATIONS

Abbreviations are used in knitting patterns to save space and printing costs and to make the instructions easier to follow. It is important to read through the list of abbreviations before beginning to knit a pattern; although they are more or less standardized, some publishers occasionally use different initials to describe the same processes. If the list of abbreviations includes a stitch or means of working which is unfamiliar, it is advisable to try this out on some spare wool before starting to knit the garment.

These are the standard abbreviations in use in British knitting patterns:

ABBREVIATIONS USED IN KNITTING

Alt. = Alternative.
Beg. = Beginning.
B. = Back (as in *C.B.*, *K.B.* — see below).
B. = Bobble (as in *Bobble Stitch*).
(—) = Brackets, the instructions written in the brackets are repeated the numbers of times stated immediately after the brackets, e.g., (k.1, p.1) twice = k.1, p.1, k.1, p.1.
C. = Cable.
C.B. = Cable Back.
C.F. = Cable Front.
Cr.B. = Cross Back.
Cr. F. = Cross Front.
D.C. = Double Crochet.
Dec. = Decrease or decreasing.
K.B. = Knit into back of stitch.
G.St. = Garter Stitch.
Inc. = Increase or increasing.

Incl. = Inclusive.
In. Ins. = Inch, inches.
K. = Knit.
M.1 = Make 1 (see *Increase*).
M.B. = Make bobble.
Over = Wool over needle.
P. = Purl.
Patt. = Pattern.
P.B. = Purl into Back of Stitch.
P.S.S.O. = Pass Slip Stitch Over.
Rep. = Repeat.
Sl. = Slip.
St. Sts. = Stitch, stitches.
T.B.L. = Through back loop.
Tog. = Together.
Tw. = Twist.
W.B. = Wool Back. Where this term occurs in knitting it means taking the wool to the back of the work and keeping it at the back while working the next stitch.
W.Ft. = Wool Front. Where this term occurs in knitting it means bringing the wool to the front of the work and keeping it at the front while working the next stitch.
W.F. or Wl.Fd. = Wool Forward.
W.O.N. = Wool On Needle.
W.R.N. = Wool Round Needle.
Y. = Yarn.

ACCESSORIES

These are simple and inexpensive but it is always advisable to buy the best quality tools available. These should include:

  Pairs of knitting needles, pointed at one end, in sizes 6 to 14.
  Sets of four needles, pointed at both ends, in sizes 9 to 16.
  A needle holder (see page 64).
  A new tape measure (old ones tend to stretch and deform the measurements given).
  A small pair of sharp scissors.
  Large safety pins or stitch holders.
  A cable needle.
  A tapestry needle for sewing up garments.
  A box of pins.
  A white cloth to wrap the knitting in.
  A knitting bag for keeping all these accessories together.

ACRILAN

An acrylic fibre (see *Synthetics,* page 89).

ANGORA

Angora wool is now understood to mean yarn spun from the hair of the Angora rabbit, the finest quality being spun in France. Originally, however, Angora wool was spun from the hair of the Angora goat (commonly known as the Mohair Goat) and was exported from Angora, now Ankara.

Angora yarns are very delicate and are best spun with wool or nylon to increase durability and also to reduce their tendency to fluff up and shed irritating hairs. Because of these traits, Angora yarn is not suitable for baby garments and can constitute a danger if the baby swallows the loose hairs. The tendency to shed loose hairs may be lessened if the Angora garment is stored overnight in a domestic refrigerator.

ARABIC KNITTING

Sandal-socks are one of the earliest forms of knitting to have been recorded and nomadic desert tribes were knitting them two or three centuries B.C. These were knitted in the round, possibly on a circular frame on the same principal as bobbin knitting today. The frame would have been a simple circle with pins inserted round the edge. A series of loops would have been made on the pins, and by winding a length of wool round the outside of the pins and drawing loops of the length of wool a circular piece of knitted fabric would be produced. The shaping of the heel and the divided toe section of these socks was a complex and perfect piece of craftsmanship, suggesting that this was the final phase of a long evolution in knitting (1).

A parallel development with the sandal-sock was Arabic colour knitting and this has played an important part in the development of the craft through the centuries The only fragment of Arabic knitting in existence is in

Sandal socks, one of the earliest forms of knitting done by nomadic desert tribes

the collection of Dr. Fritz Ikle. This fabric was discovered at Fostat, an ancient city on the site of Cairo and is dated between the seventh and ninth centuries A.D. It is an extremely elaborately patterned fabric worked on a tension of thirty-six stitches to the inch and undoubtedly inspired the exquisite Spanish and Florentine knitted silks of the twelfth and fourteenth centuries. This example points to the two-needle technique with which we are familiar today, so that it can be presumed that the Arabs used both frame knitting and needle knitting for many centuries.

ARAN KNITTING

The knitters of Aran, off the west coast of Ireland, are world famous for their sweaters knitted in coarse hand spun wool. The designs, being built up from cables, twists and bobbles, achieve the appearance of a heavily embossed piece of fabric. The garments are extremely intricate as the designs, which change on the front and back, are created by the knitters as they work.

The basic pattern is usually built up from a centre panel with two side panels, the division between the panels being emphasized by cable patterns.

It has never been discovered from where the people of Aran derived their knitting. Its general appearance suggests that it has come from Austrian or German sources but the patterns themselves are unique to this small island and have never been found in any other part of the world.

Here is a typical stitch from Aran (2).
See *Abbreviations,* page 9.
Cast on 29 sts.

1st row: K.5, p.7, k.2, make bobble as follows—(p.1, k.1, p.1, k.1, p.1) all into next st., turn, k.5, turn, p.5, sl. 2nd, 3rd, 4th and 5th sts. over 1st st., thus making one st. again—k.2, p.7, k.5.

2nd row: P.5, k.7, p.2, p.b.1, p.2, k.7, p.5.

3rd row: K.5, p.6, cr.1b. as follows—sl. next st. on cable needle and leave at back of work, k. following 2 sts., then p. st. on cable needle—k.b.1, cr.2f. as follows—sl. next 2 sts. onto cable needle and leave at front of work, p. the following st., then k.2 sts. on cable needle—p.6, k.5.

4th row: P.5, k.6, p.2, k.1, p.b.1, k.1, p.2, k.6, p.5.

5th row: K.5, p.5, cr.1b. as follows—slip next st. on to cable needle and leave at back of work, k. the following 2 sts., then k.b.1 into st. on cable needle—p.1, k.b.1, p.1, cr.2f. as follows—sl. next 2 sts. on to cable needle and leave at front of work, k.b.1 in following st., k. across 2 sts. on cable needle—p.5, k.5.

6th row: P.5, k.5, p.2, (p.b.1, k.1) twice, p.b.1, p.2, k.5, p.5.

7th row: K.2, m.b., k.2, p.4, cr.1b. as on 3rd row (k.b.1, p.1) twice, k.b.1, cr.2f. as on 3rd row, p.4, k.2, m.b., k.2.

8th row: P.5, k.4, p.2, (k.1, p.b.1) 3 times, k.1, p.2, k.4, p.5.

9th row: K.1, (m.b., k.1) twice, p.3, cr.1b. as on 5th row, (p.1, k.b.1) 3 times, p.1, cr.2f. as on 5th row, p.3, k.1 (m.b., k.1) twice.

10th row: P.5, k.3, p.2, (p.b.1, k.1) 4 times, p.b.1, p.2, k.3, p.5.

11th row: K.5, p.2, cr.1b. as on 3rd row, (k.b.1, p.1) 4 times, k.b.1, cr.2f as on 3rd row, p.2, k.5.

12th row: P.5, k.2, p.2, (k.1, p.b.1) 5 times, k.1, p.2, k.2, p.5.

These 12 rows form the pattern.

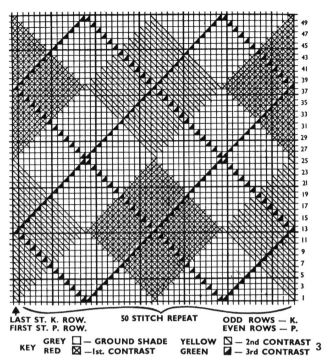

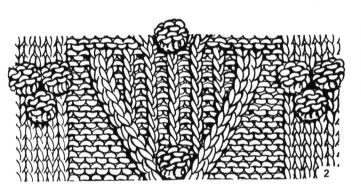

ARGYLL KNITTING

An Argyll pattern is always knitted in stocking-stitch with a multi-coloured plaid design. Starting with a neutral ground, solid diamonds of colour are knitted which are also traversed with a fine over-check in a second or third contrasting colour. The pattern is most commonly used on men's socks and occasionally on pullovers; the backgrounds are natural or grey with dark red or green diamonds, and white or dark blue as additional colours.

The pattern is derived from the Campbell tartan; the Earls and Dukes of Argyll being descended from the Campbells of Lochow.

The chart shows a typical Argyll Pattern (3).

ASTRAKHAN WOOL

This is wool spun with large loops to give the appearance of Astrakhan fur when knitted. It is suitable only for knitting in stocking-stitch, using a similar tension as for double knitting wools, but should be bordered with ordinary yarn or bound with ribbon to keep its shape.

b

BABY KNITTING

(See *Layettes,* page 60).

BABY WOOLS AND YARNS

Knitted garments for babies are usually made in the finer plys—3-ply and 4-ply—as these are soft and light for the baby to wear. Quick Knitting Baby Wool or Baby Quick Knit designates a knitting yarn which is between 4-ply and Double Knitting in weight and only patterns specifying this yarn should be used. Double Knitting Baby Wool is available for pram sets and covers and blankets. Baby wool is specially spun from the best quality Merino wool and it is not intended for garments receiving hard wear from older children, but it is very suitable for adults' bedjackets and vests. Baby Yarns in synthetics are particularly suitable for garments which need frequent washing.

BAININ WOOL

Bainin (pronounced *Bawneen*) comes from Ireland and is spun from the fleece of Irish sheep. It is of Double Knitting thickness and traditionally is used in its natural colour, which contains oils, for fishermen's and shepherds' sweaters using the old Aran and Irish patterns. The wool is scoured free of oils to be dyed for use in fashion knitting and is much used for Aran sweaters.

BALACLAVA

This close-fitting helmet with ribbed polo-neck is now popular winter wear for all sports and for school-children. The helmet derives its name from the famous Battle of Balaclava (October 25th, 1854) during the Crimean War, when it was adopted by British soldiers who suffered greatly from the icy Crimean winter, as it covers the ears and the surrounding knitted bands keep out bitter winds. Victorian ladies knitted these as comforts for the troops.

BANDS

These are knitted separately to border the neck, front, sleeves and lower edge of jumpers and cardigans and are sometimes called "strappings". These are usually knitted in k.1, p.1 rib, but can be in double rib, moss stitch, garter stitch or double stocking-stitch, and should be made on needles one size smaller than those used for the main parts of the garments; they should be slightly stretched to fit. Front bands of cardigans are often backed with petersham ribbon to keep their shape.

BEAD KNITTING

This is a decorative type of knitting in which small beads are worked in patterns on the reverse side of stocking stitch. The simplest method is to work the pattern from a chart, counting the number of beads required and threading this number on to the yarn before commencing the knitting itself. Naturally if it is a large pattern a simpler method is to thread sufficient beads on to the yarn for one row of knitting, then thread a sufficient number of beads for the next row and so on, joining in the new yarn containing the beads for the particular row at the beginning of each row. Although this type of work is not much used today it does lend itself to trimming the yokes of evening jumpers and can prove a very effective form of decoration on a garment.

For this kind of knitting work as follows:

Purl 1 stitch in the ordinary way, draw up a bead and, leaving it at the front (purl side) of the work, purl the

4

following stitch, draw up a second bead and purl the next stitch. Continue all across the row to obtain a solid row of beads across front of fabric. (4).

When a pattern is desired the work is done from a chart, the beads being brought forward to the front of the work according to the design on the chart itself.

The second and every alternate rows in bead knitting are knitted.

The chart shows a simple motif which could be used effectively in bead knitting; it is worked on 14 sts. (5).

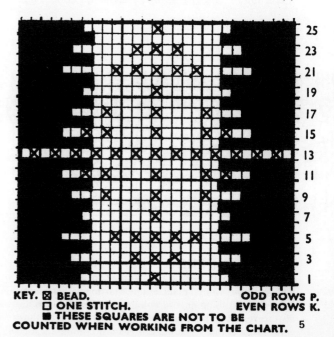

KEY. ⊠ BEAD. ODD ROWS P.
□ ONE STITCH. EVEN ROWS K.
■ THESE SQUARES ARE NOT TO BE
COUNTED WHEN WORKING FROM THE CHART. 5

BEGINNERS' KNITTING

The four basic steps to learn in knitting are:—Casting On, forming a Knit stitch, forming a Purl stitch and Casting Off. Once these actions have been mastered it will be possible to knit any pattern with practice by following the instructions carefully. Instructions for these four steps in learning to knit are given on pages 24 (Casting On), page 55 (Knit Stitch), page 68 (Purl Stitch) and page 24 (Casting Off). Where possible it is best to learn basic knitting from watching a good knitter who can demonstrate the simple actions required. Practise on large needles—at least size 8—with Double Knitting in a contrasting colour so that the stitches show up well against the needles.

Straight pieces of garter stitch (each row Knit) can be used for practice and made up into blankets later; many beginners like to use soft Dishcloth Cotton for making useful kitchen cloths. Next comes mastery of stocking-stitch, which is one row Knit, one row Purl; it is essential to produce a smooth fabric with even stitches. Again, these squares can be used to make blankets and car-rugs. Later, ribbing and moss stitch can be practised as well as the shaping of stocking stitch in decreasing and increasing.

BERETS

The beret takes its name from the Basque country where it was first knitted. Originally it was knitted much larger than its final size when completed, thoroughly soaked in water, pummelled with heavy stones while still wet (for felting purposes) and finally shaped on a wooden block ready for wear. You will notice that on a genuine beret today there is a little end of wool on the centre top. This is where the beret has been completed, as they are always knitted in rounds on four needles, the end at the centre marks the final cast-off and finish of the beret itself.

The principle of knitting a beret is to cast on the number of stitches required for it to fit comfortably yet firmly round the head. To do this, measure round the head carefully with a tape measure. Next test out the tension of the yarn being used on the needles selected. Once the number of stitches to the inch has been established, multiply this number by the measurement round the head, thus arriving at the total number of stitches required for the commencement of the beret.

Here is an example for a beret for an average head, made with wool that knits up at a tension of 8 sts. to the in. The head measurement is 21 ins. Multiply the 21 by 8, obtaining 168 sts.

At this point a minor adjustment may be needed, as the beret is decreased either by a circular graded decrease or in sectional decreases; therefore a number of stitches easily divisible into 6 or 8 sections is necessary. In the case of the number 168 we get eight 21-stitch sections.

In order to obtain a firm fitting to the band of the beret it is advisable to use a set of needles one or two sizes finer than those on which the major part of the beret is knitted.

Cast on 168 sts. on to three needles, i.e. 56 on each needle, using the Through the Stitch Method to give the looped edge cast-on.

Work ¾ in. on these needles and then knit up a hem to

form the head band by knitting together 1 st. from the needle and 1 loop from the cast-on edge all round the 3 needles.

Next work increases evenly round this band. A close fitting beret will only need one inc. to every 3 sts.

The fuller type, resembling a Tam O'Shanter, will require one inc. in every 2 sts. The inc. are worked on the "m.1" principle and it is advisable to work the inc. row while still using the finer needles.

Now change to the larger needles and work 2 inc. in rounds.

The crown shaping may be done by the circular (concentric) or sectional (octagonal) dec. method, according to the type of beret being designed. The diagrams show the shape of the crown with the decreases clearly marked.

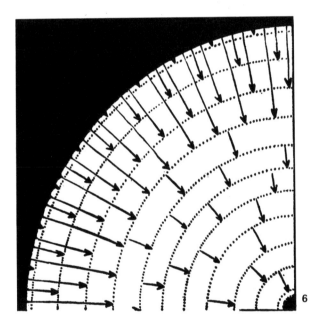

Concentric Design. The diagram (6), which covers 252 sts. in the round (thus working on the basis of the "1 in 2" inc. already referred to) shows the dec. arranged in concentric circles with 5 plain rounds between, these give a perfectly flat circular medallion forming the crown of the beret itself.

In the first dec. a 6 st. unit controls the dec. thus giving 42 dec. in all. Therefore a k.4, k.2 tog., in the dec. round.

In the next dec. a 5 st. unit is used, k.3, k.2 tog., being worked all round, thus working off 42 sts. in each dec. round.

Then work a dec. on a 4 st. unit, followed by a dec. on a

3 st. unit, thus bringing the sts. down to 84.

Now move to a series of concentric decreases worked on a 6 st. unit, thus gradually moving down until you have reached the centre of the circle with only 14 sts. remaining in the round.

The wool is broken off and threaded through these stitches, which are drawn up tightly, and then neatly finished off to hold the centre firm, giving the end of wool mentioned as being typical of a properly designed beret.

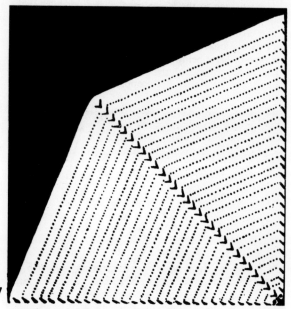

7

Octagonal Decrease. The alternative shape for the crown is worked on an octagonal decrease, the stitches being worked off on every alternate row (7).

For this type of crown commence with 248 sts. in the round, thus giving 8 sections of 31 sts. The 31 st. section forms the unit in the octagonal shape, the dec. being graded on every alt. round as follows:—

1st round: K.29, k.2 tog.; rep. all round.
2nd round: K.
3rd round: K.28, k.2 tog.; rep. all round.
4th round: K.
5th round: K.27, k.2 tog.; rep. all round.
6th round: K.

Continue decreasing on this octagonal dec. principle until only 8 sts. remain.

Break off wool, thread it through the 8 sts. and finish off as on the medallion shaped crown.

FAIR ISLE BERET

In this type of beret, the concentric method of decrease is used in conjunction with the octagonal method.

BLANKETS

Blankets (or afghans, as they are called in the States) are an excellent way of using up odd ounces of wool, and a variety of square motifs in different colours and different stitches can be joined to make a most attractive patchwork rug. Pram and cot blankets are best knitted in pastel shades, often using two or three different stitches in one colour or the same stitch in varying colours. Before starting to knit up a garment a small square should always be test-knitted so that the knitter's tension can be checked with that required by the instructions; these squares can be seamed or crocheted together to make a blanket.

BLOCKING GARMENTS

This simple operation consists firstly of pinning out the various pieces of a garment to their correct shape and size with the wrong side uppermost, ready for pressing lightly, before sewing up the seams.

First of all, place a pin in the edge of the garment at its widest point (generally this is at the beginning of the armhole), now place a tape measure across the garment and pin the piece of fabric out at this point to the exact measurement required (8).

When making up a 34 in. jumper and the front or back is being blocked it will be pinned out to a fraction over 17 ins. at this point.

Next measure the length from the armhole to the top of the ribbing and pin down again at each side (9). On a standard classic shape, the width here generally averages 3 to 4 ins. narrower than the armhole width.

Now pin out the exact length from the armhole to the shoulder, remembering again that the width across the garment at shoulder level is approximately 4 ins. narrower than at widest point (10).

The basic shape is now pinned out, and the piece of fabric is ready to block. The blocking process is done by placing pins along the edges of the fabric approximately ½ in. apart. The pins are placed all round the shaped piece and along the top edge of the ribbing (11).

It is important to remember that you *do not block the ribbing*. Where there is a neckband on a garment in ribbing, the pins blocking the shape are placed round the edge of the neckband, although in most cases it is simpler to block and press the pieces before actually knitting up the neckband. When the pieces are blocked out, press the fabric very lightly on the wrong side, using a warm iron and damp cloth. This is danger point No. 2, for if you press too heavily you may ruin the appearance of the right side of the fabric. It is essential to have a thick felt under the ironing sheet, the springiness of this type of material assists in preserving the natural texture of hand-knitting.

One of the advantages of this method of blocking the pieces before making them up into a garment is, that if

14

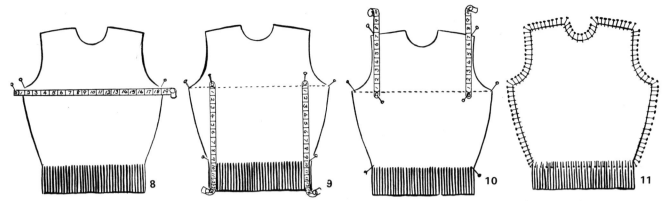

Diagrams show how to pin out the pieces of a garment before pressing and sewing seams

they are slightly on the large side you can ease them down to the correct size, or, vice versa, if they are slightly on the small side you can stretch them a little to give the correct measurements in the finished pieces.

Colour Knitting. The same principles of blocking are applied to Fair Isle and colour knitting. The pressing, however, is different, as here a hot iron and wet cloth are used, the fabric being actually steamed, thus producing a very even texture on the right side of the fabric. When Fair Isle or colour knitting is blocked there may be a slight unevenness on the front of the fabric before it is blocked, but most of this will disappear if pressed in the manner described.

Fabrics. *Angora* fabric is blocked with the right side facing. It is not actually pressed, but steamed by holding the wet cloth, which is ironed, ¾ in. above the fabric itself.

Cottons and Silks must be treated extremely carefully during the pressing, as it is easy to form a gloss on the surface of these fabrics by using an iron that is too hot or pressing on too heavily with the iron. The cloth should be slightly wetter for cottons and silks than for wool.

The following table gives a very clear picture of how to press or block pieces of fabric.

ANGORA. Hot iron and wet cloth, steam ¾ in.–1 in. above surface of fabric.

COTTON AND SILKS. Hot iron and wet cloth, press lightly, rewetting the cloth when necessary if it dries out under the iron at any point.

FAIR ISLE FABRICS AND COLOURED FABRICS. Hot iron and wet cloth, press firmly and evenly.

RIBBED AND CABLE FABRICS. Warm iron and damp cloth. Press *very* lightly.

SIMPLE WOOL FABRICS. Warm iron and damp cloth.

Garter Stitch. A point to remember about a garment in garter stitch is that a slight stretch lengthwise in blocking (allowing for this stretch when measuring the pieces as you knit them) will prevent "dropping" in wear.

Ribbing. If a garment contains fancy rib fabric as the main part of the design, or cable fabrics worked into the design, these should only be touched slightly with the iron, over a damp cloth, as the flattening down of this type of knitting ruins the garment.

Note. For all the above types of blocking use a warm iron and damp cloth.

Garter stitch and ribbed fabrics can be pressed *very lightly,* although if the ribbing is really neat and even, it is wiser not to touch it with a warm iron at all.

BLOCK PATTERNS

Simple checks can be made by casting on multiples of 6, 8 or 10 stitches and, if a multiple of 10 is used, working in blocks of 5 knit and 5 purl for 5 rows then reversing the blocks so that the purl block falls over the knit block and the knit block over the purl block for the same number of rows.

Here are typical examples of simple check patterns:

BASKET CHECK, MULTIPLE OF EIGHT
Cast on a multiple of 8 sts.
1st to 4th rows: * P.4, k.4; rep. from * to end.
5th to 8th rows: * K.4, p.4; rep. from * to end.
These 8 rows form the pattern (12).

BASKET CHECK, FANCY
Cast on a multiple of 8 sts.
1st to 4th rows: * P.4, k.4; rep. from * to end.
5th and 6th rows: * K.4, p.4; rep. from * to end.
7th and 8th rows: * P.4, k.4; rep. from * to end.
9th and 10th rows: As 5th and 6th rows.
These 10 rows form the patt. (13).

ELONGATED AND DICE CHECK
For elongated or fancy checks the number of rows on the blocks in the check are varied. Here is a simple

example of this—

Cast on a multiple of 4 sts.

1st to 4th rows: * P.2, k.2; rep. from * to end.
5th and 6th rows: * K.2, p.2; rep. from * to end.
7th and 8th rows: * P.2, k.2; rep. from * to end.
9th and 10th rows: As 5th and 6th rows.
These 10 rows form the patt. (14).

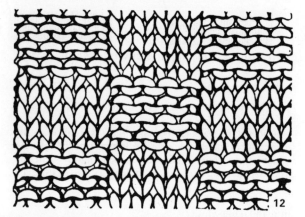

Examples of simple check patterns, multiple of eight Basket Check (12), Fancy Basket Check (13) and Elongated and Dice Check (14)

BOBBIN KNITTING

Most of us did frame knitting as children. We called it bobbin work or corkwork. The method used is to fix 4 short nails at equal distances round the hole in an ordinary cotton reel, make 4 loops (one on each nail) and then proceed to produce a circular knitted cord by winding the wool round the outside of these 4 nails and drawing the loops over the wool, repeating this action until a piece of cord the length required has been produced.

16

BOBBLE STITCH

A bobble consists of a piece of reverse stocking stitch created by stitches being increased out of one stitch of the original fabric, a small piece of fabric being knitted on these stitches and then the stitches being all drawn over the first stitch, thus creating the bobble as it appears on the front of the work. The size of the bobble is determined by the number of stitches made out of the one stitch and the number of rows worked on these stitches. For a small bobble 3 sts. are made from the one; for a medium bobble 4 sts. out of one; and for a large bobble 5 sts. out of one. The number of rows worked on these stitches is always the same, whatever the size of bobble.

The first example is a small bobble built on the "3 sts. out of one" principle.

To make this simple bobble proceed as follows:

K. into the front, back and front of the next stitch on the needle (15).

Turn the work round and k. across the 3 sts. made out of the one stitch, turn the work again and p. across the 3 sts. (16), turn the work again and k. across the sts. once, thus working 3 rows of reverse stocking stitch on the 3 sts.; turn the work again.

Now insert the point of the right-hand needle in the second st. from the point of the left-hand needle, drawing this st. over the first st. (17). Insert the point of the right-hand needle into the next st. on the left-hand needle (the second st. from the point again), and draw this over the first st.

Slip the first st. on the left-hand needle (the one over which the other 2 sts. have been drawn) on to the right-hand needle (18) and continue in stocking stitch working the bobbles as specified in the pattern.

The principle of the medium size "4 st." bobble is to make 4 sts. out of the one by knitting into the front and back of one st. twice.

Work 3 rows of reverse stocking stitch, as above, then slip 3 sts. over the first stitch in place of the 2 sts.

For the large "5 sts." bobble make 5 sts. out of the one stitch by knitting into the front and back of one st. twice, then knitting into the front of it again.

Work 3 rows in reverse stocking stitch, as above, then slip 4 sts. in place of 2 over the first st.

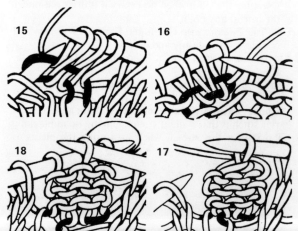

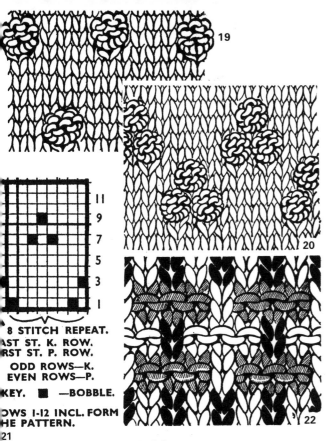

19

20

21

22

8 STITCH REPEAT.
AST ST. K. ROW.
RST ST. P. ROW.
ODD ROWS—K.
EVEN ROWS—P.
KEY. ■ —BOBBLE.
OWS 1-12 INCL. FORM
HE PATTERN.

BOBBLE FABRICS

Bobbles can be built up as simple all-over seedings or into geometrical shapes on a stocking stitch ground. They can also be used with a lacy stitch or combined with cable patterns, for sports wear and traditional Tyrolean and Aran effects.

It is quite easy to design bobble fabrics by graphing out the position of the bobbles.

BOBBLE FABRIC, SIMPLE

Cast on a multiple of 6 sts., plus 1 st.
1st row: * K.3, m.b., k.2; rep. from * to last st., k.1.
2nd row: P.
3rd row: K.
4th to 6th rows: Rep. 2nd and 3rd rows once then 2nd row once.
7th row: * M.b., k.5; rep. from * to last st., m.b.
8th to 12th rows: Rep. 2nd and 3rd rows twice, then 2nd row once.

These 12 rows form the pattern (19).

TREFOIL MOTIF

This is another example of Bobble Fabric (20) in which three bobbles have been used to form the attractive trefoil motif.

It may be worked by following the graph (21).

BOHUS KNITTING

On the outskirts of Gôteborg in Sweden is the Bohus country where peasant knitters have developed a type of colour knitting peculiar to this small area. In this type of knitting, embossed effects are obtained by working some of the stitches in reverse stocking stitch on a stocking stitch ground. Another element in Bohus designs is their clever use of slip stitches to build up multi-colour effects in the finished fabrics.

SCANDINAVIAN RHAPSODY

Here is a typical example of Bohus knitting, using blue, white, brown and red wools (22).

Cast on a multiple of 4 sts. plus 1 st.
1st row: Using blue and white, k.2 blue, * 1 white, 3 blue; rep. from * to last 3 sts., 1 white, 2 blue.
2nd row: Using blue, white and brown, p. * 1 white, 1 blue, 1 brown, 1 blue; rep. from * to last st., 1 white. Break off white.
3rd row: K.2 blue, * 1 brown, 3 blue; rep. from * to last 3 sts., 1 brown, 2 blue.
4th row: P. * 1 blue, 3 brown; rep. from * to last st., 1 blue.
5th row: * K.1 blue, bring brown to front, p.3 brown, take brown to back; rep. from * to last st., k.1 blue. Break off brown.
6th row: Using red and white, p. * 1 red, 1 white; rep. from * to last st., 1 red.
7th row: K. * 1 red, 1 white; rep. from * to last st., 1 red. Break off red.
8th row: Using blue and white, p.2 blue, * 1 white, 3 blue; rep. from * to last 3 sts., 1 white, 2 blue.
9th row: P.2 blue, * take blue to back, k.1 white, bring blue to front, p.3 blue; rep. from * to last 3 sts., take blue to back, k.1 white, bring blue to front, p.2 blue.
10th row: Using brown and white, p. * 1 brown, 3 white, rep. from * to last st., 1 brown.
11th row: * K.1 brown, bring white to front, p.3 white, take white to back; rep. from * to last st., k.1 brown. Break off brown.
12th row: As 8th row.
13th row: As 9th row.
14th row: As 6th row.
15th row: As 7th row. Break off white and red.
16th row: As 4th row.
17th row: As 5th row.
18th row: P.2 blue, * 1 brown, 3 blue; rep. from * to last 3 sts., p. 1 brown, 2 blue.
19th row: Using blue, brown and white, k. * 1 white, 1 blue, 1 brown, 1 blue; rep. from * to last st., 1 white. Break off brown.
20th row: P.2 blue, * 1 white, 3 blue; rep. from * to last 3 sts., 1 white, 2 blue.

These 20 rows complete the patt. and are repeated throughout.

17

BORDERS
(See *Bands*, page 12).

BOTANY WOOL
Botany is the best-quality wool from Merino sheep; the term is derived from Botany Bay, in Australia, where Captain Cook landed in 1770 with Sir Joseph Banks, the botanist. The first colony founded there some years later imported Merino sheep from India. They produced very thick fleeces with a short, curly staple and their wool was used to supply a good deal of the raw wool required by the new knitting machines in Britain during the Industrial Revolution. Merino sheep still flourish in Australia, which has remained the greatest exporter of raw wool in the world.

BOUCLET
This word is derived from the French word *boucler* which includes among its meanings "to curl or loop up". Bouclet wools are formed by twisting together a thick and a thin thread; the thick thread is delivered more speedily than the thin one and therefore forms loops or curls round the latter.

BRIDAL SHIRTS
One of the most interesting pages of the knitter's story is that of the introduction of the Bridal Shirt, a particularized "version" of the fisherman's sweater. These garments were knitted by the Fisherman's sweetheart, to be worn by him on his wedding day and after that on all festive occasions. Every fishing port round the coastline of England had its traditional design for this type of sweater. Many of these designs are lost and the few that remain are collectors' pieces.

BRIOCHE KNITTING
This is a type of knitting which produces a thicker fabric than ordinary knitting (23). The basic principle is a travelling thread which is worked in with the knitted stitch, the travelling thread always being worked on the "wool forward" principle, the wool forward always being followed by a slip stitch.

On the following row the slip stitch is always knitted together with the wool forward.

For brioche knitting the stitches are cast on in the ordinary way, but it is advisable to use a larger needle for the casting on than for the knitting itself. An even number of stitches is used.

In all brioche patterns the basic row (an increase row) after the cast-on row is as follows:—

K.1, * w.f., sl.1 purlwise, k.1; rep. from * to last st., k.1. This row is never repeated but forms the foundation of the fabric to be produced.

The brioche principle is worked as follows:—

K.1, * bring wool to front of needle, sl.1 purlwise (24). w.o.n., k.2 tog. (25); rep. from * to last st., k.1.

This row is repeated throughout ordinary brioche knitting.

Before casting off, the sts. should be reduced to the number cast on by working as follows:—

K.1, * k.1, k.2 tog., rep. from * to last st., k.1, across the last row.

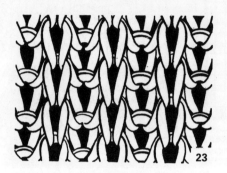

23

24

25

BRUSHING WOOLS
When a fluffy surface is required, it is possible to brush up the surface of a firm stocking-stitch fabric with a wire brush sold specifically for this purpose. The process is also called "teazling", as in former days the heads of teazle thistles were used. Knitted pieces should be brushed before making up, using a gentle rotary action with a slight lift and pull. Care must be taken to do this very delicately to avoid pulling threads and ribbing must be avoided as the result is naturally uneven.

BUTTERFLY STITCH
Butterfly stitch derives its name from the appearance of the finished stitch when it is worked in knitted fabric (26). The principle is to drop a stitch down a given number of rows, thus creating a ladderlike formation in the knitting. The ladders and stitch are then placed on the left-hand needle and are all knitted together on the right-hand needle.

Here is a simple all-over butterfly fabric:
Cast on a multiple of 16 sts. plus 12 sts.

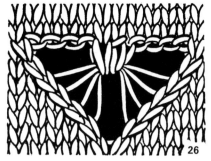

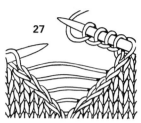

1st row: * K.4, k.2 tog., (w.f.) twice, k.2 tog. t.b.l., k.8; rep. from * to last 12 sts., k.4, k.2 tog., (w.f.) twice, k.2 tog. t.b.l., k.4.

2nd row: * P.3, p.2 tog. t.b.l., drop w.f.'s of previous row, (w.r.n.) twice, p.2. tog., p.7; rep. from * to last 12 sts., p.3, p.2 tog. t.b.l., drop w.f.'s of previous row, (w.r.n.) twice, p.2 tog., p.3.

3rd row: * K.2, k.2 tog., drop w.r.n.'s of previous row, (w.f.) twice, k.2 tog. t.b.l., k.6; rep. from * to last 10 sts., k.2, k.2 tog., drop w.r.n.'s of previous row, (w.f.) twice, k.2 tog. t.b.l., k.2.

4th row: * P.1, p.2 tog. t.b.l., drop w.f.'s of previous row, (w.r.n.) twice, p.2 tog., p.5; rep. from * to last 8 sts., p.1, p.2 tog. t.b.l., drop w.f.'s of previous row, (w.r.n.) twice, p.2 tog., p.1.

5th row: * K.2 tog., cast on 4 sts., drop w.r.n.'s of previous row (27). Work butterfly as follows:—

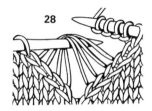

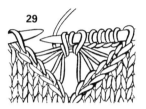

Insert point of left-hand needle under 4 strands formed by dropped sts. (28). Insert right-hand needle under the 4 strands and k.1 st., w.f., insert point of right-hand needle under 4 strands again and k.1 st. (29), (this completes action referred to as "work butterfly").

Cast on 4 sts., k.2 tog. t.b.l., k.4; rep. from * to last 6 sts., k.2 tog., cast on 4 sts., drop w.r.n.'s of previous row, work butterfly, cast on 4 sts., k.2 tog. t.b.l.

6th row: * P.6, p.2 tog., p.9; rep. from * to last 13 sts., p.6, p.2 tog., p.5.

7th row: K.

8th row: P.

9th row: K.4, * k.8, k.2 tog., (w.f.) twice, k.2 tog. t.b.l., k.4; rep. from * to last 24 sts., k.8, k.2 tog., (w.f.) twice, k.2 tog. t.b.l., k.12.

10th row: P.1, * p.10, p.2 tog. t.b.l., drop w.f.'s of previous row, (w.r.n.) twice, p.2 tog.; rep. from * to last 27 sts., p.10, p.2 tog. t.b.l., drop w.f.'s of previous row, (w.r.n.) twice, p.2. tog., p.11.

11th row: K.2, * k.8, k.2 tog., drop w.r.n.'s of previous row, (w.f.) twice, k.2 tog. t.b.l.; rep. from * to last 24 sts., k.8, k.2 tog., drop w.r.n.'s of previous row, (w.f.) twice, k.2 tog. t.b.l., k.10.

12th row: P.3, * p.6, p.2 tog. t.b.l., drop w.f.'s of previous row, (w.r.n.) twice, p.2 tog.; rep. from * to last 21 sts., p.6, p.2 tog. t.b.l., drop w.f.'s of previous row, (w.r.n.) twice, p.2 tog., p.9.

13th row: K.4, * k.4, k.2 tog., cast on 4 sts., drop w.r.n.'s of previous row, work butterfly, cast on 4 sts., k.2 tog. t.b.l.; rep. from * to last 18 sts., k.4, k.2 tog., cast on 4 sts., drop w.r.n.'s of previous row, work butterfly, cast on 4 sts., k.2 tog. t.b.l., k.8.

14th row: P.5, * p.9, p.2 tog., p.6; rep. from * to last 7 sts., p.7.

15th row: K.

16th row: P.

These 16 rows form the pattern.

BUTTONHOLES

Making buttonholes in knitted fabric is perfectly simple.

Bound Buttonholes. Where decorative buttonholes are used, in, for example, heavy knitted coats using large buttons, the cast-off and cast-on hole (see *Tailor's Buttonholes*), can be bound round with a piece of bias knitting (30). It is advisable to use a finer wool than that used for the coat itself. If you cannot match up the exact shade a contrast can be used, picking up the same colour as the button. The principle of bias knitting is to decrease at the beginning of the row and increase at the end of the row, working a plain row in between each increase and decrease.

Here is an example of a bias on eight stitches that will form a wide enough binding for buttonholes of this type (31).

Cast on 8 sts.

1st row: K.2 tog., k. to last st., inc. in last st.   **2nd row:** P.
Rep. these 2 rows for length required.

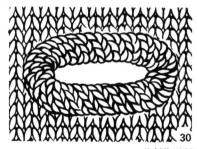

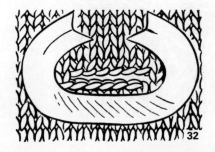

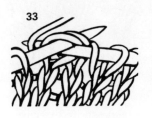

When the binding has been knitted fold it at the centre and press a crease on the right side. Neatly stitch the binding round the buttonhole, joining the bias edges together with a flat seam (32). It is advisable to make the join at the centre of the top or bottom edge of the buttonhole to keep corners smooth and strong.

Small Buttonholes. Where a small buttonhole is required as in children's garments, or where small buttons are used on adult garments, the buttonhole is made by working a "wool forward, knit 2 together" (33).

When the second row has been worked this forms a small hole in the fabric (34).

Tailor's Buttonholes. The ordinary type of tailor's buttonhole is worked over two rows of the fabric. On the first row a given number of stitches is cast off, two, three or more according to the size of button which is being used, and on the second row the same number of stitches is cast on (35).

The ideal way to cast on the stitches is simply to make a loop on the thumb and slip it on the needle.

Repeat this action until the required number has been cast on to the needle (36).

In order to avoid the loose stitch so many knitters make when casting on the second row of the buttonhole, a useful tip is to work twice (see *Increasing*, page 49) into the stitch immediately before the cast-off stitches, casting on one stitch fewer than the total number cast off, as the stitch increased counts as the first cast-on stitch.

It is important to remember not to tighten up the buttonhole when working a buttonhole stitch edge. You can use either the same wool the garment is knitted in, or the same colour in a finer wool if the actual wool used for the garment seems too heavy to finish off the buttonhole.

In children's garments where the "Small Buttonhole" principle is used, it is not advisable to work round in buttonhole stitch, as this will turn the buttonhole into a circular eyelet and tend to distort the flow of the fabric.

Vertical Buttonholes. Where a vertical buttonhole is required the knitting is "split" at the point where the buttonhole is to be worked. Two balls of wool are used from this point until the buttonhole has been completed,

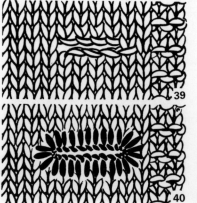

the first ball being used over the first group of stitches and the second one over the second group (37).

When the buttonhole has been completed simply break off the second ball of wool and continue the fabric using the one ball, running in the end of the wool from the second ball firmly and neatly at the back of the work (38).

In making vertical buttonholes the first stitch on every row along the edge of the buttonhole should be slipped knitwise, the same stitch being knitted on the following row; this creates a neat and firm edge.

Worked Buttonholes. A firm edge is easily made on a knitted buttonhole by working ordinary buttonhole stitch round the buttonhole opening (39 and 40).

Where the "cast-off, cast-on" (Tailor's) buttonhole principle has been used, the finished effect is exactly like a tailored buttonhole.

BUTTONHOLE STITCH

Work with a length of matching thread and a wool needle as diagram (41).

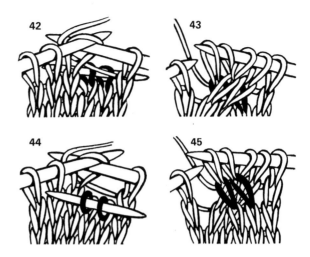

CABLE KNITTING

The principle of cable knitting is to place a stated number of stitches to the back or the front of the work, working these stitches after the stated number of stitches at the beginning of the cable have been worked.

Cable 2 Back. Slip 2 sts. on to a cable needle and leave them on this needle at the back of the work. Using the right-hand needle k. the following 2 sts. (42). Bring the cable needle forward and k. across the 2 sts. on the cable needle (43), taking care not to twist this needle during the operation.

Cable 2 Front. Slip 2 sts. on to a cable needle and leave them on the needle at the front of the work. K. the following 2 sts., using the right-hand needle (44). Take the cable needle back and k. across the 2 sts. on the cable needle (45), taking care not to twist this needle during the operation.

The above two examples illustrate the basic principle of working cable in knitting. You will have noticed that the stitches stated on the cable are multiplied by 2, i.e., C.2F and C.2B are worked over 4 stitches. Once the principle is understood the number of stitches cabled can be varied, always remembering the 2 multiple principle,

thus when working a cable 3 action work over 6 sts., a cable 4 action over 8 sts., and so on.

The operation of cabling produces a rope-like twist on the front surface of the fabric.

Cables are usually worked in stocking stitch but fancy cable patterns can be produced by varying the type of stitch used on the cable itself.

In placing the cabling principle on the knitted fabric a given number of rows are worked in the ordinary pattern e.g. knit 2, purl 2 rib base as on rows 1 and 2 in the *Ribbed Cable* pattern. The number of rows varies according to the effect the knitter desires to produce. The general principle here is to work 2 more rows between the cable than the number of stitches used on the complete cable.

Thus, where C.2F, or C.2B is worked, 4 stitches being used for the cable, the cable-row is worked on every sixth row. Where C.3F, or C.3B is worked, 6 stitches being used, the cable is worked on every eighth row.

In a pattern, where 8 stitches are used in the cable, the cable will be worked on every tenth row.

Ribbed Cable. The perfect example of the fancy cable principle is where a ribbed cable stitch is worked. The principle here is to work the pattern on a ribbed base.

Here is an example of cable worked on a knit 2, purl 2 base.

Cast on a multiple of 12 sts. plus 2.

1st row: * K.2, p.2; rep. from * to last 2 sts.; k.2.

2nd row: * P.2, k.2; rep. from * to last 2 sts.; p.2.

3rd row (on which the cable is worked): K.2, p.2; sl. the next 4 sts. on to a cable needle and leave at the back of the work. Using the right-hand needle k.2, p.2 across the next 4 sts. on the left-hand needle. Bring the cable needle forward and k.2, p.2 across the 4 sts. on the cable needle.

Now k. the last 2 sts. on the left-hand needle.

4th row (on which the cable is set): * P.2, k.2;·rep. from * to last 2 sts.; p.2.

Work 6 rows in k.2, p.2 rib (46).

Stocking Stitch Cable with Rib. In ordinary cabling on a stocking stitch base the usual practice is to work a purl stitch rib (working one or two stitches in this rib) before and after the group of stitches used for the cable. This emphasises and enhances the beauty of the cable pattern.

As an example of this principle here is a pattern embody-

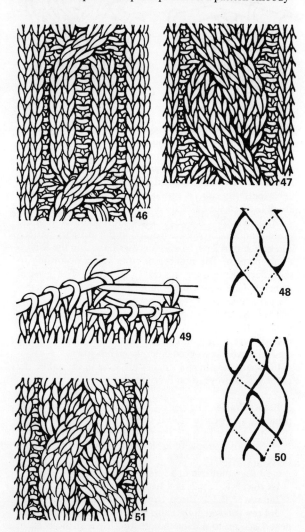

ing the C.3F principle (47 and 48).

Cast on a multiple of 10 sts. plus 4.

1st row: K.2, p.2, k.6, p.2, k.2.

2nd row: P.2, k.2, p.6, k.2, p.2.

3rd row (on which the cable is worked): K.2, p.2, sl. the next 3 sts. on to a cable needle and leave at the front of the work. Using the right-hand needle k. across the next 3 sts. on the left-hand needle (49). Take the cable needle back and using the right-hand needle k. across the 3 sts. on the cable needle, p.2, k.2 across the 4 remaining sts. on the left-hand needle.

4th row: P.2, k.2, p.6, k.2, p.2.

Repeat 1st and 2nd rows twice.

Three Plait Cable. Another variation of cabling in which the principle is to cable across a given number of stitches (one-third of the total number used for the pattern) and then after working a given number of rows to cable again across the second group of stitches (again one-third of the total number of stitches used on the pattern), thus producing the plaited cable effect as against the single cable effect in ordinary cabling.

The usual practice here is to place a purl stitch rib each side of the group of stitches used in the cable pattern to give proper emphasis to the pattern itself.

Here is an example of Plaited Cable using 9 stitches on the cable portion of the fabric. The number of stitches can be varied, thus altering the width of the cable pattern, but it must always be a number divisible by 3. In the example there are 9 stitches (3 multiplied by 3), (50).

Cast on a multiple of 13 sts. plus 4.

1st row: K.2, p.2, k.9, p.2, k.2.

2nd row: P.2, k.2, p.9, k.2, p.2.

3rd row (on which the first group of stitches is cabled): K.2, p.2, sl. the next 3 sts. on to a cable needle and leave at the front of the work; using the right-hand needle k. across the next 3 sts. on the left-hand needle. Take the cable needle back and, using the right-hand needle, k. across the 3 sts. on the cable needle. Now, using the right-hand needle k.3, p.2, k.2 on the remaining 7 sts. on the left-hand needle.

4th row: As 2nd row.

5th and 6th rows: As 1st and 2nd rows.

7th row (on which the second group of stitches is cabled): K.2, p.2, k.3; sl. the next 3 sts. on to a cable needle and leave at the back of the work; using the right-hand needle k. across the next 3 sts. on the left-hand needle. Bring the cable needle forward and using the right-hand needle k. across the 3 sts. on the cable needle. Now, using the right-hand needle p.2 k.2 across the remaining 4 sts on the left-hand needle.

8th row: As 2nd row.

9th and 10th rows: As 1st and 2nd rows.

By repeating rows 3 to 10 inclusive the cable pattern will

be worked on every 4th row of the fabric (51).

In this stitch the placing of the cable principle is slightly different to ordinary cable, it will vary according to the number of stitches used in the cable pattern, thus where 12 stitches are used the cable principle will be worked on every sixth row; where 15 stitches are used, on every eighth row.

It is a comparatively simple matter for the knitter to adjust the number of rows between the cable principle once the total number of stitches to be used in the cabled portion of the pattern has been established.

CARDIGAN

Perhaps the most popular of all knitted garments for the family, this jacket borrows its name from Lord Cardigan who was a general in the Crimean War. It is reported that he ordered a woollen jacket with sleeves and open sides to give additional warmth when on horseback, and within a few months women at home were knitting these "Cardigans" for the soldiers at the front. The term is now used to describe a classic collarless jacket (with closed side seams) and with a V or high round neck, buttoning down the front.

MAN'S CARDIGAN

The average measurements for a Man's Cardigan are given below in four sizes.

	ins.	ins.	ins.	ins.
Chest	38	40	42	44
Length from top of shoulder to lower edge	23½	23¾	24	24¼
Depth of armhole ..	8½	8¾	9	9¼
Width across back of shoulders	14½	14¾	15	15¼
Width of shoulder ..	4¾	4⅞	5	5⅛
Sleeve seam from wrist to underarm	18	18¼	18½	18¾
Length of sleeve from wrist to shoulder ..	23½	23¾	24	24¼
Width of sleeve at wrist above cuff ..	9	9⅛	9¼	9⅜
Sleeve at widest point	16½	17	17½	18

With the aid of the table of measurements, coupled with the tension of the fabric used for the cardigan, it is a comparatively simple matter to arrive at the number of stitches for each point in the work as it proceeds.

The table on page 99 gives the number of stitches and size of needles for knitting a man's cardigan in various types of wool.

WOMAN'S CARDIGAN

The table of measurements given below shows sizes for garments to fit the average figure.

	ins.	ins.	ins.	ins.	ins.
Bust	34	36	38	40	42
Length from top of shoulder to lower edge ..	22	22	22¼	22¼	22½
Depth of armhole ..	7	7¼	7½	7½	7¾
Width across back of shoulders	14	14	14¼	14¼	14½
Width of shoulder ..	4½	4½	4¾	4¾	5
Sleeve seam from wrist to underarm	18	18	18	18	18
Length of sleeve from wrist to shoulder	23	23	23¼	23¼	23½
Width of sleeve at wrist above cuff	8	8	8¼	8¼	8½
Sleeve at widest point ..	13	13	13½	13½	14

The table shown on page 99 gives the number of stitches and size of needles required for knitting a woman's cardigan in various types of wool.

CARPETS AND RUGS

In medieval times, knitted carpets were included in the work required for examination of an apprentice after he had served his six-year training and before he could be admitted as a Craftsman to the Knitters' Guild of Paris.

The carpet had to measure 8 by 12 feet and be of an extremely intricate design of foliage, birds and flowers in as many as thirty different colours. Rare examples have been preserved in continental museums. Today, knitted floor rugs are popular and packs are sold containing all materials for an Aran-type rug. An experienced knitter can design her own rugs from graphs, using thick wools.

Hearth rugs and bedside rugs can be knitted in a triple-knit or chunky yarn and because of their weight should preferably be made in synthetics for easy washing.

Larger carpets can be made up from squares, like tapestry carpets. These can be knitted in alternate diagonal patterns to form an interesting textured effect when sewn together or they can be made in Colour Knitting.

CASHMERE

Cashmere yarn is made from the long, fine silky hair of the Cashmere goat. As these are rare and the yarn is particularly soft and warm, Cashmere is very expensive and is used mainly for industrial knitting. However, a knitting yarn is obtainable which is a mixture of Cashmere and wool (about 20% wool), this is usually spun to a thickness between 3 ply and 4 ply so that a pattern expressly designed for Cashmere is essential.

23

CASTING OFF

This action is used when finishing off a piece of fabric. There are two methods of casting off.

Simple Cast Off. Knit the first 2 stitches in the ordinary way.

Place the point of the left-hand needle through the second stitch on the right-hand needle (the first stitch knitted) and draw this stitch over the first stitch on the right-hand needle (52).

Knit the next stitch on the left-hand needle (53), thus there will be 2 stitches on the right-hand needle again, and repeat the action.

Continue in this manner until all the stitches have been cast off. Cut wool and draw loop of remaining stitch through, using wool to fasten off. (54).

Single Decrease Cast Off. Using the right-hand needle, knit together the first 2 stitches on the left-hand needle (55). (See *Decreasing*, page 30).

Slip the first stitch formed by knitting the 2 stitches together back on to the left-hand needle (56).

Knit together the first 2 stitches on the left-hand needle (57). Repeat last two actions until all stitches have been cast off (58).

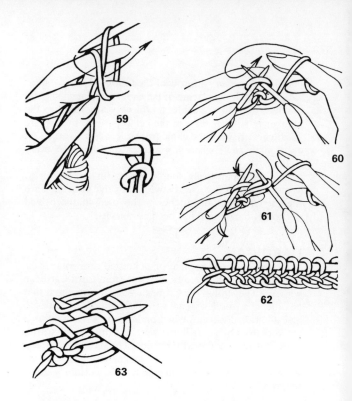

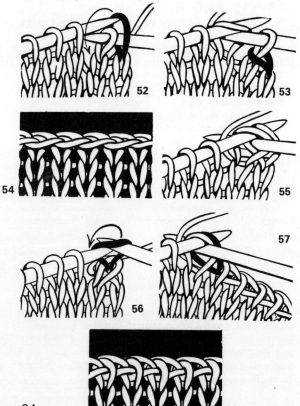

CASTING ON

This is the first action in knitting and consists of making the stitches on to the needle from a straight length of wool. There are several methods of casting on, each being suited to a particular purpose.

Through the Stitch Method. This method is always used where a knitted up hem forms part of the garment.

Make a loop at the end of wool (59) and slip it on to left-hand needle.

Place the point of the right-hand needle through the loop on the left-hand needle (60).

Using the right hand, bring the wool round the point of the right-hand needle and draw the loop formed through the stitch on left-hand needle (61).

Slip the stitch formed on to the left-hand needle.

Repeat this procedure until the required number of stitches has been cast on (62).

Between the Stitches Method. The perfect method of casting on for socks and stockings.

Commence as for the casting on *Through The Stitch Method.*

When the second stitch has been placed next to the first stitch on the left-hand needle, insert the point of the right-hand needle *between* the two stitches.

Using the right hand, wrap the wool round the point of the right-hand needle (63) and draw the loop formed through between the two stitches on the left-hand needle.

24

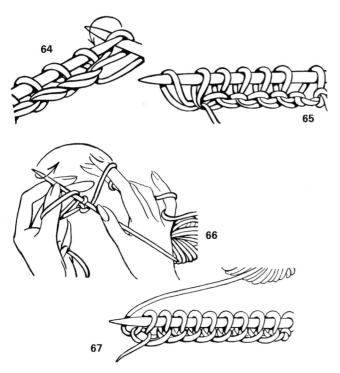

64

65

66

67

Place the stitch on the left-hand needle (64) and repeat this action until the required number of stitches has been cast on (65).

Thumb Method. The method most frequently used.

Leaving a length of wool, sufficient to make the number of stitches to be cast on, make a loop and place it on needle held in right hand.

Hold wool from ball in right hand and take the loose end of wool in left hand. Form a loop on left thumb..

Insert point of right-hand needle into loop (66), with right hand wrap wool round point of needle and draw through loop on thumb.

Slip loop off thumb and gently tighten left-hand thread. Continue until required number of stitches has been cast on (67).

CHARTS

Charts provide a simple method of following a pattern using two or more colours as in Fair Isle or Scandinavian Knitting. Squared graph paper is used and each square represents one knitted stitch. Crosses, circles and diagonals are used (with a key) to show where the different colours are used. This is a much quicker method to follow and more space-saving than printing out the pattern in full. It enables the knitter to recognise the patterns formed as she goes along.

Designers use charts to work out the basic shape of new garments and to ascertain how many stitches are required at what point in the measurement (see *Graphing*, page 31).

CIRCULAR KNITTING

(Knitting in rounds).

Circular knitting, which is carried out on four or more needles, creates either a tubular type of fabric as used in socks or stockings; a circular piece of fabric, or a square, pentagonal, hexagonal or octagonal piece of fabric. These fancy shapes are usually used as the basis for lace mats in fine cotton, or can be made up into blankets or Afghans if worked in heavy wool.

Four-Needle Method. The simplest circular fabric in knitting is the tubular type.

Cast on an equal number of stitches on each of three needles (68).

The next step is—using a fourth needle—join the three together to form a triangle by knitting the first stitch on the first needle on to the fourth needle, drawing up the last stitch on the third needle firmly (69).

Continue to knit across the stitches on the first needle with the fourth needle, thus releasing the first needle ready for use.

Now knit across the stitches on the second needle using the first needle, thus releasing the second needle.

Finally knit across the stitches on the third needle using the released second needle, thus completing the first round of the work.

Continue working in rounds in this manner (70).

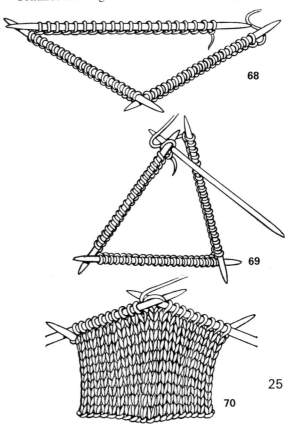

68

69

70

25

Discs, Circular. To knit a circular disc cast on 2 stitches on each of four needles. (5 needles required).

1st round: K.

2nd round: Inc. in each st., thus making 4 sts. on each needle (16 sts. in all).

3rd, 4th and 5th rounds: K. all round without inc.

6th round: Inc. in each st., thus making 8 sts. on each needle (32 sts. in all).

7th, 8th and 9th rounds: K. all round without inc.

10th round: Inc. in every 2nd st., thus making 12 sts. on each needle (48 sts. in all).

11th, 12th and 13th rounds: K. all round without inc.

14th round: Inc. in every 3rd st., thus making 16 sts. on each needle (64 sts. in all).

15th, 16th and 17th rounds: K. all round without inc.

Continue increasing on the same principle as on 10th and 14th rounds, *noting* that three plain rounds are worked between each set of increases and that the increases move up numerically in position one stitch on every increase round, always giving a stable 4 stitch increase on each needle on each increase round.

The next round (the increase round) will be "inc. in every 4th st." on each needle, the following increase round will be "inc. in every 5th st." and so on, until a circle has been knitted to the desired size (71).

71

72

At the top of the page is an example of a knitted circular disc using four needles (71) and above (72) is the method of working a square in circular knitting using five needles

Square. To work a square in circular knitting the principle is the same as knitting in rounds except that an increase is made at both ends of each needle while the circular knitting action is in progress. In this type of circular knitting five needles are used.

Commence by casting on 2 stitches on each of four needles.

Using fifth needle join up as for knitting in rounds and work one round over all four needles.

Commence to shape the square as follows:—

1st round: Using the spare needle inc. in each of the 2 sts. on the first needle, thus making 4 sts. out of 2 and releasing the first needle. Work in the same manner over the 2 sts. on each of the other three needles.

2nd round: Work one round without inc.

3rd round: * Inc. in first st., k.2, inc. in last st. * across 4 sts. on first needle; rep. from * to * across each needle.

4th round: As 2nd round.

5th round: * Inc. in first st., k.4, inc. in last st. * on first needle; rep. from * to * across each needle.

6th round: As 2nd round.

Continue increasing as above on next and every alternate round, *noting* that there will be 2 sts. more in the group of sts. knitted between the increases on each needle, on next and every alternate round (72).

Varied Geometric Shapes—Pentagon, Hexagon, Octagon Shapes can be knitted by using six, seven, or nine needles, working on exactly the same principle as the square, i.e., commencing by casting on 2 stitches on five, six or eight needles, working in rounds and increasing in same way as a square.

COLOUR KNITTING

This term applies to knitting carried out in two colours or more, the colours being worked as an actual pattern in the fabric. The general practice is to work the fabric in stocking stitch, knitting in the coloured pattern from a chart. Although the term "Fair Isle Knitting" has come to be applied generally to colour knitting this is a complete anomaly, as this type of knitting falls into various groups—

Argyle Knitting, Bohus Knitting, Fair Isle Knitting, Faroe Isle Knitting, Florentine Knitting, Jacquard Knitting, Mid-European Knitting, Scandinavian Knitting, Shetland Knitting. All these types of colour knitting are described in detail under their respective heading.

Charts. Colour patterns are all worked from charts. The reading of these charts is a perfectly simple matter providing you remember that each square represents a stitch and each row of squares a row in the knitting.

The patterns are worked in stocking stitch, i.e. one row knit, one row purl, so that when reading the first row of the chart from right to left it is a k. row and the second row, from left to right, is a p. row. Continue to work on this principle until the design is completed.

Here is an example of a Fair Isle design. In this a white ground has been used and the pattern is in traditional royal blue and scarlet. In Fair Isle knitting the general tendency is for a natural or white ground and vivid coloured patterns. This design may be worked from the chart (73) or the written instructions below.

The row by row instructions are as follows:—
Abbreviations: W. White, S. Scarlet, R. Royal Blue.
Join in colours at beginning of rows and break off at end, as required.
Cast on with w. a multiple of 33 sts. plus 1 st.

1st row: K. * 1w., 1s., 2w., 2s., 2w., 1s., 1w., 1s., 5w., 2s., 5w., 1s., 1w., 1s., 2w., 2s., 2w., 1s.; rep. from * to last st., 1w.

2nd row: P. 1w., * 1s., 1w., 2s., 2w., 1s., 1w., 1s., 5w., 1s., 2w., 1s., 5w., 1s., 1w., 1s., 2w., 2s., 1w., 1s., 1w.; rep. from * to end.

3rd row: K. * 1w., 3s., 2w., 1s., 1w., 1s., 5w., 1s., 4w., 1s., 5w., 1s., 1w., 1s., 2w., 3s.; rep. from * to last st., 1w.

4th row: P. 1w., * 2s., 2w., 1s., 1w., 1s., 2w., 5s., 4w., 5s., 2w., 1s., 1w., 1s., 2w., 2s., 1w.; rep. from * to end.

5th row: K. * 1w., 1s., 2w., 1s., 1w., 1s., 3w., 1s., 2w., 1s., 1w., 1s., 2w., 1s., 1w., 1s., 2w., 1s., 3w., 1s., 1w., 1s., 2w., 1s.; rep. from * to last st., 1w.

6th row: P. 1w., * (1s., 1w.) twice, 1s., 4w., (1s., 2w.) twice, 2s., (2w., 1s.) twice, 4w., (1s., 1w.) 3 times; rep. from * to end.

7th row: K. * 1w., 2s., 1w., 1s., 5w., 5s., 1w., 2s., 1w., 5s., 5w., 1s., 1w., 2s.; rep. from * to last st., 1w. Break off scarlet.

8th row: P. 1w., * 1r., 1w., 1r., 5w., 2r., 4w., 1r., 2w., 1r., 4w., 2r., 5w., (1r., 1w.) twice; rep. from * to end.

9th row: K. * 1w., 2r., 5w., (1r., 2w.) twice, 1r., 4w., (1r., 2w.) twice, 1r., 5w., 2r.; rep. from * to last st., 1w.

10th row: P. 1w., * 1r., 5w., 1r., 4w., (2r., 2w.) twice, 2r., 4w., 1r., 5w., 1r., 1w.; rep. from * to end.

11th to 20th rows: Rep. rows 10 to 1 in backward rotation, i.e. 10, 9, 8, 7, 6, etc., reading k. for p. and p. for k.

These 20 rows form the pattern.

Fair Isle designs usually have broad patterns interspaced with narrow patterns, which are usually worked in a neutral colour such as black, brown, dark green or navy, thus emphasising the lovely contrast colourings.

The common practice is to vary the patterning right through the garment, thus distinguishing Fair Isle colour knitting from Shetland colour knitting.

Here are the instructions for a smaller linking pattern as shown in chart (74).
Abbreviations: B. Brown, W. White.
Cast on a multiple of 12 sts. plus 1 st.

1st row: K. * 2b., 2w., 5b., 2w., 1b.; rep. from * to last st., 1b.

2nd row: P. 1w., * 2b., 2w., 3b., 2w., 2b., 1w.; rep. from * to end.

3rd row: K. * 1b., 1w., 2b., 2w., 1b., 2w., 2b., 1w.; rep. from * to last st., 1b.

4th row: As 2nd row.

5th row: As 1st row.

Principles of Colour Knitting. There are two distinct methods of working colour knit fabrics.
Strand the Colour. The first method, common to most types of colour knitting, is to strand the colour not in

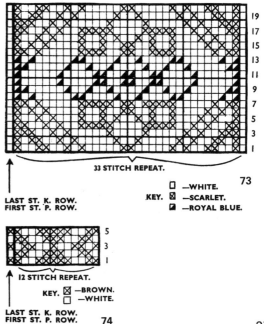

33 STITCH REPEAT.

LAST ST. K. ROW.
FIRST ST. P. ROW.

73

KEY.   □ —WHITE.
      ☒ —SCARLET.
      ◪ —ROYAL BLUE.

12 STITCH REPEAT.

KEY. ☒ —BROWN.
      □ —WHITE.

LAST ST. K. ROW.
FIRST ST. P. ROW.   74

27

use across the back of the work. The simplest way to do this is to hold one colour in the right hand and one colour in the left (75).

Knit with each colour according to the sequence from the charts, letting the colour not in use strand itself loosely across the back of the fabric (76).

Here are a few points to remember when working colour knitting.

a. Always strand the wools loosely across the back, as this helps to preserve the natural elasticity of the knitted fabric.

b. Be sure that the wools used for the coloured parts of a garment, if they are oddments from your workbasket, are the same thickness as the ground shade, otherwise the patternings will not stand out boldly when the knitting is completed.

c. Always run in the coloured ends of wool securely at the back of the work.

d. If stranding wool over more than 5 stitches it is advisable to twist the colours over and under each other at the centre of each group of 5, thus preventing long strands.

e. Be sure that the wools used are dyed in fast colours, otherwise when the garment is washed the colours may run into the ground, thus ruining a fine piece of work.

Weave the Colour. The second principle is weaving the colour not in use under and over the colour in use (77). The method of weaving is perfectly simple, as the colour not in use is passed over the colour in use when knitting one stitch (78), and under the colour in use (79) when knitting the following stitch.

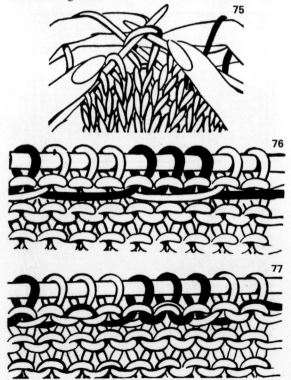

CONTINENTAL KNITTING

This is a type of knitting, the action of which resembles the movement of crochet rather than the normal knitting technique. It has been claimed that it is much quicker to knit by the continental method, but as it is much more difficult to sustain an even tension by this method and as the completed fabric always has a tendency to be looser than a fabric produced on the same size needle by the English method, it is doubtful whether any advantage is gained by mastering this rather clumsy technique.

To knit a stitch in the continental method the wool is held in the left hand above the needle (80).

The point of the right-hand needle is placed through the stitch to be knitted and then the needle point is inserted under the wool to draw the wool through the stitch on the needle (81).

The big difference here is that, whereas in English knitting the wool is wrapped over the point of the right-hand needle, in Continental knitting the point of the right-hand needle is placed over and under the wool after it has been inserted in the stitch which is to be knitted.

To purl a stitch by the Continental method the same principle applies as in knitting a stitch except that the action is carried out on the purl side of work (82 and 83).

COPTIC KNITTING

Coptic Caps, which are worked in patterned designs, have been found in various parts of North Africa and the tradition of knitting these appears to date from the second or third centuries B.C. They show the development of the needle-knitting technique and it is probable that early traders carried these from Egypt to Spain and thus inspired early Spanish colour knitting, which later spread to Fair Isle and Scandinavia.

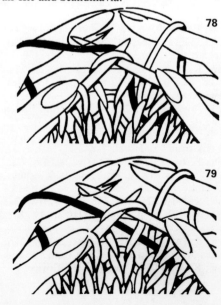

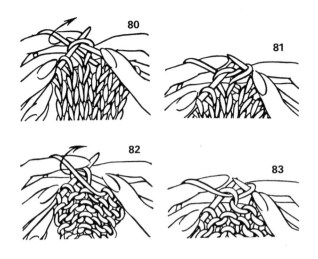

CORD

A most useful cord for trimming on knitted garments or for use as belts and ties can be made from twisted strands of wool or yarn. Cut several lengths, each three times the length required for the finished cord; knot together tightly at one end and then twist together tightly until they begin to crimp or kink up. Quickly fold in half and twist again to form a cord.

COSIES

Knitted covers to retain the warmth of tea-pots, coffee-pots and egg cups can be made from oddments of wool and are always good sellers at bazaars and fetes. A pattern for a tea cosy is given on page 100.

COTTON

Cotton knitting yarn is popular for summer garments, gloves, table centres, doilies and lace work. Great care should be taken when washing to dry the article flat and to pin it out to shape before ironing, as the mesh tends to close up when the threads are wet.

COURTELLE

(See *Synthetics*, page 89).

CREPE

Crepe wool or yarn is hard wearing and knits up well into a smooth fabric which does not fluff up or "pill" yet retains an interesting texture. The effect is produced by an extra twisting process during manufacture.

CROCHET CHAIN

Sometimes used in conjunction with knitting, work as diagram (84).

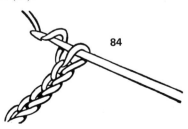

CROSSING STITCHES

Crossing stitches in knitted fabric creates the effect of a moving stitch on the surface of the fabric itself. The movement is determined by the direction in which the stitch is crossed, i.e., whether it moves inwards or outwards across the following stitch.

Cross 1 Back. Sl. the point of the right-hand needle into back of 2nd stitch on left-hand needle (85), bring the wool round the point of the needle and draw a stitch through the 2nd stitch, leaving the 2nd stitch on the left-hand needle. Now insert the point of the right-hand needle into the front of the 1st stitch on the left-hand needle, bring the wool round the point of the right-hand needle (86) and draw another stitch through the 1st stitch. Slip the first and second stitches off the left-hand needle (87).

Cross 1 Front. Slip the point of the right-hand needle into the front of the 2nd stitch on the left-hand needle, bring the wool round the point of right-hand needle (88) and draw the stitch through the 2nd stitch on the left-hand needle. Do not drop the stitch off the left-hand needle but insert the point of the right-hand needle into the back of the 1st stitch on the left-hand needle (89), wrap the wool round the point of the right-hand needle and draw a stitch through the 1st stitch, then drop the first and second stitches on the left-hand needle off the needle together (90).

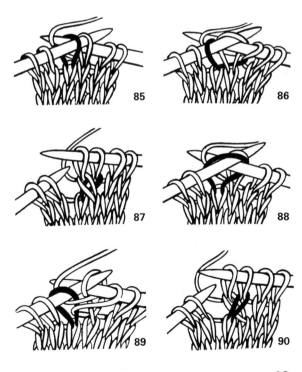

CROSS-BRED WOOL

This is a wool spun from the fleeces of English Cross-bred sheep, which have a coarser, longer fibre than those from the Merino sheep. It has a slightly harsher feel than Botany Wool and is excellent for hard-wearing outer garments and for socks and gloves.

CUTTING KNITTED FABRIC

A straight piece of knitting can be cut to make up into a shaped garment and it is often useful to cut down knitted garments to fit children. Before cutting, lay out the single piece of fabric flat and mark with tackling threads where it is to be cut; machine-stitch along this line at least twice before cutting to prevent the work unravelling, using a loose tension. Sew together with back-stitch seams or double rows of machine-stitching.

d

DARTS

Knitted garments can be darted for a better fit and it is usual to turn the fold of the dart over towards the outside seam. When thick fabric is involved, the dart must be cut open and very carefully oversewn several times—or the edges machine-stitched before the dart is opened and pressed flat. Darts can be replaced by careful decreasing during the knitting.

DECREASING

Decreasing in knitting is actually losing stitches in the fabric itself. The decreases can be worked at any point in the fabric where shaping is required, the position of these decreases being determined by the type of garment the knitter is working on.

Knit Stitches Together. The commonest form of decrease is that of knitting 2 stitches together. Insert the point of the right-hand needle through the first 2 stitches on the left-hand needle (91).

Wrap the wool round the point of the right-hand needle and draw one stitch through both the stitches through which the point of the right-hand needle has been inserted (92).

Drop the 2 stitches off the point of the left-hand needle, thus making one stitch out of two.

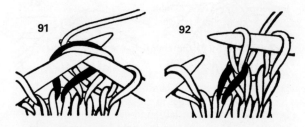

Knit Stitches Together, Double. A double decrease is worked by knitting 3 stitches together. The principle is the same as knitting 2 stitches together except that the point of the right-hand needle is placed through the first 3 stitches on the left-hand needle, the one stitch being drawn through all these 3 stitches, thus making one stitch out of three.

Knit Stitches Together, Reverse. When working the decreases to create a sloping movement across the flow of the fabric it is frequently necessary to work through the back of the stitches.

To knit 2 together through the back of the stitches insert the point of the right-hand needle through the back of the first 2 stitches on the left-hand needle.

Wrap the wool round the point of the right-hand needle and draw one stitch through the 2 stitches as in an ordinary knit 2 together decrease, dropping the 2 stitches off the left-hand needle when knitted (93).

The same principle applies on a double decrease but in this instance the point of the right-hand needle is slipped through the back of the first 3 stitches on the left-hand needle, the wool being wrapped round the point of the right-hand needle and the stitch being drawn through the 3 stitches before they are dropped from the point of the left-hand needle as in an ordinary decrease.

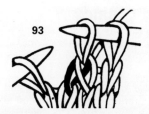

Pass Slip Stitch Over. Another method of decreasing, worked as follows:—

Using the point of the right-hand needle slip the stitch from the left-hand needle. Using the right-hand needle knit the next stitch in the ordinary way. Insert the point of the left-hand needle into the second stitch (the slipped stitch) on the right-hand needle, draw this stitch over the first stitch on the right-hand needle (94), dropping it off the point of the left-hand needle (95).

Pass Slip Stitch Over, Double. In a number of graduated patterns and lace stitches this type of double decrease is worked.

Using the point of the right-hand needle slip the first stitch off the left-hand needle.

Insert the point of the right-hand needle through the next 2 stitches on the left-hand needle, working a single decrease on these 2 stitches in the ordinary way.

Insert the point of the left-hand needle into the second stitch (the slipped stitch) on the right-hand needle, draw this stitch over the first stitch and drop it off the point of the left-hand needle.

Purl Decreases. All the above decreases have been worked on the knit principle. Decreases can be worked on the purl side of the fabric, this principle being as follows:—

For a single decrease insert the point of the right-hand needle through the first 2 stitches on the left-hand needle purlwise.

Wrap the wool round the point of the right-hand needle and then draw a stitch purlwise through the 2 stitches on the left-hand needle, dropping the 2 stitches off the left-hand needle in the ordinary way.

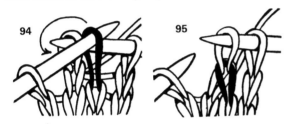

DESIGNERS
(See *Knitting Designers,* page 55).

DESIGNING FABRICS
It is a comparatively simple matter for a knitter to design her own stitches and fabrics once the principles underlying the production of the fabrics have been understood.

There are one or two points which must always be borne in mind. The first is that generally speaking any increases worked on the repeat of a pattern in any row must be balanced out by appropriate decreases. The second is that care must be taken to work out a clear repeat of the pattern.

In fabrics which move from a central double decrease, i.e., where the "sl.1, k.2 tog., p.s.s.o." principle is used, it is often necessary to have a single increase at the beginning and end of each row, thus preserving the balance of stitches throughout the production of the patterned fabric.

There is one other point which must be emphasized. In certain types of fabric, mainly where an embossed motif is worked on the surface of the fabric, the increases are often worked during the first half of the sequence of rows, without decreases being worked to balance them. In the second section of the pattern, decreases are worked without increases, thus, by the time the final row is reached the knitter will have the same number of stitches on the needle as when the pattern was started.

GRAPHING
First of all the graph of the pattern is worked out. This is done by using symbols on the graph paper, a sort of knitter's shorthand, to enable one to read how the stitch is worked from the chart prepared (96).

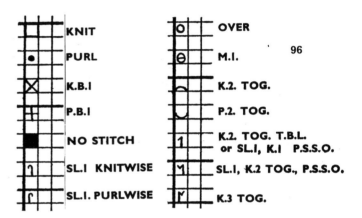

Each square on the graph represents one stitch in knitting, and each row of squares represents a row of knitting. Mark out a section of the graph paper with the number of squares necessary for one or two repeats of the pattern, plus one extra stitch. It will be necessary to work out two repeats when the double decrease principle is used.

In blocking out a graph for ribbed patterns or embossed effects, where the principle is reverse stocking stitch worked on a stocking stitch ground, the easiest method is to block out on the graph paper the rib or pattern, the solid squares representing reverse stocking stitch and the open squares stocking stitch, throughout the graph.

In using the symbols it will be noticed that each one only fills one square on the graph paper. This means that blank squares are left after the symbol where the action delineated in the symbol covers more than one stitch, e.g., where the "k.2 tog." symbol is used, the symbol will be placed in the first square, the square which follows being left blank. If however a "k.2 tog." followed by an "over" is being worked, the "k.2 tog." symbol will be placed in the first square and the "over" symbol in the second square. Where the "over" moves, and does not directly follow the "k.2 tog.", the movement is shown by placing the "over" symbol in the appropriate square.

Where a pattern is being worked with a variable number of stitches, as the rows of the pattern proceed the graph will move outwards where the increases are made and inwards again where the decreases are worked.

In uncomplicated patterns it is not advisable to mark any of the k. and p. stitches unless these are specifically part of a pattern, as in check patterns and rib designs, or in lace patterns where embossed effects are obtained by using p. stitches to create reverse stocking stitch on the right side of the work. If the basis of a pattern is stocking stitch it will be much simpler to read the graph if the k. and p. stitches are left blank throughout the pattern, and only the fancy stitches marked.

DESIGNING PATTERNS

(See also *Graphing*, page 31).

IF you examine a wide variety of knitted garments you will find that they have all been built up from a simple shape. That shape was originally a circular tube of knitting, the reason for this being that before knitting needles, as we know them today, were invented, the actual process of knitting was carried out on a frame.

The frames used were of several shapes. Some of them were oblong and others circular. The principle on all frames was the same. A number of pegs were plugged round the edges of the frame, the centre of the frame being open to allow the fabric to pass through it as it was built up on these pegs. The frames varied in size—some of the pegs were thick, for using with heavy yarns, grading down to finer pegs where finer yarns were used. The tubular knitting produced was, as explained, the foundation of every type of garment. A tube was used to encase the body, two narrow tubes for the arms, and a smaller tube than that used for the body was knitted for the neckband.

If leg coverings were needed, tubes similar to those used for the arms were made.

Thus we have the simple sweater or the overall type of garment like the knitted hose and doublet of Tudor times. The sleeves were inserted into slits cut in the main part of the garment and the raw edges of the fabric were over-stitched together.

If a coat type of garment was required, the centre front of the body tube was cut open and the edges firmly over-sewn to prevent fraying of the fabric.

It was from this simple beginning that the shapes of knitted garments as we know them today evolved, and once this principle has been understood a great variety of designs can be knitted.

DIAGONAL PATTERNS

The principle of working diagonal patterns is reverse stocking stitch on a stocking stitch base.

DIAGONAL RIB

Cast on a multiple of 4 sts. plus 2.

1st row: * K.2, p.2; rep. from * to last 2 sts., k.2.
2nd row: P.1, * k.2, p.2; rep. from * to last st., k.1.
3rd row: * P.2, k.2; rep. from * to last 2 sts., p.2.
4th row: K.1, * p.2, k.2; rep. from * to last st., p.1.
These 4 rows form the patt. (97).

97

DIAGONAL RIB AND CHECK PATTERN

Cast on a multiple of 12 sts.

1st row: * P.1, k.1, p.2, k.2, p.2, k.3, p.1; rep. from * to end.
2nd row: * K.2, p.3, k.2, p.1, k.2, p.2; rep. from * to end.
3rd row: * P.2, k.2, p.2, k.3, p.2, k.1; rep. from * to end.
4th row: * P.2, k.2, p.3, k.2, p.1, k.2; rep. from * to end.
5th row: * K.2, p.2, k.3, p.2, k.1, p.2; rep. from * to end.
6th row: * K.2, p.2, k.2, p.3, k.2, p.1; rep. from * to end.
7th row: * P.2, k.3, p.2, k.1, p.2, k.2; rep. from * to end.
8th row: * K.1, p.1, k.2, p.2, k.2, p.3, k.1; rep. from * to end.
9th row: * K.3, p.2, k.1, p.2, k.2, p.2; rep. from * to end.
10th row: * P.1, k.2, p.1, (k.2, p.2) twice; rep. from * to end.
11th row: * K.1, p.2, k.1, (p.2, k.2) twice; rep. from * to end.
12th row: * P.3, k.2, p.1, k.2, p.2, k.2; rep. from * to end.
These 12 rows form the patt.

DIAMOND CHECKS

Check patterns can be worked in knitted fabric either by using one purl stitch to emphasize the diamond shapes or by working diamonds in solid reverse stocking stitch on a stocking stitch background.

"His and Hers" sweaters knitted in the same pattern, but different colours—instructions page 158

DIAMOND PATTERN, DOUBLE

Cast on a multiple of 12 sts. plus 1 st.

1st row: P.2, * k.9, p.3; rep. from * to last 11 sts., k.9, p.2.

2nd row: K.2, * p.9, k.3; rep. from * to last 11 sts., p.9, k.2.

3rd row: * K.1, p.2, k.7, p.2; rep. from * to last st., k.1.

4th row: P.2, * k.2, p.5, k.2, p.3; rep. from * to last 11 sts., k.2, p.5, k.2, p.2.

5th row: K.3, * p.2, k.3, p.2, k.5; rep. from * to last 10 sts., p.2, k.3, p.2, k.3.

6th row: P.4, * k.2, p.1, k.2, p.7; rep. from * to last 9 sts., k.2, p.1, k.2, p.4.

7th row: K.5, * p.3, k.9; rep. from * to last 8 sts., p.3, k.5.

8th row: P.5, * k.3, p.9; rep. from * to last 8 sts., k.3, p.5.

9th row: K.4, * p.2, k.1, p.2, k.7; rep. from * to last 9 sts., p.2, k.1, p.2, k.4.

10th row: P.3, * k.2, p.3, k.2, p.5; rep. from * to last 10 sts., k.2, p.3, k.2, p.3.

11th row: K.2, * p.2, k.5, p.2, k.3; rep. from * to last 11 sts., p.2, k.5, p.2, k.2.

12th row: P.1, * k.2, p.7, k.2, p.1; rep. from * to end. These 12 rows form the patt.

DIAMOND PATTERN, SINGLE

Cast on a multiple of 6 sts. plus 1.

1st row: K.3, * p.1, k.5; rep. from * to last 4 sts., p.1, k.3.

2nd row: P.2, * k.1, p.1, k.1, p.3; rep. from * to last 5 sts., k.1, p.1, k.1, p.2.

3rd row: * K.1, p.1, k.3, p.1; rep. from * to last st., k.1.

4th row: * K.1, p.5; rep. from * to last st., k.1.

5th row: As 3rd row.

6th row: As 2nd row.

These 6 rows form the patt. and are repeated throughout to complete the fabric as in (98).

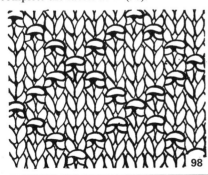

Cabled V-necked sweater in four sizes with new action-sleeves—instructions on page 118

RIBBED DIAMOND PATTERN

Cast on a multiple of 11 sts.

1st row: * P.1, k.2 tog., w.f., k.5, w.f., k.2 tog. t.b.l., p.1; rep. from * to end.

2nd and every alt. row: * K.1, p.9, k.1; rep. from * to end.

3rd row: * P.1, k.1, w.f., k.2 tog. t.b.l., k.3, k.2 tog., w.f., k.1, p.1; rep. from * to end.

5th row: * P.1, k.2, w.f., k.2 tog. t.b.l., k.1, k.2 tog., w.f., k.2, p.1; rep. from * to end.

7th row: * P.1, k.3, w.f., k.3 tog., w.f., k.3, p.1; rep. from * to end.

9th row: * P.1, k.2, k.2 tog., w.f., k.1, w.f., k.2 tog. t.b.l., k.2, p.1; rep. from * to end.

11th row: * P.1, k.1, k.2 tog., w.f., k.3, w.f., k.2 tog. t.b.l., k.1, p.1; rep. from * to end.

12th row: As 2nd row. These 12 rows form the patt. and are repeated throughout.

DOUBLE CROCHET

A useful edging which is worked as diagram (99).

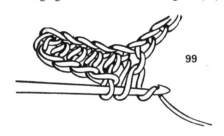

DOUBLE KNITTING

This type of knitting, tubular with closed ends, can be used for borders to cardigans and for scarves. The principle is that double the number of stitches required for the final width of fabric to be produced (an even number) is cast on. Work every row as follows:—

* K.1, bring wool to front of work, sl.1 purlwise, take wool to back of work; rep. from * to end of row.

When the length of fabric required has been completed cast off as follows:—

K.2 tog. twice, now sl. the 2nd stitch on the right-hand needle (the first 2 knitted together) over the first stitch (the second 2 knitted together), k. the next 2 sts. tog. Rep. the preceding action and continue in this way until all the stitches have been cast off.

DOUBLE KNITTING YARNS

This is one of the most useful and popular weights for knitting for all outer garments as it is quick to knit and not too bulky to wear. The quality of double knitting wools can vary considerably and it is advisable to use the brand and type of wool recommended in the pattern. Synthetic double knittings contain a greater yardage per ounce weight than wools and many synthetics are therefore sold in three-quarter ounce balls.

DOUBLE MOSS STITCH
(See *Moss Stitch Double*, page 64).

D'OYLEY
(See *Lace Knitting*, page 56)

DROPPED STITCHES
(See *Picking Up Stitches*, page 66).

DUTCH HEEL
(See *Socks*, page 84).

DYES
All branded wools and yarns are sold with a reference number on the label of the Dye Number used and it is important that all the wool used in one garment should bear the same Dye Number otherwise there may be an infinitesimal difference in tone. When buying wool, it is advisable to buy one or two ounces more than stated in the pattern to avoid the necessity of matching up Dye Numbers later on if a difference in tension takes more ounces than quoted. Left-over wools can be used up in many ways.

ELASTICISED KNITTING
(See *Waist Bands*, page 94).

EMBOSSED KNITTING
Here we have a type of knitting embodying the principle of embossed motifs being built up from a single stitch on to the front surface of the fabric. The surface fabric is usually the reverse side of stocking stitch.

The principle is to work an odd number of stitches out of a single stitch. These are then worked in ordinary stocking stitch on the reverse stocking stitch background, decreases being carried out at each side of the fabric worked on the increased stitches until the single stitch has been restored.

Small Embossed Leaf Pattern. Here is an example of an embossed leaf pattern worked on a 5 increase principle (100).

Cast on 9 sts.
1st row: P.
2nd row: K.
3rd and 4th rows: As 1st and 2nd rows.
5th row: P.4, inc. in next st., by knitting into front and back of st. twice and then knitting into the front of it again (thus making 5 sts. out of one), p.4.
6th row: K.4, p.5, k.4.
7th row: P.4, k.5, p.4.
8th row: As 6th row.
9th row (on which side decreases are commenced on embossed stocking stitch portion): P.4, k.2 tog. t.b.1, k.1, k.2 tog., p.4.
10th row: K.4, p.3, k.4.
11th row: P.4, sl.1, k.2 tog., p.s.s.o., p.4.
12th row: K.4, p.1, k.4 (original 9 sts. back on needle).
13th to 16th rows: Rep. 1st and 2nd rows twice.

The embossed leaf can be made larger by working more stitches out of a single stitch and carrying the decrease principle through the extra rows required to get rid of the extra stitches formed. These motifs form a delightful basis for a cot blanket or bedspread.

100

101

Variation. Another method by which the embossed leaf can be worked is by creating "over principle" increases at each side of the centre stitch, again working the leaf in stocking stitch on a background of reverse stocking stitch (101). A typical example of this type of embossed knitting is as follows:—

Cast on 9 sts.
1st row: P.
2nd row: K.
3rd and 4th rows: As 1st and 2nd rows.
5th row: P.4, k.1, p.4.
6th row: K.2, k.2 tog., inc. by purling into the front, back and front again of the next st., k.2 tog., k.2 (this row sets the position of the leaf. It is the only row in which

decreases are worked outside the leaf itself).

7th row: P.3, (k.1, w.f.) twice, k.1, p.3.
8th row: K.3, p.5, k.3.
9th row: P.3, k.2, w.f., k.1, w.f., k.2, p.3.
10th row: K.3, p.7, k.3.
11th row: P.3, k.3, w.f., k.1, w.f., k.3, p.3.
12th row: K.3, p.9, k.3.
13th row: P.3, k.4, w.f., k.1, w.f., k.4, p.3.
14th row: K.3, p.11, k.3.

(At this point the leaf can be widened by continuing on this principle until the size of leaf required is created).

Now work 2 rows without further increase as follows:—
15th row: P.3, k.11, p.3.
16th row: As 14th row.

You are now ready to start the decrease principle of the leaf.

17th row: P.3, k.2 tog. t.b.l., k.7, k.2 tog., p.3.
18th row: K.3, p.9, k.3.
19th row: P.3, k.2 tog. t.b.l., k.5, k.2 tog., p.3.
20th row: K.3, p.7, k.3.
21st row: P.3, k.2 tog. t.b.1, k.3, k.2 tog., p.3.
22nd row: K.3, p.5, k.3.
23rd row: P.3, k.2 tog. t.b.l, k.1, k.2 tog., p.3.
24th row: K.2, inc. by knitting into front and back of next st., p.3, inc. by knitting into front and back of next st., k.2 (in the above row the stitches have been made to balance the decrease principle in the 6th row).
25th row: P.4, sl.1, k.2 tog., p.s.s.o., p.4.
26th row: K.4, p.1, k.4.
27th to 30th rows: Rep. 1st and 2nd rows twice.

EMBROIDERY ON KNITTING

The golden rule for working embroidery on knitting is to strive to create bold effects with simple stitches. If a transfer is used the best plan is to iron the transfer on to a piece of tracing paper, tack the tracing paper over the knitting that is to be embroidered, work the embroidery through the paper and the knitted fabric and tear the paper away when the work is completed.

Embroidery on knitting links us to some of the oldest aspects of this interesting craft. In parts of Bavaria, peasant knitting has been covered with bright coloured embroidery for several centuries. The Victorian age saw a revival of embroidered knitting in this country, the development being mainly of cross stitching and Swiss darning. A delightful Victorian embroidered peasant apron can be seen in the collection at the Victoria and Albert Museum.

There are two distinct approaches to the embroidering of knitted fabric. The first and commonest is to superimpose gaily coloured designs in Swiss darning or cross stitch on a stocking stitch fabric, or sometimes portions of the design are knitted in stocking stitch specifically for this purpose.

The Tyrolean tradition is completely different. In this the embroidery forms an integral part of the pattern itself, the boldly embossed and cable fabrics being designed in such a way that the embossed portions form a background and guide to the embroidery itself.

Cross Stitch. A firm fabric is essential if the embroidery is to lie smoothly on the surface of the knitting. The diagram (102) shows quite clearly the working method for cross stitch on knitting. It is important to notice the position of the needle, as this illustrates the way to form the cross in such a way that it is not dragged out of shape by the natural elasticity of the knitted fabric.

French Knots. French knots are tiny "bobbles" embroidered on the surface of the fabric. Insert the needle, from the wrong side, at the point where the French knot is to be formed, draw the needle through, wrap the thread two or three times round the needle (103), insert the needle again at the same point where it was inserted the first time, draw the thread through the loops, thus forming a knot on the surface of the fabric.

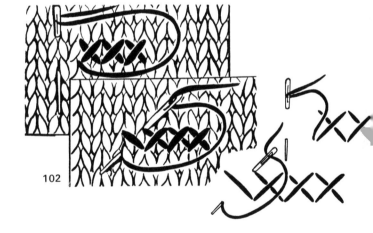

102

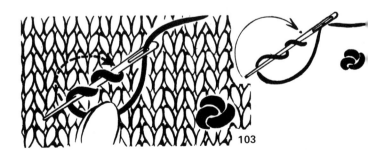

103

Lazy Daisy Stitch. Draw the needle through the fabric at the base of the stitch; now insert the needle in the same place again, then run it up behind the fabric at the point defining the size of the lazy daisy stitch to be worked. The point of the needle must come out through the loop formed by the wool on the front of the fabric (104). Insert the needle over the top of the wool, catching the loop formed and making the Lazy Daisy Stitch.

Smocking. Embroidered smocking on knitted fabric can be used to form charming yokes for babies' dresses or effective decoration for knitted blouses.

It is important to remember that the portion of a garment to be smocked should be at least a third as wide again as the finished width when the smocking is completed.

The basic fabric for knitting is an embossed rib. One-in-three forms a neat grounding.

Cast on a number of stitches divisible by 4, plus 3 over.

1st row: K.1, * k.b.1, p.3; rep. from * to last 2 sts., k.b.l, k.1.

2nd row: K.1, * p.b.1, k.3; rep. from * to last 2 sts., p.b.l, k.1. These 2 rows form the basic embossed rib on which smocking is worked when the knitting is completed.

The actual smocking may be worked with the same colour as the knitting or with a contrasting colour. The principle is perfectly simple. On the first row of smocking draw together, as shown in the diagram (ribs 1 and 2), (ribs 3 and 4), (ribs 5 and 6), etc. On the next row of smocking, worked 5 rows up the fabric, draw together (ribs 2 and 3), (ribs 4 and 5), (ribs 6 and 7), etc. etc. Repeat this until the smocking is completed (105).

Swiss Darning. The principle here is that the embroidered stitch follows the line of the knitting stitch, superimposing what appears to be coloured patterns in stocking stitch on the front surface of the fabric. Here is the working method for Swiss darning on knitted fabric.

First of all draw the needle through the 2 threads at the base of the stitch to be covered, then insert the needle again through the two threads at the top of the stitch to be covered, draw the needle through, thus covering one side of the knitted stitch. Now insert the needle again through the base of the next stitch and the second side of the stocking stitch loop on the front of the fabric will be covered (106).

105

Examples of embroidery stitches shown on knitting are Lazy Daisy (104), Smocking (105) and Swiss Darning (106), all described above

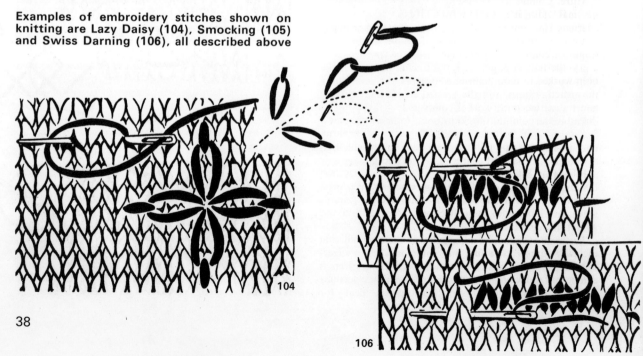

104

106

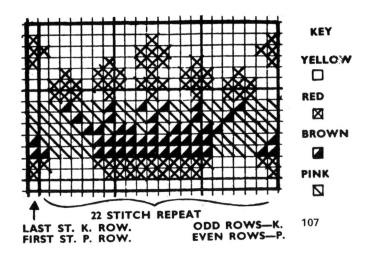

KEY

YELLOW □

RED ⊠

BROWN ◪

PINK ◻

22 STITCH REPEAT

LAST ST. K. ROW.
FIRST ST. P. ROW.

ODD ROWS—K.   107
EVEN ROWS—P.

FACINGS, Knitted

Interesting tailored effects can be obtained in knitwear by using facings knitted on to the front edge in place of ribbed bands. When this is done, the hem at the lower edge must be mitred and the facing mitred to match the hem.

Mitre. Commence by casting on 14 stitches less than the final width, increase one stitch at both ends of every alternate row until 7 sets of increases (14 stitches in all, 7 at each end) have been worked. Mark this point with a length of coloured thread. Now continue increasing on every alternate row until 7 more sets of increases have been worked (7 more stitches at each end), thus forming the mitred portion of the hem up to the coloured thread, and the mitred portion of the facing from the coloured thread to the point that has now been reached.

Buttonholes on facings will have to be worked in duplicate sets, exactly corresponding to buttonholes on fronts.

Ribbon or Bias Binding. When using ribbon or bias binding for facing front bands or shaped edges (bias binding should always be used on shaped edges) simply stitch the ribbon into position, using a flat seam on the wrong side of the work.

Buttonholes worked in ribbon facings. First of all tack the ribbon into position. Mark the position of each buttonhole with a pin or tacking stitch, take the ribbon off again, cut and work buttonholes, then stitch the facing on in the ordinary way.

FAIR ISLE KNITTING

This is knitting in multi-colours the patterns traditional to Fair Isle. Many of the designs link directly with the Catholic tradition and it is claimed, with a certain amount of historical evidence, that the Fair Islanders originally derived their knitting tradition from Spanish sources, either copying designs found on garments worn by sailors who had been wrecked on one of the vessels of the Armada, or actually learning the patterns from survivors of the wreck who stayed on the Island.

Crown of Glory. This is a typical Fair Isle design and may be worked from the chart (107).

In reading the chart remember that all odd rows are knitted and are read from right to left; all even rows are purled and are worked from left to right. Each square read horizontally represents one stitch and each square read vertically, one row.

FAIR ISLE PATTERNS

Today, all knitting where two or more colours are used is often referred to as "Fair Isle knitting." This is a misnomer, as Fair Isle knitting proper is only practised on Fair Isle. The hall marks of a genuine Fair Isle are—
a. The method in which the colour design is worked, and
b. the sequence of patternings that change all the way up the garment.
In these sequences, a broad pattern carried out in a number of colours is generally followed by a narrow pattern carried out in two to three colours only.

The patterining is always done on a ground of white, fawn, grey or brown. Bold, clear colourings are always used for the patternings, as these give the traditional effect known as Fair Isle knitting.

Colour Charts. Never more than two colours are used at the same time in any row on a Fair Isle design. The colours themselves are worked on two rows, with the

39

ground shade and pattern shade changing on alternating rows, thus giving a multi-coloured effect to the whole pattern.

The following table shows the working of a fifteen-row Fair Isle pattern.

	Background	Pattern
1st row:	Ground Shade	1st Colour
2nd row:	2nd Colour	1st Colour
3rd row:	2nd Colour	3rd Colour
4th row:	4th Colour	3rd Colour
5th row:	4th Colour	5th Colour
6th row:	6th Colour	5th Colour
7th row:	6th Colour	7th Colour
8th row:	Ground Shade	7th Colour
9th row:	As 7th row	As 7th row
10th row:	As 6th row	As 6th row
11th row:	As 5th row	As 5th row
12th row:	As 4th row	As 4th row
13th row:	As 3rd row	As 3rd row
14th row:	As 2nd row	As 2nd row
15th row:	As 1st row	As 1st row

The narrow patterns that lie between the broad patternings are worked in two or three colours. For a narrow pattern which falls over seven rows the sequence of colours will be as follows—

	Background	Pattern
1st row:	Ground Shade	1st Colour
2nd row:	Ground Shade	2nd Colour
3rd row:	3rd Colour	2nd Colour
4th row:	As 3rd row	As 3rd row
5th row:	As 3rd row	As 3rd row
6th row:	As 2nd row	As 2nd row
7th row:	As 1st row	As 1st row

Designing for Fair Isle. Designing Fair Isle garments is perfectly simple, as the design is charted out on graph paper before the actual knitting is commenced. The important point to remember is that, for the beginner, it is advisable to work patterns which have a multiple that will divide equally into the total number of stitches used on the section of the garment which is being worked, plus one extra stitch.

FAROE ISLE KNITTING

This is a traditional colour knitting peculiar to the Faroe Isles. The background of the lovely coats, for which the Faroe knitters are world famous, is always in an off-white shade and approximate to the thickness of a 4-ply Fingering wool.

The principle of Faroe knitting is the same as in Fair Isle knitting, except that the designs, usually based on simple geometric shapes, are much bolder in conception. Each section of the design is knitted in a different colour, the ground shade being constant throughout.

40

COATS

The patternings of the coats follow a very definite theme. Bold ribbing is used for the welt and cuffs, moving into a narrow border in which geometric shapes in vivid colours dominate. The body of the coat is worked in various types of seedings, i.e. single or grouped stitches forming all-over patterns on the fabric.

The yokes are literally a blaze of lovely colourings on the off-white ground, the designs again being based on bold geometric patternings. The patternings on the yoke are matched up on the tops of the sleeves, giving a typical off-the-shoulder effect, although the armhole shapings and sleeve top shapings are done in the same way as for a classic design.

The combining of these bold designs with seedings makes a lovely pattern for a garment.

The neckband is another interesting feature of these garments. This is usually knitted double. The first part of the neckband, which is knitted up in the same way as on a classic cardigan, is worked in the ground shade in 1 and 1 rib. The second part of the band, which is usually knitted on a size finer needle, is knitted in the same patterning that was used for the border immediately after the ribbing. The band is then folded over at the top of the ribbing and neatly stitched down on the right side.

The front bands are worked in 1 and 1 rib exactly the same as the front bands on a classic cardigan. Gay

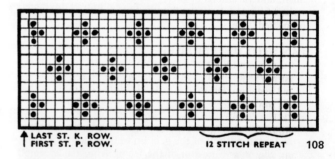

↑ **LAST ST. K. ROW.**
↑ **FIRST ST. P. ROW.**   **12 STITCH REPEAT**   **108**

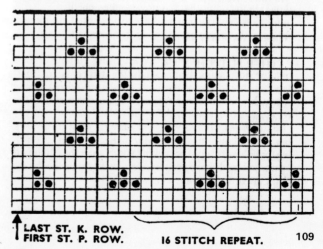

↑ **LAST ST. K. ROW.**
↑ **FIRST ST. P. ROW.**   **16 STITCH REPEAT.**   **109**

peasant buttons in wood or metal are used, picking up, if possible, the colourings used in the coat itself.

In traditional garments buttons are nearly always in wood and are hand painted, again with simple geometric patterning, repeating some of the themes used in the design on the coat itself.

SEEDINGS

A variety of seeding patterns can be devised and used in the body of the coats. The charts (108 and 109) show simple seedings used in Faroe knitting.

FEATHER PATTERNS

The basic principle of lace knitting is that holes are created in the fabric by using the "over" principle (see page 50), the holes being balanced by decreases. Generally the number of stitches on each row remains constant, as the "overs" are balanced by the decreases throughout the pattern.

There are, however, exceptions to this principle, when embossed effects or pointed lace edgings are worked, and in these patterns the number of stitches may vary from row to row but always returns to the number used on the first row of the pattern in order that the repeat can be worked successfully by the knitter.

The patterns commonly known as Fan, Feather or Shell, and variations of them, are all worked by using a series of massed decreases balanced by a succeeding series of massed "overs".

FAN STITCH, EMBOSSED

Cast on a multiple of 11 sts. plus 1 st.
1st row: * K.1, w.f., k.10, w.f.; rep. from * to last st, k.1.
2nd and every alt. row: K.1, p. to end.
3rd row: * K.2, w.f., k.10, w.f., k.1; rep. from * to last st., k.1.
5th row: * K.3, w.f., k.10, w.f., k.2; rep. from * to last st., k.1.
7th row: * K.3, (p.2 tog.) 6 times, k.2; rep. from * to last st., k.1.
8th row: K.1, p. to end.
These 8 rows form the patt. (110).

FEATHER STITCH, CASCADE

Using Through the Stitch method cast on a multiple of 17 sts.
1st row: K.
2nd row: K.
3rd row: P.
4th row: K.
5th row: * (K.2 tog.) 3 times, (over, k.1) 5 times, over, (k.2 tog.) 3 times; rep. from * to end.
6th row: P.

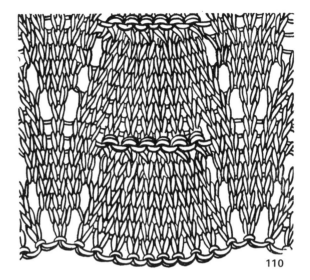

110

111

7th to 16th rows: Rep. 5th and 6th rows 5 times.
These 16 rows form the patt. (111).
Note: For dressing jackets and babies' garments, rows 1 to 4 inclusive in the pattern can be worked in a contrasting colour, this gives a lovely effect of cascades of coloured shells on the pattern.

41

FEATHER AND SHELL PATTERN

Cast on a multiple of 18 sts. plus 1 st.
1st row: * K.1, (k.2 tog. t.b.l.) 3 times, (over, k.1) 5 times, over, (k.2 tog.) 3 times; rep. from * to last st., k.1.
2nd row: K.
3rd row: K.
4th row: P.
These 4 rows form the patt. as shown in (112) and are repeated for the length throughout.

FEATHER STITCH, RIDGED

Cast on a multiple of 13 sts.
1st row: * K.4, (w.f., k.1) 5 times, w.f., k.4; rep. from * to end.
2nd row: P.
3rd row: * (P.2 tog.) 3 times, p.7, (p.2 tog.) 3 times; rep. from * to end.
4th row: K.
5th row: K.
6th row: P.
These 6 rows form the patt. (113).

FEATHER STITCH

Cast on a multiple of 18 sts., plus 1 st.
1st row: * P.1, (k.2 tog. t.b.l.) 3 times, (over, k.1) 5 times, over, (k.2 tog.) 3 times: rep. from * to last st., p.1.
2nd row: * K.1, p.17; rep. from * to last st., k.1.
3rd row: * P.1, k.17; rep. from * to last st., p.1.
4th row: As 2nd row.
These 4 rows form the patt. (114).

FELTING

Knitted garments, in particular berets and fez, are "felted" to make them weather proof. They are knitted much larger than the final size is to be and are then soaked in water and pummelled with heavy stones while still wet; they are then shaped on wooden blocks and left to dry.

Felting of home-knitted garments can take place inadvertently if the garment is roughly handled during the washing process and particularly if there are sudden changes of temperature in the washing water or if water is used which is too hot.

FINISHING

(See *Blocking Garments*, page 14, and *Seams*, page 74).

FISHERMEN'S JERSEYS

These close-fitting jerseys are designed to keep fishermen warm under oilskins and are always knitted in 4-ply wool with high-fitting polo collars. The most famous are the Bridal Shirts, which used to be knitted by the fisherman's sweetheart to be worn by him on his wedding day; these jerseys have intricate cabled and raised patterns and every

112

113

114

fishing port round the coastline of England had its own individual designs, most of which have now been lost although designs from Cornwall and Yorkshire still remain. Equally well-known is the Guernsey, the sweater worn by fishermen from the Channel Islands, which is knitted on four needles and is still popular today for sailing and ski-ing.

FISHERMEN'S RIB

(See *Ribbing*, page 69).

FLORENTINE KNITTING

Florentine (sometimes called Jacquard Knitting) is in some ways the most elaborate colour knitting. The designs consist of floral, animal and insect motifs, built up into an all-over pattern, separate lengths of wool being used for each colour in each motif, the colour first used is twisted round the next shade used, throughout, thus preventing gaps in the work.

These designs are frequently knitted in silk on a woollen ground and are sometimes enriched with embroidery in stem stitch or chain stitch in gold or silver thread round the edges of the motifs. When this is done, it represents the full flowering of the Florentine tradition of the sixteenth century and it is sometimes referred to as "Brocaded Knitting."

Jacquard knitting, which resembles Florentine knitting of the sixteenth and seventeenth centuries in that any number of colours can be used in the design, is worked in exactly the same way as Fair Isle knitting. It is advisable to use short lengths of wool for the coloured patterning, as this makes it easier to knit up this type of design.

Motifs of this type can be worked on the fronts of jumpers or cardigans, in fact they can be used for decorative effects on all types of knitting.

The charts show typical Jacquard motifs (115, 116, 117).

FRAME KNITTING

The origins of frame knitting are completely unknown. Traces of frames have been found in excavations in parts of Arabia and it was certainly an established section of the craft during the reign of Queen Elizabeth I. At this period it played a very significant part in the development of the hosiery industry, as the Rev. W. Lee, a Church of England clergyman, invented on the basis of the simple frame a mechanical frame which was to lay the foundations of the machine-knitting industry all over Europe.

Bobbin Work. Most of us did frame knitting as children. We called it bobbin work or corkwork. The method used is to fix 4 short nails at equal distances round the hole in an ordinary cotton reel, make 4 loops (one on each nail) and then proceed to produce a circular knitted cord by winding the wool round the outside of these 4 nails and drawing the loops over the wool, repeating this action until a piece of cord the length required has been produced in the centre of frame (118).

Circular Frames. In the early days, circular frames with pegs numbering up to 200 and 300 were produced. On these tubular fabric could be made on exactly the same principle as bobbin work.

The frame knitting method is probably the ideal one for teaching young children how to knit, giving them an interest in the development of the craft.

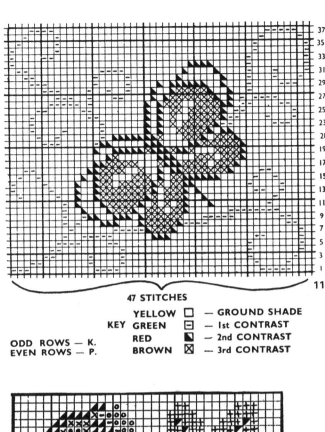

47 STITCHES   115

	KEY		
YELLOW	□	—	GROUND SHADE
GREEN	⊟	—	1st CONTRAST
RED	◣	—	2nd CONTRAST
BROWN	☒	—	3rd CONTRAST

ODD ROWS — K.
EVEN ROWS — P.

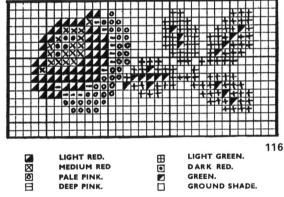

116

◪	LIGHT RED.	⊞	LIGHT GREEN.
☒	MEDIUM RED	⊡	DARK RED.
⊙	PALE PINK.	◩	GREEN.
⊟	DEEP PINK.	□	GROUND SHADE.

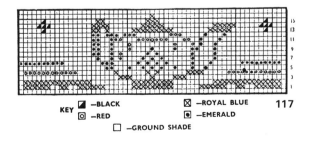

117

KEY	◪ —BLACK	☒ —ROYAL BLUE
	⊙ —RED	⊡ —EMERALD
	□ —GROUND SHADE	

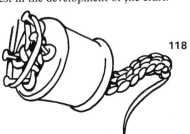

118

43

FRINGING

(See also *Scarves,* page 74).

To make a fringe on a scarf or other garment, take a length of cardboard about 3 inches wide. Wind the wool round the cardboard and then cut along one edge. Take 3 or 4 strands, hold the ends together between the fingers, slip a crochet hook through the edge of the scarf and through the loop formed by holding the strands of wool between the fingers. Draw this loop through the knitted fabric. Now insert the crochet hook under the strands of wool held between the fingers, draw this through the loop already formed and pull tightly into a knot. Continue to fringe across the ends of the scarf in this way, trimming the ends neatly to a uniform length. (See diagram, page 74).

GARTER STITCH

This stitch, as its name suggests, was originally used for long woollen garters which were wrapped round the tops of stockings.

To produce Garter Stitch fabric when working on two needles, every row is knitted in Knit Stitch. When working on four needles or more in rounds, one round is Knitted and the next is Purled; these two rounds are repeated throughout the fabric.

g

GAUGE OF NEEDLES

Knitting needles are numbered (gauged) according to size. (See the chart below).

The English gauge system, where a bell type gauge (119) is used to check the size of the needle, numbers from 1-20, size 1 being the coarsest and size 20 the finest needle. Sizes 1-14 are usually made in metal, plastic or steel, the very coarse needles are also made in wood. The perfect knitting needle should have a smooth surface along which the stitches move easily and a short, rounded "point" which will not catch on the wool.

The finest gauges, from 15-20, are usually used for lace knitting. The next group, from 12-15, are used for sock and stocking knitting while the coarser gauges, size 1-6, are frequently used for knitting blankets in heavy wools.

Here is a list of gauges with notes as to the most suitable material to use these needles with.

1-6   Heavy wools, mainly used for blankets and rugs.
6-9   Double knitting, forming ideal fabrics for sports-wear of all types.
8-10 4-ply wools.
9-12 3-ply wools.
10-14 2-ply wools.
12-15 Sock wools of various thicknesses.
15-20 Cotton for lace, or fine garments in 1-ply wool.

119

GLOVES

The traditional way of knitting gloves is to work in rounds, using 4 or 5 needles. The hand portion of the glove is actually a piece of circular knitting with a gusset shaping for the thumb.

The thumb and fingers are also pieces of circular knitting shaped off at the top to fit the thumb and fingers.

All types of yarn, cotton, silk or wool can be used for gloves. It is essential however that fine needles should be used, as a firm fabric must be produced, even if it is in a lacy pattern in cotton or silk; this enables the glove to retain its shape in wear and wash.

In order to knit a pair of gloves to the right size it is essential to take the measurements from your own hand. Diagram (120) shows you quite clearly how these measurements are taken.

It is important to remember that the controlling measurement will be the width round the top of the hand at a point between the beginning of thumb and beginning

Comparative Gauges of Knitting Needles (Continental, American and British)

Metric (m.m.) European	9	8½	8	7½	7	6½	6	5½	5	4½	4	3½	3¼	3	2½	2¼	2
British	000	00	0	1	2	3	4	5	6	7	8	9	10	11	12	13	14
American	15	13	12	11	10½	10	9	8	7	6	5	4	3	2	1	0	00

of the fingers. This line is marked A on the measurement chart. Once you have obtained this measurement, it is a simple matter to arrive at the number of stitches to cast on. Check the tension by knitting a small square with the particular type of yarn you are using on the needles on which you are going to knit the gloves. Multiply the number of stitches to the inch by the hand measurement to get the total required.

For a 6½ size glove the measurement round the hand is 7½ ins. If you are working at a tension of 12 sts. to the in. you will require 90 sts. It is always advisable to use needles one or two sizes finer for the ribbing at the wrist, as these give a nice firm grip to the wrist band and thus aid the proper fitting of the finished glove.

The next measurement, point B on the diagram, is round the hand at the base of the thumb, as this will give the extra stitches required in the thumb gusset. For a size 6½, the measurement here is 9¼ ins., 1¾ in. more than the first measurement (the width round the hand). On a 12 st. tension this would give you 21 sts. As an even number is needed for the thumb increases add 22 sts. The thumb gusset is worked in graded inc., therefore there will be 11 sets of inc. in the gusset.

Now measure the length of the thumb gusset, point C on the chart. This is approximately 2 ins. for a 6½ size glove. If your tension is 14 rows to the in., as it probably will be on a 12 st. tension, this means there will be 28 rounds in which to work the 11 sets of increases. Therefore, the inc. are worked on every alt. round for 22 rounds. Work 6 rounds after the last set of inc., thus completing the gusset base for the thumb.

Placing and Working the Gusset. The placing of the gusset is a very simple matter. When you have completed the ribbing (and in the gloves already referred to you will have cast on 90 sts.), work 4 rounds in stocking stitch.

Commence the gusset thus—

Divide 90 by 2; this gives you 45 sts. You will need 2 sts. at the centre of the gusset, these lying between the 2 made sts. on the first inc. round. Thus the round will be worked as—K.44, m.1, k.2, m.1, k.44.

The gusset increases move outwards, thus creating a "V" formation in the fabric; until you have completed 11 sets of increases (121).

You will notice that in the 2nd inc. round 4 sts. are worked between the 2 made sts., in the 3rd inc. round 6 sts. and so on. The number before and after the made sts. remains constant throughout the shaping, i.e. 44 sts. on each side of the made sts.

When the 28 rounds have been worked the gusset is completed.

Knit the Thumb. This is worked in rounds on the 22 made sts. plus 4 sts. which are cast on to form a bridge in the gusset itself.

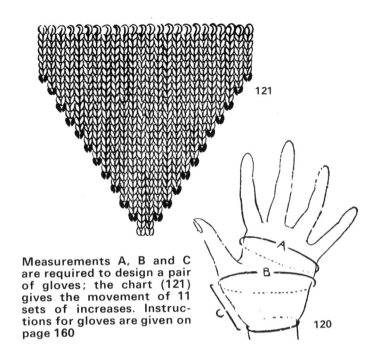

121

120

Measurements A, B and C are required to design a pair of gloves; the chart (121) gives the movement of 11 sets of increases. Instructions for gloves are given on page 160

To set the thumb, work across 45 sts., slip the next 22 sts. on to a length of wool.

Cast on 4 sts. (thus there will be 49 in place of 45 sts. on the needle), then work across the remaining 45 sts., working these sts. (94) into a round again, 30 on each of 2 needles and 34 on the 3rd needle. It is advisable that the round shall break the centre of the 4 cast-on sts. as this means that when you come to the fingers it is a simple matter to place them in the correct position.

Work in rounds until the point for the fingers is reached, thus completing the straight bag with thumb gusset, which forms the hand part of the glove.

Stitches for Fingers, Divided. The number of stitches required for the first 3 fingers is the same, but 2 or 3 less are used for the little finger.

The round has 94 sts. which can be worked on the 1st, 2nd and 3rd fingers thus, 26 sts. for the first finger, 23 sts. each for the 2nd and 3rd fingers (a total of 72 sts.), leaving 22 for the little finger.

As the palm is narrower than the back of the hand, allow more stitches for the back than for the front of each finger. Thus, on the 26-stitch finger, use 11 from the front of the hand and 15 from the back; for the 23-stitch fingers 11 from the front and 12 from the back, and for the 22-stitch finger 10 from the front and 12 from the back.

Place the Fingers. Working from the 2 sts. worked up from the 4 cast-on which form a bridge on thumb, slip 43 sts. on to a length of wool. Slip the remaining 51 sts. on to a 2nd length of wool, (94 sts on the round) the 43 sts. forming the fronts of the fingers, the 51 sts. the backs of the fingers.

A bridge consisting of cast-on sts. is formed between the 1st and 2nd, 2nd and 3rd, 3rd and 4th fingers. In the glove given as an example 3 cast-on sts. will be sufficient.

If a coarser yarn were used, probably only 2 would be required. With a finer yarn you may need from 4 to 5 sts. The point of this bridge is that it allows for free play of the fingers when the gloves are worn.

The First Finger. Slip 11 sts. from the thumb gusset end on to a needle, (these 11 being from the 43 group of sts.), sl. 15 sts. from the 51-st. group on to a 2nd needle.

Cast on 3 sts. at the opposite end of the needle to the thumb end, giving a total of 29 sts.

Now slip 10 sts. on to each of 2 needles and 9 sts. on to the 3rd needle and work in rounds for the finger.

To complete the finger, when the length required has been worked dec. for the top by working the first set of dec. in every 3 sts. of the round on the "k.2 tog., k.1" principle. This will leave 2 sts. at the end of the round. K. these 2 tog. (19 sts.).

Work 2 rounds, then work the 2nd set of dec. on every 2 sts. of the round on the "k.2 tog." principle, thus leaving 1 st., k. this st. (10 sts.).

Break off the wool, thread it through a needle and draw the length of wool through the 10 sts.

Draw up and fasten off securely.

The Second, Third and Fourth Fingers. K. up 3 sts. through the bridge formed by the cast-on sts. at the base of the 1st, 2nd and 3rd fingers, making a similar bridge on the opposite side of the 2nd and 3rd fingers by casting on 3 sts. Complete the fingers in rounds as for the first finger.

The Thumb. This is worked in the same way as the fingers on the 22 sts. which have been left on the length of wool, knitting up through the 4 cast-on sts. which form the bridge. Divide the sts. on to 3 needles to work the thumb and finish off the top as for the fingers.

Once the above principles have been understood you will find it an easy enough matter to design gloves in any type of yarn.

CONTINENTAL METHOD OF KNITTING THUMBS

Among the peasants in France, Germany and Switzerland, a simple method of knitting thumbs has been devised, which does not necessitate the creation of a thumb gusset.

The ribbed wrist is knitted as in an ordinary glove but when this is completed the number of stitches in the round is increased to the number required for the width round the broadest part of the hand at the base of the thumb.

When the point where the thumb itself is to be worked is reached (this being approximately 2 ins. from the ribbing at the wrist), k. across ¾ in. of the next round (2 sts. in from the beg. of the first needle) with different coloured wool or thread, stranding the original colour across the back of these sts. In the following round you k. across the group of coloured sts. with the ordinary wool and then complete the glove and fingers as for an ordinary glove.

To Place the Thumb. Remove the coloured thread.

This action will release the stitches required for the thumb. These are now picked up on 3 needles to form a round and the thumb is knitted in the ordinary way.

To work the thumb on the 2nd glove place the coloured thread stitches so that they terminate 2 stitches from the *end* of the round, thus reversing the position of the thumb.

GLOVE MITTENS

These are virtually gloves without fingers (122). They are knitted exactly the same as gloves to "Place the Fingers" then each finger is worked with 4 rounds of stocking stitch and 2 rounds of ribbing and cast off.

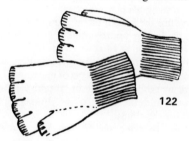

122

GRAFTING

This is a method of joining, invisibly and without a ridge, stitches on two separate needles, e.g. the toe of a sock. Divide stitches equally on two needles, right side outside.

Thread a needle with wool and commence at right-hand side of work as follows:—

* Insert wool needle knitwise into first stitch on front needle, draw wool through the stitch, slipping the latter off the needle. Insert needle purlwise into second stitch on front needle, now draw wool through and leave stitch on needle. Take wool under front needle, and insert wool needle purlwise into first stitch on the back needle, draw wool through stitch and slip latter off needle.

125

46

123

Insert wool needle knitwise into second stitch on back needle, draw wool through and leave stitch on needle. Bring wool forward and repeat from * all across.

Grafting, Alternative Method. With *wrong* sides of work outside * insert darning needle knitwise through first st. on each needle, sl. first st. off back needle, draw wool through; insert darning needle purlwise through first st. on each needle, sl. first st. off front needle, draw wool through; rep. from * until all sts. are worked off.

Ribbing. Many experienced knitters find it extremely difficult to graft in k.1, p.1 rib. There is however a continental method which makes this a very simple process indeed.

You will need a set of 4 needles and the method is as follows:—

Slip the stitches off the needle and pick up all the k. stitches on one needle and leave at the front of the work, pick up all the p. stitches on a second needle and leave at the back of work (123).

Repeat this action with the second piece of ribbing which is to be grafted to the first.

Graft together the two sets of k. stitches in the ordinary way (124).

Turn the work round (thus p. stitches become k. stitches) and graft these together in the ordinary way.

GRAPHING

(See *Designing Fabrics,* page 31)

GUERNSEY

Probably the most famous sweater of all is the Guernsey (or "gansey" as it is sometimes called). These are always knitted in a crossbred wool, usually of a 4-ply weight, fine needles being used to create a firm fabric that serves as an ideal protection against the wind and the rain.

Casting On. A special method of cast-on is used for these garments to create a knotted edge, it is worked as follows—

Using the thumb method, cast on 2 sts., sl. the 2nd st. on the needle over the first st., * cast on 2 more sts., then draw the 2nd st. on the needle over the first st., thus leaving 2 sts. on the needle; rep. from * until the correct number of sts. are cast on (125).

Although the Guernsey type of sweater is knitted on 4 needles the back and front are both commenced on 2 needles, thus creating two flaps.

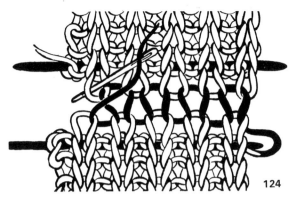

124

TRADITIONAL GUERNSEY DESIGN

Materials. 17 ozs. Wendy Family 4-ply wool; 4 No. 12 needles.

Measurements. 38/40 inch chest.

Tension 7 stitches to 1 inch.

Using No. 12 needles, cast on 140 sts., by the method given above. K.16 rows. Break off the wool, then work a 2nd piece in the same manner.

Now work the sts. of both pieces on to 3 needles, using a 4th needle to work with throughout (140 sts. on the 1st needle, 70 on each of the 2nd and 3rd needles).

Work 8 rounds in k.2, p.2, rib.

Now work in st.st. with a single g. st. at side seams.

1st round: K.

2nd round: P.1, k.139, p.1, k. to end.

Rep. these 2 rounds until work measures 15 ins., finishing at end of a 2nd round.

Divide for the Armholes. To do this, k. the first st. on to the end of the 3rd needle. Now proceed to work the front in rows, working backwards and forwards as follows—

1st row: K.3, p.4, k.126, p.4, k.3.

2nd row: P.

Rep. these 2 rows until work measures 11 ins. from division, finishing with a p. row. Break off wool and leave sts. on needle.

Rejoin wool to remaining sts. and work back to match.

Do not break off wool, but, placing back and front together, join the shoulders by casting off 42 sts. knitwise, 1 st. from the front and 1 from the back counting as 1 st. Sl. the st. remaining on the right-hand needle, after the cast-off, on to the sts. of back on left-hand needle. Break off wool, sl. sts. to other end of the needles, rejoin the wool and cast off 42 sts., 1 from the back and 1 from the front as before, *purlwise*.

The st. that remains on the right-hand needle after the cast-off should now be slipped on to sts. of front on left-hand needle. There will now be 55 sts. on each of 2 needles.

Neck Gusset. Divide the 55 sts. of back on to 2 needles and work in rounds shaping the neck gusset.

Commencing with the needle with the 55 sts. on it, proceed in rounds as follows—

1st round: 1st needle: (55 sts.) K.1, k.2 tog., k. to last st.,

47

sl. this st. on to next needle; **2nd needle:** K.2, k.2 tog., k. to end; **3rd needle:** K. to last st., sl. last st. on to next needle.

2nd round: 1st needle: Inc. in each of first 2 sts., k. to end; **2nd needle:** As 1st needle. **3rd needle:** K.

3rd round: 1st needle: Inc. in first st., k.2, inc. in next st., k. to end. **2nd needle:** As 1st needle. **3rd needle:** K.

4th round: 1st needle: Inc. in first st., k.4, inc. in next st., k. to end. **2nd needle:** As first needle. **3rd needle:** K.

Continue working in this way, noting that there are 2 sts. more between inc. of neck gusset on every round, until 8 rounds have been worked (12 sts. between inc., 136 sts. in round).

Work 14 rounds in k.2, p.2 rib.
Next round: P.
Cast off loosely, knitwise.

Sleeves: Cast on 80 sts. (26 on 1st needle, 28 on 2nd needle, and 26 on 3rd needle).

Work in rounds of k.2, p.2 rib for 3 ins.

Now proceed in st. st. with g. st. seam as follows—
1st round: K.
2nd round: P.1, k. to end.

Continue in rounds, inc. 1 st. at each side, the "p.1" forming the g. st. seam, on 7th and every following 7th round, until there are 120 sts. on needle. Continue on 120 sts. until work measures 19½ ins. from beg., finishing at end of a 2nd round.

Shape the Sleeve Gusset. This is worked in rounds as follows—

1st round: K.1, inc. in next st., k. to last 2 sts., inc. in next stitch, k.1.

2nd round: P.1, k. to end.

3rd round: K.2, inc. in next st., k. to last 3 sts., inc. in next stitch, k.2.

4th round: As 2nd round.

5th round: K.3, inc. in next st., k. to last 4 sts., inc. in next stitch, k.3.

6th round: As 2nd round.

Continue inc. in this manner until 13 sets of inc. in all have been worked, finishing at end of a 2nd round.

The sleeve top now moves to ribbing, the gusset stitches being worked in st. st. as follows—
1st round: K.17, (p.2, k.2) 28 times, p.2, k. to end.
2nd round: P.1, k.16, (p.2, k.2) 28 times, p.2, k. to end.

Rep. 1st and 2nd rounds once then 1st round once.

Next round: P.1, k.14, cast off in rib to last 13 sts., sl. all sts. on to one needle (29 sts.).

Working in rows, complete gusset as follows:—
1st row: K.2 tog. t.b.l., k. to last 2 sts., k.2 tog.
2nd row: P.13, k.1, p. to end.
3rd row: As 1st row.
4th row: P.12, k.1, p. to end.

Continue to dec. in this manner until 3 sts. remain.

Cast off.

To make the sleeves and body into a complete garment simply stitch the sleeves into position in the armholes, using a flat seam.

This traditional sweater is the basic shape on which sweaters of this type are always made.

In traditional fishermen's sweaters, sometimes called Bridal Shirts, patternings are incorporated in the back, front and sleeves of the garment. The patternings vary from stripes formed of garter stitch, embossed patterns in reversed stocking stitch on a stocking stitch foundation, and elaborate cable and bobble stitches. The latter types of stitches are usually found in Aran sweaters.

GUNNISTER MAN

The Gunnister Man is an interesting part of the history of knitting. He was a Shetland Tax Gatherer who was murdered and flung into the bog at Gunnister, Shetland, about 1745. Two hundred years later his body was recovered and his suit, waistcoat, stockings and cap, all hand-knitted in Shetland wool, were found intact and perfectly preserved and are now on view in a museum in Edinburgh, the only examples of knitted everyday garments which have survived so long.

HEELS

(See *Socks*, page 82).

HEMS

There are two methods of making the hems used on knitted garments.

Knitted-up Hem. Cast on, using the *Two Needle Through the Stitch Method.* When double the depth of fabric required for the hem has been knitted (always noting that you must finish on a purl row so that the right side of work will be facing when working the next row), on the next row make the hem by knitting together one stitch from the needle and one loop from the cast-on edge, all across the row, thus, pick up loop from cast-on edge and put it on left-hand needle, knit this and next stitch together.

Sewn Hem. This is the simplest method of making a hem in knitting. Knit in pattern the extra amount of material required for the hem.

48

Fold over and press the hem lightly in position on the inside of the work.

Run in a tacking thread to hold the hem in position whilst it is being sewn.

Neatly sew the edge with hem stitch, making sure that the sewing is worked stitch by stitch where the cast-on edge meets the row of knitted fabric. Work the hemming stitches diagonally and take great care that they do not show on the right side of the work.

HERRINGBONE STITCH

A sewing stitch used for the stitching of hems and waist belts. Work from left to right as diagram (126).

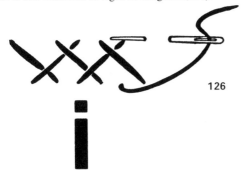

INCREASING

Increasing means making a stitch or stitches in the fabric. There are several methods by which this can be done, the methods varying according to the type of knitting that is being worked.

Invisible increase. This method of increase is where a stitch is made out of the fabric, the increase being practically invisible on the right side of the work.

Insert the point of the right-hand needle into the back of the stitch below the first stitch on left-hand needle.

Then insert the point of the left-hand needle into the front of the loop picked up on the right-hand needle (127).

Knit this loop off the needle.

An alternative method is to insert the point of the left-hand needle into the front of the stitch below the first stitch on the right-hand needle.

Slip the point of the right-hand needle through this loop as though to knit it.

Knit the loop off the needle.

Knit Between Stitches. This method of increasing is to make stitches out of the fabric itself. It is commonly used when creating dart shapings in pieces of knitted fabric.

Insert the point of the right-hand needle in the strand that lies between the stitch just knitted and the following stitch (128). Place this loop on the point of the left-hand

needle and then knit into the back of this loop in the ordinary way.

Purl. If the Knit Between Stitches type of increase is worked on the purl side of the fabric, the same principle is followed, except that you purl into the back of the strand that has been slipped on to the point of the left-hand needle, instead of knitting into the back of it.

Knit into Front and Back of Stitch. The commonest form of increase, used mainly for edge shapings in garments.

Insert the point of the right-hand needle into the first stitch on the left-hand needle, wrap the wool round the point of the right-hand needle. Draw a stitch through but do not drop the stitch off the needle (129).

Next insert the point of the right-hand needle through the back of the first stitch on the left-hand needle (130).

Wrap the wool round the point of the right-hand needle and draw the second stitch through, then drop stitch off left-hand needle in the ordinary way (131).

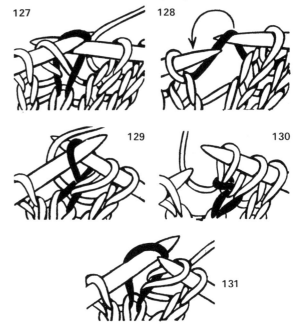

Double. When working a double increase work as for Knit into Front and Back of Stitch until the second stitch (the one knitted through the back of the first stitch on the left-hand needle) has been knitted. Do not drop the first stitch off the left-hand needle, but insert the point of the right-hand needle into the front of the stitch once more. Now wrap the wool round the point of the right-hand needle and knit a third stitch, then drop the stitch off the left-hand needle in the usual way.

Purl. If the Knit into Front and Back of Stitch type of

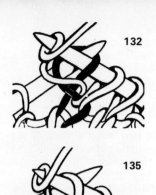

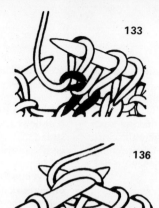

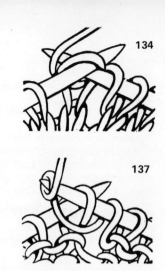

increase is worked on the purl side of the fabric the principle is exactly the same, except that the operation is carried out purlwise as follows:—

Insert the point of the right-hand needle purlwise through the first stitch on the left-hand needle.

Wrap the wool round the point of the right-hand needle and draw a stitch through, but do not drop the stitch off the needle. Next insert the point of the right-hand needle purlwise through the back of the first stitch on the left-hand needle.

Wrap the wool round the point of the right-hand needle and draw a second stitch through, then drop the stitch off the left-hand needle.

Rib. Another method of working the Knit into Front and Back Stitch type of increase (used mainly when working on ribbed fabrics) is to knit and purl into the same stitch.

Insert the point of the right-hand needle knitwise into the first stitch on the left-hand needle, wrap the wool round the right-hand needle and draw a stitch through but do not slip the stitch off the left-hand needle.

Insert the point of the right-hand needle purlwise into the back of the first stitch on the left-hand needle, wrap the wool round the point of the right-hand needle (132) and draw a stitch through, then drop the stitch off the left-hand needle (133).

Over Type of Increase. The "over" type of increase is used mainly in lace patterns. The operation here is perfectly simple as it merely means wrapping the wool over the right-hand needle before working the following stitch.

For the "over" that lies between two knit stitches, knit the first stitch, bring the wool forward from the back to the front of the work, take it over the top of the right-hand needle, then knit the next stitch in the ordinary way (134).

When the "over" falls between a knit and a purl stitch, knit the first stitch, then bring the wool to the front of the work, take it over the point of the right-hand needle, bring it to the front of the work again and purl the follow-

ing stitch (135).

When the "over" falls between a purl and a knit stitch, simply take the wool over the point of the right-hand needle and knit the next stitch in the ordinary way (136).

When the "over" lies between two purl stitches, take the wool over the point of the right-hand needle, bring it to the front of the work again and purl the following stitch (137).

IRONING
(See *Blocking Garments*, page 14).

j

JACQUARD KNITTING
(See *Florentine Knitting*, page 42).

JERSEYS

This is probably one of the original types of knitted garments. In its old form it was made as a straight tunic which slipped over the head, it had long or short sleeves. When worn as an outer garment it was referred to as a jersey and when used for underwear was referred to as a vest. Closely akin to the jersey is the Guernsey or Gansey worn by fishermen, as, although this is more elaborate than

Machine-knitted cardigan and pullover for school children—instructions for the cardigan are on page 197 and for the pullover, page 122

A complete layette which looks equally pretty in pink with white trimming. Instructions on page 178

the simple jersey, the basic principles of knitting it are the same.

The correct way to knit a jersey is in rounds with no armhole shaping, the sleeves being grafted in to the armhole, the shoulders are also grafted, thus giving the appearance of a seamless garment. The principles of knitting a round jersey are to take the chest measurement, and, using this against the tension of the type of wool to be used, work a circular tube of stocking stitch, bordered with either a hem or ribbing. At the armholes the work is divided on to 2 needles, half the stitches being used for the back and the other half for the front. The neck opening commences approximately 2 to 3 ins. below the shoulder line. The shoulders are worked by a series of turns, the stitches being placed on lengths of wool or stitch-holders ready for grafting.

The stitches at the front and back of the neck are not cast off but are again left on lengths of wool and are knitted up when working the neckband, which is usually in k.1, p.1 rib.

If the jersey is knitted on 2 needles then exactly half the number of stitches are cast on for the front. The front is worked straight up to the neck opening and is finished off as in the design worked in rounds. The back is knitted to match the front, the neck opening being omitted.

The sleeves are knitted as the sleeves of a cardigan.

This type of jersey can be made up with back-stitch seams in which case the shoulder stitches will be cast off instead of being left on lengths of wool for grafting.

Front Neck. The neck opening covers approximately $4\frac{1}{2}$ ins. at the centre front. Thus, when working at a tension of 8 sts. to the in., the centre group of 36 sts. will be lost in the neck opening of the fronts. This is done by slipping the centre 16 sts. on to a length of wool (these being knitted up later into the neckband). Dec. 10 sts. at each side of these centre sts., working the dec. on every row. The work is then continued without further dec. until the shoulder shaping is reached.

Shoulders. As the traditional type of jersey has the drop shoulder effect, the remaining sts. after the neck opening has been worked are divided into 3 or 4 groups. If working on a jersey with 8 sts. to the in. tension for a 40-in. chest, there will be 160 sts. across the front at the point where the neck opening commences; 36 of these are used for the neck opening, leaving 124 sts., i.e. 2 groups of 62.

Divide these 62 sts. into 3 groups: 20, 20, 22.

To work the shoulder shaping start at the neck edge and work across to the last 20 sts., turn and work back to the neck edge.

Next work to the last 40 sts., turn work again and work across to the neck edge. The sts. are then slipped on to a length of wool and left ready for grafting.

The same principle applies to the back but as there is no neck opening work across the whole group of 160 sts. Thus on the first 2 rows of the shoulder shaping work to the last 20 sts.; on the second 2 rows to the last 40 sts. and on the third group to the last 62 sts. All the sts. are now slipped on to a length of wool, the 62 at each end being grafted to the 62 at each side of the neck opening on the front, the centre group of 36 being left on a length of wool to be utilised when knitting up the neckband.

Knitting up Neckband. The neckband is worked on 4 needles. A common practice is to use needles two sizes finer than the ones on which the body of the jersey has been knitted, the finer needles being used also for the cuffs.

First of all, with right side of work facing, k. across the stitches left on the length of wool for the back of the neck. Now, using a 2nd needle k. up 1 st. through each edge st. round the neck shaping, and then across half the sts. which have been left on the length of wool at the front of the neck, using a 3rd needle k. across the other half of the sts. from the length of wool at the front of the neck, then k. up the other side of the neck to match the first side. The sts. are now on 3 needles and you are ready to work the rib neckband in rounds.

The following table gives the number of stitches in the round for chest measurements from 30 to 44 inches in different types of wool.

	3-ply			4-ply			Double Knitting		
Size of Needle	10	11	12	9	10	11	7	8	9
Chest Measurement ins.	Stitches			Stitches			Stitches		
30	224	240	254	194	210	224	158	164	172
32	240	256	272	208	224	240	168	176	184
34	254	272	288	220	238	254	178	186	196
36	270	288	306	234	252	270	189	198	208
38	284	304	322	246	266	284	200	208	218
40	300	320	340	260	280	300	210	220	230
42	314	336	356	272	294	314	220	230	242
44	330	352	374	286	308	330	230	242	254

JOINING YARN

Always join in a new ball of yarn or wool at the beginning of a row. If you are in doubt as to whether the remaining length of yarn will carry you to the end of the row, measure it; you will need four times the width of the row to complete it. If you have not quite enough, join on the new ball before starting the row.

When a join has to be made in the middle of the row (as in circular knitting) it must be spliced. Unravel the ends and cut away short pieces of one or two strands from each side, twisting the remaining long strands together so that you get the original thickness of the yarn. Knit this section carefully, taking care not to pull the yarn, and later cut off any stray ends.

JUMPERS AND PULLOVERS

The jumper presents one of the most interesting aspects of modern knitting. After the First World War, women suddenly appeared wearing long tube-like garments, copied from sailors' uniforms. Fashion magazines featured the "twenty's" girl and satirical skits were written about her in reviews.

The jumper itself has endless variations, from the plain stocking stitch classic to the elaborate lace-like blouse; basically it consists of a back, front and two sleeves, with a ribbed neckband or collar and ribbed cuffs.

A pullover is a knitted garment consisting of back and front (unlike the jersey which is knitted in rounds in one piece) and can be made sleeveless, when it is more usually known as a slipover, or with sleeves. Welt, cuffs and neckline are ribbed. A pullover is generally accepted to be a garment for a man or for children and is designed with the minimum of shaping at the sides; loose-fitting jumpers for women for sportswear in heavier plys are also often referred to as pullovers.

SLEEVES
(See *Sleeves*, page 82).

VARIOUS JUMPER NECKLINES

The rounded neck with neckband is given for the basic classic jumper, but there are a number of variations of the neckline theme which may be used to give distinctive style.

Collar Neckline. If a collar neckline is worked, instead of casting off the stitches at the front of the neck and across the back of the neck, the stitches at the front of the neck are left on a stitch-holder, and stitches across the back of the neck are slipped on to a second stitch-holder. The back is worked without an opening. The reason for placing these stitches on the stitch-holders is that this allows a greater elasticity than the cast-off principle, enabling the garment to be pulled over the head easily. The stitches for the collar are then knitted up on the same principle as knitting up a neckband. After a couple of rounds of ribbing have been worked, the collar is divided at the centre front, the knitting now being worked in rows instead of rounds. The stitch at the beginning and end of each row is knitted to give a firm edge to the collar.

Continue in ribbing for the depth required for the collar itself.

Cast off loosely.

In working this type of collar it is advisable to work half the number of rows required for the total depth on No. 13 needles, and the other half of the total number of rows on No. 11 needles, as this gives a neat flow and shape to the collar.

A Fancy Collar. It is advisable to knit this separately, stitching it neatly into the neck opening when the jumper is made up.

If you prefer a back opening with a collar, the collar itself can be knitted in two halves. This means that when the neckband stitches have been knitted up in the ordinary way, you work in rows to the centre front on each half in exactly the same way as the collar above is worked.

Polo Neck. When working a jumper with a polo neck the front of the neck should be $\frac{1}{2}$ in. higher than in the ordinary classic type of neckline. No back opening is worked and the stitches for the front and back of the neck are placed on stitch-holders instead of being cast off as in the case with a back opening.

The sts. are then knitted up on 4 needles and approximately 5 ins. of k.1, p.1 ribbing are worked before casting off.

If a k.2, p.2 rib or a twisted rib has been used for the welt and cuffs of the jumper, the same ribbing is worked on the polo neck.

The neatest way to work a polo neck in twisted rib is to work the first 2 ins. in k.1, p.1 rib and then work the remainder of the ribbing in the twisted rib. It is important to remember that the twisted side of the rib must be on the inside of the ribbed neckband when working, so that it will fall on the right side when the polo neck is turned over in wear.

"V" Neck. When knitting up the neckband on a "V" neck it is important to knit up a centre stitch through the cast-off stitch at the centre front of the neck. Decreases are then worked on every round of the neckband, at each side of this centre stitch.

JUMPERS FOR THE FULLER FIGURE

Jumpers for the fuller figure are basically the same in shape as those used for the standard size. The one difference is that darts are worked at the underarms on the front of the garment to ease the bustline.

These cross darts are worked as follows—

1st and 2nd rows: Work to the last 7 sts., turn.
3rd and 4th rows: Work to the last 13 sts., turn.
5th and 6th rows: Work to the last 19 sts., turn.
7th and 8th rows: Work to the last 25 sts., turn.

The above dart will be perfectly adequate when working in 3- and 4-ply wools.

If you are working in a 2-ply, however, add 9th and 10th rows which will read as follows—

9th and 10th rows: Work to last 31 sts., turn.

These turns will form a series of gaps in the row (138). The gaps are closed up in the row which is worked right across the stitches, immediately after the "turn" row sequence has been completed, by picking up the loop that lies just below the gap caused by the "turn" action.

Work into the back of this loop, slip it on to the left-hand needle and then knit together this loop with the first stitch on the left-hand needle.

The table shown gives the number of stitches at various points in a jumper when worked in 2-ply on size No. 13 and No. 11 needles for sizes ranging from a 40- to 50-in. bust.

The table shown overleaf gives the number of stitches required at various points for making a 3-ply jumper worked on No. 12 and No. 10 needles.

BODICE

For the fuller figure it is always advisable to break the stocking stitch on the front of the jumper with a broad centre panel in a fancy patterning, as this definitely tends to give a slimmer line to the garment. The panel can be either of an embossed nature or in an open lace stitch.

The important thing to remember is that lines should always move vertically for the fuller figure, as if these move across the garment there is a tendency to add width.

Another method of creating the slimming line is to work in a contrasting colour, lighter preferably, just above the bustline, breaking from one colour to the other with a Vandyke or scalloped movement; this will give a charming effect in the finished garment.

Generally speaking, the low or medium "V" type of neck is preferable in this larger size garment as it is softer and kinder to the figure than the classic round neckline.

A simple collar with a tie bow at the front of the "V" can be added if trimming is desired, as a slight fussiness on the neckline is often flattering to the larger woman.

KNITTERS' GUILDS

Knitters' Guilds thrived in medieval Europe, when the knitters were always men. An apprentice served three years in which he learned the fundamentals of knitting and was then sent abroad for a further three years to study knitting techniques different from his own.

At the end of his six-year apprenticeship he had to submit to an examination by the master craftsman of his

138

own Guild. The work he had to undertake included knitting a carpet to measure eight by twelve feet, a woollen shirt, a beret and a pair of woollen socks with clocks. All this work had to be completed in thirteen weeks and specimens of these carpets shown in continental museums contain the most intricate designs in as many as twenty to thirty colours. In order to protect the good name of the Guild, heavy penalties were imposed upon any craftsman who violated the regulations of his craft. If he produced shoddy work he could be heavily fined or, in extreme circumstances, expelled from the Guild. As the Guild controlled the sale of work produced this would cause him extreme economic privation.

KNITTING DESIGNERS

The designs for hand-knitting which are photographed in magazines and leaflets are planned by designers who work out the garments stitch by stitch on a graph before writing out the instructions from which one of a team of expert knitters will produce the finished article. Many of our most brilliant designers have been self-taught, learning the intricacies of their craft through many years of hard work, but it is now possible for the new generation of designers to take a diploma course at a College of Art.

The theory and practice of the design of knitted fabrics are included briefly in many courses at Technical Colleges throughout the country, but the Leicester College of Art is the only one to have a course specialising in hand-knitting design. The Faculty of Fashion and Textiles includes in its syllabus a three-year course in the design and production of machine-knit fabrics, jersey, pattern cutting as well as hand-knitting design and the Diploma in Art & Design which can be obtained at the end of this training is equivalent to degree status.

KNITTING IN ROUNDS

(See *Circular Knitting*, page 25).

KNIT STITCH

(always carried out with the wool at the back of the work).

The fundamental principle on which the whole of knitting is built is the simple action of knitting stitches.

Insert the point of the right-hand needle into the first stitch on the left-hand needle.

Holding the wool in the right hand bring the wool round

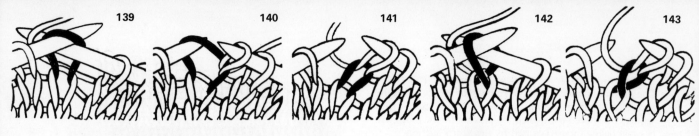

the point of the right-hand needle (139).

Draw the loop, formed by wrapping the wool round the point of the right-hand needle through the first stitch on the left-hand needle (140). Drop the stitch off the point of the left-hand needle (141). Repeat these actions across all the stitches.

Knit Into the Back of Stitch. In certain types of fabric the knit action is carried out in the back instead of the front of the stitch.

Insert the point of the right-hand needle through the back loop of the first stitch on the left-hand needle.

Holding the wool in the right hand, bring it round the point of the right-hand needle (142). Draw stitch through the first stitch on the left-hand needle.

Drop the stitch off the needle in the ordinary way (143).

KNOT STITCH

This is really a variation of bobble stitch (see page 16), creating small knots on the surface of the fabric in place of bobbles (144).

The principle is to work a purl increase on the first row, turn the work and knit together the stitches created by the purl increase, turn, and slip the one stitch back on to the right-hand needle.

On the next row work into the back of the stitch out of which the knot has been formed, thus emphasising the knot on the front surface of the work.

Here is a typical knot worked on a three increase principle:—

When the stitch on which the knot is to be worked is reached purl into the front, back and front of the same stitch, thus forming 3 stitches out of the one stitch. Turn the work round and knit the 3 stitches together, then turn the work again and slip the stitch on to the right-hand needle, then continue working across the row in the ordinary way. On the next row work to the stitch out of which the knot has been made, work into the back of this stitch, then complete the work in the ordinary way.

If larger knots are required work a 4 or a 5 increase on the same principle as the 3 increase given above, knitting the 4 or 5 stitches together after turn to complete knot.

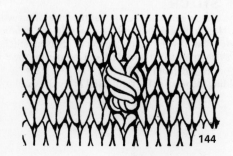

144

LACE KNITTING

(See also *Shetland Lace*, page 79, and *Viennese Lace*, page 93).

Knitted laces are found in many parts of Europe. Vienna and Paris were at one time the centres of knitting of this type and it is to these two centres that most designers have turned for inspiration and ideas in the creation of lovely laces and lace fabrics.

BASIC PRINCIPLES OF LACE KNITTING

Knitted laces are built up from decorative units formed mainly on the "over" principle. To form edgings, single increases are used on every alternate row, followed in certain types of edgings with single decreases matching the increases on every alternate row.

Overs. In all knitted laces the made stitches consist of either a "w.f." between 2 k. actions, a "w.o.n." between a p. and a k. action, a "w.r.n." between 2 p. actions. In this section all these actions are referred to as "over" as they are commonly written of in lace patternings as the "over principle," the action itself making a lace hole or looped edge to lace fabrics.

Note: The basic principle that applies to all laces is that there must be a static number of stitches at the beginning of each lace pattern. Thus, if at the beginning of the lace pattern 15 stitches have been cast on, 7 increases are worked to form the point (thus giving 22 stitches), 7 decreases must be worked either by casting off 7 in the serrated edge type of lace or by working 7 decreases in the triangular or scalloped edge type of lace, thus reducing the stitches to the original 15 stitches before the repeat of the lace pattern is worked.

Pointed Edges. The principles of forming pointed edgings vary according to the shape of the point. The first method is to work a single increase on the first and every odd row in the next to the last stitch until the number of increases to make the length of point required has been completed. The increases are then lost by a single cast-off, the same number of stitches being cast off as were increased in shaping the point of the lace itself.

In graphing a cross is used to mark each increase, the cast-off stitches being marked by the half circles along the cast-off edge itself (145).

If a more decorative edge to the point is required the increases are not worked on the first and every odd row, but on the second and every even row. The method of increase here is to work an "over" on the needle before knitting the first stitch of the second and every even row.

DRAFT

To draft a lace pattern, first of all draw the basic shape on graph paper, mark the increases and decreases. Next build up the lace units into the type of design to be used on the lace itself. In the following series of patterns, where the above principles are applied, the drafting method is shown in the diagrams relating to the first lace pattern.

Basic Shapes

Cast on 12 sts.

1st row: K.

2nd row: Wrap the wool round the needle before knitting the first stitch, k. to end.

Repeat these 2 rows 7 times more.

Next row: K.

Next row: Cast off 8 sts., k. to the end, thus there will be 12 sts. on the needle again.

By adding "overs" and decreases to the basic simple pointed lace, a design is built up (146).

The principle is exactly the same but a patterning is introduced to turn the plain knitted shape into an attractive lace edging.

Graduated Points. If a graduated type of edge is desired it can be worked by a series of increases balanced by a series of decreases.

The increases worked in the next to the last stitch on the row. The decreases are also worked on the odd rows, marked with a cross, this being a simple "k.2 tog." principle at the end of the rows.

If the decorative looped edge is required on these graduated points, the principle is to work an "over" at the beginning of the 2nd and every even row until sufficient increases have been worked to give the depth required to the point. To balance the looped edge on the other side of the lace where the decreases are worked, a single decrease is made on the centre row and every alternate row; the following row (to the centre row) is worked with an "over, k.2 tog." at the beginning of the row. This action is repeated on every alternate row until the decreases have been worked to balance out the increases at the commencement of the point.

The series of increases and decreases which are worked along the top edge give an even movement to both sides of the point.

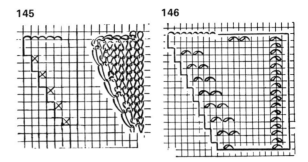

145   146

Medium Pointed Lace

Cast on 10 sts.

1st row: Sl.1, k.2, over, k.2 tog., k.1, (over twice, k.2 tog.) twice.

2nd row: Sl.1, k.1, p.1, k.2, p.1, k.3, over, k.2 tog., k.1.

3rd row: Sl.1, k.2, over, k.2 tog., k.3, (over twice, k.2 tog.) twice.

4th row: Sl.1, k.1, p.1, k.2, p.1, k.5, over, k.2 tog., k.1.

5th row: Sl.1, k.2, over, k.2 tog., k.5, (over twice, k.2 tog.) twice.

6th row: Sl.1, k.1, p.1, k.2, p.1, k.7, over, k.2 tog., k.1.

7th row: Sl.1, k.2, over, k.2 tog., k.11.

8th row: Cast off 6, k.6 (7 sts. on right-hand needle after cast-off), over, k.2 tog., k.1.

These 8 rows form the patt. (147).

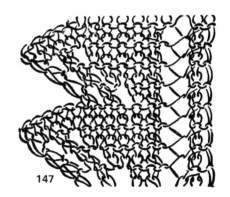

147

EDGES, SCALLOPED

For scalloped edgings the principle is exactly the same as for the triangular edged laces except that in place of 3 rows being worked at the centre of the point, 5 or 7 rows are worked. The looped edge is by far the most attractive in scalloped laces.

In the scalloped edge diagram (148) the looped edge is marked with a half circle on the second and every alternate row until all the increases have been completed; on the centre row of the lace, marked with a cross at the lower edge, an "over, k.2 tog." is worked at the top edge to form

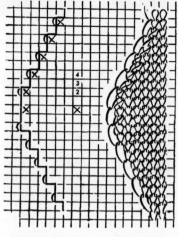

148

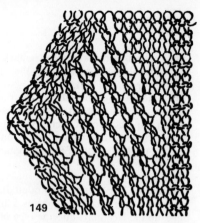

149

Scalloped effects are obtained by graduating increases and decreases worked symmetrically throughout the pattern. The bold lace with a scalloped edge (149) has a matching insertion, instructions below

the loop, the same principle being worked on the following alternate row, marked with a figure 2, and the straight edge of the diagram; on the row marked with a figure 3 and every alternate row, a "k.2 tog." is worked at the end of the row, and on the row marked with a 4, and every alternate row, an "over, k.2 tog." is worked at the beginning of the row, thus forming the looped edge.

Scalloped effects are in fact obtained in lace edgings, by graduating increases and decreases worked symmetrically throughout the patterning.

A lovely scalloped lace, where the looped edge is used on both the straight and scalloped edges of the design, is a lace pattern of large holes which are worked by making two stitches in place of one.

This distinctive type of lace hole is used mainly in the knitted laces found between Belgrade and Novi Sad and is referred to as Smyrna open-work.

Bold Lace with Scallops

This bold lace with a scalloped edge (149) has a diamond design in each scallop.

Cast on 13 sts. and k. 1 row.

Now commence the pattern as follows—

1st row: K.7, over, k.2 tog., over, k.4.

2nd and every alt. row: K.2, p. to last 2 sts., k.2.

3rd row: K.6, (over, k.2 tog.) twice, over, k.4.

5th row: K.5, (over, k.2 tog.) 3 times, over, k.4.

7th row: K.4, (over, k.2 tog.) 4 times, over, k.4.

9th row: K.3, (over, k.2 tog.) 5 times, over, k.4.

11th row: K.4, (over, k.2 tog.) 5 times, k.2 tog., k.2.

13th row: K.5, (over, k.2 tog.) 4 times, k.2 tog., k.2.

15th row: K.6, (over, k.2 tog.) 3 times, k.2 tog., k.2.

17th row: K.7, (over, k.2 tog.) twice, k.2 tog., k.2.

19th row: K.8, (over, k.2 tog.) twice, k.2.

20th row: K.2, p. to last 2 sts., k.2.

These 20 rows form the patt.

LACE BORDERS

Knitted lace is a derived craft and when one studies the patterns it is obvious that many of them have been copied from other types of lace. Lace knitted in fine cotton

had a tremendous vogue during the middle period of the Victorian age and today there is a reviving interest in this delightful and delicate aspect of the knitter's craft.

This selection of lace edgings and insertions illustrates the constructional details, and once the knitter has grasped the application of the main principles in these designs, she should, with practice, be able to create lace edgings to suit her own particular taste.

HEART AND DIAMOND LACE, WITH CORNER

Cast on 25 sts.

1st row: Over, k.2 tog., over, k.1, (over, sl.1, k.1, p.s.s.o.) twice, over, k.9, (over, k.2 tog.) 3 times, k.3.

2nd row: Sl.1, k.2, p.24.

3rd row: Over, k.2 tog., over, k.3, (over, sl.1, k.1, p.s.s.o.) 3 times, k.5, (k.2 tog., over) 4 times, k.3.

4th row: Sl.1, k.2, p.25.

5th row: (Over, k.2 tog.) twice, over, k.1, (over, sl.1, k.1, p.s.s.o.) 4 times, k.3, (k.2 tog., over) 4 times, k.4.

6th row: Sl.1, k.2, p.26.

7th row: (Over, k.2 tog.) twice, over, k.3, (over, sl.1, k.1, p.s.s.o.) 4 times, k.1, (k.2 tog., over) 4 times, k.1, over, sl.1, k.1, p.s.s.o., k.2.

8th row: Sl.1, k.2, p.27.

9th row: (Over, k.2 tog.) twice, over, k.5, (over, sl.1, k.1, p.s.s.o.) 3 times, over, sl.1, k.2 tog., p.s.s.o., (over, k.2 tog.) twice, over, k.1, (over, k.2 tog.) twice, k.3.

10th row: Sl.1, k.2, p.28.

11th row: (Over, k.2 tog.) twice, over, k.7, (over, sl.1, k.1, p.s.s.o.) 3 times, k.1, (k.2 tog., over) 3 times, k.1, (over, sl.1, k.1, p.s.s.o.) twice, k.2.

12th row: Sl.1, k.2, p.29.

13th row: (Over, k.2 tog.) twice, over, k.9, (over, sl.1, k.1, p.s.s.o.) twice, over, sl.1, k.2 tog., p.s.s.o., (over, k.2 tog.) twice, over, k.1, (over, sl.1, k.1, p.s.s.o.) twice, k.3.

14th row: Sl.1, k.2, p.30.

15th row: Over, sl.1, k.2 tog., p.s.s.o., (over, sl.1, k.1, p.s.s.o.) twice, k.8, (over, sl.1, k.1, p.s.s.o.) twice, k.1, (k.2 tog., over) twice, k.1, (over, sl.1, k.1, p.s.s.o.) 3 times, k.2.

16th row: As 12th row.

58

17th row: Over, sl.1, k.2 tog., p.s.s.o., (over, sl.1, k.1, p.s.s.o.) twice, k.8, over, sl.1, k.1, p.s.s.o., over, sl.1, k.2 tog., p.s.s.o., over, k.2 tog., over, k.1, (over, sl.1, k.1, p.s.s.o.) 3 times, k.3.

18th row: As 10th row.

19th row: Over, sl.1, k.2 tog., p.s.s.o., (over, sl.1, k.1, p.s.s.o.) twice, k.8, over, sl.1, k.1, p.s.s.o., k.1, k.2 tog., over. k.1, (over, sl.1, k.1, p.s.s.o.) 4 times, k.2.

20th row: As 8th row.

21st row: Over, sl.1, k.2 tog., p.s.s.o., (over, sl.1, k.1, p.s.s.o.) twice, k.8, over, sl.1, k.2 tog., p.s.s.o., over, k.1, (over, sl.1, k.1, p.s.s.o.) 4 times, k.3.

22nd row: As 6th row.

23rd row: (Over, k.2 tog.) twice, over, k.8, k.2 tog., over, k.3, over, sl.1, k.2 tog., p.s.s.o., (over, k.2 tog.) 3 times, over, k.3.

24th row: As 8th row.

25th row: (Over, k.2 tog.) twice, over, k.8, (k.2 tog., over) twice, k.1, over, sl.1, k.1, p.s.s.o., over, sl.1, k.2 tog., p.s.s.o., (over, k.2 tog.) twice, over, k.4.

26th row: As 10th row.

27th row: (Over, k.2 tog.) twice, over, k.8, (k.2 tog., over) twice, k.3, over, sl.1, k.1, p.s.s.o., over, sl.1, k.2 tog., p.s.s.o., (over, k.2 tog.) twice, over, k.3.

28th row: As 12th row.

29th row: (Over, k.2 tog.) twice, over, k.8, (k.2 tog., over) 3 times, k.1, (over, sl.1, k.1, p.s.s.o.) twice, over, sl.1, k.2 tog., p.s.s.o., over, k.2 tog., over, k.4.

30th row: As 14th row

31st row: Over, sl.1, k.2 tog., p.s.s.o., (over, sl.1, k.1, p.s.s.o.) twice, k.5, (k.2 tog., over) 3 times, k.3, (over, sl.1, k.1, p.s.s.o.) twice, over, sl.1, k.2 tog., p.s.s.o., over, k.2 tog., over, k.3.

32nd row: As 12th row.

33rd row: Over, sl.1, k.2 tog., p.s.s.o., (over, sl.1, k.1, p.s.s.o.) twice, k.3, (k.2 tog., over) 4 times, k.1, (over, sl.1, k.1, p.s.s.o) 3 times, over, sl.1, k.2 tog., p.s.s.o., over, k.4.

34th row: As 10th row.

35th row: Over, sl.1, k.2 tog., p.s.s.o., (over, sl.1, k.1, p.s.s.o.) twice, k.1, k.2 tog., over) 4 times, k.3, (over, sl.1, k.1, p.s.s.o.) 3 times, over, sl.1, k.2 tog., p.s.s.o., over, k.3.

36th row: As 8th row.

37th row: Over, sl.1, k.2 tog., p.s.s.o., over, sl.1, k.1, p.s.s.o., over, sl.1, k.2 tog., p.s.s.o., (over, k.2 tog.) 3 times, over, k.5, (over, sl.1, k.1, p.s.s.o.) 4 times, k.3.

38th row: As 6th row.

39th row: Over, sl.1, k.2 tog., p.s.s.o., over, sl.1, k.1, p.s.s.o., k.1, (k.2 tog., over) 3 times, k.7, (over, sl.1, k.1, p.s.s.o.) 4 times, k.2.

40th row: As 4th row.

41st row: (Over, sl.1, k.2 tog., p.s.s.o.) twice, (over, sl.1, k.1, p.s.s.o.) twice, over, k.9, (over, k.2 tog.) 3 times, k.3.

2nd to 41st rows incl. form the patt. (150).

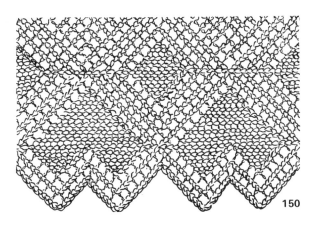

150

LEAF MOTIF

This lace pattern has a double leaf motif forming a scalloped edging to the lace itself.

Cast on 23 sts.

1st row: * Over, k.1, over, k.2, (k.2 tog.) twice, k.2; rep. from * once, (over, k.2 tog.) twice, k.1.

2nd and every alt. row: P.

3rd row: * Over, k.3, over, k.1, (k.2 tog.) twice, k.1; rep. from * once, (over, k.2 tog.) twice, k.1.

5th row: * Over, k.5, over, (k.2 tog.) twice; rep. from * once, (over, k.2 tog.) twice, k.1.

7th row: * Over, k.3, k.2 tog., k.2, over, k.2 tog.; rep. from * once, (over, k.2 tog.) twice, k.1.

8th row: P.

These 8 rows form the patt. (151).

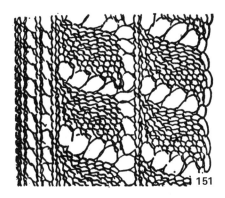

151

OPEN DIAMOND LACE

Cast on 36 sts.

1st row: Sl.1, k.1, w.f., k.3, w.f., k.2 tog., k.13, k.2 tog., w.f., k.3, w.f., k.2 tog., k.9.

2nd row: K.8, k.2 tog., w.f., k.5, .w.f., k.2 tog., k.11, k.2 tog., w.f., k.5, w.f., k.2.

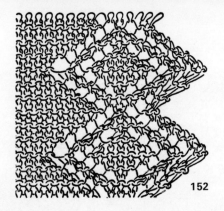

152

3rd row: Sl.1, k.1, w.f., k.1, k.2 tog., w.f., (k.1, w.f., k.2 tog.) twice, k.9, (k.2 tog., w.f., k.1) twice, w.f., k.2 tog., k.1, w.f., k.2 tog., k.7.

4th row: Sl.1, k.5, k.2 tog., w.f., k.1, k.2 tog., w.f., k.3, w.f., k.2 tog., k.1, w.f., k.2 tog., k.7, k.2 tog., w.f., k.1, k.2 tog., w.f., k.3, w.f., k.2 tog., k.1, w.f., k.2.

5th row: Sl.1, k.1, w.f., k.1, k.2 tog., w.f., k.5, w.f., k.2 tog., k.1, w.f., k.2 tog., k.5, k.2 tog., w.f., k.1, k.2 tog., w.f., k.5, w.f., k.2 tog., k.1, w.f., k.2 tog., k.5.

6th row: Sl.1, k.3, k.2 tog., w.f., k.1, k.2 tog., w.f., k.7, w.f., k.2 tog., k.1, w.f., k.2 tog., k.3, k.2 tog., k.1, k.2 tog., w.f., k.7, w.f., k.2 tog., k.1, w.f., k.2.

7th row: K.2 tog., (k.1, w.f., k.2 tog.) twice, k.3, (k.2 tog., w.f.) twice, k.7, w.f., k.2 tog., k.1, w.f., k.2 tog., k.3, k.2 tog., w.f., k.1, k.2 tog., w.f., k.6.

8th row: K.7, (w.f., k.2 tog., k.1) twice, k.2 tog., w.f., k.1, k.2 tog., w.f., k.9, w.f., k.2, w.f.. k.2 tog., k.1, k.2 tog., (w.f., k.1, k.2 tog.) twice.

9th row: (K.2 tog., k.1, w.f.) twice, sl.1, k.2 tog., p.s.s.o., w.f., k.1, k.2 tog., w.f., k.1, w.f., k.11, w.f., k.1, w.f., sl.1, k.2 tog., p.s.s.o., w.f., k.1, k.2 tog., w.f., k.8.

10th row: K.9, w.f., k.2 tog., k.3, k.2 tog., w.f., k.13, w.f., k.2 tog., k.3, k.2 tog., w.f., k.1, k.2 tog.

11th row: K.2 tog., k.1, w.f., k.2 tog., k.1, k.2 tog., w.f., k.15, w.f., k.2 tog., k.1, k.2 tog., w.f., k.10.

12th row: K.11, w.f., sl.1, k.2 tog., p.s.s.o., w.f., k.17, w.f., sl.1, k.2 tog., p.s.s.o., w.f., k.1, k.2 tog.

These 12 rows form the patt. (152).

LAUNDERING

(See *Washing,* page 95).

LAYETTES

Knitting for a baby is one of the most delightful forms of knitting because the garments are so attractive and, being so small, are very quick to knit. When knitting for a friend's baby it is wise to knit second-size garments, otherwise the new mother finds that she has too many first-size woollies which are outgrown by three months.

First-size knitting should be as simple as possible, avoiding open patterns in which a baby could catch its fingers. Buttons and bobbles within reach of the mouth must also be avoided. Washing is made easier if ties are of nylon ribbon or cord made from the knitting yarn; this eliminates ironing.

A classic Layette is usually knitted in a fine yarn, 3-ply or 4-ply, and includes the following items:

First-size (Birth to 3-4 months): 3 vests; 3 prs. bootees; 3 matinée jackets; a big shawl and a head shawl; dresses; bonnets.

Second-size (3 to 6-8 months): 3 vests; 3 prs. bootees; 3 matinée jackets or tiny cardigans; 2 pram sets with leggings.

Third-size (8 months to 1 year): 3 vests; 3 cardigans; 3 pram sets.

In addition, extra dresses, romper suits, pullovers, pram rugs and cot covers are always useful.

It must be appreciated that the ages given are approximate; where a compact 6-lb. baby can wear his first-size clothes for a full four months, a strapping 10-lb. baby may be ready for the second-size in a few weeks.

LEARNING TO KNIT

(See *Beginners' Knitting,* page 12).

LINING

(See *Mounting,* page 64).

LOOP KNITTING

This type of knitting forms a delightful trimming for a bed-jacket or for baby garments.

It consists of a series of loops which are created by wrapping loops round one or two fingers, according to the size of loop required and working these loops into the fabric in the actual knitting of the stitch where the loop is formed.

To work loop fabric proceed as follows—

Cast on an odd number of sts.

1st row: K.

2nd row: * K.1, insert needle into next st. without knitting it, sl. two fingers from left hand under point of right-hand needle, wrap wool round fingers and point of right-hand needle 3 times (153), draw loops through stitch on left-hand needle, sl. sts. thus formed back on to left-hand needle and k. all loops as one st. (154), slip the loops off the left-hand needle in the usual way (155); rep. from * to last st., k.1.

These two rows form the loop-stitch patt. and are repeated throughout to create the fabric shown in (156).

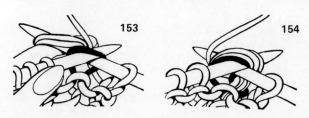

153 **154**

MACHINE KNITTING

The knitting machines of today are the logical and intricate developments of the original frame knitting and many women find them as essential as a sewing machine. A knitting machine is particularly useful to a large family as it can be used to make warm garments for every age group with remarkable speed and at a considerable saving on ready-made clothes.

Whereas hand knitting is a sociable pastime which can be picked up at leisure, it is important to realise when acquiring a knitting machine that it will need space and concentration just as the sewing machine does. Many enthusiastic knitters find that a machine is ideal for producing smooth, classic knitwear, such as school pullovers and men's cardigans, thus leaving them free to choose delicate, lacy garments for hand-knitting in the evenings. However, many of the new machines can also produce the most intricate fabrics.

When choosing a knitting machine it is advisable to see as many models as possible and to decide for oneself which type, size and price of machine is the most suitable. The merits of single bed machines, double bed machines and more advanced machines which can both knit and weave or can work automatically should be considered.

A small machine specially designed for children and for handicapped people may well be the first introduction to machine knitting; this produces fabric up to 10 inches wide, suitable for scarves, small pullovers, babies' clothes etc.

A single bed machine can produce all simple patterns and fabrics and Fair Isle designs and is very easy to work; a special ribbing attachment is usually needed for rib stitches. These machines are probably the most suitable for beginners and family use as they are relatively easy to store.

Double bed machines are more expensive and can produce more complicated patterns as well as ribbing, circular and semi-circular knitting, but as they are heavier must generally be kept in a permanent position. They are suitable for those who intend to knit for profit as well as for their own requirements.

Some single bed machines can now be changed into double bed machines with special additions, and many of the double bed machines can be changed into single bed machines for stocking stitch.

Tuition is given by the majority of manufacturers but it is important to find out about this before purchasing the machine; it is generally considered that three lessons are sufficient to give a beginner enough confidence to continue to practise on her own. In some parts of the country, evening classes are available at technical institutes for beginners and for more advanced students.

3-ply and 4-ply wools and yarns are the most suitable for machine knitting and double knitting is also successful although it usually has to be waxed during winding. Chunky wools are not recommended unless there is a special attachment for them.

Patterns for knitting up on machines can be obtained from the manufacturers, many of whom publish regular pattern books, and designs are also shown in magazines. In this book we give machine-knitting instructions for the three most popular designs—a cardigan and a pullover for children of school age and a man's classic cardigan.

MACHINE-WASHABLE WOOLS

Garments hand-knitted in wool should, as a general rule, be washed very carefully by hand, but the development of the new Machine-Washable Wools in this country means that knitted garments can now be washed in a washing-machine at suitably low temperatures. This is a great advantage for children's clothes, toys and sports wear and was pioneered in Great Britain by Robin Wools, advised by the International Wool Secretariat.

MAKING UP

(See *Blocking Garments*, page 14, and *Seams*, page 74).

MESH PATTERNS

In these patterns open-work mesh stitches are worked to give a simple all-over lace effect.

CANDELABRA MESH STITCH

Cast on a multiple of 10 sts. plus 1 st.

1st row: * K.1, w.f., k.2 tog. t.b.l., k.5, k.2 tog., w.f.; rep. from * to last st., k.1.

2ns and every alt. row: P.

3rd row: * K.1, w.f., k.1, k.2 tog. t.b.l., k.3, k.2 tog., k.1, w.f.; rep. from * to last st., k.1.

5th row: * K.1, w.f., k.2, k.2 tog. t.b.l., k.1, k.2 tog., k.2, w.f.; rep. from * to last st., k.1.

7th row: * K.1, w.f., k.3, k.3 tog., k.3, w.f.; rep. from * to last st., k.1.

9th row: * K.3, k.2 tog., w.f., k.1, w.f., k.2 tog. t.b.l., k.2; rep. from * to last st., k.1.

11th row: * K.2, k.2 tog., (k.1, w.f.) twice, k.1, k.2 tog. t.b.l., k.1; rep. from * to last st., k.1.

13th row: * K.1, k.2 tog., k.2, w.f., k.1, w.f., k.2, k.2 tog.

155

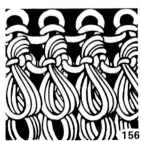

156

t.b.l.; rep. from * to last st., k.1.

15th row: K.2 tog., * k.3, w.f., k.1, w.f., k.3, k.3 tog.; rep. from * to last 9 sts., k.3, w.f., k.1, w.f., k.3, k.2 tog. t.b.l.

16th row: As 2nd row.

These 16 rows form the patt. (157).

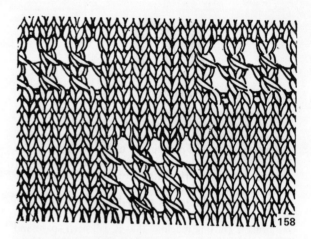

CHEQUERED MESH STITCH

Cast on a multiple of 12 sts. plus 1 st.

1st row: K.1, * k.6, (w.f., k.2 tog. t.b.l.) 3 times; rep. from * to end.

2nd and every alt. row: P.

3rd and 5th rows: As 1st row.

7th and 9th rows: K.

11th and 13th rows: K.1, * (w.f., k.2 tog. t.b.l.) 3 times, k.6; rep. from * to end.

15th and 17th rows: K.

18th row: P.

These 18 rows form the patt. (158).

LATTICE MESH STITCH

Cast on a multiple of 4 sts.

1st row: * K.2, w.f., k.2 tog. t.b.l.; rep. from * to end.

2nd row: * P.2, w.r.n., p.2 tog.; rep. from * to end.

These 2 rows form the patt. (159).

PINE TREE MESH STITCH

Cast on a multiple of 14 sts. plus 1 st.

1st row: * K.1, w.f., sl.1, k.1, p.s.s.o., k.9, k.2 tog., w.f.; rep. from * to last st., k.1.

2nd and every alt. row: P.

3rd row: * K.2, w.f., sl.1, k.1, p.s.s.o., k.7, k.2 tog., w.f., k.1; rep. from * to last st., k.1.

5th row: * K.1, (w.f., sl.1, k.1, p.s.s.o.) twice, k.5, (k.2 tog., w.f.) twice; rep. from * to last st., k.1.

7th row: * K.2, (w.f., sl.1, k.1, p.s.s.o.) twice, k.3, (k.2 tog., w.f.) twice, k.1; rep. from * to last st, k.1.

9th row: * K.1, (w.f., sl.1, k.1, p.s.s.o.) 3 times, k.1, (k.2 tog., w.f.) 3 times; rep. from * to last st., k.1.

11th row: * K.2, (w.f., sl.1, k.1, p.s.s.o.) twice, k.3, (k.2 tog., w.f.) twice, k.1; rep. from * to last st., k.1.

13th row: As 5th row.

15th row: As 3rd row.

17th row: * K.1, w.f., k.2 tog., k.2, k.2 tog., w.f., k.1, w.f., sl.1, k.1, p.s.s.o., k.2, k.2 tog., w.f.; rep. from * to last st., k.1.

19th row: * K.4, k.2 tog., w.f., k.3, w.f., sl.1, k.1, p.s.s.o., k.3; rep. from * to last st., k.1.

21st row: * K.3, (k.2 tog., w.f.) twice, k.1, (w.f., sl.1, k.1, p.s.s.o.) twice, k.2; rep. from * to last st., k.1.

23rd row: * K.2, (k.2 tog., w.f.) twice, k.3, (w.f., sl.1, k.1, p.s.s.o.) twice, k.1; rep. from * to last st., k.1.

25th row: * K.1, (k.2 tog., w.f.) 3 times, k.1, (w.f., sl.1, k.1, p.s.s.o.) 3 times; rep. from * to last st., k.1.

27th row: As 23rd row.

29th row: As 21st row.

31st row: As 19th row.

33rd row: * K.1, w.f., sl.1, k.1, p.s.s.o., k.2, k.2 tog., w.f., k.1, w.f., sl.1, k.1, p.s.s.o., k.2, k.2 tog., w.f., rep. from * to last st., k.1.

34th row: P.

Rows 3 to 34 incl. form the patt. and are repeated throughout (160).

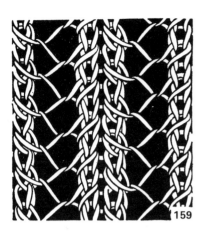

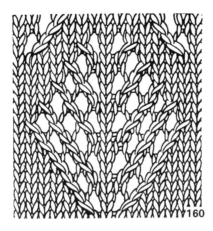

159

160

161

SQUARED MESH STITCH

Cast on a multiple of 8 sts. plus 4 sts.

1st row: K.1, * w.f., sl.1, k.1, p.s.s.o., k.6; rep. from * to last 3 sts., w.f., sl.1, k.1, p.s.s.o., k.1.

2nd and every alt. row: P.

3rd row: K.1, * sl.1, k.1, p.s.s.o., w.f., k.6; rep. from * to last 3 sts., sl.1, k.1, p.s.s.o., w.f., k.1.

4th row: P.

5th to 10th rows: Rep. rows 1 to 4 incl. once, then 1st and 2nd rows once.

11th row: K.1, * sl.1, k.1, p.s.s.o., w.f.; rep. from * to last st., k.1.

12th row: P.

These 12 rows form the patt. and are repeated throughout for (161).

VANDYKE AND RIB MESH STITCH

Cast on a multiple of 12 sts. plus 1 st.

1st row: * P.2, k.3, k.2 tog., w.f., k.4, p.1; rep. from * to last st., p.1.

2nd and every alt. row: K.1, * k.1, p.9, k.2; rep. from * to end.

3rd row: * P.2, k.2, k.2 tog., w.f., k.1, w.f., k.2 tog. t.b.l., k.2, p.1; rep. from * to last st., p.1.

5th row: * P.2, k.1, k.2 tog., w.f., k.3, w.f., k.2 tog. t.b.l., k.1, p.1; rep. from * to last st., p.1.

7th row: * P.2, k.2 tog., w.f., k.5, w.f., k.2 tog. t.b.l., p.1; rep. from * to last st., p.1.

8th row: As 2nd row.

These 8 rows form the patt. (162).

MID-EUROPEAN COLOUR KNITTING

It is doubtful if there has been a great deal of original colour knitting in the mid-European countries. The few examples which survive in museums reflect the embroidery tradition of the country and are undoubtedly knitted designs based on older embroidered specimens. There is a much freer use of colour than in the Scandinavian knitting, in fact the work seems to be the spontaneous life flow of a peasant people who have embodied in their culture all the gaiety of a folk tradition.

The knitting is carried out on the same basis as that of Scandinavia, using borders, motifs and seedings, which are worked from charts.

MITRE

(See *Facings,* page 39).

MITTENS

The mitten, as distinct from the glove mitten takes the form of a large bag for the four fingers and a smaller bag for the thumb. These can be worked in any weight of wool from a 3-ply to a double knitting and many of them have very attractive coloured designs in peasant knitting which add interest and excitement to the finished work.

The principle of knitting mittens is the same as gloves, work until the fingers are reached (see *Gloves,* page 44).

At this point, instead of dividing the stitches for the fingers as on the glove, continue in rounds until the work is long enough to reach the tip of the little finger.

The top shaping is worked to form a diagonal movement at each side of the front and back of the mitten, 2 sts. are

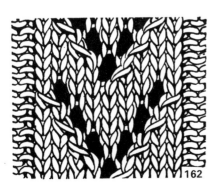

162

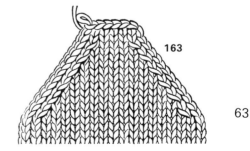

163

63

kept as a "constant" between the decreases at each side.

Diagram (163) shows the decreases marked for the top of a mitten to fit an average hand, knitted in a double knitting weight.

The knitting can either be worked in stocking stitch or you might like to decorate it with a heavy cable pattern down the centre back.

Simple all-over colour patterns form another variation but the most interesting types are the peasant mittens, which are always worked from charts.

MOHAIR

This is very fine, fluffy wool spun from the fleece of the mohair goat; it produces a garment with a brushed, fluffy surface but because of its extreme delicacy and rarity it is often mixed with wool for knitting yarns. In spite of its delicate appearance it washes extremely well.

MOSS STITCH

The origin of this stitch is completely unknown. Specimens of it have been found on fragments of very early knitted fabric. When closely knitted it has the appearance of a woven fabric (164).

To produce moss stitch, cast on an odd number of stitches and work * k.1, p.1; rep. from * to last st., k.1, on every row of the fabric.

When working on four or more needles use an even number of stitches.

Work as follows:—

1st round: * K.1, p.1; rep. from * to end.
2nd round: * P.1, k.1; rep. from * to end.

MOSS STITCH, DOUBLE

Cast on a multiple of 4 sts.
1st and 2nd rows: * P.2, k.2; rep. from * to end.
3rd and 4th rows: * K.2, p.2; rep. from * to end.
These 4 rows form the pattern (165).
The "Double Moss Stitch" principle form the basis of knitted *Check Patterns*.

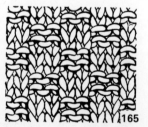

Closely knitted Moss Stitch resembles a woven fabric (164). Double Moss Stitch (165) forms the basis of knitted check patterns (page 15)

MOTHPROOFING

Synthetic yarns are naturally resistant to attack by moths and many hand-knitted wools are now subjected to a special process which renders them moth-proof and they carry a label to this effect. Some dry-cleaners will undertake mothproofing as part of their service, but it is simple to treat a garment at home with a special mothproofing spray. The garment should be very carefully washed and when dried and pressed it should be spread flat and sprayed with a D.D.T. mothproofing spray on both sides. The garment can then be stored in a plastic bag (airproof) until required. This form of mothproofing must be repeated after every washing.

MOUNTING

Net mounting is used mainly for lacy garments knitted in 1-ply and 2-ply wools, or it can be used to form a foundation for garments knitted in fine cotton or silk. When the separate pieces of the garments are knitted pin them out, block and press them (as described under *Blocking Garments* page 14).

Lay these pieces on the net that is to be used for the foundation, tacking them carefully on to the net. Now, using sharp scissors, cut the net shapes to match the knitted shapes. When making up, join the pieces with back-stitch seams stitching the net foundation and knitted fabric together at the same time.

NEEDLES

Knitting needles—or pins as they used to be known—should be strong but lightweight and it is always worth-while buying the best quality available. Modern knitting needles are usually made from nylon or a metal alloy; plastic needles are not advisable as they bend and can break under the weight of a heavy garment. Sets of four needles are often steel but are also now made in nylon. It is important to check that there is no roughness on the needles before beginning work, particularly if they have been stored away for some time or used by children.

Knitting needles are made in different sizes to suit different yarns and stitches. (See *Gauge of Needles*, page 44).

NEEDLE HOLDER

Holder for Knitting Needles. A useful holder for knitting needles can be made out of two pieces of material, one

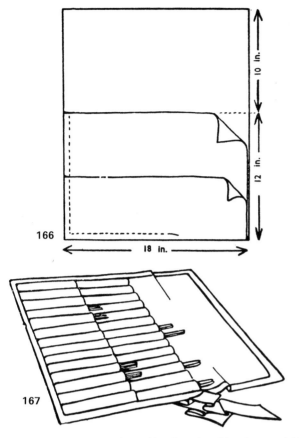

166

167

ODDMENTS

Attractive gifts, toys and articles for the home can be made from oddments of wool left over from knitting garments. These include dolls' clothes; knitted animals and other toys; hot water bottle covers; tea cosies and egg cosies; mittens and caps; cushions and blankets from squares. Instructions for many of these are given at the end of this book.

OILED WOOL

Wool in its natural state includes a considerable amount of oil and it undergoes a number of chemical processes to remove this for everyday knitting. However, wool with its natural oils is used for knitting up certain garments which need to be more waterproof than most, including seaboot stockings, sailing sweaters and Aran sweaters.

ORLON
(See *Synthetics*, page 89).

OVER PRINCIPLE
(See *Increasing*, page 50).

34 ins. long and 18 ins. wide, the other 6 ins. long and 18 ins. wide. Neatly hem both pieces of material. Now fold over 12 ins. of the 34 in. material, place the 6 in. material on top of the piece folded over (166).

Machine all round the sides and bottom edge of these pieces of material, thus forming an envelope with two pockets, one 12 ins. deep, the other 6 ins. deep. Work rows of machining, 1 in. apart from the bottom edge to the top of the 12 in. flap, thus making a series of narrow pockets in the knitting needle holder. The sets of four needles are inserted in the 6 in. pockets and the pairs in the 12 in. pockets (167). Fold the flap over, roll the holder up and tie round with a piece of tape.

NORWEGIAN KNITTING

Norwegian knitting includes many intricate and colourful designs on a natural background and the main pattern —as with most Scandinavian knitting—is shown in a rounded yoke. Pine trees and stags are among the most popular motifs in Norway, as shown in these two charts. Colourings are very subtle and include a warm grey and a wonderful smoky blue. (See also *Scandinavian Colour Knitting*, page 71).

NYLON
(See *Synthetics*, page 89).

PANELS

In knitting, a panel is a strip or wide stripe of different stitches from the rest of the garment, as shown in Tyrolean and cabled garments. The main part of the garment may be in stocking-stitch, garter-stitch or rib and then a decorative panel of cable or seedings will be set up the centre or on either side of centre front fastenings; this is often repeated down the sleeve and back.

PASS SLIP STITCH OVER

This action is usually carried out when decreasing or in lace fabrics, it can be on either the knit or the purl row in the fabric. Always slip the stitch in the same way as the row is being worked, i.e. knitwise on a knit row, purlwise on a purl row.

Insert the point of the right-hand needle into the next

stitch on the left-hand needle, slipping the stitch from the left to the right-hand needle (168).

Work the number of stitches over which the slipped stitch is to be passed (169). Now insert the point of the left-hand needle through the front of the slipped stitch, draw it over the stitches that have been worked, dropping it off the point of the left-hand needle over these stitches (as shown in diagram 170).

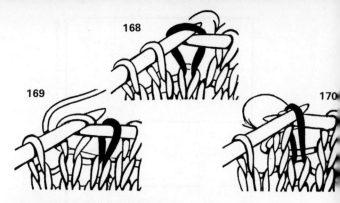

PATTERN MAKING

(See also *Designing Fabrics*, page 31 and *Designing Patterns*, page 32)

Many knitters prefer to make their own patterns for garments in order to obtain a perfect fit. This is particularly useful when knitting for figures which are not stock size as variations can be made in length, sleeve length, shoulder and chest widths. Measurements are taken and the garment drawn out on squared graph paper (see Graphing), using one square to one stitch and taking into account the ply of the wool, tension and needle size. Details of the number of stitches, etc., required are given under the different headings Cardigans, Jumpers, Gloves and Vests.

PATCHWORK KNITTING

Patchwork can be assembled from simple squares (see *Beginners' Knitting and Blankets*, pages 12 and 14) or it can be made from more complex shapes, hexagons and pentagons as instructed in Circular Knitting. These shapes are then joined together by careful seaming, as for a fabric patchwork quilt, or preferably by crochet insertion.

PERUVIAN KNITTING

During excavations in Peru, a collection of very interesting fringes were discovered which have been called "Peruvian Needle Knitting". On examining the texture of these fringes, a fabric is discovered which is much more closely akin to knitting as we know it today than was Sprang. It would appear that a series of loops has been built up with a needle on a single thread, a second series built up through the first ones and this action repeated to produce a type of knitted fabric. It is impossible to place a date on Peruvian Needle Knitting but it has been said to belong to the first centuries of the Christian era. (171).

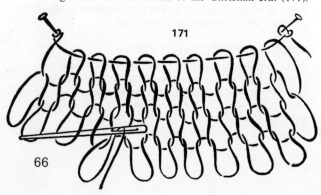

171

66

PICKING UP STITCHES

Dropped stitches can most easily be picked up with a crochet hook; slip the hook through the loop which has been dropped and push it through to pick up also the strand of wool left across the gap. Pull the wool back through the loop and a stitch has been made; continue up the work in this way, working on the right side of garment for stocking stitch or from alternate sides for garter stitch. Slip the stitch back on to the needle and work as usual.

Stitches can also be picked up along a cast-off edge, as when knitting a neckband. To do this, join yarn to first stitch and work with one needle only held in right hand. Holding work in left hand (right side of garment towards you) insert the needle from front to back of the edge stitch and knit a stitch. Continue in this way, picking up the number of stitches specified in the pattern over the space, which is usually one stitch to every stitch or row of stitches.

PICOT EDGE

This edge forms a charming finish to the necks of lacy garments and to the edges of dressing jackets and matinee coats. In fact it has many uses and the skilful knitter can use a picot edge to give a finishing touch to her work.

The principle of picot edge worked on a stocking stitch base is as follows:

Using two needles cast on an odd number of stitches as for an ordinary hem. Work 4 rows in stocking stitch. On the next row (which will be a knit row), a row of holes is introduced into the fabric, which later forms the picot (172). These are worked as follows:—

K.1, * w.f., k.2 tog.; rep. from * to end of row.

Work 3 more rows in stocking stitch and then knit up the hem as *Knitted Up Hem* (page 48). This action folds the work over at the centre of the row of holes, forming a picot as shown in the diagram (173).

Once the principle of the picot has been understood, it can be worked on a reverse stocking stitch base or a k.1, p.1 rib base.

PIP EDGE

(See *Seams, Lacing Action*, page 75).

PLAIN

(See *Knit Stitch*, page 55).

PLEATING

A delightful pleated effect can be produced in knitted fabric on a ribbed base by working a slip stitch every alternate row 3 or 4 stitches from the end of the rib which is to form the pleat (174). On the final row the stitches which complete the rib after the slip stitch are cast off, and the pleat is made by folding these stitches to the back of the work and stitching them into position. The pleat is pressed along the slip-stitch edge. This type of fabric will stand up to wear and washing and retain the pleated effect, as the pleats can be re-pressed into position each time the garment has been washed.

Here is an example of pleated fabric—

Cast on a multiple of 13 sts.

Proceed as follows:—

1st row: * K.5, keeping wool at back of work, sl.1 purlwise, k.3, p.4; rep. from * to end of row (175).

2nd row: * K.4, p.9; rep. from * to end of row.

Rep. these two rows for required length.

When the pleating is complete, finish the work at the end of a 2nd row and proceed as follows:—

Next row: * K.6, cast off 3, p.3 (4 sts. on needle after cast-off); rep. from * to end of row.

Next row: * K.4, p.6, drawing firmly together the 2 sts. between the cast off stitches of the previous row (176).

Work a few rows in the k.6, p.4, rib before casting off. Neatly stitch the cast-off stitches down flat on the wrong side of the work, finally pressing the pleats in position.

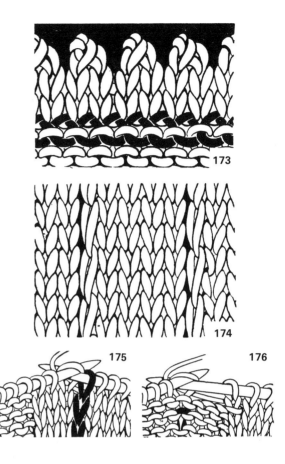

173
174
175
176

172

PLYS

Plys are the thickness of yarns formed by twisting several threads of the spun yarn together (See *Wool Processing*, page 96); 1-ply is the finest, for lace work, and is seldom used; 2-ply is more often used for delicate shawls and jumpers; 3-ply and 4-ply are used mainly for baby wear and for fine jumpers; Double Knitting is the most popular thickness for outer-wear; Triple or Treble Knitting is thicker again than D.K., and finally one comes to the Chunky or thick wools which may be composed of a number of fine threads or fewer thick threads.

POCKETS

There are several ways of making pockets in knitting, they may be purely utilitarian or decorative.

Flap Pocket. If a pocket with a flap is required, the simplest way is to knit the flap first, finishing the work so that the right side will be facing when working next row.

Cast off the stitches as for a Slit Pocket. On the following row, instead of slipping the stitches from the lining (which has not yet been knitted) on to the left-hand needle, slip the stitches from the knitted flap on to this needle, working across them in pattern as in the slit-pocket method. The lining for this pocket is knitted separately and neatly stitched into position on the wrong side of the work.

Patch Pocket. In garments where a decorative patch pocket is wanted, knit the pocket separately, knitting the first and the last stitch of every row. Place the pocket in position on the right side of the garment and after the pocket has been stitched into position, work a line of crochet slip stitch round the edge of the pocket thus neatening the appearance of the work.

67

Slit Pocket. The neatest type of pocket for a knitted garment. First knit the lining of the pocket. To do this cast on the number of stitches required (according to the width of the pocket), and knit the lining to the length required in stocking stitch, finishing at the end of a purl row (177).

When the point in the garment where the pocket is to be placed is reached (this will be at the top of the pocket of course), finish the piece of knitting with the wrong side of the work facing, then proceed as follows:—

Work along the number of stitches to the commencement of the pocket top, cast off the same number of stitches which has been cast on for the lining, then work along the remainder of the stitches to the end of the row (178). On the next row work along the first group of stitches, (i.e., to the commencement of the cast-off stitches on the previous row), now slip the stitches from the pocket lining on to the left-hand needle, and work in pattern across these stitches (179), then work across the remaining stitches to the end of the row.

The lining is now in position and the pocket is completed by neatly stitching it down. This will give a simple slit pocket without a flap.

POM-PONS

To make a pom-pon, cut two cardboard circles the size of finished bobble; cut holes in centre of each, about one third of diameter. Place circles together and wind yarn round, passing through the hole each time until cardboard is completely covered. Continue to wind evenly until hole is filled. With sharp scissors cut all round outer edge of circle between the two pieces of cardboard. Tie a piece of yarn very tightly between circles, cut them away and trim.

PULLOVER

(See *Jumpers and Pullovers*, page 54)

PRESSING

(See *Blocking Garments,* page 14).

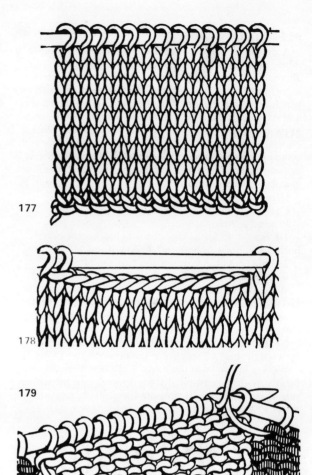

177

178

179

STITCH PURL

(Always carried out with the wool at the front of the work). Insert the point of the right-hand needle into the front of first stitch on the left-hand needle.

Holding the wool in the right hand, wrap it round the point of the right-hand needle (180).

Draw this loop through the first stitch on the left-hand needle (181) to make a stitch.

Drop the left-hand stitch off the left-hand needle in the ordinary way.

Purl Into the Back of Stitch. To purl into the back of the stitch insert the point of the right-hand needle into the back of the first stitch on the left-hand needle, bringing the point of the right-hand needle to the front of the point of the left-hand needle. Wrap the wool round the point of the right-hand needle and then drop the stitch off the needle in the ordinary way.

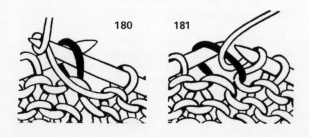

180   181

q

QUANTITIES

When buying wool or yarn it is essential to buy enough ounces with the same Dye Number to complete the garment. If the garment is worked exactly at the tension stated it will require the number of ounces of the specific wool quoted in the pattern, but if this tension is not strictly maintained or if a different brand of yarn is used, then the garment may take one or two ounces extra, or even more. It is therefore always advisable to buy extra ounces; if not required, these can be used to knit small articles or blanket squares. Alternatively, some wool shops will agree to reserve a small quantity of extra wool for a limited time.

QUICK KNITTING WOOLS

Wools with the designation "Quick Knit" or "Quick Knitting" are usually baby wools of a thickness between 4-ply and Double Knitting. They knit up more quickly than 4-ply but are not as bulky in wear as D.K. It is important to use the brand specified in the pattern as the yardage per ounce can vary considerably with different brands. (See also *Thick Wools*, page 90).

r

RE-KNITTING WOOLS

A hand-knitted garment in good condition can be unravelled (pulled back) and used to knit something else.

Unpick seams carefully and, starting from the cast-off edge, wind the wool into a loose loop or skein. As each ounce is unwound, tie the skein at two or three places with wool to keep it under control. The wool will be crimped up. If the article has not long been knitted it may be possible to steam out the crimping over a kettle, but it is usually necessary to wash the wool. Hold carefully in skein shape and swish lightly in warm water in which some pure soap flakes or a special liquid detergent for wools has been dissolved. Rinse thoroughly at same temperature and roll up in a towel to remove excess moisture. Suspend skein of wool in an airy place to dry, not near direct heat. When completely dry, the skein may be wound up into a ball for re-knitting.

RIBBED PATTERNS

The principle on which all ribbed patterns are built is alternating panels of stocking stitch and reverse stocking stitch. In narrow ribs this gives an elastic fabric and is mainly used for the welts of garments or in vests and underwear. The broader types of rib giving a vertical striped effect can be used for a variety of garments from men's pullovers to ladies' jumpers and cardigans. Ribbed fabrics are ideal for children's wear, as the natural elasticity in the fabric itself enables the knitter to create a garment that will, to a certain extent, stretch with the growth of the child.

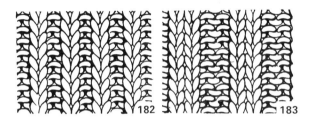

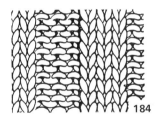

RIBBING

Basic. This type of ribbing is always carried out with an even number of stitches, using a multiple of 2, 4, 6, 8 or more to create narrow or broad ribbed effects.

K.1, P.1 Rib. Cast on a multiple of 2 sts., work every row * k.1, p.1; rep. from * to end (182).

K.2, P.2 Rib. Cast on a multiple of 4 sts., work every row * k.2, p.2; rep. from * to end (183).

K.3, P.3 Rib. Cast on a multiple of 6 sts., work every row * k.3, p.3; rep. from * to end (184).

French. In French or Continental ribbing an effect is obtained which gives the appearance of a finer version of brioche stitch.

The principle of this ribbing is that in every purl stitch

on every row the purl stitch of the row below is worked into (185).

The "purling into the stitch below" action is as follows:—

Slip the point of the right-hand needle purlwise through the stitch below (186).

Purl a stitch through this stitch then drop the first stitch (the stitch that normally would have been purled) off the left-hand needle (187).

Twisted. An interesting variation of basic ribbing can be worked by knitting into the back of one row and purling into the back of the next row on the stocking stitch surface, on the right side of the ribbed fabric.

Knitting or purling into the back of the stitch is carried out in exactly the same way as ordinary knitting and purling, except that the point of the needle, before the stitch is worked, is inserted into the back instead of the front of stitch.

Here are typical examples of twisted ribbing using the "working into the back of the stitch principle" as specified above.

K.1, P.1 Rib. Cast on a multiple of 2 sts.

1st row: * K. into back of 1 st., p.1; rep. from * to end.

2nd row: * K.1, p. into back of 1 st.; rep. from * to end.
These 2 rows form the pattern (188).

K.2, P.2 Rib. Cast on a multiple of 4 sts.

1st row: * K. into back of 2 sts., p.2; rep. from * to end.

2nd row: * K.2, p. into back of 2 sts.; rep. from * to end.
These 2 rows form the pattern (189).

K.3, P.3 Rib. Cast on a multiple of 6 sts.

1st row: * K. into back of 3 sts., p.3; rep. from * to end.

2nd row: * K.3, p. into back of 3 sts.; rep. from * to end.
These 2 rows form the pattern (190).

FANCY RIB PATTERN

Cast on a multiple of 8 sts.

1st row: * P.2, k. into back of next st., p.2, k.3; rep. from * to end.

2nd row: * P.3, k.2, p. into back of next st., k.2; rep. from * to end.
These 2 rows form the patt. (191).

FANCY RIB PATTERN, VARIATION

Cast on a multiple of 9 sts.

1st row: * P.1, k.5, p.1, k.2; rep. from * to end.

2nd row: * P.2, k.1; rep. from * to end.
These 2 rows form the patt. (192).

FANCY RIB PATTERN, SECOND VARIATION

Cast on a multiple of 11 sts.

1st row: * P.2, k.6, p.2, k.1; rep. from * to end.

2nd row: * P.1, k.3, p.4, k.3; rep. from * to end.
These 2 rows form the patt. (193).

PLEATED RIB

Cast on a multiple of 7 sts.

1st row: * K.3, keeping wool at back of work sl.1 purlwise, k.1, p.2; rep. from * to end.

2nd row: * K.2, p.5; rep. from * to end.
These 2 rows form the patt.

Fishermen's Rib

Cast on an even number of stitches.

1st row: * K.1, p.1; rep. from * to end.

2nd and every following row: K.B.1, * purl into next st. one row below *at same time* slipping off stitch above,

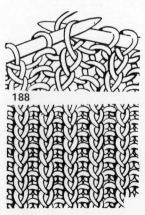

188

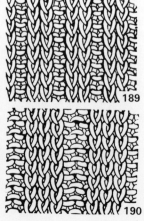

189

190

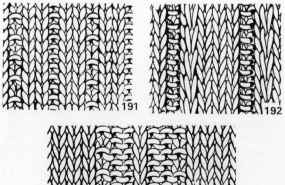

191

192

193

K.B.1, rep. from * to last st., p.1.

These two rows form the pattern.

This stitch is usually knitted in Double Knitting for sweaters and cardigans, but it can be knitted in finer wools and when worked up in 2-ply wool on coarse gauge needles it makes a very attractive lacy rib fabric.

RIBBON KNITTING

Very attractive garments may be knitted from ribbon which is sold specifically for the purpose. The principles used are the same as for yarn knitting but of course a special pattern is required which has been specially designed for ribbon knitting.

SAMPLERS

Following the increase in popularity of hand-knitting during the Crimean War, a knitted sampler of all the stitches learned became a familiar school-room task. Expert knitters were able to work their names and various motifs in Colour Knitting just as they did in needlework samplers. Examples are rare but a clever knitter who had grasped the basic principles of Graphing could chart herself a most attractive multicoloured sampler or a a picture to be framed.

SCANDINAVIAN COLOUR KNITTING

Denmark, Sweden and Norway have a very fine heritage of colour knitting that sprang up among the peasant communities several centuries ago and which still flourishes today in parts of Scandinavia. Here we find very simple designs inspired by the natural surroundings.

Under this heading knitting from as far north as Finland and as far south as Denmark and the Faroes are grouped together, as all the countries within this orbit have been inspired by the same tradition. In Finland gaily coloured peasant figures are knitted on to a natural background; in Norway stags and pine trees form the main theme; the Swedish knitting has become much more self-conscious and sophisticated and the designs used are typical of Swedish textiles and embroideries. In Denmark simpler themes, mainly seedings with simple borders or motifs are used; while in the Faroes there is a blending of the Norwegian and Swedish traditions.

Colour knitting varies from that discovered on the Fair Isle and Shetland, in that self-coloured effects on white and natural grounds are the dominating themes. The basis to the Scandinavian traditions, however, is seedings, simple all-over patternings breaking up the stocking stitch fabric, combined with borders and motifs. Overleaf are graphs of typical motifs which can be used in designing Scandinavian sweaters.

SEEDINGS

The seeding pattern is always worked in a contrasting dark shade on a natural or white background. Red, brown, dark green and navy are the colours most frequently used in these seedings; but gay effects can be obtained by interspacing a bright colour with a dark shade.

Spotted Seedings. *Abbreviations:* D.—Dark; L.—Light.
1st row: K. * 1 D., 5 L.; rep. from * to last st., 1 D.
2nd row: Using light, p.
3rd row: Using light, k.
4th row: Using light, p.
5th row: * 3 L., 1 D., 2 L.; rep. from * to last st., 1 L.
6th row: Using light, p.
7th row: Using light, k.
8th row: Using light, p.
These 8 rows form patt. and are repeated throughout (194).

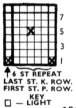

7
5
3
1

↑ 6 ST REPEAT
LAST ST. K. ROW.
FIRST ST. P. ROW.
KEY
□ — LIGHT
☒ — DARK   194

On the left is the chart for the seeding pattern. Below are illustrated alternative seeding patterns which may be worked by following the simple charts

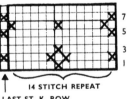

7
5
3
1

↑ 14 STITCH REPEAT

LAST ST. K. ROW.
FIRST ST. P. ROW.

7
5
3
1

↑ 8 STITCH REPEAT

LAST ST. K. ROW.
FIRST ST. P. ROW.

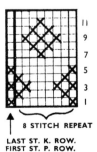

11
9
7
5
3
1

↑ 8 STITCH REPEAT

LAST ST. K. ROW.
FIRST ST. P. ROW.

9
7
5
3
1

↑ 8 STITCH REPEAT

LAST ST. K. ROW.
FIRST ST. P. ROW.

KEY
□ — LIGHT
☒ — DARK
◪ — MEDIUM

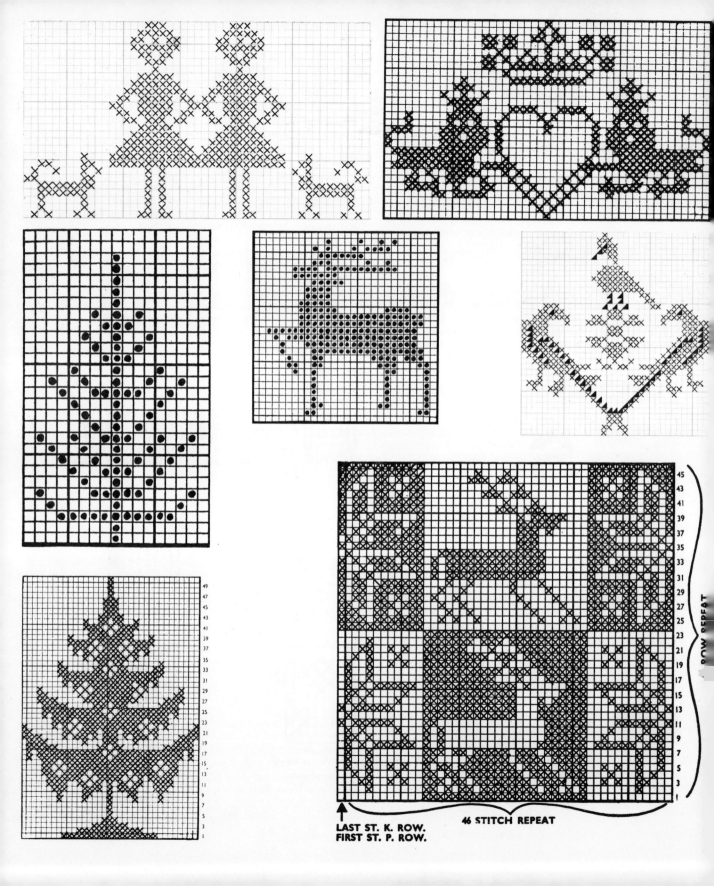

LAST ST. K. ROW.
FIRST ST. P. ROW.

46 STITCH REPEAT

ROW REPEAT

45
43
41
39
37
35
33
31
29
27
25
23
21
19
17
15
13
11
9
7
5
3
1

49
47
45
43
41
39
37
35
33
31
29
27
25
23
21
19
17
15
13
11
9
7
5
3
1

Opposite page and above: Some examples of Scandinavian Colour Knitting

SWEATERS

The Scandinavian sweaters are knitted in heavy wools approximating to what are known as double knitting wools in this country. The ground shades are usually navy, rich brown or bottle green, the patternings generally being carried out in white or a natural, although in Norway bold splashes of primary colours—reds, yellows and blues, are used to give striking effects to the sweaters.

The reindeer motifs are typical of Scandinavian knitting. Pine trees are always popular. The pine tree and reindeer design is a typical Scandinavian sweater motif.

These sweaters are knitted without any shapings. The welt and cuffs are worked in k.1, p.1, rib and a neckband, worked on four needles, is again in rib. The sweaters may be finished with either an ordinary crew neck 1¼ ins. in depth, or a roll over polo neck 5 ins. in depth.

The armholes are not shaped at all, but a square gusset is always knitted and stitched into the sleeve at the side seams, giving ease to the fit of the sweater itself.

The gussets are knitted with seeding to match the main pattern on the body of the garment.

73

SCARVES

Scarves are narrow oblong pieces of knitted fabric with the ends fringed. A common practice is to knit in a rib pattern, although a very useful type of scarf can be made in double knitting (see page 35). Wool of 2- or 3-ply will produce an ideal fabric in double knitting for either a light weight or medium weight scarf.

Another useful stitch, particularly if 4-ply or double knitting weights are used, is *French Ribbing*.

Another effective stitch for scarves is *Brioche Knitting*.

If striped effects are desired, either double knitting or k.1, p.1 rib is an ideal fabric.

DIAGONAL EFFECTS

Interesting effects for scarves with diagonal ends can be created by working the fabric on the bias. Bias knitting is worked on the simple principle of increasing in first st. and knitting the last 2 sts. tog. on alt. rows.

Diagonal striped effects can be created by using bias fabrics; or you can knit a charming lace scarf but remember that you must keep 2 k. sts. at the beg. and end of every row.

FRINGE

The fringing of scarves is a very simple matter. Take a length of cardboard about 3 ins. wide. Wind the wool round the cardboard, then cut along one edge.

Now take 3 or 4 strands, hold the ends together between the fingers, slip a crochet hook through the edge of the scarf and through the loop formed by holding the strands of wool between the fingers, draw this loop through the edge of the knitted fabric. Now insert the crochet hook under the 6 or 8 strands of wool held between the fingers, draw this through the loop already formed and pull tightly into a knot (195).

Fringe across the ends of the scarf in this manner, trimming the fringe off neatly to the length desired.

SHETLAND LACE SCARF

This is a traditional scarf, which is always knitted in *Fan and Feather* pattern, a delightful variation of *Feather Stitch*. The pattern row is worked exactly as in Feather Stitch, 3 knit rows being worked after each pattern row. The usual practice is to knit these scarves in a 2- or 3-ply weight of wool, using a comparatively coarse needle,

approximately size 5 for a 3-ply and size 7 for a 2-ply.

Broad bands of colour can be worked into the scarf, keeping the patterning going all the time.

The edge when finished will be scalloped and the usual finish to the ends is to work 6 knit rows before commencing the pattern, completing the scarf by working 5 knit rows before casting off.

A remarkable point that must be emphasized here is that in this type of scarf the cast-on and cast-off rows must be worked very loosely, as this enables the fabric to flow attractively into its natural scallops.

Here is the variation of Feather Stitch used on a Shetland scarf—

Fan and Feather Stitch. Cast on a multiple of 18 sts. plus 1 st.

1st row: * K.1, (k.2 tog.) 3 times, (w.f., k.1) 5 times, w.f., (k.2 tog.) 3 times; rep. from * to last st., k.1.

2nd, 3rd and 4th rows: K.

These 4 rows form the pattern.

SEAMS

Making up the finished pieces of knitted fabrics into garments is as important a part of the knitters' craft as the knitting of the pieces of fabric themselves. So many people ruin a garment by not paying sufficient attention to "make up detail" when they are finishing their work.

It can take from six to eight hours to block and make up a simple jumper properly and as long as ten to twelve hours to make up cardigans, coats and more elaborate garments.

Three types of seam are used in making up knitteds.

Back-Stitch Seam. The seam most commonly used is one sewn with back stitch. Lay the two pieces of fabric together, right side to right side (reverse sides outside), matching up as nearly as possible row by row on the two pieces of fabric, tack about $\frac{1}{4}$ inch in from the edge (196).

Tacking stitches about $\frac{1}{2}$ inch long are the most useful for this purpose and it is advisable to do the tacking stitches in a different coloured wool or thread so that they can be clearly seen and drawn out easily when the seam is completed.

Now, with the same material as that used for knitting the garment and a blunt pointed (tapestry) needle, neatly back-stitch the pieces together approximately one and a half knitted stitches from the outside edge (197).

When the seams are completed draw out tacking threads and neatly press seams open, using the point of the iron (198).

Flat Seam. When joining ribbing and stitching on front bands a flat seam is used, the action here consists of drawing together the edge stitches of each piece of fabric.

195

74

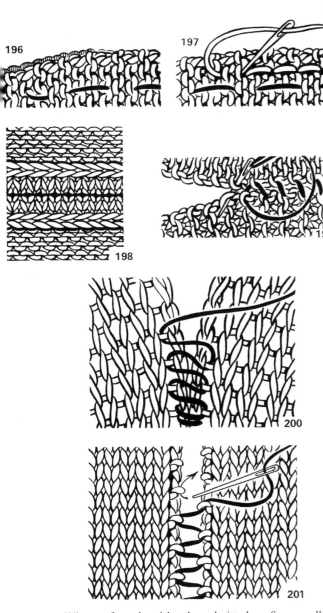

196

197

198

199

200

201

there are no shapings breaking the line of the fabric at the edge.

Placing the first finger of the left hand between the two pieces to be seamed together, hold them edge to edge with the right side of work to the outside. Draw the needle through the bottom edge and fasten ready to commence seaming. Note that the needle must be on the right side of the work when starting the actual seaming.

Taking needle over to the second edge, insert it under the thread that lies between the first and second stitch, the point of the needle pointing to the top of the pieces being seamed (200). Repeat this operation between the first and second stitch on the second piece of fabric and then continue until the two pieces have been joined together, taking care to work in every stitch.

The above type of seaming is ideal for classic cardigans and jumpers and panel skirts, for, when it is finished, it makes an invisible seam in the fabric.

Lacing Action. In certain garments, baby garments in particular, a different type of flat seam is used, as each piece of fabric has a "pip" edge. This edge is formed by knitting the first and last stitch in every row and forms a series of one stitch ridges down the edge of the piece of fabric.

The flat seam here is a lacing action, drawing together the two pieces of fabric, matching the rows pip stitch by pip stitch all along the edge. The method is to work the oversewing action on an under and over lacing principle.

Insert the needle between the first two ridges made by the pip edge, take the needle to the right side of the second piece, bring the point of the needle up through the first two ridges, draw the two pieces together (201). Now take it to the right side of the second piece and bring the point of the needle up through the second and third ridges.

Repeat this action, alternating from one edge to the other, until the two pieces of fabric have been neatly drawn together.

General Principles. The general principle of making up knitted garments (except for baby garments or other garments where the pip edge method is used) is to use a flat seam for the ribbed portions and a back-stitch seam for the remainder of the garment.

Let us take as an example a classic jumper.

After the pieces have been blocked and pressed, the make up finish is as follows:—

Using a flat seam, join the ribbing of the back and fronts and of the cuffs.

Using a back-stitch seam join side and sleeve seams.

Using a back-stitch seam join the shoulders before knitting up the neckband itself.

Using a back-stitch seam stitch sleeves into position.

Press all back-stitch seams open with the point of a warm iron, covering the seam itself with a damp cloth.

Where a front band has been knitted on finer needles than the piece of fabric to which it is to be seamed, it will not be possible to match the flat seam stitch by stitch; they must be adjusted so that the band lies absolutely even when the seam is completed. Hold the two pieces of fabric together, with the finger in between, at the point where the flat seam is to be made.

Using an Oversewing Stitch, neatly seam together the two pieces, taking great care not to form a ridge (199).

Invisible Seam. This method of seaming is only used where dart shapings are worked in the fabric and where

SEEDING
(See *Scandinavian Colour Knitting*, page 71)

SHAPING

A beginner learns to knit a straight piece of fabric; as soon as the basic stitches are mastered it becomes necessary to learn how to shape knitting into a garment or useful article. This is done by Increasing during the knitting or by Casting On extra stitches, or alternatively by Decreasing during knitting or by Casting Off (as for an armhole). In this way the outline of the garment can be shaped during knitting just as a piece of woven cloth can be cut and sewn to a particular shape. Practise the instructions given under the sections Increasing and Decreasing in order to perfect the various methods, then by following the pattern instructions carefully it will be easy to shape a simple knitted garment.

SHAWLS

Shawls have always had their place in the world of fashion. One immediately thinks of the lovely embroidered specimens from China and Spain, or the delightful woven ones from Persia and India. Coming nearer home the Paisley shawl in fine cashmere at one time ranked very highly as an accessory for the well dressed woman. Indeed shawls have always been popular favourites. They can be square, triangular or round. Some of them, the traditional Shetland christening shawls for instance, are so lacy and cobweb-like that as one gazes at them in sheer admiration one is inclined to think that celestial spiders have been at work creating the lovely, lacy effects. Babies' shawls in 2-ply or 3-ply have always been popular, while shawls in heavier weights—4-ply and double knitting—have won a place in the modern woman's heart.

CIRCULAR SHAWLS

The first method of knitting these shawls is on the same principle as for the circular disc, (see *Circular Knitting*). By knitting one round and purling the following round, you will produce a circle of garter stitch. If, on the other hand, you knit every round you will produce stocking stitch.

Delightful lace patternings can be worked into these shawls, providing it is remembered that the lace pattern must be built up to fall into the number of stitches between the increases.

Lace Pattern, Simple. This design embodying the lace medallion on a target principle can be worked as follows—
Cast on 8 sts., arranging 2 on each needle, using 5 needles in all to work the rounds.

1st round: K. into back of all sts.
2nd round: K. into front and back of each st. (16 sts.).
3rd round: K.
4th round: * W.f., k.2 tog.; rep. from * to end.
5th round: K.
6th round: K. into front and back of each st. (32 sts.).
7th round: K.
8th round: * K.2, w.f., k.2 tog.; rep. from * to end.
9th round: K.1, * w.f., k.2 tog., k.2; rep. from * to last 3 sts. of round, w.f., k.2 tog., k.1.
10th round: * W.f., k.2 tog., k.2; rep. from * to end.
11th round: K.
12th round: K. into front and back of every st. (64 sts.). These 12 rounds are shown in detail in (202).
13th round: K.
14th to 16th rounds: As 8th to 10th.
17th round: K.
18th round: * K.1, k. into front and back of next st.; rep. from * to end (96 sts.).

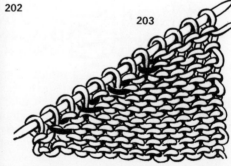

202

203

204

19th and 20th rounds: K.

21st round: * W.f., k.2 tog.; rep. from * to end.

22nd and 23rd rounds: K.

24th round: * K.2, k. into front and back of next st.; rep. from * to end.

25th to 29th rounds: As 13th to 17th.

30th round: * K.3, k. into front and back of next st.; rep. from * to end.

31st to 35th rounds: As 19th to 23rd.

Continue in this manner, working 5 rounds between each two sets of increases, *noting* that 1 st. more is knitted before the inc. in each inc. round.

You can alternate the lace pattern in the 5 rounds throughout completing the shawl by knitting a narrow border on 2 needles and sewing it on neatly all round the edge, taking care not to draw up the circle.

Sections, Knitting In. Another method of knitting circular shawls, using two needles only, is to knit the shawl in sections, the sections being created by turning and working back to the outside edge.

When the first section has been completed work a second one in a similar way continuing until sufficient sections to form a flat circle have been worked, then join the cast-on and cast-off edges together with a flat seam.

If you cast on using the two needle method to form a looped edge, the stitches on the needle can be grafted (without casting off) to the loops formed by the Through the Stitch method cast-on.

The principle of working the sections is as follows—

Cast on 12 sts.

1st row: K.

2nd row: P. to last 2 sts., turn. (See *Note* below).

3rd row: K.

4th row: P. to last 4 sts., turn.

5th row: K.

6th row: P. to last 6 sts., turn.

7th row: K.

8th row: P. to last 8 sts., turn.

9th row: K.

10th row: P. all across.

11th row: K.

Diagram shows one section completed (203).

Rep. rows 2 to 11 incl. until a complete circle has been formed.

Once the principle of section knitting has been grasped it is a simple enough matter to adjust the stitches to the size of shawl being made.

Note. An important point on turning; to prevent holes in the work slip the stitch after the point where the turn is made from the left-hand to the right-hand needle without knitting it, take the wool round this stitch to the back, returning the slipped stitch to the left-hand needle again

(204). This action would be worked as follows on the 2nd row of the instructions given above.

P. to last 2 sts., sl. the next st. from the left-hand to the right-hand needle without purling it, take the wool to the back of the work, so that it lies across the front of the st. just slipped, now sl. the st. back again on to the left-hand needle, turn and k. 3rd row.

SQUARE SHAWLS

These can be knitted in several ways. The simplest type is a square of knitted fabric either in garter stitch or an all-over lace patterning, to which is added afterwards a lace border.

The principle here is perfectly simple.

Cast on the number of sts. required for the width of the shawl, less the width of the border, thus if the finished shawl is to measure 72 ins. square and the border pattern measures 4 ins. at its widest point, the centre square will have to be 64 ins. across.

If a garter stitch centre is used, simply multiply the number of stitches to the inch in the appropriate type of wool by the width of the shawl (64 ins.) and proceed to knit every row until a length of garter stitch approximately 60 inches long has been produced. The extra 4 ins. are added when you "dress" the shawl by stretching the knitted fabric lengthwise until it measures the required 64 ins. (See *Blocking Garments,* page 14).

Second Method. Another method of knitting a square shawl is to work from the centre outwards (see instructions for *Square Disc* on page 26). The principle here is to cast on 3 sts. on each of 4 needles (5 needles will be required for knitting the shawl), 12 sts. in all. Then work an increase principle at each side of the centre stitch on each needle on every alternate round, working in rounds all the time.

When working a garter stitch centre on this principle purl every alternate round.

The following instructions illustrate this principle when worked in garter stitch. The action on each round is worked on each of the 4 needles.

1st round: K.1, m.1, k.1, m.1, k.1.

2nd round: P.

3rd round: K.2, m.1, k.1, m.1, k.2.

4th round: P.

5th round: K.3, m.1, k.1, m.1, k.3.

6th round: P.

Continue working in this manner until a square the required size has been completed.

The increases can either be worked on the "m.1" principle (the solid increase, where you pick up the loop between the stitch just worked and the following stitch and knit into the back of it), or on the ordinary "w.f." principle (lace hole increase), which will give you effective lace stripes moving diagonally up to each corner of the shawl.

The border is knitted afterwards on two needles, using

a lace pattern and allowing sufficient at the corners to gather in slightly on turning the corners with the lace.

A favourite design on Shetland has a garter stitch centre, working on the principle of knitting from the centre in rounds as given above, with a *Shell and Feather Pattern* border knitted in with the shawl. The principle here is perfectly simple. Start the border when you have a multiple of the number of stitches required for Shell and Feather Pattern, working outwards in this pattern as multiples are added in the increasing, thus enabling you to include additional patterns in the border itself.

TRIANGULAR SHAWLS

These are worked on a simple increase principle.

The simplest stitch is garter stitch and this can look very attractive if a fine wool and coarse needle are used, with a lace border sewn on the triangle after it has been completed. The principle here is to work side increases until the bottom corner of the triangle has been completed, following this by parallel increases up each side of the shawl until the desired size has been obtained.

Work as follows—

Cast on 3 sts.

1st row: K.

2nd row: (K.1, m.1) twice, k.1.

3rd and every alt. row: K.

4th row: K.1, m.1, k.3, m.1, k.1.

6th row: K.1, m.1, k.5, m.1, k.1.

8th row: K.1, m.1, k.7, m.1, k.1.

10th row: K.1, m.1, k.9, m.1, k.1.

Continue in this manner, working increases on every alt. row as before until the row "k.1, m.1, k.23, m.1, k.1" has been worked.

Proceed to work parallel increases as follows—

1st row: K.1, m.1, k.10, m.1, k.5, m.1, k.10, m.1, k.1.

2nd row: K.

3rd row: K.1, m.1, k.10, m.1, k.9, m.1, k.10, m.1, k.1.

4th row: K.

5th row: K.1, m.1, k.10, m.1, k.13, m.1, k.10, m.1, k.1.

6th row: K.

Continue increasing in this manner until a triangle the desired size has been completed. Cast off loosely.

SHELL KNITTING

The method of working shell knitting is to cluster together groups of stitches worked on a drop stitch principle, increasing in the next stitch to balance out the clustered stitch. The shells can be composed of four to six stitches.

Here is an example of shell knitting which can be seen in (205):

Cast on a multiple of 6 plus 2.

1st row: K.

2nd row: K.

3rd row: K.1, * (w.r.n.) 3 times, k.1 (206); rep. from * to end.

4th row: K.1, * drop 3 w.r.n. of previous row, k.1 (207); rep. from * to end.

5th row: K.1, * sl.3, k.2 tog., pass 3 sl. sts. over, (k.1, p.1, k.1, p.1, k.1, all into next st.); rep. from * to last st., k.1.

6th to 8th rows: K.

9th row: As 3rd row.

10th row: As 4th row.

11th row: K.1, * (k.1, p.1, k.1, p.1, k.1, all into next st.), sl.3, k.2 tog., pass 3 sl. sts. over; rep. from * to last st., k.1.

12th row: K.

These 12 rows form the patt. and are repeated throughout.

The diagrams show how the shell principle is worked and placed on knitted fabric.

The fabric produced is light and airy and consequently highly suitable for making shawls, bedwraps and dressing-jackets.

SHETLAND COLOUR KNITTING

It is fascinating to note that although Shetland is so near to Fair Isle, the tradition in Shetland knitting is derived much more from Scandinavian than from Fair Isle sources.

The early settlers on Shetland in the nineteenth century were exiles from Norway and they probably brought with them the symbolic patterns rooted in the peasant crafts of their country. Generally speaking pure Shetland designs are all-over patterns worked in a variety of colours, the ground shade again remaining constant.

205

206

207

Shetland colour knitting differs from Fair Isle knitting, in that the designs fall into two distinct categories. The first type of design has bands of coloured patternings which are always carried out in natural shades, moving from a dark pattern on a light ground to a light pattern on a dark ground. In the chart (208) this type of design is shown and may be adapted to the basic shape for a man's pullover. Here the shades graduate from light to dark by a series of small diamonds, the pattern bands being worked in one colour only, the lightest shade is used on the dark ground and the darkest on the light ground.

In some cases the actual patterning in the diamond varies as the design proceeds, while in others striped effects are obtained in the patterning.

The second type of Shetland design is worked in an all-over patterning. Any number of colours can be used, but these are graded, and the colours are used in the sequence given in the twelve-row colour sequence below.

This twelve-row colour sequence is followed throughout the pattern. Thus, if there are fifteen pattern rows the colour sequence will change as the patterning proceeds.

	Background	Pattern
1st row:	1st Colour	2nd Colour
2nd row:	1st Colour	2nd Colour
3rd row:	3rd Colour	2nd Colour
4th row:	3rd Colour	4th Colour
5th row:	3rd Colour	4th Colour
6th row:	5th Colour	4th Colour
7th row:	5th Colour	6th Colour
8th row:	5th Colour	6th Colour
9th row:	7th Colour	6th Colour
10th row:	7th Colour	8th Colour
11th row:	7th Colour	8th Colour
12th row:	9th Colour	8th Colour

SHETLAND LACE

It is important to remember that few of the traditional patterns in Shetland have ever been written down. Lace knitting there is an oral tradition, the patterns have been handed down from one generation to another for the last two centuries.

The origin of Shetland lace knitting is quite unknown, although in tradition it links with the lace hose for which the Knitters' Guild of Paris was famous from 1400 onwards. We do know that Mrs. Jessie Saxby, who was a great collector of lace, visited Shetland in the nineteenth century, taking with her specimens from her collection and it has been stated with authority, by one of the Shetlanders whose grandmother met Mrs. Saxby, that the lovely laces in this collection definitely helped to give a renewed impetus to lace knitting in Shetland.

Shetland lace knitting is usually carried out in very fine wool, similar to 1-ply or lace wool, which is hand spun by the people themselves and knitted on very fine needles,

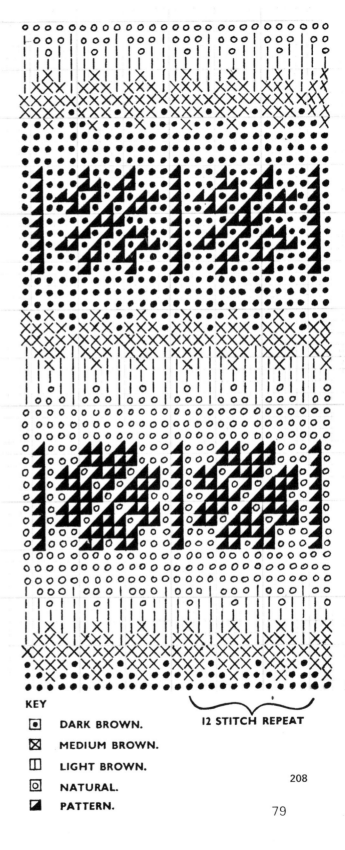

KEY

⊡	DARK BROWN.
⊠	MEDIUM BROWN.
⊞	LIGHT BROWN.
⊙	NATURAL.
◪	PATTERN.

12 STITCH REPEAT

208

79

the sizes used range from No. 16 to No. 18. This fine wool and needles create the lovely cobweb effect.

When the work is completed it is stretched on a frame, dampened and allowed to dry. As the ordinary knitter does not necessarily possess the facilities for carrying out this operation, a simpler way is to stretch the work well on an ordinary ironing board over a felt, pin it out evenly round the edges and press well, using a hot iron and wet cloth.

BASIC STITCHES

The main stitches used in Shetland lace are given in the following instructions, these merely lay down the principles of each stitch.

Bead Stitch. This is generally grouped to form part of the background of designs.
Cast on 9 sts. for each pattern.
1st row: K.2, k.2 tog., w.f., k.1, w.f., k.2 tog., k.2.
2nd row: K.1, k.2 tog., w.f., k.3, w.f., k.2 tog., k.1.
3rd row: K.2, w.f., k.2 tog., k.1, k.2 tog., w.f., k.2.
4th row: K.3, w.f., k.3 tog., w.f., k.3.
These 4 rows form the patt.

Cat's Paw Stitch. This stitch is used to emphasize the lace aspect of the design. It takes its name from the simple fact that the stitch when completed looks like the imprint of a cat's paw.
Cast on 11 sts. for each pattern.
1st row: K.3, k.2 tog., w.f., k.1, w.f., k.2 tog., k.3.
2nd row: P.
3rd row: K.2, k.2 tog., w.f., k.3, w.f., k.2 tog., k.2.
4th row: P.
5th row: K.4, w.f., k.3 tog., w.f., k.4.
6th row: P.
These 6 rows form the patt. (209).

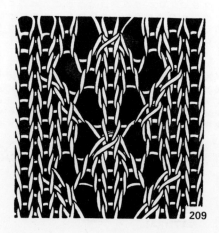
209

Lace Holes. This is a stitch used mainly for background work or building up into diamond formations in combination with other stitches to give variety to the lace patterns themselves. (See *Overs,* page 56).

Madeira Stitch. This consists of a fan-shaped open-work lace pattern worked against either a plain or a bead stitch background. The Madeiras can either be simple fan formations or more intricate ladder-like sequences worked into the Madeira itself.

Cast on 13 sts. for each pattern.
1st row: K.6, w.f., k.2 tog., k.5.
2nd row: K.5, w.f., k.3 tog., w.f., k.5.
3rd row: K.3, w.f., k.2 tog., w.f., k.3 tog., w.f., k.2 tog., w.f., k.3.
4th row: K.1, w.f., (k.2 tog., w.f.) twice, k.3 tog., (w.f., k.2 tog.) twice, w.f., k.1. These 4 rows form patt.
Shetland lace designs are worked from charts as in Viennese Lace knitting. The basis of the fabric is Garter Stitch, thus creating patternings that are completely reversible.

TRADITIONAL ALL-OVER PATTERN

This is a traditional Shetland pattern which has a beautiful all-over design suitable for the centre of a shawl or for a lacy bed jacket. It embodies "Madeiras" "Cat's Paw" stitch and "Lace Holes".
Here are the instructions for first 6 rows:
Cast on a multiple of 28 sts. plus 2.
1st row: K.1, * k.5, k.2 tog., w.f., k.1, w.f., k.2 tog., k.9, k.2 tog., w.f., k.1, w.f., k.2 tog., k.4; rep. from * to last st., k.1.
2nd row: K.1, * k.3, k.2 tog., w.f., k.3, w.f., k.2 tog., k.7, k.2 tog., w.f., k.3, w.f., k.2 tog., k.4; rep. from * to last st., k.1.
3rd row: K.1, * k.3, (k.2 tog., w.f.) twice, k.1, (w.f., k.2 tog.) twice, k.5, (k.2 tog., w.f.) twice, k.1, (w.f., k.2 tog.) twice, k.2; rep. from * to last st., k.1.
4th row: K.1, * k.1, k.2 tog., w.f., k.7, w.f., k.2 tog., k.3, (k.2 tog., w.f.) twice, k.3, (w.f., k.2 tog.) twice, k.2; rep. from * to last st., k.1.
5th row: K.1, * k.1, (k.2 tog., w.f., k.2, w.f., k.2 tog., k.1) twice, (k.2 tog., w.f.) twice, k.1, w.f., sl.1, k.2 tog., p.s.s.o., w.f., k.1, (w.f., k.2 tog.) twice, rep. from * to last st., k.1.
6th row: K.1, * w.f., k.2 tog., k.9, k.2 tog., w.f., k.1, w.f., k.2 tog., k.3, w.f., sl.1, k.2 tog., p.s.s.o., w.f., k.3, k.2 tog., w.f., k.1; rep. from * to last st., k.1.
Continue working from chart (210).
Once the principles of charting and knitting Shetland laces, along the lines outlined in this section, have been mastered, it should be a comparatively simple matter for the knitter to experiment with designing her own laces.
It will be noticed that most of the patterns fall into

80

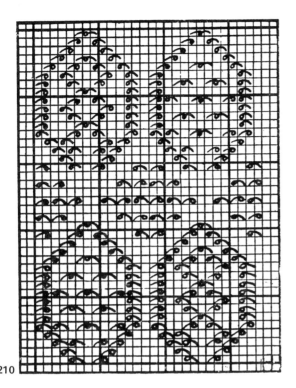

210

simple geometrical shapes. Triangles, diamonds and hexagons are the main shapes used in building up the foundation of the pattern.

Mark out the basic shapes to be embodied into the pattern, on graph paper.

Next fill in each shape with the particular type of lace stitch to be used. It is advisable to have one or two plain stitches outlining the edges of the shapes, thus giving a clear definition to the finished piece of knitting.

Start with simple patterns, moving on to more intricate designs as your ability to design this fascinating material in knitting improves.

SHETLAND LACE SCARF

(See *Scarves*, page 74)

SHRINKAGE

Synthetic yarns are unshrinkable if washing temperatures and instructions are followed to the letter. Wool, as a natural fibre, is more subject to shrinkage from rough handling or high temperatures during washing and drying and once a garment has shrunk there is very little to be done about it so that prevention, as always, is preferable to remedy.

A slight shrinkage may be remedied by re-washing the article in luke-warm water with a special detergent for delicate fabrics (do not use ordinary powder detergents).

Follow the instructions, rinse carefully, pulling out the garment very slightly in the water. Roll in a towel to remove excess moisture, then lay flat on a sheet of white paper on which you have pencilled the shape and original measurements of the article. Pull it very gently into shape and pin to the measurements required. Dry flat in an airy place away from a direct source of heat.

SKIRTS

Skirts can be knitted either in the round, using a circular needle, or in sections, on two needles, the various sections being stitched together after they have been knitted. The principle of skirt knitting is to work on a series of graded decreases forming what is virtually a tubular piece of fabric wider at one end (the lower edge of the skirt) than the other end (the waist band).

Wools in 4-ply weights or with a bouclet twist are the best for this type of garment. If a 2-ply or 3-ply wool is used this necessitates extremely fine needles in order to get a close texture in the fabric, which is an important factor in a knitted skirt.

FLARED SKIRT

Flaring in a knitted skirt is created by moving the graded decreases inwards so that they move in diagonal lines towards each other, forming a series of triangular points on each section of the skirt (211).

If each section consists of 90 sts. the graded decreases

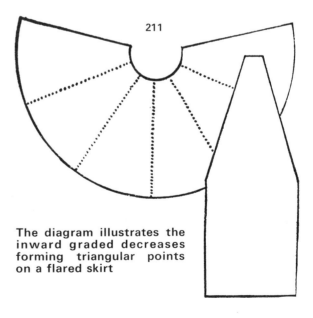

The diagram illustrates the inward graded decreases forming triangular points on a flared skirt

will be worked as follows—

1st row: K.1, k.2 tog., k.85, k.2 tog.
2nd row: P.
3rd row: K.
4th row: P.
5th and 6th rows: As 3rd and 4th.
7th row: K.2, k.2 tog., k.81, k.2 tog., k.1.
8th row: P.
9th row: K.
10th row: P.
11th and 12th rows: As 9th and 10th.
13th row: K.3, k.2 tog., k.77, k.2 tog., k.2.
14th row: P.
15th row: K.
16th row: P.
17th and 18th rows: As 15th and 16th.

Continue decreasing in this manner on next and every following 6th row until 40 sts. remain.

Working on the basis of six 90-st. sections, (540 sts. all round), there will be 240 sts. at waist band when all the decreases have been worked.

You will need 145 rows to work the decreases so that each section moves from 90 to 40 sts. This means that 140 rows will be worked before commencing the flaring on the skirt itself.

PLEATED SKIRT

The easiest method of working a pleated skirt is to create a ribbed fabric, working the decreases in the reverse stocking stitch portion of the rib and then in the stocking stitch portion of the rib so that you get what appears to be a series of graded pleats in the fabric itself.

SLEEVES

The sleeves of a knitted garment can be either raglan style or set-in, depending upon the style and design, and the current fashion. Generally, raglan sleeves are to be preferred as they give a smoother fit over the shoulders and are also suitable to any width of shoulders. A jumper with set-in sleeves may need darting or alterations to fit someone with shoulders which are narrower than the width allowed for in the pattern.

In order to ensure that both sleeves are identical, it is a good idea to knit both sleeves at once. Cast on the stitches for the first sleeve with one ball of wool, and then continuing on the same needle, cast on stitches for a second sleeve with a second ball of wool. Continue to knit up the sleeves using these different balls of wool; the shaping of both sleeves will come on exactly the same row without constant checking.

SLIPOVERS

A slipover (sometimes called a pullover) is, as the name suggests, a loose fitting sleeveless garment with a casual line and can be worn either by man or a woman. The important thing in this type of garment is that there is no side shaping, the straight line giving a sleek fit.

All weights of wool from a 2-ply to a double knitting can be used for these types of garment. Usually, however, a 3-ply or 4-ply weight is used, as these form fabrics of an ideal weight and texture for slipovers for men and women.

SLIP STITCH

Slip stitches are often used for edge stitches as these facilitate the making up of a flat seam, and also along the sides of the heel flap on socks and stockings, making the series of stitches which are picked up when completing the heel.

Edges. The slip stitch principle for edges (212) is always to slip the first stitch knitwise and knit the last stitch on every row irrespective of the pattern. The easiest way to do this is to add 2 extra stitches to the number used for the pattern.

Heel Flap. In slipping the stitches of a heel flap (213), on the knit row slip the first stitch knitwise and knit the last stitch; on the purl row slip the first stitch purlwise and purl the last stitch, thus making a chain edge up each side of the heel flap.

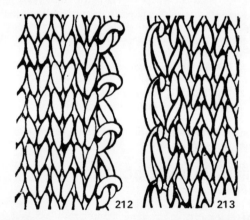

212   213

SOCKS

Hosiery forms a very interesting part of the knitter's tale. The earliest examples of such items were found in the tombs in the desert places of Egypt, and it is interesting to note that, although the fabric used for these pre-Christian specimens was crossed stocking stitch (i.e. knitting into the back of every stitch on every round), the principles of shaping heels and toes were identical with the methods we use today.

The knitting of fancy stockings was an important

82

industry in France right up to the time of Charles II and there are records telling us that Edward IV, Princess Mary, sister of Henry VIII, Henry VIII himself and the first Queen Elizabeth were all proud possessors of hosiery knitted under the supervision of the Knitters' Guild in Paris.

It is arising out of the fact that so much hosiery was imported from France that one type of heel in use today is called the "French Heel".

Stocking knitting appears to have been carried on in England as early as the 16th century, and from the middle of the 17th to the middle of the 18th century hosiery knitting was a thriving industry in the Yorkshire Dales. During the period of the Commonwealth Walloons and Dutchmen emigrated from the Continent to England, bringing with them weaving and knitting as part of their industrial heritage. It is from these immigrants we derive the type of heel used in socks commonly known as the "Dutch Heel".

The principle of knitting socks and stockings is to knit in the round a straight or shaped tube for the leg, a similar tube for the foot, linking these two tubes with a heel and finishing the tube that forms the foot with a toe.

There are two types of toe shaping—the round toe and the flat toe.

Ribbing. The top of a sock is always ribbed for approximately 3½ to 4 ins. as this gives a good grip for the leg. It is quite a common practice among experienced sock knitters to work the ribbing on finer needles to give additional grip.

An easy grip top can be knitted into the ribbing by working the first 1½ ins. in crossed ribbing, i.e. knitting into the back of every knit stitch and purling into the back of every purl stitch throughout. On the next round cast off half the total number of stitches on the round and on the following round cast these stitches on again.

Continue in ordinary ribbing until 3½ or 4 ins. of ribbing have been completed.

Seam Stitch. Another important principle that all experienced sock knitters use, if they are knitting a sock in stocking stitch, is to work a "seam" stitch down the centre back of the leg working increases at each side of this "seam" during the leg shaping. The "seam" is a "made" stitch worked in after the ribbing has been completed and the best place for the stitch is in the centre of the first needle. Thus, if you are working on 60 stitches for the round (20 on each of 3 needles), on the first round after the ribbing work the first needle as follows—

K.10, then m.1 by picking up the loop that lies between the st. just knitted and the following st., purling into the back of this loop. This stitch is then purled on every round, thus creating the effect of a seam down the centre back of the sock.

If a rib pattern is used for the sock it is advisable to see that one of the ribs runs down the centre back.

The increases can then be worked at each side of the rib, working them into the rib pattern.

Shaping. The normal number of decreases worked to shape the leg is roughly 5 sets, thus making 10 stitches less in the round when they have all been worked. It is important to remember that the decreases must be paired and are usually worked at a point 1 or 2 stitches at each side of the seam stitch.

The first decrease, i.e. the one prior to the seam stitch, is worked on a simple "k.2 tog." principle, while the decrease on the other side of the seam stitch is worked on the "sl.1, k.1, p.s.s.o." basis.

When the decreases are worked on a ribbed fabric, the simplest plan is to work them at the beginning of the rib before the centre back point is reached and at the end of the rib after the centre back is reached. The number of decreases can be varied slightly in order that when they are completed you are still working in the rib pattern used before the decreases commenced. Thus, if you are working a "4 and 1" rib, by working 5 sets of decreases you will lose one rib pattern at each side of the centre stitch.

HEEL FLAP, MAKING A

K. across the quarter of the total number of sts. (less the seam st.) before the seam, k. the seam st., then k. across another quarter of the total number of sts., thus having half the total number on the round plus 1 to form the heel flap.

The flap itself is always worked in st. st. on 2 needles, sl. the first st. knitwise on all k. rows and the first st. purlwise on all p. rows, thus forming a chain edge along each side.

Continue until heel flap is a square of st. st. finishing at end of a p. row (214).

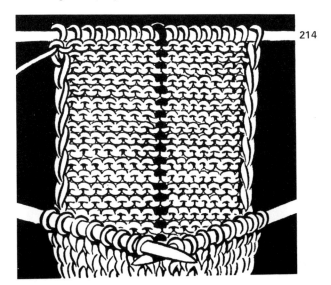

214

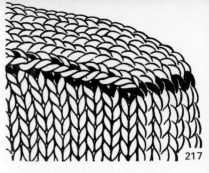

HEEL, TURNING THE

As already explained, there are two methods of turning the heel, the French Heel and the Dutch Heel.

Dutch Heel. After the heel flap has been worked the decreases are regular, the stitch formed by the first decrease becoming the first stitch of the second decrease, thus leaving the same number of stitches at the centre of the heel throughout.

Work 3, 4 or 5 sts. beyond the centre st. (approximately two-thirds of the number of sts. on the heel flap); dec. the next st. by sl.1, k.1, p.s.s.o., (215) turn, p. the dec. st., then p. across the same number of sts. at the other side of the centre, p.2 tog. (216), turn; now k. to the dec. stitch of the previous row, then sl.1, k.1, p.s.s.o., turn, p. back to the dec. stitch of previous row, then p.2 tog., continuing to work in this manner until all the sts. are worked on to one needle (217).

French Heel. This heel is turned by working a series of decreases at each side of a centre portion of the heel, each decrease using 2 stitches; the number of stitches at each side of the centre portion must be a multiple of 2.

To Turn the Heel. Work to 2 or 3 sts. past the centre, leaving a multiple of 2 on the end of the needle. Dec. the first 2 sts. of this multiple by working sl.1, k.1, p.s.s.o.; turn the work, p.1 st., (i.e. the st. which was decreased on the previous row), then p. across to the same number of sts. at the other side of the centre st., p. the next 2 sts. tog.; turn the work, k. back to the dec. st., k. this st., then work sl.1, k.1, p.s.s.o. again (218); turn the work once more, p. back to the p. dec. at the end of the previous row, p. the dec. st., p.2 tog. (219); turn the work again and continue decreasing in this manner until all the sts. have been worked on to one needle (220).

Instep. The turning of the heel having been completed on a p. row the gusset that forms the instep is then worked.
K. to the centre st. of the heel sts.

Sl. the instep sts. on to one needle.

Using spare needle k. the other half of the heel sts., now k. up the sts. along one side of the heel flap, knitting up one st. through both loops of the chain edge.

Using a 2nd needle work across the instep sts.

Using a 3rd needle k. up the same number of sts. along the 2nd side of the heel flap as on the 1st needle, then k. across the remaining heel sts., thus completing the round.

The Instep Gusset is formed by a series of decreases, which are worked until the combined number of stitches on the 1st and 3rd needles equals the total number of stitches that are on the 2nd needle.

The decreases themselves are worked as follows—

1st round: K. to last 3 sts. of 1st needle, k.2 tog., k.1; k. across instep sts. on 2nd needle; now k.1, k.2 tog. at the beg. of 3rd needle, k. to end of round.

2nd round: K.

Continue working these 2 rounds until the correct number of sts. is obtained.

Now work the foot.

HEEL-LESS SOCK

This type of sock is knitted on the spiral principle on the basis of a k.3, p.1 rib worked in the round, the purled stitch moving 1 st. to the left on every 3 rounds.

Spiral Knitting. Here is the principle of spiral knitting—
Cast on to 3 needles a number of sts. divisible by 4.
Join up to form a round.
Work as follows—

Rounds 1 to 3: * P.1, k.3; rep. from * to end of round.

Rounds 4 to 6: * K.1, p.1, k.2; rep. from * to end of round.

Rounds 7 to 9: * K.2, p.1, k.1; rep. from * to end of round.

Rounds 10 to 12: * K.3, p.1; rep. from * to end of round.
These 12 rounds form the spiral pattern (221).

The toe of these socks is shaped in the ordinary way, a Round Toe always being used.

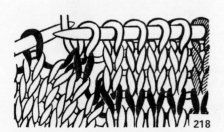

A warm set in Fair Isle and a Tyrolean cardigan. Instructions are on pages 143 and 146

A Scandinavian sweater in double knitting, perfect for winter. Instructions on page 141

TOES

Before commencing to shape the toe, lose the odd stitch (i.e. the stitch which was originally made for the seam stitch down the centre back of the leg) by k.2 tog. (the stitch that was originally the seam stitch and the following stitch) on the round immediately before you commence the toe shaping.

Flat Toe. 1st round: K. to last 3 sts. on 1st needle, k.2 tog., k.1. On the 2nd needle, k.1, k.2 tog. t.b.l., k. to last 3 sts., k.2 tog., k.1. On the 3rd needle, k.1, k.2 tog. t.b.l., k. to end.

2nd round: K.

Rep. these 2 rounds until approximately half the number of sts. as at the commencement of the toe remain.

K. the sts. from first needle on to 3rd needle, then either graft the 2 sets of sts. together or cast off from 2 needles together (220).

Round Toe. This type of toe is worked in a series of spiral decreases and is commonly found in socks knitted by peasants from all parts of Europe. This is rarely a really satisfactory type of toe shaping but in exceptional cases as on a Spiral Sock or where the foot is rather more pointed than is usual, it can be a very useful method. When the point for shaping the toe is reached, take the total number of stitches and divide them so that there are six sets, each of the same number of stitches. To arrive at this figure it may be necessary to work one or two decreases on the round prior to shaping the toe. If there are 61 stitches on the round at this point. On the round prior to the toe shaping, decrease the odd stitch (the seam stitch), thus leaving 60 stitches. This will give you 6 sets of 10 stitches.

1st round: * K.8, k.2 tog.; rep. from * to end of round.

2nd round: K.

3rd round: K.9, * k.2 tog., k.7; rep. from * to end of round.

Note. The last dec. will be formed by knitting together the first 2 sts. from the 1st needle on to the end of the 3rd needle.

4th round: K.

Continue decreasing in this manner, noting that the dec. moves 1 st. further along the needle on each dec. round until 10 sts. remain.

Divide these sts. on to 2 needles (5 sts. on each needle) and graft them together (see page 46).

Toes and Heels, Reinforcing. A common practice is to reinforce heels and toes by knitting in a length of strong cotton or thread with the wool, in the heel and toe of the sock.

Another method of reinforcing is to use a pure nylon yarn for the heel and toe making sure that this is approximately the same ply and thickness as the wool used for the sock.

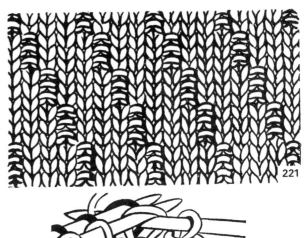

SPANISH KNITTING

It is presumed that the principles of knitting were carried to Spain from Egypt by early traders, and the tradition of exquisite Spanish colour knitting was then built up. In the Middle Ages the craft spread throughout Europe, notably to Florence and Paris and eventually to the north of Scotland. A vessel of the Spanish Armada was wrecked on Sheep Rock, Fair Isle, and the islanders copied the delicate and intricate colour knitting of garments brought ashore in the home-spun wools available to them. The patterns which go to make up the rich tradition of Fair Isle Colour Knitting bear witness to their early Catholic ancestry with such names as "The Sacred Heart", "Star of Bethlehem", "Crown of Glory" and "Rose of Sharon".

SPLICING

(See *Joining Yarn,* page 53).

SPRANG

In the northern parts of Scandinavia, and in some of the Viking tombs in Norway, fragments of material marking the transitional point from weaving to knitting have been discovered. They are known as Sprang, and are in fact an interlocked fabric built up on a weaving principle.

Sprang is produced by first of all setting up on a simple rectangular framework a series of vertical threads running closely together, resembling the warp in weaving. Using a simple needle a chain stitch is worked up the first thread. Commencing again at the bottom of the second thread, a second chain stitch is worked up this thread, interlacing the second row of chain stitch through the side loops of the first set made. This action is continued up each thread until the interlaced chain stitch fabric completely covers the whole of the warp. The warp threads are then withdrawn, leaving a piece of fabric resembling stocking stitch in knitting, but with the interlocking action through the sides of the loops instead of through the top of the loops as in knitting. The fabric so closely resembles knitting that in many cases specimens of Sprang have been wrongly labelled as knitted fabric.

The technical difference between knitting and weaving is that the former is produced from a single thread of yarn, whereas in the latter two threads are used, one moving horizontally across the fabric and the other vertically up the fabric.

STITCHES

Knitting consists of just two simple basic stitches—Knit Stitch and Purl Stitch (also known as Plain and Purl). Every other stitch and variation is built on these, however intricate and lacy the resulting fabric. Other popular stitches include Rib, Fishermen's Rib, Moss Stitch, Shell Stitch, Bobble, Brioche, Cable, Twist Stitches and Lace Stitches. Details of all these are given under their alphabetical headings.

STOCKING STITCH

This is the basic fabric in knitting, used originally for smooth stockings in wool and silk. To produce stocking stitch when working on two needles, one row is knitted and the next row is purled and these two rows are repeated throughout the fabric. When working on four or more needles in rounds every round is knitted. The right side of the fabric is the knit side or "plain" side (223).

Reverse Stocking Stitch

This is the purl side of stocking stitch and is worked in the same way as stocking stitch, but it is made up with the knit side inside and the purl side outside (224).

STOCKINGS

The knitting of stockings is worked on exactly the same principle as that given for socks. If long stockings are being knitted it is advisable to shape the calf by working 2 sets of increases, approximately 8 or 10 rows apart above the calf, and 5 or 6 sets of decreases below the calf. Work the decreases on the same principle as those worked in the shaping of the leg of a sock.

The increases can be worked on the "m.1" principle, i.e. by lifting up the loop between the stitch just knitted and the following stitch and knitting into the back of it, an important point being that the increases and decreases must move in a straight line up each side of the centre seam stitch. Thus, if the decreases are being worked 2 or 3 stitches from each side of the centre seam stitch, the increases will be worked 2 or 3 stitches from each side.

STRAPPING

(See *Bands*, page 12).

STRETCHING

Hand-knitted garments in either synthetic or natural fibres will stretch if they are not handled with sufficient care during washing and drying. Avoid pulling a garment out of shape during the washing and avoid wringing and twisting. Remove moisture by spin-drying (30 seconds) or rolling in a towel, as the weight of water can drag a garment down to considerable lengths. Do not peg up by shoulders or side seams but dry flat, preferably on a special hammock which allows the air to circulate and maintains correct shape. Squares and rectangles such as pram covers should always be pinned out to shape and dried flat with great care to prevent distortion.

SWEATERS

Traditional jerseys which were commonly worn by fishermen as they plied their trade are the true sweaters. They were then knitted on four needles, in the round. The shoulder stitches were joined by casting off the stitches from both needles together and the sleeves were sewn in with an invisible seam.

Today, the word "sweater" refers to any loose pullover, usually knitted in double knitting or thicker yarns.

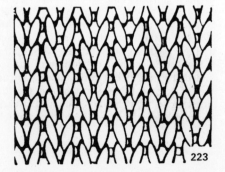

223

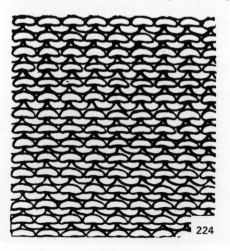

224

225

SWEDISH KNITTING
(See *Scandinavian Colour Knitting*, page 71)

SYNTHETICS
Acrilan, Bri-Nylon, Courtelle, Orlon and Terylene are the most popular man-made fibres used for hand-knitting yarns. Their chief advantages lie in ease of washing (they do not "absorb" dirt into their fibres as natural fibres do); quickness of drying and the fact that, if carefully handled, they never need pressing. They do not become matted from frequent washings and are completely resistant to moths and dampness during storage. Because of the lightness of these yarns the yardage for one ounce is considerably longer than that of wool; as a result, many synthetic yarns are marketed in balls of less than one ounce —often ¾ oz. balls—which the spinners claim will go as far as one ounce of wool.

It is important to note when buying yarn to knit up a pattern, that synthetics of a particular ply are not necessarily interchangeable with other synthetics or with wool of the same ply. For example, a pattern which quotes Double Knitting Courtelle should be knitted up in that yarn; if knitted in D.K. wool or D.K. Bri-Nylon the garment may come up in a different size unless tension and needles are adjusted.

TAILORING OF KNITTING
The ancient craft of knitting has passed through several evolutions during its period of development. Beginning as a simple means of making utilitarian garments for the working folk of the world, the craft was later organised into a Trade Guild that perfected fashions and fabrics in which to dress and flatter the Kings and Courtiers of Europe. After a period of decline in the 19th century, knitting has now become one of the ideal handicrafts for every woman in the home.

The 1920's and the jumper age brought these modern evolutions in knitting to the forefront. Almost impercep-

tibly, new trends were developing in knitted garments allying them to the tailored lines of the Couture Houses of Paris, London and New York.

In some cases, straight pieces of knitting were used as a basic fabric to make up into garments, and this tendency definitely influenced the development of tailored lines that are a most significant contribution to this undying craft.

Perfect knitting demands perfect make-up and it is here that so many fail. Women will spend countless hours knitting the pieces which are later to be made into a garment and they stitch them together as though they were pieces from the rag bag. Careful attention to detail, using the right method of seaming and finishing are the points which give home knitting a professional appearance.

TAPING
Seams of knitted garments may be strengthened by taping and this is particularly useful on shoulder seams of heavy jackets or pullovers or wherever there may be strain on the seam. Tape must be ready-shrunk, of course, and special tape for seams is obtainable from haberdashery counters. It may be sewn in with the seam (as in dress-making) or for a flat seam the tape may be stitched down on either side of the seam. Care must be taken not to stretch the knitting when taping.

TEAZLING
(See *Brushing Wools*, page 18)

TENSION
The word "tension" in knitting means the number of stitches and number of rows to each square inch of fabric. The usual practice is to measure over stocking stitch as once the knitter perfects her tension in the fabric other types of fabric will automatically knit up correctly (226).

The secret of working in tension is to let the wool

226

"flow" smoothly through the fingers, so that it forms even loops on the needle as the stitches are worked.

Here is the standard list of tensions for various ply wools. Synthetic yarns differ and must be tested separately.

Needles	2-ply		3-ply		4-ply		Double Knitting	
	Sts.	Rows	Sts.	Rows	Sts.	Rows	Sts.	Rows
4	5	7	4½	6½	4	6	3	5
5	5½	7½	5	7	4½	6½	3½	5½
6	6	8	5½	7½	5	7	4	6
7	6½	8½	6	8	5½	7½	4½	6½
8	7	9	6½	8½	6	8	5	7
9	7½	9½	7	9	6½	8½	5½	7½
10	8	10	7½	9½	7	9	6	8
11	8½	10½	8	10	7½	9½	6½	8½
12	9	11	8½	10½	8	10	7	9
13	9½	11½	9	11	8½	10½	7½	9½
14	10	12	9½	11½	9	11	8	10

TERYLENE
(See *Synthetics*, page 89)

TOYS
Knitted toys make delightful gifts and are always popular items at bazaars, as they can be knitted up from small amounts of wool. It is important to make sure that they are fully washable—and for this reason the new machine-washable wools are ideal for toys—and that the filling also is washable. Old nylon stockings are the best stuffing, cut up into strips; unwashable filling such as kapok should be avoided. Beads and buttons used as eyes should also be avoided in toys for children but may be used for teenagers' animal mascots. Eyes and features can be embroidered on to faces or small circles of felt can be sewn firmly in place.

THICK WOOLS
Thick wools, from Triple Knitting upwards to wools which are nearly as thick as rug wools, are popular for outer garments as they are so quick to knit. Each brand, however, can differ so greatly in thickness that it is most important to use a pattern recommending the particular brand you choose otherwise the finished garment may be inches larger or smaller than intended. The designation "Chunky" does not apply to any standard thickness of yarn or wool.

THUMB METHOD
(See *Casting On*, page 24)

TUBULAR KNITTING
(See *Double Knitting*, page 35)

TURNING
When shaping knitting, it is sometimes necessary to turn in the middle of a row. This is perfectly simple. Work the number of stitches stated in the pattern, turn the work round and knit from the other side back along the stitches just worked, leaving the unworked stitches still on the right-hand needle. Where instructions are given to turn in order to divide for a neck opening, for example, the stitches which are not being worked are slipped on to a stitch-holder or large safety-pin while the first side of the opening is completed and are then picked up and knitted to match.

TWIST STITCH
The action here consists of twisting two or three stitches, forming cord-like vertical stripes up the fabric.

As in cable fabrics a purl stitch is often worked up each side of the group of twisted stitches to give emphasis to the pattern.

Twist Two. To twist 2 stitches pass the point of the right-hand needle in front of the first stitch on the left-hand needle, insert the point of the right-hand needle knitwise through the second stitch on left-hand needle (227).

Knit up a stitch through the second stitch but do not slip it off the needle.

Insert the point of the right-hand needle knitwise through the first stitch on the left-hand needle (228). Knit up a stitch through this stitch.

Now slip the 1st and 2nd stitches off the left-hand needle (229).

Here is an instruction for a simple twisted stitch fabric (230):

Cast on a number of stitches divisible by 3 and one stitch over.

1st row: * P.1, Tw.2; rep. from * to last st., p.1.
2nd row: * K.1, p.2; rep. from * to last st., k.1.
These 2 rows form the patt.

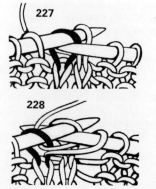

Twist Three. To twist 3 stitches take the point of the right-hand needle over the first 2 stitches on the left-hand needle. Insert the point of the right-hand needle knitwise into the next stitch (3rd stitch on the left-hand needle), knit up a stitch through this stitch. Still keeping the point of the right-hand needle to the front of the work insert it knitwise into the front of the 2nd stitch on the left-hand needle, knit up a stitch through this stitch. Insert the point of the right-hand needle knitwise through the first stitch on the left-hand needle, knit up a stitch through this stitch, then drop the 3 end stitches off the left-hand needle.

Mock Cable. A mock cable can be obtained by the Tw.3 principle, working a purl stitch rib up each side of the 3 twisted stitches (231).

Cast on a number of stitches divisible by 5 plus 2 over.

1st row: * P.2, k.3; rep. from * to last 2 sts., p.2.
2nd row: * K.2, p.3; rep. from * to last 2 sts., k.2.
3rd row: * P.2, Tw.3; rep. from * to last 2 sts., p.2.
4th row: As 2nd row.

These 4 rows form the mock cable patt.

TYROLEAN KNITTING

In Tyrolean knitting a common practice is to work cable and bobble patterns, enlivening them with gaily coloured embroidery carried out in simple stitches. Transfers are never used for this type of work, the embroidered motifs being built up in such a way that they can be easily copied on to the knitting from a simple chart. In many cases the pattern used in the knitted fabric serves as a foundation for the embroidery.

The most important thing to remember about this type of embroidery is that the stitches must be bold and simple. Gay colours must be used, the general effect being one of brightness and lucidity of colouring. The following stitches are all useful in this type of work:

Blanket stitch, Chain stitch, French Knots, Lazy Daisy stitch, Running stitch, Satin stitch and Stem stitch.

The peasants of the Austrian Tyrol are famous for their gaily embroidered coats. These are generally knitted in a heavy wool (double knitting wool is ideal for this purpose), the designs being built up from bobbles and cables,

230

231

occasionally lace motifs are used to give emphasis to the pattern on the coat itself. They are usually knitted in white and then heavily embroidered in brightly coloured wools to give a gay contrast to the white ground of the coat itself.

Here is a typical Tyrolean pattern with embroidered motifs:

Abbreviations:

Cr.1f.—Cross 1 front by working across next 4 sts as follows—sl. next st. on to cable needle and leave at front of work, k. following 3 sts., then k. st. from cable needle.

Cr.3b.—Cross 3 back by working across next 4 sts. as follows—sl. next 3 sts. on to cable needle and leave at back of work, k. the next st., then k.3 sts. from cable needle.

Cast on a multiple of 51 sts.

1st row: K.6, (leave wool at back of work), sl.1, k.1, sl.1, k.9, (m.b. make bobble by p.1, k.1, p.1, k.1, into next st., thus making 4 sts. out of next st., turn, k.4, turn, p.4, sl. 2nd, 3rd and 4th sts. over first st., k.2) twice, w.f., sl.1, k.2 tog., p.s.s.o., w.f., (k.2, m.b.) twice, k.9, sl.1, k.1, sl.1, k.6.

2nd row: P.6, sl.1, p.1, sl.1, p. to last 9 sts., sl.1, p.1, sl.1, p.6.

3rd row: K.3, cr.3b., k.1, cr.1f., k.5, (m.b., k.2) twice, k.2 tog., w.f., k.1, w.f., k.2 tog. t.b.l., (k.2, m.b.) twice, k.5, cr.3b., k.1, cr.1f., k.3.

4th row: P.

5th row: K.6, sl.1, k.1, sl.1, k.7, (m.b., k.2) twice, k.2 tog., w.f., k.3, w.f., k.2 tog. t.b.l., (k.2, m.b.) twice, k.7, sl.1, k.1, sl.1, k.6.

6th row: As 2nd row.

7th row: K.3, cr.3b., k.1, cr.1f., k.3, (m.b., k.2) twice, k.2 tog., w.f., k.5, w.f., k.2 tog. t.b.l., (k.2, m.b.) twice, k.3, cr.3b., k.1, cr.1f., k.3.

8th row: P.

9th row: K.6, sl.1, k.1, sl.1, k.5, (m.b., k.2) twice, k.2 tog., w.f., k.7, w.f., k.2 tog. t.b.l., (k.2, m.b.) twice, k.5, sl.1, k.1, sl.1, k.6.

10th row: As 2nd row.

11th row: K.3, cr.3b., k.1, cr.1f., k.1, (m.b., k.2) twice, k.2 tog., w.f., k.9, w.f., k.2 tog. t.b.l., (k.2, m.b.) twice, k.1, cr.3b., k.1, cr.1f., k.3.

12th row: P.
13th row: As 9th row.
14th row: As 2nd row.
15th row: As 7th row.
16th row: P.
17th row: As 5th row.
18th row: As 2nd row.
19th row: As 3rd row.
20th row: P.

The diagram (232, overleaf) shows the method of working the embroidered pattern.

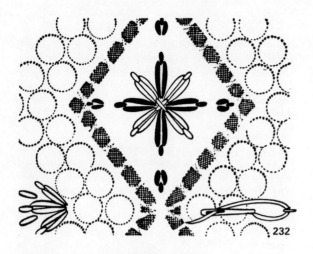

232

U

UNPICKING KNITTING

If it is necessary to unravel work because of a mistake, take a blunt-ended tapestry needle threaded with contrasting wool and run this across the work in the row below that in which the mistake occurred. Pick up every stitch on the thread and make it fast at both ends of the work. Pull back the wool to this row, rewinding and smoothing the wool on to the ball. Slip these stitches on to a needle (making sure that the row will be re-started from the point of the needle) and withdraw the contrasting wool.

UNST LACE

(See *Shetland Lace*, page 79).

V

VESTS

Traditionally vests have always been knitted on a ribbed basis. A soft 3-ply wool is the ideal yarn for the purpose and it is wise to knit with slightly coarser needles than the ones usually used for outerwear garments.

A "k.1, p.1", a "k.2, p.2" or a "k.3, p.1" rib are all equally suitable.

A vest is really a tube of knitting with holes left for the neck and arms. It is advantageous to knit the waist line for 2 or 3 ins. on finer needles.

When working in a k.2, p.2 or a k.3, p.1 rib, the waist-band can be knitted in a k.1, p.1 rib on the finer needles,

thus giving it a firmer, more comfortable grip to the figure.

As the basic shape is virtually the same as a sweater or pullover you should be able to design your own vests quite simply from the following table, which gives the number of stitches on a No. 9 needle at various points in knitting the vest.

The decreases and increases can be worked according to the shape desired when finished.

Bust Measurement	ins. 30	ins. 32	ins. 34	ins. 36	ins. 38	ins. 40
	sts.	sts.	sts.	sts.	sts.	sts.
Cast on	104	110	118	124	132	140
Waist	98	104	112	118	124	130
Bust	106	112	120	126	134	142

The top of a vest can be—cast off straight and ribbon shoulder straps attached, shaped on a "V" or rounded principle, or worked with a buttoned-up neck and a placket front. A charming finish to a straight topped vest may be added by working a simple lace pattern for the last 2 ins. and completing it with a picot edge.

PLACKET FRONT OPENING

This type of neck is used for children's and men's vests, it is worked by casting on an underflap. If working a 36-in. size vest with 126 sts. on the front, work the opening as follows—

Take 10 sts. away from 126=116 sts. Thus, to place the opening work 58 plus 10 plus 58=126 sts. When dividing for the placket opening knit across 68 sts. Work the 2 sts. at the inside edge in garter stitch, making the buttonholes at equal distances apart, 4 sts. from the inside edge.

For the underflap, cast on 10 sts., k. across the remaining 58 sts., and working the 2 sts. at the inside edge in garter stitch as before (this gives a flat edge); complete to match the other half of the front.

Neatly flat stitch the cast-on stitches to the base of the placket opening, thus completing the underflap.

VANDYKE PATTERNS

This type of pattern is similar in method of work to *Diagonal Patterns*, in that vandyke stripes of stocking stitch are worked on a ground of reverse stocking stitch.

FANCY VANDYKE

Cast on a multiple of 22 sts.

1st row: * P.1, k.1, p.3, (k.1, p.1) twice, k.1, p.5, (k.1, p.1) twice, k.1, p.2; rep. from * to end.

2nd row: * K.3, p.1, (k.1, p.1) twice, k.3, p.1, (k.1, p.1) twice, k.3, p.3; rep. from * to end.

3rd row: * K.4, p.3, (k.1, p.1) 5 times, k.1, p.3, k.1; rep. from * to end.

4th row: * P.2, k.3, p.1, (k.1, p.1) 4 times, k.3, p.3, k.1, p.1; rep. from * to end.

5th row: * P.3, k.3, p.3, (k.1, p.1) 3 times, k.1, p.3, k.3; rep. from * to end.

6th row: * K.1, p.3, k.3, p.1, (k.1, p.1) twice, k.3, p.3, k.4; rep. from * to end.

7th row: * P.1, k.1, p.3, k.3, p.3, k.1, p.1, k.1, p.3, k.3, p.2; rep. from * to end.

8th row: * (K.3, p.3, k.3, p.1) twice, k.1, p.1; rep. from * to end.

9th row: * (P.1, k.1) twice, p.3, k.3, p.5, k.3, p.3, k.1; rep. from * to end.

10th row: * K.1, p.1, (k.3, p.3) twice, k.3, p.1, (k.1, p.1) twice; rep. from * to end.

11th row: * (P.1, k.1) 3 times, p.3, k.3, p.1, k.3, p.3, k.1, p.1, k.1; rep. from * to end.

12th row: * (K.1, p.1) twice, k.3, p.5, k.3, p.1, (k.1, p.1) 3 times; rep. from * to end.

13th row: * P.3, (k.1, p.1) twice, k.1, p.3, k.3, p.3, (k.1, p.1) twice, k.1; rep. from * to end.

14th row: * (K.1, p.1) 3 times, (k.3, p.1) twice, (k.1, p.1) twice, k.4; rep. from * to end.

These 14 rows form the patt.

VICTORIAN KNITTING

Hand-knitting, which had for long been regarded as a peasant industry, became fashionable during the reign of Queen Victoria. Balaclavas, cardigans, socks and mufflers were knitted for the troops during the Crimean War; petticoats, camisoles and spencers were knitted for the warmth of the ladies at home and with the Victorian flair for decorated objects, exquisite bead-knitted bags and reticules and bell-pulls were made. Baby clothes were also decorated with beading and embroidery, and some intricate examples have been preserved in museums, notably the Victoria & Albert Museum in London.

VIENNESE LACE

For several centuries the knitters of Vienna have specialised in knitted laces, producing beautiful doilies. cloths and edgings, all of which are extremely elaborate and are knitted mainly from charts.

Leaves and floral shapes grow within filigree backgrounds, giving a very dainty effect to the finished design.

The laces themselves are worked in fine cotton or silk and are afterwards either mounted on a fine net, or stiffened slightly with a very weak solution of glycerine and water, or starch.

Blocking and Pressing the Lace. The pinning out and blocking of these laces is very important for, unless this has been done well, they lose a great deal of their beauty. The process of pinning out is perfectly simple. With circular or square shapes pin out the full width from the centre to the outside edge, then pin out the full width again at right angles to first pins, thus dividing the work into four segments or sections. Now pin out carefully between the four pins already in place, pinning down each point and working the knitting carefully into a circle or square as the case may be. Finally, press the work well, using a warm iron and damp cloth.

Method. The edgings are carried out on five needles and the knitting is done in rounds throughout. This means that when measuring for the knitting, measure up the four sides of the cloth being trimmed with edging and cast on sufficient stitches on each of four needles for each side of the cloth. If it is a circular cloth measure the circumference of the circle (round the outside edge), that will be approximately three times the diameter of the circle (i.e., the width across at the widest point).

Symbols. Various symbols are used on Viennese lace charts, these are shown in diagram (233).

Note: Where two "overs" occur together, on following row, k. into front of first "over", then into back of second over. This applies to all instructions for Viennese lace. On the next page are the instructions for Leaf Edging.

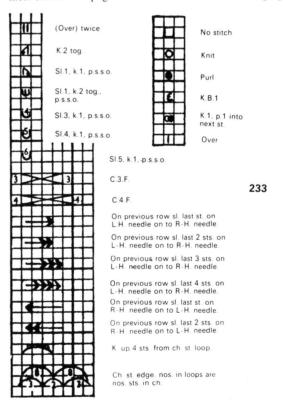

233

95

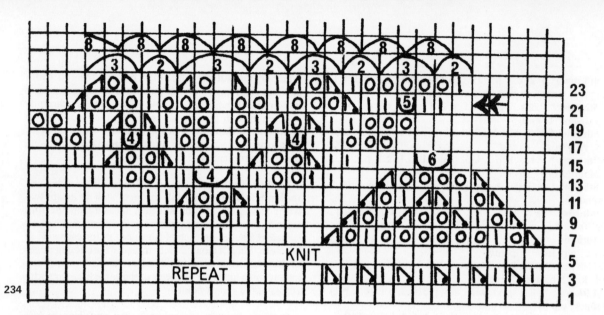

234

LEAF EDGING

Cast on a multiple of 12 sts. to each of 4 needles and using 5 needles work row by row following the chart (234).

In this example the working of the chart is translated in round by round instructions. Notice that every alternate round is a knit round.

1st round: K.

2nd and every alt. row: K.

3rd round: * Over, sl.1, k.1, p.s.s.o.; rep. from * to end.

5th round: K.

7th round: * Sl.1, k.1, p.s.s.o., k.1, over, k.6, over, k.1, k.2 tog., (over) twice; rep. from * to end.

9th round: * Sl.1, k.1, p.s.s.o., k.1, over, sl.1, k.1, p.s.s.o., k.2, k.2 tog., over, k.1, k.2 tog., (over) twice, k.2, (over) twice; rep. from * to end.

11th round: * Sl.1, k.1, p.s.s.o., k.1, over, sl.1, k.1, p.s.s.o., k.2 tog., over, k.1, k.2 tog., (over) twice, sl.1, k.1, p.s.s.o., k.2, k.2 tog., (over) twice; rep. from * to end.

13th round: * Sl.1, k.1, p.s.s.o., k.4, k.2 tog., (over) twice, k.2, (over) twice, sl.4, k.1, p.4 s.s.o., (over) twice, k.2, (over) twice, rep. from * to end.

15th round: * Sl.5, k.1, p.5 s.s.o., (over) twice, sl.1, k.1, p.s.s.o., k.2, k.2 tog., over, k.1, over, sl.1, k.1, p.s.s.o., k.2, k.2 tog., (over) twice; rep. from * to end.

17th round: * K.3, (over) twice, sl.3, k.1, p.3 s.s.o., (over) twice, k.3, (over) twice, sl.3, k.1, p.3 s.s.o., (over) twice, k.2; rep. from * to end.

19th round: * K.3, (over) twice, sl.1, k.1, p.s.s.o., k.1, k.2 tog., over, k.3, over, sl.1, k.1, p.s.s.o., k.1, k.2 tog., (over) twice, k.2; rep. from * to end.

20th round: K., sl. last 2 sts. on right-hand needle on to left-hand needle thus moving patt. 2 sts. to the right.

21st round: * (Over) twice, sl.4, k.1, p.4 s.s.o., (over) twice, sl.1, k.1, p.s.s.o., k.3, over, k.5, over, k.3, k.2 tog.; rep. from * to end.

23rd round: * Over, k.5, over, sl.1, k.1, p.s.s.o., k.1, k.2 tog., (over) twice, sl.1, k.1, p.s.s.o., k.1, k.2 tog., (over) twice, sl.1, k.1, p.s.s.o., k.1, k.2 tog.

24th round: K.

Cast off loosely.

This edging is typical of Viennese lace. Notice how it moves from a bold half leaf formation on to a delightful filigree of leaves.

To complete the edging, a crochet chain is worked thus: slip stitch into the edging and work chain half circles.

WAIST BANDS

There are several ways of finishing the waists of jumpers and skirts. Here the methods of attaching elastic or petersham bands are described.

Elastic, Broad. When broad elastic has to be stitched in the waist band of a skirt, or in any part of a garment where a slot hem has not been worked, cut the elastic ½ inch longer than the required length, fold over ¾ inch at each end and firmly backstitch it. Tuck the elastic in position. Now work Herringbone stitch over the elastic to hold it firmly round the waist of skirt, inserting the needle above and below the elastic each side (235).

Elastic, Shirring. Another method of creating elastic waist bands is to weave a thread of shirring elastic in with

94

the waist ribbing. This can be worked on every 3rd row.

Here is an example of how elastic is woven on a k.1, p.1, rib.

After the first two rows of the rib have been knitted, join in the elastic and purl or knit it with the first stitch. Presume that the first stitch has been knitted. Keeping the elastic at the back of the work purl the next stitch, then weave the elastic round the wool before knitting the following stitch. If the elastic is woven by laying it over the wool before the first stitch to be knitted, and under the wool on every alternate stitch to be knitted, the tangle that is often created by twisting the elastic round the wool will be avoided.

Repeat the weaving action on every knitted stitch along the row of ribbing, working the last stitch with both the elastic and wool.

Work 2 rows of ribbing. On the next row, the elastic must be at the front of the work and is woven over and under the purl stitches on the rib as follows:—

Using elastic and wool together, purl the first stitch. Keeping the elastic at the front of the work knit the following stitch, but before purling the next stitch weave the elastic over the wool.

Continue in this manner all across the row, remembering that the elastic is woven in each case over and under the alternating purl stitches.

Petersham Bands. First of all cut a length of petersham ½ inch longer than required. Neatly fold in ¼ inch at each end and oversew along the edges Tack the top of the skirt into position, easing in the skirt into the width of the petersham band. Oversew the petersham and knitted fabric together along the top edge.

Where petersham bands are used they must be stitched into position before the zip-fastener is sewn into the placket of the skirt, so that the tape round the zip-fastener will cover the edges of the petersham. Stitch the ends of the petersham band firmly in position.

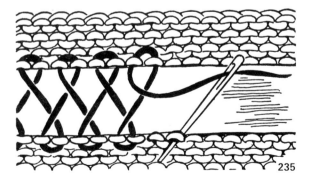
235

WAISTCOATS

Waistcoats form a very interesting chapter in the history of clothes. Originally they were exactly what they state— a waist length coat with full sleeves—and were worn as an outer garment. In Regency days the elongated front was developed, changing in the Victorian period into the shaped and pointed fronts as we know them today.

The simplest way to knit quite an attractive waistcoat is to make the fronts straight and work back ribbing for 4 ins. on fine needles. This draws the fronts apart, giving a pointed effect.

FULLY FASHIONED WAISTCOAT

Commence at the point, casting on 3 sts. Then increase on every alt. row at the front edge, casting on in groups of 4, 5 or 6 sts. (according to the depth of point required) at the other side of the point, thus obtaining the graduated point effect needed for a fully fashioned styling.

The armholes and "V" neck are worked as on the front of a cardigan.

Any all-over fabric stitch is ideal for a waistcoat.

Front Bands are knitted separately and mitred at the bottom corners. Thus you will need a band with buttonholes and two mitred ends for round the fronts of the waistcoat and a second band with mitred corners for round the front waist edges and back of the waistcoat. These bands should be knitted in k.1, p.1 rib, the principle of mitring the points being as follows—

Cast on 1 st.

1st row: K. and p. into st.
2nd row: K.1, p.1.
3rd row: K.1, p. and k. into next st.
4th row: P.1, k.1, p.1.
5th row: K.1, p.1, k. and p. into last st.
6th row: (K.1, p.1) twice.

Continue in this manner until number of sts. for the required width of a front band are on the needle.

The mitred corners are joined with a flat seam, care being taken to match the k. and p. sts. in joining.

WASHING

Knitted garments can be completely ruined by careless washing and drying and it is always worth taking care with articles which have taken much time and trouble to knit. If the following rules are followed, the results will always be successful:

(1) Water should be warm — never hot — and the temperature should be constant for washing and rinsing; a sudden change of temperature from lukewarm to hot for rinsing can cause felting.

(2) All fibres are more vulnerable when wet than they are dry, so no hand-knitted garment should be rubbed

hard, pulled about or twisted roughly.

(3) Good quality soapflakes, soap powder or detergents may be used but it is important to see that these are thoroughly dissolved in the water before washing. Detergents containing bleach should not be used.

(4) Articles should be very thoroughly rinsed.

(5) Very gently squeeze out surplus water. Remove excess moisture by rolling in a towel, spin-drying for about 30 seconds or folding to pass through a wringer.

(6) Dry flat in a current of air away from direct heat. Never peg hand-knitted garments up by the seams, sleeves or shoulders or allow them to hang wet over a clothes-horse or line as the weight of moisture will drag them out of shape.

(7) When dry, pin out to the correct shape and press as explained for *Blocking Garments*, page 14.

WELSH WOOL

This wool from the fleeces of Welsh hill sheep is used mainly in Wales for the weaving of blankets, tweeds and rugs but small quantities are spun for hand-knitting in lovat and heather-mixture shades and a pullover in this wool is the perfect complement to a skirt in Welsh tweed.

WELT

A welt is a hem or edging and in a knitted garment refers to the borders beginning the main parts of the body and sleeves.

WINDING WOOL

Nowadays wool and synthetic fibres are usually already made up into balls when they are sold; however, some cheaper yarns may be sold in hank or skein form and must be wound into balls before knitting. The quickest way is for one person to hold the hank between both hands whilst a second person winds the wool into a neat, compact ball, taking care not to pull the wool or it will be stretched out of shape. Alternatively the wool can be looped over a chair back and wound off from there.

WOOLMARK

The Woolmark is an international symbol sponsored by the International Wool Secretariat and is seen on the labels of knitting wools from many spinners. It signifies that the knitting yarn is made up wholly from pure new wool with a maximum tolerance of 5% for non-wool fibres used for visible decorative effect and 0.3% for inadvertent impurities. The symbol has the same significance in every country using it and is already registered in 90 countries. The International Wool Secretariat maintains a constant testing programme to ensure that Woolmark merchandise at all times comes up to the standards specified.

WOOL PROCESSING

Raw wool, as it is clipped from the sheep, is submitted to a number of very important processes before it becomes knitting wool. It is first sorted and graded into categories depending on its fineness, and then scoured by washing in a solution of soap and soda to remove dirt and grease. Next it is carded between a series of wire-covered rollers and emerges as a continuous rope known as sliver. This is combed—perhaps the most important of all processes—to remove short fibres and leave those remaining lying smoothly in one direction; this combed sliver is known as top. The top is now drawn by pulling between heavy rollers to obtain the correct thickness and is wound on to bobbins; it is now known as roving, and is finally spun into yarn. Twisting is the next process, to produce the ply required—two or more threads being twisted together —the resulting yarn being dyed and then balled ready for sale.

WOOL TYPES

Wool which is processed into hand-knitting yarn is produced mainly in Australia, New Zealand, South Africa and the United Kingdom. Two main types of sheep are used—Merino and Crossbred—and both are grown in the first three countries but the United Kingdom produces only Crossbred wools. Merino sheep produce the fleeces which are processed into Botany Wool, the finest quality wool for hand-knitting. Kent or Romney Marsh sheep produce Crossbred wool which is thicker and coarser than Botany wool and consequently harder-wearing. The Border Leicester sheep produce wools used mainly for carpets and for very chunky knitting wools.

WOOL-WEIGHTS

Wool-weights are of great interest in the history of the wool trade and examples can be seen in provincial museums as well as in the Victoria and Albert Museum and the Science Museum.

These weights were originally thin, flat, stirrup-shaped castings in lead, about six inches deep; after 1494 they were cast in bronze and from 1600 were usually shield-shaped. The tod (28 lbs.) was the unit of weight used in the wool trade and wool-weights were commonly 7 lbs. each or 14 lbs., known as half-tods.

Fine English wool was in great demand for exporting to the Continent and wool taxes were levied on all wool exports. The fleeces were weighed by travelling tax officials or tronagers; they carried with them their own weights, each with the royal arms moulded upon one side, which they used to check the accuracy of the wool staplers' scales. They inspected the wool for quality and cleanliness as well as weight before sealing each bale and assessing the tax; the sealed bales were then sold at the wool market, or staple, and approved merchants were granted the right to purchase them for exporting.

Wool-weights were cast with the arms of each successive monarch as well as the marks of the Founders who cast them and were subjected to stringent checks. They are a most unusual and rewarding subject for collectors.

WOVEN KNITTING

The type of fabric produced in woven knitting resembles hopsack in appearance. It is much firmer than ordinary knitted fabric and lacks the elasticity one usually finds. The principle of woven knitting is to slip alternate stitches, bringing the wool to the front of the slipped stitch and taking it to the back of the work again before knitting the following stitch. On the second row the stitches which were slipped on the first row are purled, the woven principle being carried out at the back of the knitted stitches of the previous row.

To work woven knitting, proceed as follows—

Cast on an odd number of stitches.

1st row: K.1, * bring wool to front of needle (236), sl. next st. purlwise, take wool to back of needle, k. next stitch; rep. from * to end of row.

2nd row: K.1, * p.1, take wool to back of needle, sl. the following stitch purlwise, bring wool to front of needle; rep. from * to last 2 sts., p.1, k.1.

These 2 rows form the patt. for woven knitted fabric (237).

An important point to remember in producing woven knitting is that it should be worked on a finer needle than ordinary stocking stitch.

When using 2-ply wool a No. 12 needle is recommended, for 3-ply a No. 11 needle, for 4-ply a No. 10 needle and for double knitting wool a No. 8 needle.

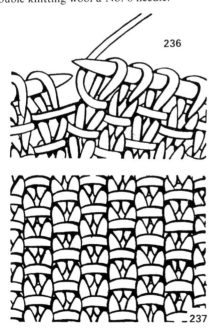

236

237

YARNS

Yarn is the spun thread used for knitting and may be made from any fibre. The term is used when knitting synthetics—in abbreviations and instructions—in place of the commonly used word "wool" which is obviously incorrect when "synthetic yarn" is intended.

Z

ZIP-FASTENERS

To stitch in zip-fasteners, place the zip-fastener in position and tack down round the centre of the material at the edge of the top and take special care to see that the fastener lies completely flat before commencing to stitch it in position (238).

Using an ordinary back-stitch neatly stitch down the edge of the piece of knitted fabric to the tape round the zip-fastener, working on the right side (239 shows wrong side).

Working on the wrong side, make neat short hemming stirches round the outside edge of the tape on the zip-fastener (240).

A useful tip when sewing in zip-fasteners is to oversew the edges of the opening together, then sew on the fastener as described above.

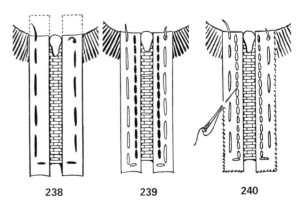

238   239   240

97

tables of stitches for cardigans and jumpers

jumpers for the fuller figure

2-ply wools

Back and Front							Size					
							40 ins.	42 ins.	44 ins.	46 ins.	48 ins.	50 ins.
							sts.	sts.	sts.	sts.	sts.	sts.
Cast on							132	140	148	156	164	172
Inc. for waistline							143	151	159	167	175	183
No. of sts. at bustline							159	167	175	183	191	199
No. of sts. after armhole shaping has been worked							127	131	135	139	143	147
No. of sts. at shoulder							38	40	42	44	46	48
Sleeves, Long												
Cast on							62	64	66	68	70	72
Inc. at top of urist							73	75	77	79	81	83
No. of sts. at top of sleeve							111	115	119	123	127	131
Sleeves, Short												
Cast on							86	88	90	92	94	96
Inc. above ribbing							97	99	101	103	105	107
No. of sts. at top of sleeve							111	115	119	123	127	131

3-ply wools

Back and Front							Size					
							40 ins.	42 ins.	44 ins.	46 ins.	48 ins.	50 ins.
							sts.	sts.	sts.	sts.	sts.	sts.
Cast on							124	128	132	136	140	144
Inc. for waistline							135	141	147	153	159	165
No. of sts. at bustline							149	155	163	171	177	183
No. of sts. after armhole shaping has been worked							109	113	117	121	125	129
No. of sts. at shoulder							36	38	40	42	44	46
Sleeves, Long												
Cast on							60	62	64	66	68	70
Inc. at top of wrist							69	71	73	75	77	79
No. of sts. at top of sleeve							103	107	111	115	119	123
Sleeves, Short												
Cast on							84	86	88	90	92	94
Inc. above ribbing							95	97	99	101	103	105
No. of sts. at top of sleeve							103	107	111	115	119	123

woman's cardigan

	No. 11					No. 9					No. 7				
Size of needle	3-ply					4-ply					Double Knitting				
Type of wool	3-ply					4-ply					Double Knitting				
Size of garment	ins. 34	ins. 36	ins. 38	ins. 40	ins. 42	ins. 34	ins. 36	ins. 38	ins. 40	ins. 42	ins. 34	ins. 36	ins. 38	ins. 40	ins. 42
	sts.	sts.	sts.	sts.	sts.	sts.	sts.	sts.	sts.	sts.	sts.	sts.	sts.	sts.	sts.
Cast on for front ($\frac{1}{4}$ bust measurement less $\frac{1}{2}$ in.)	64	68	72	76	80	51	55	58	62	65	44	47	49	52	55
Cast on for back ($\frac{1}{2}$ bust measurement)	136	144	152	160	168	110	117	123	130	137	93	99	105	110	116
Width after armhole shaping ..	112	112	114	114	116	91	91	93	93	94	77	77	78	78	80
Shoulder	36	36	38	38	40	29	29	31	31	33	25	25	26	26	27
Cast on for sleeves	58	58	60	60	62	48	48	50	50	52	40	40	42	42	44
Sts. above cuff	64	64	66	66	68	52	52	54	54	55	44	44	45	45	47
Sts. at widest point on sleeve ..	104	104	108	108	112	84	84	87	87	91	71	71	74	74	77

man's cardigan

	No. 11				No. 9				No. 7			
Size of needle	3-ply				4-ply				Double Knitting			
Type of wool	3-ply				4-ply				Double Knitting			
Size of garment	ins. 38	ins. 40	ins. 42	ins. 44	ins. 38	ins. 40	ins. 42	ins. 44	ins. 38	ins. 40	ins. 42	ins. 44
	sts.	sts.	sts.	sts.	sts.	sts.	sts.	sts.	sts.	sts.	sts.	sts.
Cast on for front ($\frac{1}{4}$ chest measurement less $\frac{1}{2}$ in.)	72	76	80	84	59	62	65	68	40	42	44	46
Cast on for back ($\frac{1}{2}$ chest measurement)	152	160	168	176	124	130	136	142	86	90	94	98
Width after armhole shaping ..	116	118	120	122	94	96	98	100	64	66	66	68
Shoulder	38	39	40	41	31	32	33	34	21	22	23	24
Cast on for sleeve	64	64	66	66	52	54	56	58	36	38	40	42
Sts. above cuff	72	73	74	75	58	60	62	64	40	42	44	46
Sts. at widest point on sleeve ..	132	136	140	144	106	110	114	118	74	76	78	80

part two

SUPPLEMENT OF GARMENTS TO MAKE

patterns from odd ounces

Abbreviations (for all Odd-Ounce Patterns). K. knit, p. purl, st(s). stitch(es), rem. remain, rep. repeat, cont. continue, str. straight, st.st. stocking stitch, patt. pattern, foll. following, alt. alternate, beg. beginning, tog. together, t.b.l. through back of loop(s), inc. increase, dec. decrease, make 1 *or* make 1k. lift yarn between sts. on row below and knit it t.b.l., make 1p. lift yarn between sts. on row below and purl it t.b.l., sl.p. slip 1 purlwise, w.o. wool over, w.f. wool forward, w.b. wool back.

tea cosy

Materials. 3 ozs. Main Colour and 3 ozs. White, both in Double Knitting Wool. A pair of No. 8 needles.

Measurements. To fit an average-size tea-pot.

Tension 5 stitches to 1 inch over garter stitch.

Abbreviations. MC Main Colour, W White.

Note—*Keep strands to wrong side of work throughout. The pleats are formed by drawing each strand of wool tight when work with this colour re-commences.*

Using MC, cast on 98 sts. and k.6 rows.

Colour pattern
  1st row: K.1 W, (k.8 MC, k.8 W) until 1 st. remains, k.1 MC.
  2nd row: (Twisting wools at beginning of row) K.1 MC, (k.8 W, k.8 MC) until 1 st. remains, k.1 W. Rep. these last 2 rows once more.
  5th row: K.1 MC, (k.8 W, k.8 MC) until 1 st. remains, k.1 W.
  6th row: K.1 W, (k.8 MC, k.8 W) until 1 st. remains, k.1 MC.
  Rep. these last 2 rows once. Rep. these 8 rows once more and then cont. to rep. the 5th and 6th rows until work

measures 6½ ins. from cast-on edge, ending after a wrong-side row.

Shape Top

1st row: K.1 MC, (using W, k.2 tog., k.4, k.2 tog., using MC, k.2 tog., k.4, k.2 tog.) until 1 st. remains, k.1 W.

2nd row: K.1 W, (k.6 MC, k.6 W) until 1 st. remains, k.1 MC.

3rd row: K.1 MC, (using W, k.2 tog., k.2, k.2 tog., using MC, k.2 tog., k.2, k.2 tog.) until 1 st. remains, k.1 W.

4th row: K.1 W, (k.4 MC, k.4 W) until 1 st. remains, k.1 MC.

5th row: K.1 MC, (using W, k.2 tog. twice, using MC, k.2 tog. twice) until 1 st. remains, k.1 W.

6th row: K.1 W, (k.2 MC, k.2 W) until 1 st. remains, k.1 MC.

7th row: K.1 MC, (k.2 tog. W, k.2 tog. MC) until 1 st. remains, k.1 W.

Thread remaining 14 sts. on to double yarn, pull tight and knot on inside.

Work another, identical piece.

To Make Up. Do not press. Stitch side seams, leaving openings for spout and handle. Make a pompon and stitch securely on top.

egg cosy

Materials. 1 oz. Main Colour and 1 oz. White Double Knitting Wool. A pair of No. 8 needles.

Using MC, cast on 74 sts., and k.2 rows.

Colour pattern

1st row: K.1 W, (k.6 MC, k.6 W) until 1 st. remains, k.1 MC.

2nd row: K.1 MC, (k.6 W, k.6 MC) until 1 st. remains, k.1 W.

Rep. these last 2 rows once more.

5th row: K.1 MC, (k.6 W, k.6 MC) until 1 st. remains, k.1 W.

6th row: K.1 W, (k.6 MC, k.6 W) until 1 st. remains, k.1 MC.

Rep. these last 2 rows once.

Cont. to rep. 1st and 2nd rows until work measures 3 ins. from cast-on edge, ending after a wrong side row.

Shape Top

1st row: K.1 W, (using MC, k.2 tog., k.2, k.2 tog., using W, k.2 tog., k.2, k.2 tog.) until 1 st. remains, k.1 MC.

Cont. and complete as from 4th row of Shaping Top of Tea Cosy, reversing colours.

To Make Up. Do not press. Sew side seam. Make a pompon and stitch securely on top.

his and her aran sweaters

Pictured on the cover and overleaf

Materials. 23 [31] ozs. Wendy Double Knitting Nylonised. One pair each Nos. 10 and 7 needles. Set of 4 No. 10 needles, points at both ends. 1 Cable needle. Stitch holder.

Measurements. Length from top of shoulder—24½ [29¼] inches. To fit—34/36 inch bust, 42/44 inch chest. Actual measurements—38 [44] inches. Sleeve seam—16½ [18] inches.

Tension 7 stitches to 1 inch over Diamond Pattern on No. 7 needles.

Abbreviations. K. knit, p. purl, sl.1 slip one, st(s). stitch(es), ins. inches, dec. decrease, inc. increase, beg. beginning, alt. alternate, t.b.l. through back of loop, rep. repeat, tog. together.

Note—*Instructions given for 34/36 inch bust, 42/44 inch chest given in brackets.*

The Back. ** Using No. 10 needles, cast on 136 [164] sts. Work 3 ins. in k.2, p.2 rib, inc. 1 st. at each end of the needle on the last row.

Change to No. 7 needles and commence pattern.

1st row: (Right side of work.) P.7, slip next 2 sts. on to cable needle and leave at front of work, k.2, k.2 from cable needle (this will be referred to as C. 2F.), rep. twice [4 times], p.3, C. 2F., k.2, p.3, k.2 t.b.l., p.8, k.2 t.b.l., p.3, C. 2F., k.2, p.3, [C. 2F.] 7 [10] times, p.3, C. 2F., k.2, p.3, k.2 t.b.l., p.8, k.2 t.b.l., p.3, C. 2F., k.2, p.3, C. 2F.. 3 [5] times, p.7.

2nd row: K.7, p.12 [20], k.3, p.6, k.3, p.2 t.b.l., k.8, p.2 t.b.l., k.3, p.6, k.3, p.28 [40], k.3, p.6, k.3, p.2 t.b.l., k.8, p.2 t.b.l., k.3, p.6, k.3, p.12 [20], k.7.

3rd row: P.7, k.2, slip next 2 sts. on to cable needle and leave at back of work, k.2, k.2 from cable needle (this will be referred to as C. 2B.), rep. once [3 times], k.2, p.3, k.2, C. 2B., p.3, slip next 2 sts. on to cable needle and leave at front of work, p.1, k.2 t.b.l. from cable needle (this will be referred to as Front Twist), p.6, slip next st. on to cable needle and leave at back of work, k.2 t.b.l., p.1 from cable needle (this will be referred to as Back Twist), p.3, k.2, C. 2B., p.3, k.2, [C. 2B] 6 [9] times, k.2, p.3, k.2, C. 2B.,

continued overleaf

continued from previous page

p.3, Front Twist, p.6, Back Twist, p.3, k.2, C. 2B., p.3, k.2, [C. 2B.] twice [4 times], k.2, p.7.

4th row: K.7, p.12 [20], k.3, p.6, k.4, p.2 t.b.l., k.6, p.2 t.b.l., k.4, p.6, k.3, p.28 [40], k.3, p.6, k.4, p.2 t.b.l., k.6, p.2 t.b.l., k.4, p.6, k.3, p.12 [20], k.7.

5th row: P.7, [C. 2F.] 3 [5] times, p.3, C. 2F., k.2, p.4, Front Twist, p.4, Back Twist, p.4, C. 2F., k.2, p.3, [C. 2F.] 7 [10] times, p.3, C. 2F., k.2, p.4, Front Twist, p.4, Back Twist, p.4, C. 2F., k.2, p.3, [C. 2F.] 3 [5] times, p.7.

6th row: K.7, p.12 [20], k.3, p.6, k.5, p.2 t.b.l., k.4, p.2 t.b.l., k.5, p.6, k.3, p.28 [40], k.3, p.6, k.5, p.2 t.b.l., k.4, p.2 t.b.l., k.5, p.6, k.3, p.12 [20], k.7.

7th row: P.7, k.2, [C. 2B.] twice [4 times], k.2, p.3, k.2, C. 2B., p.5, Front Twist, p.2, Back Twist, p.5, k.2, C. 2B., p.3, k.2, [C. 2B.] 6 [9] times, k.2, p.3, k.2, C. 2B., p.5, Front Twist, p.2, Back Twist, p.5, k.2, C. 2B., p.3, k.2, [C. 2B.] twice [4 times], k.2, p.7.

8th row: K.7, p.12 [20], k.3, p.6, k.6, p.2, t.b.l., k.2, p.2 t.b.l., k.6, p.6, k.3, p.28 [40], k.3, p.6, k.6, p.2 t.b.l., k.2, p.2 t.b.l., k.6, p.6, k.3, p.12 [20], k.7.

9th row: P.7, [C. 2F.] 3 [5] times, p.3, C. 2F., k.2., p.6, Front Twist, Back Twist, p.6, C. 2F., k.2, p.3, [C. 2F.] 7 [10] times, p.3, C. 2F., k.2, p.6, Front Twist, Back Twist, p.6, C. 2F., k.2, p.3, [C. 2F.] 3 [5] times, p.7.

10th row: K.7, p.12 [20], k.3, p.6, k.7, slip 2 purl sts. on to cable needle and leave at front of work, p.2 t.b.l., p.2 t.b.l. from cable needle, k.7, p.6, k.3, p.28 [40], k.3, p.6, k.7, slip 2 sts. on to cable needle and leave at front of work, p.2 t.b.l., p.2 t.b.l. from cable needle, k.7, p.6, k.3, p.12 [20], k.7.

11th row: P.7, k.2, [C. 2B.] twice [4 times], k.2, p.3, k.2, C. 2B., p.6, Back Twist, Front Twist, p.6, k.2, C. 2B., p.3, k.2, [C. 2B.] 6 [9] times, k.2, p.3, k.2, C. 2B., p.6, Back Twist, Front Twist, p.6, k.2, C. 2B., p.3, k.2, [C. 2B.] twice [4 times], k.2, p.7.

12th row: K.7, p.12 [20], k.3, p.6, k.6, p.2 t.b.l., k.2, p.2 t.b.l., k.6, p.6, k.3, p.28 [40], k.3, p.6, k.6, p.2 t.b.l., k.2, p.2 t.b.l., k.6, p.6, k.3, p.12 [20], k.7.

13th row: P.7, [C. 2F.] 3 [5] times, p.3, C. 2F., k.2, p.5, Back Twist, p.2, Front Twist, p.5, C. 2F., k.2, p.3, [C. 2F.] 7 [10] times, p.3, C. 2F., k.2, p.5, Back Twist, p.2, Front Twist, p.5, C. 2F., k.2, p.3, [C. 2F.] 3 [5] times, p.7.

14th row: K.7, p.12 [20], k.3, p.6, k.5, p.2 t.b.l., k.4, p.2 t.b.l., k.5, p.6, k.3, p.28 [40], k.3, p.6, k.5, p.2 t.b.l., k.4, p.2 t.b.l., k.5, p.6, k.3, p.12 [20], k.7.

15th row: P.7, k.2, [C. 2B.] twice [4 times], k.2, p.3, k.2,

C. 2B., p.4, Back Twist, p.4, Front Twist, p.4, k.2, C. 2B., p.3, k.2, [C. 2B.] 6 [9] times, k.2, p.3, k.2, C. 2B., p.4, Back Twist, p.4, Front Twist, p.4, k.2, C. 2B., p.3, k.2, [C. 2B.] twice [4 times], k.2, p.7.

16th row: As 4th row.

17th row: P.7, [C. 2F.] 3 [5] times, p.3, C. 2F., k.2, p.3, Back Twist, p.6, Front Twist, p.3, C. 2F., k.2, p.3, [C. 2F.] 7 [10] times, p.3, C. 2F., k.2, p.3, Back Twist, p.6, Front Twist, p.3, C. 2F., k.2, p.3, [C. 2F.] 3 [5] times, p.7.

18th row: K.7, p.12 [20], k.3, p.6, k.3, p.2 t.b.l., k.8, p.2 t.b.l., k.3, p.6, k.3, p.28 [40], k.3, p.6, k.3, p.2 t.b.l., k.8, p.2 t.b.l., k.3, p.6, k.3, p.12 [20], k.7.

Rows 3 to 18 inclusive form the pattern.

Continue in pattern until work measures 16 [19] ins. from beginning, finishing on a wrong side row.

Shape Armholes

Keeping the pattern correct, cast off 6 [16] sts. at beg. of the next 2 rows.

K.2 tog. at each end of the needle on the next and every following alt. row until 102 [112] sts. remain. **

Continue without further dec. until armhole measures 8½ [10¼] ins. from beginning, measured straight.

Shape Shoulders
34/36 inch size only

Cast off 11 sts. at beg. of next 6 rows.

42/44 inch size only

Cast off 11 sts. at beg. of next 4 rows. Cast off 12 sts at beg. of next 2 rows.

Both sizes

Cast off remaining 36 [44] sts.

The Front. Work exactly as instructions given for Back from ** to **.

Continue without further dec. until armhole measures 6½ [7] ins. from beginning, finishing on a wrong side row.

Shape Neck

Next row: Pattern across 43 [46] sts., turn.

Slip remaining sts. on to a st. holder.

K.2 tog. at neck edge on every row until 38 [40] sts. remain.

K.2 tog. at neck edge on every following alt. row until 33 [34] sts. remain.

Continue without further dec. until armhole measures 8½ [10¼] ins. from beginning, measured straight, finishing at armhole edge.

continued overleaf

ribbed casual sweater

Materials. 24 [25] balls of Lister Palazzo Double Crepe (a ¾ oz. ball knits up as 1 oz. D.K.). 1 pair each Nos. 10 and 8 needles. 1 set of No. 10 needles. 1 Cable Needle.

Measurements. To fit a 40 [42] inch chest. Length 27 [27½] inches. Sleeve seam 19½ [19¾] inches. (Instructions for larger size in brackets.)

Tension 7 stitches and 8 rows to 1 inch on No. 8 needles.

Abbreviations. K. knit, p. purl, rep. repeat, inc. increase, dec. decrease, beg. beginning, tog. together, sl. slip, p.s.s.o. pass slip stitch over, st(s). stitch(es), ins. inches, patt. pattern, rem. remain.
2C.R—2 stitches crossed to the right—pass needle in front of 1st stitch, knit 2nd stitch, then purl the 1st stitch.
3C.R—3 stitches crossed to the right—pass needle in front of first 2 stitches, knit into 3rd stitch, then into 2nd stitch and purl into the 1st stitch.
2C.L—2 stitches crossed to the left—put 1st stitch on

continued from previous page
Shape Shoulders
34/36 inch size only
Cast off 11 sts. at beg. of the next and following 2 alt. rows.

42/44 inch size only
Cast off 11 sts. at beg. of following 2 alt. rows. Cast off 12 sts. at beg. of the following alt. row.

Both sizes
Slip 43 [46] sts. from st. holder on to a No. 7 needle, leave 16 [20] sts. on st. holder for front neck.
Rejoin wool at neck edge and work to correspond with other side.

The Sleeves (both alike). Using No. 10 needles, cast on 60 (76) sts.
Work 3 [4] ins. in k.2, p.2 rib.
Inc. row: Rib 5 [3]. * inc. in next st., rib 4, rep. from * to last 5 [3] sts., rib 5 [3]. 70 [90] sts.
Change to No. 7 needles and commence pattern.
1st row: K.1 [0], p.2 [3], k.2 t.b.l., p.8, k.2 t.b.l., p.2 [3],

cable needle, pass needle behind and purl into the back of 2nd stitch, then knit into the back of stitch on cable needle.

3C.L—put 2 first stitches on cable needle, purl into the back of 3rd stitch, then knit into the back of 2nd stitch, then 1st stitch on cable needle.

The Front. With No. 10 needles cast on 144 [144] sts., and work as follows, beg. right side of work:-

K.1 for the edge, p.1, * 15 sts. in k.1, p.1, rib, p.2, rep. from * 7 times, 5 sts. in k.1, p.1, rib, k.1.

Keep the sts. in these blocks, knitting the knit sts. and purling the purl sts., until work measures 2 ins. Change to No. 8 needles and continue in main pattern.

1st row: K.1, * 2C.R 3 times, p.1, 3C.R 3 times, p.1, rep. from * ending with 2C.R 3 times, k.1.

2nd, 3rd and 4th rows: Knit the knit sts., and purl the purl sts.

5th row: K.1, * 2C.L 3 times, p.1, 3C.L 3 times, p.1, rep. from * ending with 2C.L 3 times, k.1.

6th, 7th and 8th rows: As 2nd, 3rd and 4th rows.

These 8 rows form the main pattern.

Larger Size only

Inc. 1 st. each end of 11th and every following 10th row 4 times. (152 sts.)

Both sizes

Cont. in pattern until work measures $16\frac{1}{4}$ [$16\frac{1}{2}$] ins. (or desired length).

Shape Raglan

Cast off 6 sts. at beg. next 2 rows.

1st row: K.1, rib 4, sl.1, k.1, p.s.s.o. patt. to last 7 sts., k.2 tog., rib 4, k.1.

2nd row: Knit the knit sts. and purl the purl sts.

Repeat these 2 rows until there are 66 sts. left.

Shape Neck

With wrong side of work facing, patt. 22, cast off 22, patt. to end. Finish this side first.

2nd row: K.1, rib 4, sl.1, k.1, p.s.s.o., patt. to end.

3rd row: (neck edge). Cast off 5, patt. to end.

Repeat 2nd and 3rd rows twice.

8th row: Rib to end. Cast off rem. 4 sts.

Rejoin wool to rem. sts. at centre front.

1st row: Cast off 5 sts., rib to last 7 sts., k.2 tog., rib 4, k.1.

2nd row: Rib to end. Rep. last 2 rows once.

5th row: Cast off 5, rib to end.

6th row: Rib to end.

Cast off.

The Back. Work as for Front up to armhole, then shape raglan as follows:-

Cast off 6 sts. at beg. of next 2 rows.

1st row: K.1, (k.1, p.1) twice, sl.1, k.3 tog., p.s.s.o., patt. to last 8 sts., k.3 tog., (p.1, k.1) twice, k.1.

2nd and all even number rows: Knit the knit sts., and purl the purl sts.

continued overleaf

C. 2F., k.2, p.2 [3], [C. 2F.] 5 [9] times, p.2 [3], C. 2F., k.2, p.2 [3], k.2 t.b.l., p.8, k.2 t.b.l., p.2 [3], k.1 [0].

2nd row: P.1 [0], k.2 [3], p.2 t.b.l., k.8, p.2 t.b.l., k.2 [3], p.6, k.2 [3], p.20 [36], k.2 [3], p.6, k.2 [3], p.2 t.b.l., k.8, p.2 t.b.l., k.2 [3], p.1 [0].

These two rows set the pattern for the sleeve.

Commencing on the 3rd row of pattern and keeping the 16 rows of pattern correct, and working all inc. sts. into pattern inc. 1 st. at each end of the needle on the next and every following 6th [8th] row until 94 [110] sts. are on the needle.

Continue without further inc. until work measures 17 [18] ins. from beginning, finishing on a wrong side row.

Shape Top
34/36 inch size only

Keeping the pattern correct, cast off 6 sts. at beg. of the next 2 rows.

Both sizes

K.2 tog. at each end of the needle on the next and every following alt. [3rd] row until 62 [84] sts. remain.

Work 1 row.

34/36 inch size only

Cast off 2 sts. at beg. of the next 8 rows, 3 sts. at beg. of following 6 rows and 4 sts. at beg. of following 2 rows.

Cast off.

42/44 inch size only

Cast off 3 sts. at beg. of the next 16 rows.

Cast off.

The Neckband. Join shoulder seams by back stitching.

With right side of work facing, using set of No. 10 needles, pick up and k.36 [44] sts. across back of neck, 38 [42] sts. to st. holder, k. across 16 [20] sts. from st. holder, pick up and k.38 [42] sts. to shoulder seam.

Divide sts. evenly on to 3 needles.

Work $3\frac{1}{2}$ [3] ins. in k.2, p.2 rib.

Cast off loosely in rib.

To Make Up. With wrong side of work facing, pin out all pieces to measurements given. Using a warm iron and damp cloth, press carefully.

Join side and sleeve seams by back stitching, omitting rib, join rib by top sewing. Pin sleeves into position, sew in by back stitching. Fold neckband in half on to wrong side and slip stitch. Press all seams flat.

continued from previous page

3rd row: As 1st row.
5th row: As 1st row of Front armhole decreasing.
6th row: Knit the knit sts. and purl the purl sts.
Rep. these last 2 rows until there are 58 sts. left.

Shape Back Neck.

With wrong side of work facing, patt. 17, cast off 24, patt. to end and finish this side first.
2nd row: K.1, rib 4, sl.1, k.1, p.s.s.o. patt. to end.
3rd row: Cast off 10, patt. to end.
4th row: K.1, rib 3, sl.1, k.1, p.s.s.o.
Cast off. Rejoin wool to rem. sts. at centre neck.
1st row: Cast off 10 sts., place last st. on left needle, k.2 tog., rib 4, k.1.
2nd row: Patt. to last 2 sts., k.2 tog. Cast off.

The Sleeves. With No. 10 needles cast on 69 sts. and work as follows:-
K.1, p.1, work 3 sts. in rib, * p.2, 15 sts. in rib, rep. from * ending p.2, 10 sts. in rib, k.1.
When work measures 3 ins. change to No. 8 needles and main pattern.
1st row: K.1, p.1, 3C.R, * p.1, 2C.R 3 times, p.1, 3C.R 3 times; rep. from * ending with p.1, 2C.R 3 times, p.1, 3C.R, p.1, k.1.
Cont. in patt. and inc. 1 st. each end on 4th then 6th rows alternatively, (working increased sts. in patt.) until there are 105 [113] sts. When sleeve measures 19½ [19¾] ins. or desired length, shape raglan.
Decrease as for Back armhole shaping until there are 23 sts. left.
1st row: K.1, (k.1, p.1) twice, sl.1, k.1, p.s.s.o., patt. 2, put needle through 3rd, 2nd and 1st sts. in that order and slip off, knit next 2 sts. tog., pass 3 sl. sts., over, patt. 2, k.2 tog., rib to end.
2nd row: Work in pattern.
3rd row: K.1, (k.1, p.1) twice, sl.1, k.1, p.s.s.o., sl.1, k.2 tog., p.s.s.o., k.2 tog., rib to end.
4th row: As 2nd.
5th row: Rib 4, dec. as row 3, rib 4.
6th row: As 2nd row.
7th row: Rib 2, dec. as row 3, rib 2.
9th row: Work in pattern. Cast off.

To Make Up. Sew the side and sleeve seams and sew the sleeves into the armholes.
With the set of No. 10 needles and right side of work facing, pick up and knit 5 sts. at top of sleeve, 60 sts. along the front neck, 5 sts. from second sleeve, and 54 sts. across the back. Work round in k.1, p.1 rib, and on the 3rd round k.3 tog., each side of neck. Work 6 more rounds in rib, and on 7th round make 2 incs. at each side above the decs. of 3rd round. Work 2 more rounds. Cast off in rib.

polo necked sweater in three sizes

The attractive cable panels are worked on the back as well as the front

Materials. 15 [16] [17] ozs. Hayfield Gaylon Double Knitting. 1 Pair each Nos. 9 and 10 Knitting Needles.

Measurements. To fit chest/bust 28 [30] [32] inches. Length from shoulder 19 [20½] [22] inches. Sleeve seam 12½ [13½] [14½] inches.

Tension 12½ stitches and 17 rows to 2 inches over stocking-stitch on No. 9 needles.

Abbreviations. K knit, p. purl, st(s). stitch(es), st.st. stocking stitch, patt. pattern, rep. repeat, beg. beginning, t.b.l. through back of loops, dec. decrease, inc. increase, tog. together, tw.2, twist 2 (knit into front of 2nd stitch on left-hand needle, then knit 1st stitch, letting both stitches drop off needle in the usual way), c.4, cable 4 (slip next 2 stitches on to cable needle and leave at back of work, k.2, then knit the stitches from cable needle), ins. inches.

Note—*Instructions for the larger sizes are in brackets in size order. Where one figure only is given, this applies to all sizes.*

The Back. With No. 10 needles cast on 104 [110] [116] sts. and work 2½ ins. k.1, p.1 rib.
Change to No. 9 needles and proceed as follows:
1st row: (Right side) K.41 [44] [47], p.1, tw.2, (p.1, k.4) 3 times, p.1, tw.2, p.1, k.41 [44] [47].
2nd row: P.41 [44] [47], k.1, p.2, k.1, (p.4, k.1) 3 times, p.2, k.1, purl to end.
3rd row: K.41 [44] [47], p.1, tw.2, p.1, k.4, p.1, c.4, p.1, k.4, p.1, tw.2, p.1, knit to end.
4th row: As 2nd row.
These 4 rows form the patt. Rep. them until the back measures 10½ [11½] [12½] ins. from cast-on edge, ending with a wrong-side row.

Shape Raglan

Cast off 3 sts. at the beg. of the next 2 rows.

3rd row: K.3, k.2 tog. t.b.l., work to last 5 sts., k.2 tog., k.3.

4th row: Work to end.

Rep. rows 3 and 4 until 30 [32] [34] sts. remain.

Cut off yarn. Leave sts. on a holder.

The Front. Work as given for back until 48 [52] [56] sts. remain when shaping raglan, ending with a wrong-side row.

Shape Neck

Next row: K.3, k.2 tog. t.b.l., work 11 [12] [13] sts., turn and leave remaining sts. on a spare needle until required.

Work on the first set of sts. as follows:

* Continuing raglan shaping as before, dec. 1 st. at neck edge on every row until 6 [7] [8] sts. remain.

Now continue raglan shaping only until 4 sts. remain. Dec. 1 st. at neck edge on following 2 alternate rows. Work 1 row. Cast off. *

Return to the sts. on the spare needle.

With right-side facing, slip next 16 [18] [20] sts. on a holder, join yarn to next st., work to last 5 sts., k.2 tog., k.3. Now work as given for first side from * to *.

The Sleeves (both alike). With No. 10 needles cast on 50 [52] [54] sts. and work 2½ ins. k.1, p.1 rib.

Change to No. 9 needles and proceed in st.st., but inc. 1 st. each end of 5th and every following 6th row until there are 62 [66] [70] sts., then each end of every 4th row until there are 82 [86] [90] sts.

Work straight until the sleeve measures 12½ [13½] [14½] ins. from cast-on edge, ending with a p. row.

Shape Raglan

Work as given for back raglan shaping until 8 sts. remain, ending p. row.

Cut off yarn. Leave sts. on a holder.

The Polo Collar. Join raglan seams, leaving left back seam open. With right-side facing, join on yarn and using a No. 10 needle knit the sts. of left sleeve from holder, knit up 17 [18] [19] sts. from left side of front neck, knit the sts. from holder, knit up 17 [18] [19] sts. from right side of front neck, then knit the remaining sts. from holders. 96 [102] [108] sts.

Work 2½ ins. k.1, p.1 rib.

Change to No. 9 needles and rib 2½ ins. more.

Cast off in rib.

To Make Up. Press work on wrong side with a warm iron over a damp cloth. Join remaining raglan and collar seam, then join side and sleeve seams. Fold the collar over to the right side.

Press all the seams carefully.

107

two lacy

A light weight bouclet jumper with a tie neck and a two-ply cardigan that is as soft as thistledown

LACY IN BOUCLET

Materials. 13 [13] [14] ozs. Patons Bouclet; 1 pair each No. 12 and No. 10 knitting needles.

Measurements. To fit 34 [36] [38] inch bust; length, 22½ [23¼] [23½] inches; sleeve seam, 12 inches.

Tension 7 stitches to 1 inch on No. 10 needles.

Abbreviations. K. knit, p. purl, tog. together, st(s). stitch(es), st.st. stocking stitch, patt. pattern, beg. beginning, cont. continue, dec. decrease, inc. increase, ins. inches, foll. following, alt. alternate, rem. remaining, w.o.n. wool over needle, w.r.n. wool round needle.

Note—*Figures in brackets refer to larger sizes in size order, where only one figure is given, this refers to all sizes.*

The Back. With No. 12 needles, cast on 130 [138] [146] sts.
1st row: K.2, (p.2, k.2) to end.
2nd row: P.2, (k.2, p.2) to end.
Rep. last 2 rows 4 times more.
Change to No. 10 needles and patt.
1st row: K.2, (p.2, k.2) to end.
2nd row (right side): P.2, (w.o.n., k.2 tog., p.2) to end.
3rd row: As 1st row.
4th row: P.2, (k.2 tog., w.r.n., p.2) to end.
These 4 rows form the patt. Cont. in patt. until work measures 15½ [16] [16] ins. from beg.

Shape Armholes
Cast off 12 sts. at beg. of next 2 rows. ** Cont. straight until armhole measures 7 [7¼] [7½] ins.

Shape Shoulders
Cast off 8 sts. at beg. of next 4 rows; 6 [7] [8] sts. at beg. of foll. 6 rows. Cast off.

The Front. Work as Back to **. Cont. straight until armholes measure 4 [4] [4½] ins.

patterns

Shape Neck

Next row: Patt. 53 [57] [61], turn, and keeping patt. correct complete this side first. Dec. 1 st. at neck edge on every row to 34 [37] [40] sts. Cont. straight until armhole matches Back to shoulder, ending at armhole edge.

Shape Shoulder

Cast off 8 sts. at beg. of next and foll. alt. row; 6 [7] [8] sts. on foll. 3 alt. rows. Join wool to neck edge of rem. sts. and complete to match first side.

The Sleeves (both alike). With No. 12 needles, cast on 70 [74] [74] sts. Work 10 rows rib as for Back welt.

Change to No. 10 needles and cont. in main patt. as Back, inc. 1 st. at both ends of 25th and every foll. 8th row to 86 [90] [90] sts. Cont. straight until sleeve measures 14 ins. from beg.

Shape Top

Cast off 5 sts. at beg. of next 12 rows. Cast off rem. sts.

The Tie. With No. 12 needles, cast on 34 sts.
1st row: K.
2nd row: K.2 tog., k. to last st., inc. in last st.
Rep. last 2 rows for 40 ins. Cast off.

To Make Up. Press tie only. Join shoulder and side seams. Join sleeve seams, leaving 2 ins. open at top. Sew in sleeves, the open portion at top of sleeve to cast-off at underarm. Sew tie to neck, centre of tie to centre back neck, and leave 3 ins. at each side of centre V free to allow for tie. Press all seams lightly.

SOFT AS THISTLEDOWN

This cardigan is knitted in an all-over traditional lacy pattern called horseshoe and is ideal to wear on sunny spring and summer days.

Materials. 7 ozs. Sirdar Majestic 2 ply. 1 pair each No. 11 and No. 12 Knitting Needles. 9 Buttons.

Measurements. To fit 34 to 36 inch bust. Length 21½ inches. Sleeve 21 inches from shoulder.

continued overleaf

continued from previous page
Tension 8 stitches to 1 inch on No. 11 needles.

Abbreviations. K. knit, p. purl, st(s). stitch(es), ins. inches, patt. pattern, beg. beginning, tog. together, w.f. wool forward, sl. slip, p.s.s.o. pass slipped stitch over, t.b.l. through back of loop, m.st. moss stitch, rep. repeat.

The Back. With No. 12 needles cast on 145 sts. Work 2½ ins. in k.1, p.1 rib, *beg. 2nd row p.*1.

Change to No. 11 needles. K.1 row, p.1 row. Now patt. thus:

1st row: K.2, (w.f., k.3, k.3 tog., k.3, w.f., k.3) to last 11 sts., w.f., k.3., k.3 tog., k.3, w.f., k.2.

2nd and every alternate row: Purl.

3rd row: K.3, (w.f., k.2, k.3 tog., k.2, w.f., k.5) to last 10 sts., w.f., k.2, k.3 tog., k.2, w.f., k.3.

5th row: K.4, (w.f., k.1, k.3 tog., k.1, w.f., k.7) to last 9 sts., w.f., k.1, k.3 tog., k.1, w.f., k.4.

7th row: K.5, (w.f., k.3 tog., w.f., k.9) to last 8 sts., w.f., k.3 tog., w.f., k.5.

8th row: Purl.

These 8 rows form patt. Continue in patt. until work measures 14½ ins., ending with a 7th patt. row.

Shape Armhole

Next row: Break wool. Sl. first 12 sts. on to a safety-pin. Rejoin wool and p. to last 12 sts., turn. Leave these last 12 sts. on a safety-pin.

Next row: K.1, sl.1, k.1, p.s.s.o., patt. to last 3 sts., k.2 tog., k.1.

Next row: P.1, p.2 tog., p. to last 3 sts., p.2 tog. t.b.l., p.1. Rep. last 2 rows 5 times more. (97 sts.) Continue until work measures 21 ins., ending with a 2nd patt. row.

Shape Neck and Shoulder

Next row: Patt. 30, turn. Work on these sts. only, dec. 1 st. at neck edge on next 5 rows. Cast off loosely. Place centre 37 sts. on a stitch-holder. Complete other side to match.

The Right Front. With No. 12 needles cast on 83 sts.

1st row: (K.1, p.1) 5 times, (p.1, k.1) to end.

2nd row: (P.1, k.1) to end.

Continue thus in rib with 10 sts. at front edge in m.st. for ½ in., ending with a wrong side row.

Next row: (Make buttonhole.) M.st. 4, cast off 2, m.st. 4, rib to end.

Next row: Rib to last 8 sts., m.st. 4, cast on 2, m.st. 4.

Continue in rib with m.st. until work measures 2½ ins., ending with a wrong side row.

Change to No. 11 needles.

Next row: M.st. 10, k. to end.

Next row: P. to last 10 sts., m.st. 10.

Now patt. as back, keeping 10 sts. at front in m.st. and making buttonholes as before 2½ ins. apart (measure from base of previous buttonhole) until work measures 14½ ins., ending with a 7th patt. row.

Shape Armhole

Next row: Break wool. Sl. first 12 sts. on to a safety-pin. Rejoin wool, p. to last 10 sts., m.st. 10.

Next row: Work to last 3 sts., k.2 tog., k.1.

Next row: P.1, p.2 tog., work to end.

Making buttonholes as before, rep. last 2 rows 5 times more. (59 sts.)

Continue, making buttonholes as before until there are 8 in all. Work 2 ins. more, ending with a 7th patt. row.

Shape Neck

Next row: P.37, turn, leave remaining 22 sts. on a stitch-holder. Dec. 1 st. at neck edge on next 12 rows. Work 4 rows straight. Cast off.

The Left Front. With No. 12 needles cast on 83 sts.

1st row: (K.1, p.1) to last 10 sts., (p.1, k.1) 5 times.

2nd row: (K.1, p.1) to end. Rep. last 2 rows for 2½ ins., ending with a 2nd row. Change to No. 11 needles.

Next row: K. to last 10 sts., m.st. 10.

Next row: M.st. 10, p. to end.

Now patt. as Back, keeping 10 sts. at front edge in m.st. and complete to match Right Front, omitting buttonholes, reversing shapings and working sl.1, k.1, p.s.s.o. for k.2 tog. and p.2 tog. t.b.l. for p.2 tog. on armhole shaping.

The Sleeves. Join shoulders.

Right Sleeve: Sl. 12 sts. from Right Back Armhole on to a No. 11 needle, then pick up and k. 73 sts. around armhole edge, break wool, then sl. 12 sts. from Right Front Armhole on to needle. (97 sts.)

Rejoin wool. p. 1 row. Now work 16 ins. in patt. as back. beg. with a 1st patt. row and ending with an 8th patt. row.

Next row: K.1, (k.2 tog., k.1) to end. (65 sts.)

P.1 row. Change to No. 12 needles. Work 5 ins in k.1, p.1 rib, beg. 2nd row p.1. Cast off ribwise. Work left sleeve to match, beg. at left front armhole.

The Neckband. Sl. 22 sts. at right front edge on to a No. 12 needle, then pick up and k. 18 sts. around front and back neck shapings, k. 37 sts. from back, pick up and k. 18 sts. around back and front neck shapings, then rib 12, m.st. 10 across 22 sts. at left front edge. Work 13 rows in rib, keeping 10 sts. each end in m.st. and making 9th buttonhole as before on 6th row. Cast off in m.st. and rib.

To Make Up. Press work lightly with warm iron over damp cloth. Join side and sleeve seams. Press seams. Sew on buttons.

4 bouclet hats

Any one of these four easy-to-knit styles can be made in an evening

Abbreviations. K. knit, p. purl, p.s.s.o. pass slip stitch over, st(s) stitch(es), beg. beginning, tog. together, ins. inches, rep. repeat, cont. continue, alt. alternate, inc. increase by working into front and back of stitch, patt. pattern, sl.1 slip 1 stitch, dec. decrease by working 2 sts. together.

Tension 10 stitches and 14 rows to 2 inches measured over stocking stitch.

continued overleaf

continued from previous page

STYLE 1 (top left of picture)

Materials. 4 ozs. Bairnswear Castanet Double Knitting. 1 set of 4 each No. 9 and No. 7 Needles.

Measurements. To fit 22 inch crown.

Using set of No. 9 needles cast on 104 sts. and work in rounds of k.1, p.1 rib until work measures 3 ins. from beg.
Next round: Purl. (This marks the hemline.)
Work in rounds of k.1, p.1 rib until work measures 6 ins. from beg.
Change to set of No. 7 needles.
Next round: * Inc. in next st., p.9, inc. in next st., k.2; rep. from * to end of round.
Next round: Purl, keeping the sts. between the shapings k. on every round. Rep. the last round twice more. Cont. to inc. 1 st. on each side of k. sts. on next and every following 4th round, until 152 sts. on needles.
Next round: * P.2 tog., p.13, sl.1, p.1, p.s.s.o., k.2; rep. from * to end of round.
Next round: Purl, keeping the sts. in between the shapings k. on every round. Rep. last round twice more. Cont. to dec. 1 st. on each side of k. sts. on next and every following 4th round until 40 sts. remain. Work 3 rounds without shaping.
Next round: * P.3 tog., k.2; rep. from * to end of round (24 sts.).
Draw up and fasten off.

To Make Up. Fold rib under for 3 ins. and slip stitch to wrong side. Press lightly on wrong side with warm iron.

STYLE 2 (bottom left of picture)

Materials. 4 ozs. Bairnswear Castanet Double Knitting. 1 set of 4 No. 7 Needles.

Measurements. To fit 22 inch crown.

Using set of No. 7 needles, cast on 112 sts., arrange on three needles, work in rounds of k.2, p.2 rib until work measures 9 ins. from beg.

Shape Crown
1st round: * K.11, sl.1, k.1, p.s.s.o., k.1, k.2 tog.; rep. from * to end of round. Cont. decreasing each side of k. stitch until 28 sts. on needles.
Next round: * Sl.1, k.1, p.s.s.o., k.2 tog.; rep. from * to end. (14 sts.).
Draw up and fasten off.

To Make up. Fold the rib to form double band.

STYLE 3 (top right of picture)

Materials. 4 ozs. Bairnswear Castanet Double Knitting. 1 set of 4 No. 7 Needles.

Measurements. To fit 22 inch crown.

Using set of No. 7 needles cast on 112 sts. and arrange on three needles, then work in rounds of k.2, p.2 rib until work measures 2½ ins. from beg.
Next round: Purl. (This forms hemline.)
Next round: Work in rounds of p.2, k.2 rib until work measures 5 ins. from beg.
Next round: Knit.
Cont. in garter st. until work measures 5 ins. from hemline.

Shape Crown
Next round: * K.2 tog., k.9, sl.1, k.1, p.s.s.o., k.1; rep. from * to end of round. Cont. decreasing on each side of k. st. on every following 4th round until 32 sts. remain. Work 3 rounds without shaping.
Next round: * K.2 tog., sl.1, k.1, p.s.s.o.; rep. from * to end of round. (16 sts.)
Break yarn and draw together.

To Make Up. Fold under 2½ ins. of rib and slip stitch to wrong side of work. Press lightly on wrong side with warm iron.

STYLE 4 (bottom right of picture)

Materials. 4 ozs. Bairnswear Castanet Double Knitting. 1 set of 4 each No. 9 and No. 7 Needles.

Measurements. To fit 21 inch crown

Using set of No. 9 needles cast on 104 sts., arrange these on three needles and work in rounds of k.1, p.1 rib until work measures 1 inch from beg.
Change to set of No. 7 needles.
1st round: * K.10, inc. in next st., k.1, inc. in next st.; rep. from * to end of round. Cont. to inc. each side of k. st. on every following 4th round until there are 184 sts.
Next round: K. to last 3 sts. of round and place these 3 sts. on the 1st needle.
Next round: * K.2 tog., k.18, sl.1, k.1, p.s.s.o., k.1; rep. from * to end of round. Cont. decreasing on each side of k. st. on every following 4th round until 40 sts. remain.
Knit 3 rounds.
Next round: * K.2 tog., sl.1, k.1, p.s.s.o., k.1; rep. from * to end of round. (24 sts.)
Draw up and fasten off.

shirt-style sweater

Materials. 9 [10] [10] [11] ozs. Jaeger Celtic Spin. 1 pair each No. 8 and No. 11 Knitting Needles. 2 Buttons.

Measurements. To fit 34 [36] [38] [40] inch bust sizes. Length 23½ [23½] [24] [24] inches. Sleeve seam 17 [17] [17½] [17½] inches.

Tension 5½ stitches and 7½ rows to 1 inch on No. 8 needles.

Abbreviations. K. knit, p. purl, sts. stitches, rep. repeat, inc. increase, dec. decrease, ins. inches, st.st. stocking stitch, beg. beginning, alt. alternate, sl. slip, foll. following, rem. remain(ing).

Note—*Instructions are given for size 34. Figures in brackets refer to larger sizes in size order.*

The Front. With No. 11 needles cast on 94 [102] [106] [114] sts.
1st row: * P.2, k.2; rep. from * to last 2 sts., p.2.
2nd row: * K.2, p.2; rep. from * to last 2 sts., k.2.
Rep. these 2 rows 6 times more.
Change to No. 8 needles and work in st.st., until front measures 10¾ [10¾] [11] [11] ins. from cast on edge, ending on a k. row. **

Divide for Neck
P.42 [46] [48] [52], cast off 10 sts. Purl to end. Work each side separately, keeping neck edge straight, inc. 1 st. at beg. of next side edge row and every foll. 8th row until 46 [50] [52] [56] sts. rem. Work 7 rows straight.

Shape Armhole
Cast off at beg. of next and alt. rows 5 sts. once, 2 sts. once [twice] [twice] [3 times] and then dec. 1 st. at beg. of every alt. row 3 times, ending at centre front edge. 36 [38] [40] [42] sts.

34 inch only
Work 4 more rows.

36 inch and 38 inch
Work 2 rows.

All sizes
Shape Front
Keeping armhole edge straight, dec. 1 st. at beg. of next and every following 4th row until 25 [27] [28] [30] sts. remain ending at armhole edge.

Shape Shoulder
At beg. of side edge row cast off 5 [6] [6] [6] sts. On alt. rows cast off 5 [5] [5] [6] sts. once, 5 [5] [5] [6] once, and 5 [5] [6] [6] once; on next alt. row cast off rem. sts.
Rejoin wool to rem. sts. at front opening and, keeping front edge straight, inc. 1 st. at end of next row then on every 8th row until 46 [50] [52] [56] sts. are on needle.
Work 8 rows. Shape armhole and complete to match first side.

The Back. Work exactly as for Front to ** but end with a p. row. Inc. 1 st. at both ends of next and every 8th row until there are 102 [106] [114] [118] sts. Work 7 rows.
continued overleaf

continued from previous page

Shape Armholes

At beg. of next 2 rows cast off 5 sts. then 2 sts. at beg. of next 2 [2] [4] [4] rows. Dec. 1 st. at beg. of every row until 82 [86] [90] [94] sts. rem. Work straight until work measures 7½ [7½] [7¾] [7¾] ins. from beg. of armhole shaping, ending on a p. row.

Shape Shoulders

At beg. of next 2 rows cast off 5 [6] [6] [6] sts. At beg. of next 4 rows cast off 5 [5] [5] [6] sts. On foll. 2 rows cast off 5 [5] [6] [6] sts. and on last 2 rows cast off 5 [6] [6] [6] sts. Cast off rem. sts.

The Sleeves (both alike). With No. 11 needles cast on 46 [46] [50] [50] sts. and work 14 rows rib as for Back.

Change to No. 8 needles and st.st., work 4 rows. Inc. 1 st. at both ends of next and every 6th row until there are 52 [52] [56] [56] sts. then inc. 1 st. at both ends of every 8th row until there are 72 [72] [76] [76] sts. Work straight until sleeve is 17 [17] [17½] [17½] ins. from beg., end with a p. row.

Shape Top

At beg. of next 2 rows cast off 5 sts. then 2 sts. at beg. of next 4 [4] [6] [6] rows. Dec. 1 st. at beg. of every row until 34 sts. rem. At beg. of next 8 rows cast off 2 sts. Cast off rem. 18 sts.

The Band. Right Front Opening: With No. 11 needles cast on 19 sts.

1st row: Sl.1, k.1, * p.1, k.1; rep. from * to last st., k1.
2nd row: Sl.1, * p.1, k.1; rep. from * to end.
Rep. these 2 rib rows 9 times more.

Make Buttonhole

Next row: Work 8 sts., cast off 3 sts., work to end.
Next row: Cast on 3 sts. over those cast off.
Work 24 rows. Make a second buttonhole. Work 38 [38] [42] [42] rows. Cast off in rib.

Work Left Front Band to match Right Front Band but omit buttonholes.

The Collar. With No. 11 needles cast on 116 sts.
1st row: Sl.1, * k.2, p.2; rep. from * to last 3 sts., k.3.
2nd row: Sl.1, * p.2, k.2; rep. from * to last 3 sts., p.3.
Rep. these 2 rows for 4½ ins. Cast off firmly in rib.

To Make Up. Press pieces carefully with a warm iron over damp cloth. Join all seams. Set in sleeves. Sew bands to front opening with buttonhole band to right front, cast-off edge will be about 3¾ ins. from shoulder seam. Sew cast-on edge of collar to neck edge and side edges of collar to top of bands. Sew on buttons.

smart for a small boy

Materials. 6 [7] [7] [8] ozs. Bairnswear Crepe Laine 4 ply. One pair each No. 12 and No. 13 Knitting Needles. 3 Buttons.

Measurements. To fit 18 [20] [22] [24] inch chest. Length 11 [12½] [14] [15½] inches. Sleeve 7½ [8½] [10] [11½] inches.

Tension 8 stitches and 11 rows to 1 inch on No. 12 needles.

Abbreviations. K. knit, p. purl, st(s). stitch(es), ins. inches, st.st. stocking stitch, inc. increase, dec. decrease, tog. together, sl. slip, p.s.s.o. pass slip stitch over, t.b.l. through back of loop, beg. beginning, rep. repeat.

Note—*Instructions are for smallest size with larger sizes in brackets in size order.*

The Back. With No. 13 needles cast on 81 [89] [97] [105] sts.
1st row: P.1, (k.1 t.b.l., p.1) to end.
2nd row: K.1, (p.1 t.b.l., k.1) to end.
These 2 rows form twisted rib. Continue in twisted rib until work measures 1½ [1½] [2] [2] ins., ending with a 2nd row.

Change to No. 12 needles. Continue in st.st., beg. with a k. row until work measures 6½ [7½] [8½] [9½] ins., ending with a p. row.

Shape Raglan

1st row: K.3, k.3 tog., k. to last 6 sts., sl.1, k.2 tog., p.s.s.o., k.3. Work 3 rows straight, beg. with a p. row. Rep. last 4 rows until 33 [33] [37] [37] sts. remain. Work 3 [1] [3] [1] rows more. Cast off.

The Front. Work as Back until 77 [77] [81] [81] sts. remain. Work 2 [0] [2] [0] rows.
Next row: (Wrong side.) P.34 [34] [36] [36], cast off 9, p. to end. Work on last sts. only, shaping raglan as for Back until 24 [24] [26] [26] sts. remain. Work 2 [0] [2] [0] rows.

Shape Neck

Still shaping raglan as before, cast off 5 [5] [7] [7] sts. at beg. of next row then dec. 1 st. at neck edge on every alternate row until all sts. are worked off. Complete other side of neck to match.

The Sleeves (both alike): With No. 13 needles cast on 39 [43] [45] [47] sts. Work 1¾ [1¾] [2¼] 2¼ ins. in twisted rib, ending with a 2nd row. Change to No. 12 needles.

Continue in st.st., beg. with a k. row and inc. 1 st. each end of every 6th row until there are 57 [65] [69] [77] sts.

Continue until work measures 7½ [8½] [10] [11½] ins., ending with a p. row. Shape raglan as Back until 9 [9] [9] [9] sts. remain. Cast off.

Front Bands. With No. 13 needles pick up and k. 21 sts. along straight edge of left front opening. (Right front for a girl.) Work 6 rows in twisted rib, beg. with a 2nd row.

Buttonhole row: Rib 3, cast off 2, (rib 5, cast off 2) twice, rib 2.

Next row: Rib, casting on 2 sts. over those cast off. Work 5 rows more. Cast off in twisted rib. With No. 13 needles pick up and k. 21 sts. along right side of front opening. (Left for a girl.) Work 13 rows in twisted rib, beg. with a 2nd row. Cast off in twisted rib.

The Collar. Join all raglan seams. With No. 13 needles beg. at centre of right front band and pick up and k. 99 [103] [107] [111] sts. around neck edge, ending at centre of left front band. Work 3 [3] [3¼] [3½] ins. in twisted rib, beg. with a 1st row. Cast off in twisted rib.

To Make Up. Press work with warm iron over damp cloth. Join side and sleeve seams. Sew down lower edges of front bands, placing left band over right. (Reverse for a girl.) Press seams. Sew on buttons.

This is a fully fashioned sweater shirt for one to four year olds. Reverse button band for a girl

ribbed for big brother

For four to eight year olds the perfect sweater shirt with set-in sleeves and single rib collar for sunny but cool days when a boy likes to be out in the open air

Materials. 7 [8] [9] ozs. Emu Scotch 4 ply. 1 pair each No. 9 and No. 11 Knitting Needles. 3 Buttons.

Measurements. To fit 24 [26] [28] inch chest. Length 15 [16½] [18] inches. Sleeve 11½ [13] [14½] inches.

Tension 7 stitches and 9 rows to 1 inch (slightly stretched) on No. 9 needles.

Abbreviations. K. knit, p. purl, st(s). stitch(es), ins. inches, inc. increase, dec. decrease, tog. together, beg. beginning, patt. pattern.

Note—*Instructions are for smallest size with larger sizes in brackets in size order.*

The Back. With No. 11 needles cast on 86 [94] [102] sts. Work 2 ins. in k.1, p.1 rib, inc. 1 st. at end of last row. 87 [95] [103] sts.
Change to No. 9 needles and patt. thus:
Next row: K.3, (p.2, k.2) to end.
This one row forms patt. Continue in patt. until work measures 9 [10] [11] ins. *.

Shape Armhole
Cast off 4 sts. at beg. of next 2 rows. Dec. 1 st. at beg. of next 16 rows. 63 [71] [79] sts. Continue until work measures 15 [16½] [18] ins.

Shape Shoulder
Cast off 6 [7] [8] sts. at beg. of next 6 rows. Cast off.

The Front. Work as Back to *.
Front dividing row: Patt. 38 [42] [46], cast off 11 sts. in patt., patt. 38 [42] [46]. Work on last sts. only.

Shape Armhole
Cast off 4 sts. at beg. of next row then dec. 1 st. at armhole edge on next 8 alternate rows, at same time dec. 1 st. at neck edge on every 6th row until 18 [21] [24] sts. remain.

Continue until work measures 15 [16½] [18] ins. ending at armhole edge.

Shape Shoulder
Cast off 6 [7] [8] sts. at beg. of next and following 2 alternate rows. Complete other side of front to match.

The Sleeves (both alike). With No. 11 needles cast on 38 [46] [54] sts. Work 2 ins. in k.1, p.1 rib, inc. 1 st. at end of last row. 39 [47] [55] sts.
Change to No. 9 needles. Patt. as Back, inc. 1 st. each end of every 6th [6th] [8th] row until there are 63 [71] [79] sts. Continue until work measures 11½ [13] [14½] ins. To shape top cast off 4 sts. at beg. of next 2 rows. Dec. 1 st. at beg. of every row until 47 [51] [55] sts. remain. Dec. 1 st. each end of next 12 rows. Cast off.

Front Insets. With No. 11 needles cast on 12 sts. for left inset. Work 18 rows in k.1, p.1 rib, inc. 1 st. at end of 6th, 12th and 18th rows.
Buttonhole row: Rib to last 7 sts., cast off 3, rib 4.
Next row: Rib 4, cast on 3, rib to end.
Continue in rib, making 2 more buttonholes 14 [16] [18] rows apart and at same time inc. at end of 4th and every following 6th row until there are 20 [21] [21] sts. Work 3 rows after 3rd buttonhole is completed.

Shape Neck
Cast off 9 [10] [10] sts. at beg. of next row. Dec. 1 st. at neck on every row until all sts. are worked off. Work right inset to match left but omit buttonholes.

The Collar. With No. 11 needles cast on 116 [120] [124] sts. Work 2 [2¼] [2½] ins. in k.1, p.1 rib. Cast off loosely ribwise.

To Make Up. Press lightly with warm iron over damp cloth. Join shoulder, side and sleeve seams. Set in sleeves. Sew in insets. Sew cast-on edge of collar to neck, beg. and ending 4 sts. from front edges. Press seams lightly. Sew buttons to right inset.

white cable sweater with coloured trim

The coloured band adds a touch of individuality to this ideal sports sweater and could be knitted in club colours

Materials. 24 [25] [27] [28] ozs. in White Sirdar Double Crepe. 1 oz. each in Red and Blue. 1 pair each No. 8 and No. 10 Knitting Needles. 1 Cable Needle.

Tension 6 stitches to one inch in moss stitch with No. 8 needles. 19 stitch pattern measures $2\frac{3}{4}$ inches on No. 8 needles.

Abbreviations. K. knit, p. purl, st(s). stitch(es), ins. inches, inc. increase, dec. decrease, beg. beginning, cont. continue, foll. following, patt. pattern, tog. together, tbl. through back loops, rem. remain(ing), rep. repeat(ed), C8 cable 8 thus (slip next 4 sts. on cable needle and leave at back of work, knit next 4 sts., then knit the 4 sts. from cable needle), W White, R Red, B Blue.

Measurements. 36 [38] [40] [42] inch chest sizes. Length from shoulder—28 [28] [29] [29] inches. Length of sleeve seam—20 [20] [21] [21] inches.

Note—*Figures in brackets are for the three larger sizes in size order. One figure only refers to all sizes.*

The Back. With No. 10 needles and W, cast on 127 [135] [141] [149] sts.
1st row: K.1, * p.1, k.1; rep. from * to end.
2nd row: P.1, * k.1, p.1; rep. from * to end.
Repeat these 2 rows 13 times more, and dec. 1 st. at end

of last row. 126 [134] [140] [148] sts.
Change to No. 8 needles and patt. as follows:
1st row: (K.1, p.1) 9 [11] [3] [5] times, * k.1, p.2, k.8, p.2, (K.1, p.1) 3 times; rep. from * to last 13 [17] [1] [5] sts., (K.1, p.1) 6 [8] [0] [2] times, k.1.
2nd row: (K.1, p.1) 9 [11] [3] [5] times, * p.1, k.2, p.8, k.2, p.2, (k.1, p.1) twice; rep. from * to last 13 [17] [1] [5] sts., (k.1, p.1) 6 [8] [0] [2] times, k.1.
Rep. 1st and 2nd rows of pattern once.
5th row: (K.1, p.1) 9 [11] [3] [5] times, * k.1, p.2, C8, p.2, (k.1, p.1) 3 times; rep. from * to last 13 [17] [1] [5] sts., (k.1, p.1) 6 [8] [0] [2] times, k.1.
6th row: As 2nd row.
7th and 9th rows: As 1st row.
8th and 10th rows: As 2nd row. These 10 rows form one pattern and are repeated throughout.
Cont. straight until work measures 18 in. from beginning ending with a 10th row of patt. Break off wool.

Shape Armholes
Slip the first 14 [18] [18] [22] sts. on to a st. holder, rejoin wool and patt. to last 14 [18] [18] [22] sts. Slip these last sts. on to a st. holder. ***
Keeping continuity of patt. work straight on rem. 98 [98] [104] [104] sts. until 8 [8] [9] [9] complete patts. have been worked from start of armholes.

Shape Shoulder and Back Neck
Next row: Cast off 10 [10] [11] [11] sts., patt. until there are 21 [21] [23] [23] sts. on right needle, cast off next 36 sts., patt. to end. Cont. on rem. 31 [31] [34] [34] sts. as follows:
1st row: Cast off 10 [10] [11] [11] sts., patt. to last 2 sts., k.2 tog.
2nd row: Work in patt.
3rd row: As 1st row.
4th row: Work in patt. Cast off rem. 9 [9] [10] [10] sts.
With wrong side facing, rejoin wool to rem. 21 [21] [23] [23] sts., k.2 tog., patt. to end.
Next row: Cast off 10 [10] [11] [11] sts. and patt. to end.
Next row: K.2 tog., patt. to end. Cast off rem. 9 [9] [10] [10] sts.
The Front. Work as for Back to ***, then work 18 rows straight. 98 [98] [104] [104] sts.
Divide for Neck
Next row: Patt. 47 [47] [50] [50] sts., k.2 tog., turn, keeping patt. correct, and work on these sts. only to finish this side first. Dec. 1 st. at neck edge at end of every foll. 4th row until 47 [47] [42] [42] sts. rem., then dec. 1 st. at neck at end of every foll. 3rd row until 29 [29] [32] [32] sts. rem.
Work 1 [1] [3] [3] rows, thus ending at side edge.

Shape Shoulders
Cast off 10 [10] [11] [11] sts. at beg. of next and foll. alt.

row. Work 1 row. Cast off rem. 9 [9] [10] [10] sts.

Rejoin wool to rem. 49 [49] [52] [52] sts., k.2 tog., and patt. to end. Dec. 1 st. at neck edge at beg. of every 4th row until 47 [47] [42] [42] sts. rem., then dec. at neck edge every 3rd row until 29 [29] [32] [32] sts. rem.

Work 2 [2] [4] [4] rows, ending at side edge.

Shape shoulder as for first side.

The Sleeves (both alike). Join shoulders of back and front.

With right side facing, No. 8 needles and W, (k.1, p.1) across the 14 [18] [18] [22] sts. left on holder, pick up and knit 112 [112] [127] [127] sts. evenly across armhole, then work in (p.1, k.1) across the 14 [18] [18] [22] sts. left on other holder. 140 [148] [163] [171] sts.

1st row: (K.1, p.1) 7 [9] [8] [10] times, k.1, p.2, * k.2, p.1, (p.1, k.1) twice, p.2, k.2, p.8, rep. from * to last 28 [32] [30] [34] sts., k.2, p.1, (k.1, k.1) twice, p.2, k.2, p.1, (p.1, k.1) 8 [10] [9] [11] times.

2nd row: (K.1, p.1) 7 [9] [8] [10] times, k.1, k.2 tog., p.2, k.1 (p.1, k.1) twice, p.1, * k.1, p.2, k.8, p.2, k.1, (p.1, k.1) twice, p.1, rep. from * to last 20 [24] [22] [26] sts., k.1, p.2, k.2 tog. tbl., (k.1, p.1) 7 [9] [8] [10] times, k.1.

3rd row: (K.1, p.1) 7 [9] [8] [10] times, p.2 tog. tbl., k.2, p.1, (p.1, k1) twice, p.1, * p.1, k.2, p.8, k.2, p.1, (p.1, k.1) twice, p.1., rep. from * to last 19 [23] [21] [25] sts., p.1, k.2, p.2 tog., (p.1, k.1) 7 [9] [8] [10] times.

4th row: (K.1, p.1) 6 [8] [7] [9] times, k.1, k.2 tog., p.2, k.1, (p.1, k.1) twice, p.1, * k.1, p.2, k.8, p.2, k.1, (p.1, k.1) twice, p.1, rep. from * to last 18 [22] [20] [24] sts., k.1, p.2, k.2 tog. tbl., (k.1, p.1) 6 [8] [7] [9] times, k.1.

5th row: (K.1, p.1) 6 [8] [7] [9] times, p.2 tog. tbl., k.2, p.1, (p.1, k.1) twice, p.1, * p.1, k.2, p.8, k.2, p.1, (p.1, k.1) twice, p.1, rep. from * to last 17 [21] [19] [23] sts., p.1, k.2, p.2 tog., (p.1, k.1) 6 [8] [7] [9] times.

6th row: (K.1, p.1) 5 [7] [6] [8] times, k.1, k.2 tog., p.2, k.1, (p.1, k.1) twice, p.1, * k.1, p.2, k.8, p.2, k.1, (p.1, k.1) twice, p.1, rep. from * to last 16 [20] [18] [22] sts., k.1, p.2, k.2 tog. tbl., (k.1, p.1) to last st., k.1.

7th row: (K.1, p.1) 5 [7] [6] [8] times, p.2 tog. tbl., k.2, p.1, (p.1, k.1) twice, p.1, * p.1, k.2, p.8, k.2, p.1, (p.1, k.1) twice, p.1, rep. from * to last 15 [19] [17] [21] sts., p.1, k.2, p.2 tog., (p.1, k.1) to end.

8th row: (K.1, p.1) 4 [6] [5] [7] times, k.1, k.2 tog., p.2, k.1, (p.1, k.1) twice, p.1, * k.1, p.2, C8, p.2, k.1, (p.1, k.1) twice, p.1, rep. from * to last 14 [18] [16] [20] sts., k.1, p.2, k.2 tog. tbl., (k.1, p.1) to last st., k.1.

Keeping patt. correct, and working cables every foll. 8th row, cont. to dec. 2 sts. in every row in this way by working 1 st. less in moss st. at outer edge of decreasings every row until the wrong side row beg. with p.2 tog. tbl., and ending with p.2 tog. has been worked and 112 [112] [127] [127] sts. rem.

Now dec. 1 st. each end of next and every foll. 6th [6th]

[4th] [4th] row until 100 [100] [71] [71] sts. rem. Dec. 1 st. each end of every foll. 4th [4th] [3rd] [3rd] row until 52 [54] [59] [59] sts. rem. Cont. straight until sleeve measures 17 [17] [18] [18] ins. from the picked up sts. For the 2 smallest sizes, dec. 1 st. at beg. of last row.

All Sizes

Change to No. 10 needles and work the 2 rows of rib as for Back for 3 ins. Cast off in rib.

The Neckband. With No. 10 needles and W, cast on 235 [235] [255] [255] sts.

1st row: K.3 tog., * k.1, p.1, rep. from * to last 4 sts., k.1, k.3 tog.

2nd row: K.2 tog., * k.1, p.1, rep. from * to last 3 sts., k.1, k.2 tog.

Break off W. Join on B.

3rd row: K.3 tog., knit to last 3 sts., k.3 tog.

4th row: K.2 tog., * p.1, k.1, rep. from * to last 3 sts., p.1, k.2 tog.

Break off B. Join on R.

5th row: With R, k.3 tog., knit to last 3 sts., k.3 tog.

6th row: With R, as 2nd row.

7th row: K.3 tog., * p.1, k.1, rep. from * to last 4 sts., p.1, k.3 tog.

8th row: With R, as 4th row.

9th row: With R, as 1st row.

10th row: With R, as 6th row.

Repeat 7th and 8th rows once. Break off R. Join on B.

13th row: With B, as 3rd row.

14th row; With B., as 2nd row.

Break off B and cont. only with W.

Rep. 3rd and 4th rows once.

17th row: As 1st row.

18th row: As 2nd row.

19th row: As 7th row.

20th row: As 4th row.

Repeat 17th, 18th, 19th and 20th rows twice more. 151 [151] [171] [171] sts.

29th row: Inc. in each of the first 2 sts., * p.1, k.1, rep. from * to last 3 sts., p.1, inc. in each of the last 2 sts.

30th row: Inc. in first st., * p.1, k.1, rep. from * to last 2 sts., p.1, inc. in last st.

31st row: Inc. in each of the first 2 sts., * k.1, p.1, rep. from * to last 3 sts., k.1, inc. in each of the last 2 sts.

32nd row: Inc. in first st., * k.1, p.1, rep. from * to last 2 sts., k.1, inc. in last st. Repeat the last 4 rows three times more. 199 [199] [219] [219] sts.

Cast off loosely in rib.

To Make Up. Press lightly with warm iron and damp cloth. Join ends of the neckband. Sew cast on edge of neckband to neck edge, with right sides facing, turn over and lightly slip st. the cast off edge to last row of R. Join side and sleeve seams. Press seams.

smart stripes

Back-buttoned overblouse with gay flowers embroidered between the stripes

Materials. 15 [16] [16] ozs. Lister Lavenda Double Knitting in White, and 4 [4] [4] ozs. in Black. 1 Pair each Nos. 9 and 11 Knitting Needles. 6 Buttons. Press Stud.

Measurements. To fit a 34 [36] [38] inch bust. Length 22½ inches. Sleeve seam 12 inches.

Tension 6 stitches and 8 rows to 1 inch.

Abbreviations. K. knit, p. purl, st(s). stitch(es), tog. together, rep. repeat, inc. increase, dec. decrease, ins. inches, beg. beginning, st.st. stocking stitch, patt. pattern, W White, B Black.

Note—*Instructions are for smallest size with larger sizes in brackets in size order.*
Important: *Design is knitted sideways, starting at underarm seam.*

The Right Back. * Beg. at right-side edge, with No. 9 needles and W cast-on 88 [88] [88] sts. Work 0 [4] [8] rows st.st. Continue in patt. thus: Work 8 rows st.st. in W. Join in B.
Next row: K. (3B, 1W) to end.
Next row: Purl in W then cast on 44 sts. for armhole. (132 sts.)
Work 7 rows st.st. in W, beg. with a knit row.
Next row: Purl (1W, 3B) to end. The last 18 rows (omitting the cast-on 44 sts. for armhole) form the patt. Continue in patt., inc. 1 st. at beg. of next and every 6th row until there are 136 sts. Work 3 rows.

Shape the Neck
Dec. 1 st. at beg. of next and same edge of following 9 rows. (126 sts.) Now work 2 rows B, 2 rows W, 2 rows B and 4 rows W.
Next row: K.1B, 1W (3B, 1W) to end. Work 4 rows W, beg. with a purl row. Fasten off W and work 7 [9] [11] rows B. *
Next row: (Make buttonholes) K.6 (cast off 4 sts., k.16) 6 times.
Next row: (P.16, cast on 4) 6 times, p.6.
Work 5 rows. K.2 rows. Cast off.

The Bindings
With right-side facing and using No. 11 needles and W pick up and k.60 [66] [72] sts. along lower edge.
Work 7 rows reversed st.st., beg. with a knit row.

Cast off. Work bindings on neck edge to match, picking up 30 [32] [34] sts.

The Left Back. With B cast on 126 sts. K.2 rows. Work 13 [15] [17] rows st.st., beg. with a knit row, then join in W and work 4 rows W. **
Next row: Purl (1W, 3B) to last 2 sts., 1W, 1B.
Work 4 rows W, 2 rows B, 2 rows W and 2 rows B. Continue in patt. as right back, working 5 rows W, then a 2-colour row, *at same time* inc. 1 st. at neck edge on next 10 rows. (136 sts.)
Work 3 rows. Dec. 1 st. at shoulder end on next and every following 6th row until 132 sts. remain. Work 8 rows. Cast off 44 sts. at beg. of next row.
Work 9 rows, then work 0 [4] [8] rows. Cast off. Work bindings to match right back and neck edge.

The Front. Work as Right Back from * to *.
Work a further 9 [11] [13] rows B, then work 4 rows W. Now complete as Left Back from ** to end. With right side facing and using No. 11 needles and W pick up and k.108 [114] [120] sts. along lower edge. Work 7 rows reversed st.st., beg. with a knit row. Cast off. Work binding on neck to match, picking up 60 [62] [64] sts.

The Sleeves (both alike). With No. 9 needles and W cast on 12 sts.
Work 8 rows st.st., casting on 15 sts. at beg. of 2nd, 4th, 6th and 8th rows. (72 sts.)
9th row: Knit (3B, 1W) to end. Continue in patt. as back, inc. 1 st. at end of next row and same edge of every row until there are 96 sts.
Work 32 rows straight. Dec. 1 st. at shaped edge on next row and at this edge of every row until 72 sts. remain. Cast off 15 sts. at beg. of next and 3 following alternate rows. Work 1 row. Cast off 12 sts. With right side facing and using No. 11 needles and W pick up and k.60 sts. along lower edge of sleeve. Work 7 rows reversed st.st., beg. with a knit row. Cast off.

To Make Up. Press work lightly with a warm iron over a damp cloth. Join shoulder and binding seams. Set in sleeves. Join side and sleeve seams. Fold all bindings in half to wrong side and sew down. With B wool work flowers on the broken lines, setting them about 4 ins. apart and in alternate positions as shown. Work the petals of each flower in groups of lazy daisy stitches. Sew on buttons. Sew press stud to neck.

smart boy's pullover

A good design for a six to ten year old boy or girl to wear on school days

Materials. 7 [9] [10] ozs. Sirdar Fontein Crepe Wool, or 6 [8] [9] ozs. Sirdar Majestic Wool 4-ply, or 7 [9] [10] ozs. Sirdar Talisman Knitting Wool 4-ply, or 6 [8] [9] ozs. Sirdar Gaiety Nylon 4-ply.

Measurements. To fit 26 [28] [30] inch chest, (actual measurement 27 [29] [31] inches). Length from top of shoulder—16 [18] [20] inches. Length of sleeve seam—12½ [14½] [16½] inches.

Tension. This paragraph is most important—read it carefully before starting your garment.

To obtain the correct measurements it is essential that you work to the correct tension.

We suggest you work a small sample in the stitch before starting your garment. It is advisable to remove the sample from the machine and as most machines stretch the fabric slightly, leave for a few hours before measuring when the fabric will have returned to the normal tension.

Tension 7¼ stitches to 1 inch measured over the stocking stitch. The ribbed welts are worked at 2 tension settings tighter than the stocking stitch.

Abbreviations. K. knit, p. purl, st(s). stitch(es), beg. beginning, st.st. stocking stitch, h.p. holding position, w.p. working position.

Note—*For the 6 year size read the instructions as given. For larger sizes read the figures within the first brackets, in size order.*

The Back. Cast on 97 [105] [113] sts.
Tension setting for ribbing.
1st row: Knit in k.1, p.1 rib.
Repeat the 1st row 29 times.
Change to tension setting for st.st.
1st row: Knit.
2nd row: Knit.
Continue knitting in st.st. without shaping until the work measures 8 [10] [11] inches from the beginning,

ending with the wool at the right hand side.

Shape Armholes
Cast off 4 [5] [6] sts. at the beg. of each of the next 2 rows. **
Proceed as follows:
1st row: Decrease 1 st. at each end of the row, by transferring the 3rd st. on to the 4th needle at each end (2 sts. now on the 4th needle), then the 2nd st. on to the 3rd needle and the 1st st. on to the 2nd needle at each end. Knit the row. (All decreasings worked at the armhole edge should be worked in this manner).
2nd row: Knit.
3rd row: Knit.
Repeat from the 1st to the 3rd row (inclusive) 16 [12] [18] times, then the 1st and 2nd rows 14 [20] [16] times. 27 [29] [31] sts.
Place the end 23 [25] [27] needles at the right hand side into the h.p., working on the remaining 4 [4] [4] sts. proceed as follows:
1st row: Decrease 1 st. at the neck edge. Knit.
2nd row: Knit.
Repeat the last two rows once then the 1st row once. (1 st.).
Break off the wool and fasten off.
With the carriage at the left hand edge, replace the 23 [25] [27] needles left in the h.p. back into the w.p., rejoin the wool to the left hand edge.
1st row: Cast off 19 [21] [23] sts. at the beg. of the row, decrease 1 st. (as before) at the armhole edge. Knit.
2nd row: Knit.
3rd row: Decrease 1 st. at the neck edge. Knit.
Repeat the 2nd and 3rd rows once. (1 st.).
Break off the wool and fasten off.

The Front. Cast on 97 [105] [113] sts.
Work exactly as given for the Back until ** is reached.
Proceed as follows:
1st row: Decrease 1 st. (as given for the Back) at each end of the row. Knit.
2nd row: Knit.
3rd row: Knit.
Repeat from the 1st to the 3rd row (inclusive) twice. 83 [89] [95] sts.

Divide Neck
Place the end 42 [45] [48] needles at the right hand side into the h.p., working on the remaining 41 [44] [47] sts. proceed as follows:
1st row: Decrease 1 st. (as before) at the armhole edge. Knit.
2nd row: Knit.
*** Knit 40 [28] [46] rows decreasing 1 st. (as before) at the armhole edge on the 2nd and every following 3rd row.

At the same time decrease 1 st. at the neck edge on the next and every following 4th row. 17 [27] [19] sts.

Knit 5 [21] [7] rows decreasing 1 st. (as before) at the armhole edge on the next and every alternate row at the same time decreasing 1 st. at the neck edge on the 1st [1st] [3rd] row and every following 4th row. 12 [10] [13] sts.

Continue knitting decreasing 1 st. (as before) at the armhole edge **only** on the 2nd and every alternate row until 1 [1] [1] st. remains. ***

Break off the wool and fasten off.

With the carriage at the left hand side, replace the 42 [45] [48] needles left in the h.p. back into the w.p., rejoin the wool to the left hand edge.

1st row: Cast off 1 st. at the beg. of row, decrease 1 st. (as before) at the armhole edge. Knit.

2nd row: Knit.

Repeat from *** to *** once.

Break off the wool and fasten off.

The Left Sleeve. Cast on 59 [61] [63] sts.

Tension setting for ribbing.

1st row: Knit in k.1, p.1 rib.

Repeat the 1st row 31 times.

Change to tension setting for st.st.

1st row: Knit.

2nd row: Knit.

Continue knitting increasing 1 st. at both ends of the next and every following 6th row until there are 87 [91] [95] sts.

Continue knitting in st.st. without shaping until the work measure 12½ [14½] [16½] inches from the beginning, ending with the wool at the right hand side.

Shape Top

Cast off 4 [5] [6] sts. at the beg. of each of the next 2 rows.

Proceed as follows:

1st row: Decrease 1 st. (as given for the Back) at each end of the row. Knit.

2nd row: Knit.

3rd row: Knit.

Repeat from the 1st to the 3rd row (inclusive) 8 [6] [14] times, the 1st and 2nd rows 25 [28] [21] times then the 1st row once. 9 [9] [9] sts. ****

Proceed as follows:

1st row: Cast off 4 sts. at the beg. of the row. Knit.

2nd row: Decrease 1 st. (as before) at the left hand edge. Knit.

3rd row: Decrease 1 st. at the right hand edge. Knit.

4th row: Knit.

Repeat the 3rd row twice. (1 st.).

Break off the wool and fasten off.

The Right Sleeve. Cast on 59 [61] [63] sts.

Work exactly as given for the Left Sleeve until **** is

reached.

Proceed as follows:

1st row: Knit.

2nd row: Cast off 4 sts. at the beg. of row, decrease 1 st. (as before) at the right hand edge. Knit.

3rd row: Decrease 1 st. at the left hand edge. Knit.

4th row: Knit.

Repeat the 3rd row twice. (1 st.).

Break off the wool and fasten off.

The Back Neckband. With the carriage at the right hand side and the wrong side of the work facing, pick up and place on to the machine 25 [27] [29] sts. evenly across the back of the neck.

Tension setting for ribbing.

Rejoin the wool to the right hand edge.

1st row: Knit in k.1, p.1 rib.

Repeat the 1st row 9 times.

Cast off loosely in rib.

The Front Neckband. Sew the decreased edges of the sleeves to the decreased edges of the front bodice **only.**

The Left Half. With the carriage at the right hand side and the wrong side of the work facing, pick up and place on to the machine 8 [8] [8] sts. from the top of the left sleeve and 53 [55] [61] sts. evenly along the left side of the neck to the centre V. 61 [63] [69] sts.

Tension setting for ribbing.

Rejoin the wool to the right hand edge.

1st row: Knit in k.1, p.1 rib.

2nd row: Decrease 1 st. at the right hand edge. Knit in k.1, p.1 rib.

Repeat the 1st and 2nd rows 4 times. 56 [58] [64] sts.

Cast off loosely in rib.

The Right Half. With the carriage at the right hand side and the wrong side of the work facing, pick up and place on to the machine 53 [55] [61] sts. evenly along the right side of the neck from the centre V and 8 [8] [8] sts. from the top to the right sleeve. 61 [63] [69] sts.

Tension setting for ribbing.

Rejoin the wool to the right hand edge.

1st row: Knit in k.1, p.1 rib.

2nd row: Decrease 1 st. at the left hand edge. Knit in k.1, p.1 rib.

Repeat the 1st and 2nd rows 4 times. 56 [58] [64] sts.

Cast off loosely in rib.

To Make Up. Press each piece separately on the wrong side under a damp cloth with a warm iron. Sew up the side and sleeve seams. Sew the decreased edges of the sleeves to the decreased edges of the back bodice. Join the ends of the neckband together.

Press all seams.

123

child's fair isle sweater

A classic sweater with bands of Fair Isle in two colours on either sleeve and around the neck and waist to add interest

Materials. 6 [7] [7] ozs. of Emu Scotch 4-ply in White. 1 oz. each in Pink and Green. A pair each of Nos. 10 and 12 knitting needles. A set each of Nos. 10 and 12 double pointed knitting needles.

Measurements. To fit 22 [24] [26] inch chest sizes. Length from shoulders 12 [13½] [15] inches. Sleeve seam 8½ [10½] [12] inches.

Tension 7½ stitches and 9½ rows to 1 inch on No. 10 needles.

Abbreviations. W White, G Green, Pk Pink, st(s) stitch(es), k. knit, p. purl, inc. increase(ing), beg. beginning, st.st. stocking stitch (1 row knit, 1 row purl alternately), patt. pattern, rep. repeat, in. inch(es), dec. decrease, sl. slip, p.s.s.o. pass slipped stitch over, tog. together.

Note—*Instructions are given for 1st size; figures in brackets are for 2nd and 3rd sizes, in size order.*
Where one figure only is given, this applies to all three sizes.

The Back. With No. 12 needles and W. Wool, cast on 90 [98] [106] sts. Work 16 rows in k.1, p.1 rib, inc. 1 st. at end of last row. 91 [99] [107] sts.
Change to No. 10 needles. Beg. with a knit row, work 2 rows st.st. Join in G, then work Fair Isle patt. as follows:-
1st row: K. * 1 W, 1 G, rep. from * to last st., 1 W.
2nd row: P. * 1 G, 1 W, rep. from * to last st., 1 G.
3rd row: K. in W.

1st and 3rd sizes only. Join in Pk.
4th row: P.11 W, * 2 Pk, 1 W, 2 Pk, 11 W, rep. from * to end.

2nd size only. Join in Pk.
4th row: P.1 Pk, 1 W, 2 Pk, 11 W, * 2 Pk, 1 W, 2 Pk, 11 W, rep. from * to last 4 sts., 2 Pk, 1 W, 1 Pk.

All sizes
5th row: As 4th row, but knit instead of purl.

1st and 3rd sizes only
6th row: P.2 Pk, * 7 W, 2 Pk, (1 W, 1 Pk) twice, 1 W, 2 Pk, rep. from * to last 9 sts., 7 W, 2 Pk.

2nd size only
6th row: P.1 Pk, 1 W, 1 Pk, 1 W, 2 Pk, * 7 W, 2 Pk, (1 W, 1 Pk) twice, 1 W, 2 Pk, rep. from * to last 13 sts., 7 W, 2 Pk, (1 W, 1 Pk) twice.

1st and 3rd sizes only
7th row: K.2 Pk, * (2 W, 3 Pk) twice, 1 W, 1 Pk, 1 W, 3 Pk, rep. from * to last 9 sts., 2 W, 3 Pk, 2 W, 2 Pk.

2nd size only
7th row: K.1 W, 1 Pk, 1 W, 3 Pk, * (2 W, 3 Pk) twice, 1 W, 1 Pk, 1 W, 3 Pk, rep. from * to last 13 sts., 2 W, 3 Pk, 2 W, 3 Pk, 1 W, 1 Pk, 1 W.

1st and 3rd sizes only
8th row: P.3 W, * 2 Pk, 1 W, 2 Pk, 4 W, 3 Pk, 4 W, rep. from * to last 8 sts., 2 Pk, 1 W, 2 Pk, 3 W.

2nd size only
8th row: P.3 Pk, 4 W, * 2 Pk, 1 W, 2 Pk, 4 W, 3 Pk, 4 W, rep. from * to last 12 sts., 2 Pk, 1 W, 2 Pk, 4 W, 3 Pk.

All sizes
9th row: As 7th row.
10th row: As 6th row.
11th row: As 5th row.
12th row: As 4th row.
13th row: Knit in W.
14th row: As 2nd row.
15th row: As 1st row.
16th row: Purl in W.
Break off Contrast wools. Beg. with a knit row, continue in st.st. to end. Work straight until back measures 7 [8] [9] in. from beg., ending at finish of a purl row.

Shape Armholes
Cast off 3 [4] [5] sts. at beg. of next 2 rows, then dec. 1 st. at both ends of next row and 5 following alternate rows. 73 [79] [85] sts. Work straight for 17 [21] [27] rows.

Shape Neck

Next row: K.25 [28] [31] sts., cast off next 23 sts., knit to end. Continue on 2nd set of sts. thus:-

*** Cast off 4 sts. at beg. of next 2 rows that start from neck end, then 3 sts. at beg. of following 2 alternate rows, and 2 sts. at beg. of next 2 alternate rows. ***

Work 3 rows straight. Cast off.

With wrong side of work facing, rejoin wool to inner end of 1st set of sts. and complete to match left side.

The Front. Work as for Back until armhole shapings have been completed. Then work 11 [15] [21] rows straight.

Shape Neck

Next row: K.27 [30] [33] sts., cast off next 19 sts., knit to end. Work on 2nd set of 27 [30] [33] sts. as for Back neck shaping from *** to ***. Work 1 row straight then dec. 1 st. at neck edge on next row and following alternate row. Work 5 rows straight. Cast off.

With wrong side of work facing, rejoin wool to inner end of 1st set of sts. and complete to match right side.

The Yoke. Join shoulders and press seams. With 1st of the set of 4 No. 10 needles, W wool and right side of work facing, pick up and knit 81 sts. round front neck. On 2nd needle pick up and knit 36 sts. as far as centre back neck. On 3rd needle pick up and knit 35 sts. from remainder of back neck. 152 sts. Join in G and Pk.
Work Fair Isle patt. in rounds of all knit, as follows:-

1st round: * 1 W, 1 G; rep. from * to end.

2nd round: * 1 G, 1 W; rep. from * to end.

3rd round: Knit in W.

4th round: 2 Pk, 1 W, 2 Pk, (1 W, sl.1, k.1 W, p.s.s.o.) twice, 3 W, (k.2 tog. W, 1 W) twice, * 2 Pk, 1 W, 2 Pk, 1 W, sl. 1, k.1 W, p.s.s.o., 7 W, k.2 tog. W, 1 W * rep. from * to * once more, ** 2 Pk, 1 W, 2 Pk, (1 W, sl.1, k.1 W, p.s.s.o.) twice, 3 W, (k.2 tog. W, 1 W) twice **; rep. from ** to ** once more, then rep. from * to * twice more, 2 Pk, 1 W, 2 Pk, (1 W, sl.1, k.1 W, p.s.s.o.) twice, 3 W, (k.2 tog. W, 1 W) twice. 128 sts.

5th round: * 2 Pk, 1 W, 2 Pk, 11 W; rep. from * to end.

6th round: * (1 W, 1 Pk) twice, 1 W, 2 Pk, 7 W, 2 Pk; rep. from * to end.

7th round: * (1 Pk, 1 W) twice, (3 Pk, 2 W) twice, 2 Pk; rep. from * to end.

8th round: * 1 W, 3 Pk, 4 W, 2 Pk, 1 W, 2 Pk, 3 W; rep. from * to end.

9th round: As 7th round.

10th round: As 6th round.

11th round: As 5th round.

12th round: As 5th round.

13th round: In W * k.5, (k.2 tog., k.1) 3 times, k.2 tog., rep. from * to end. 96 sts.

14th round: As 2nd round.

15th round: As 1st round.

16th round: Knit in W.

Change to the set of No. 12 needles and work 6 rounds in k.1, p.1 rib. Cast off loosely in rib.

The Sleeves (both alike). With No. 12 needles and W wool, cast on 48 [50] [52] sts. Work 16 rows in k.1, p.1 rib, inc. 1 st. at end of last row. 49 [51] [53] sts. Change to No. 10 needles. Beg. with a knit row, work 2 rows in st.st. Join in G. Now work Fair Isle patt. thus:-

1st row: K.1 W, * 1 G, 1 W; rep. from * to end.

2nd row: P.1 G, * 1 W, 1 G; rep. from * to end.

3rd row: Knit in W. Join in Pk.

4th row: P.6 [7] [8] W, * 2 Pk, 1 W, 2 Pk, 11 W; rep. from *, ending last rep. with 6 [7] [8] W, instead of 11 W.

5th row: Knit as 4th row.

6th row: P.4 [5] [6] W, * 2 Pk, (1 W, 1 Pk) twice, 1 W, 2 Pk, 7 W; rep. from *, ending last rep. with 4 [5] [6] W, instead of 7 W.

1st and 2nd sizes only

7th row: K.2 [3] Pk, * 2 W, 3 Pk, 1 W, 1 Pk, 1 W, 3 Pk, 2 W, 3 Pk; rep. from *, ending last rep. with 2 [3] Pk, instead of 3 Pk.

3rd size only

7th row: K.1 W, 3 Pk, * 2 W, 3 Pk, 1 W, 1 Pk, 1 W, 3 Pk, 2 W, 3 Pk; rep. from * to last st., 1 W.

1st size only

8th row: P.1 W, * 2 Pk, 4 W, 3 Pk, 4 W, 2 Pk, 1 W; rep from * to end.

2nd and 3rd sizes only

8th row: P.1 [2] Pk, 1 W, * 2 Pk, 4 W, 3 Pk, 4 W, 2 Pk, 1 W; rep. from * to last 1 [2] sts., 1 [2] Pk.

Now work backwards, from 7th row to 1st row inclusive. Break off Contrast colours.

Next row: P. in W. Continue working in st.st. to end. Inc. 1 st. at each end of next row and every following 6th row, until there are 65 [71] [77] sts. Work straight until sleeve measures 8½ [10½] [12] in. from beg., ending with a purl row.

Shape Top

Cast off 3 [4] [5] sts. at beg. of next 2 rows, then dec. 1 st. at both ends of next row and following 12 [13] [14] alternate rows. Purl next row, then cast off 2 sts. at beg. of next 6 rows. Cast off remaining sts.

To Make Up. Press pieces on wrong sides with a warm iron over a damp cloth, avoiding ribbing. Sew sleeves into armholes, then join side and sleeve seams. Press seams.

Materials. 10 [11] [12] ozs. Bairnswear La Laine 4-ply in Main Colour (M), 1 oz. in Contrast (C). 1 Pair Nos. 10 and 12 Knitting Needles. A 4 inch Zip Fastener.

Measurements. To fit bust 34 [36] [38] inches. Length 23¾ [24] [24¼] inches. Sleeve seam 14½ [14½] [15] inches.

Tension 7 stitches to 1 inch on No. 10 needles.

Abbreviations. K. knit, p. purl, sts. stitches, st.st. stocking stitch, rem. remain, cont. continue, patt. pattern, rep. repeat, inc. increase, dec. decrease, beg. beginning, alt. alternate, foll. following, ins. inches.

The Front. With No. 12 needles and C, cast on 126 [134] [140] sts. Beg. with purl row, work 5 rows st.st. Break off C, join in M. With M, beg. with purl row, work 3 rows st.st.

Change to No. 10 needles and work in st.st. in patt. from chart, odd rows knit, even rows purl. Blank squares indicate M sts., crosses C stitches. Each leaf motif requires approx. 2½ yards of C wool.

1st row: K.3 [5] [6] M, * work 36-st. patt. as chart (1st row), k.6 [8] [10] M. Rep. from * once more, work 36-st. patt. as chart, k.3 [5] [6] M.

2nd row: P.3 [5] [6] M, * work 36-st. patt. as chart (2nd row), p.6 [8] [10] M. Rep. from * once more, work 36-st. patt. as chart, p.3 [5] [6] M.

Cont. in patt. as set until 20 rows have been completed. Break off C and cont. in st.st. in M until work measures 15½ ins. from beg.

Shape Armholes

Cast off 7 [8] [9] sts. at beg. of next 2 rows. Dec. 1 st. at both ends of next and alt. rows to 96 [100] [104] sts. ** Cont. straight until armholes measure 5¼ [6] [6¼] ins., ending after purl row.

Shape Neck

Next row: K.41 [42] [43], turn. Leave rem. sts. on spare needle.

Next row: Purl.

Dec. 1 st. at neck edge on next and alt. rows to 32 [33] [34] sts. Cont. straight until armhole measures 8¼ [8½] [8¾] ins., ending at armhole edge.

light and leafy

A fine-knit classic sweater bordered with leaves in a contrast colour

Shape Shoulder

Cast off 11 sts. at beg. of next and foll. alt. row. 10 [11] [12] sts. on foll. alt. row. Return to sts. on spare needle, sl. first 14 [16] [18] sts. on to needle and leave for neck, join wool to rem. sts. and work 2 rows. Complete to match other side.

The Back. Work as front to **. Cont. straight until armholes measure 4 [4½] [4½] ins., ending after purl row.

Divide for Back Opening

Next row: K.48 [50] [52], turn. Leave rem. sts. on spare needle. Work on 1st set of sts. until armhole measures as front to shoulder, ending armhole edge.

Shape Shoulder

Cast off 11 sts. at beg. of next and foll. alt. row. 10 [11] [12] sts. on foll. alt. row. Leave rem. sts. on spare needle. Join wool to rem. sts. and complete to match.

The Sleeves (both alike). With No. 12 needles and C, cast on 62 [68] [72] sts.

Beg. with purl row, work 5 rows st.st. Break off C, join in M.

Beg. with purl row, cont. in st.st., inc. 1 st. at both ends of 4th and every foll. 6th row to 100 [106] [112] sts. Cont. straight until sleeve measures 14½ [14½] [15] ins.

Shape Top

Cast off 7 [8] [9] sts. at beg. of next 2 rows. Dec. 1 st. at both ends of next and every foll. 4th row to 80 [84] [88] sts., at both ends of alt. rows to 58 sts. Dec. 1 st. at both ends of every row to 34 sts. Cast off.

The Neckband. Join shoulder seams. With No. 12 needles and C and right-side facing, beg. at left back neck, knit up 102 [106] [110] sts. round neck. Beg. with knit row, work 5 rows st.st. Cast off loosely.

To Make Up. Press lightly with a warm iron over a damp cloth. Join side and sleeve seams. Sew in sleeves. Sew in zip. Press seams.

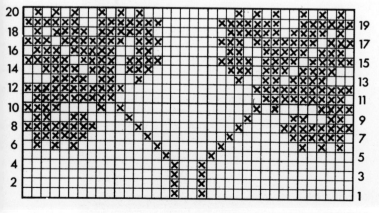

snug little rug

Materials. 10 two-oz. balls Sirdar Pullman Main Colour; 8 two-oz. balls of White; two long No. 4 knitting needles.

Size. 30 inches by 22 inches.

Tension 11 stitches to 2 inches.

Abbreviations. K. knit, p. purl, st(s). stitch(es), ins. inches, tog. together, patt. pattern, rep. repeat, MC main wool colour.

Main Part. With MC cast on 110 sts.
1st row (wrong side): P.1, * work (k.1, p.1, k.1, p.1, k.1) all in next st., p.5 tog.; rep. from * to last st., k.1.
2nd row: P.
3rd row: P.1, * p.5 tog., work (k.1, p.1, k.1, p.1, k.1) all in next st.; rep. from * to last st., p.1.
4th row: P.
These 4 rows form patt. Continue until work measures 28 ins., ending with a 1st or 3rd patt. row. Cast off.
Make another piece in White to match. Press pieces.

Borders. With MC, place 2 Main Pieces tog. and with White side towards you, pick up and k. 88 sts. working through both cast-off edges tog. **Join another length of MC and using wool double work 3 rows in k.1, p.1 rib, inc. 1 st. each end of 2nd row. Cast off loosely ribwise **. Work along cast-on edges to match. With MC pick up and k.118 sts. along one side edge, with White side towards you and working through both edges tog. as before. Rep. from ** to **. Work along other side edge to match. Join the corners. Sew in ends.

four toys they will treasure

Mother and Baby Zebra and the Lion and Lion Cub (overleaf) are soft cuddly toys that will bring joy at bedtime and will be a pleasure to make

MOTHER AND BABY ZEBRA

Materials. *Mother:* 2 two-oz. hanks Patons Big Ben in Black. 4 two-oz. hanks in White. 1 oz. Patons Double Knitting in Black. 1 pair each No. 7 and No. 11 Knitting Needles.
Baby: 2 oz. Patons Double Knitting in White, 1 oz. in Black. 1 pair No. 11 Knitting Needles.
Washable stuffing. Red Ribbon: 1 yd., $1\frac{1}{2}$ ins. wide for Mother; $\frac{1}{2}$ yd., 1 in. wide for Baby.

Measurements. *Mother:* Length of body, 12 inches. Height to top of Head 17 inches.
Baby: Length of body, 8 inches. Height, 12 inches.

Tension *Mother:* **4 stitches to 1 inch.** *Baby:* **7 stitches to 1 inch.**

Abbreviations. K. knit, st(s). stitch(es), ins. inches, g.st. garter stitch, inc. increase, dec. decrease, tog. together, beg. beginning, patt. pattern, rep. repeat, ch. chain, B Black, W White, D.K. Double Knitting.

Note—*Toys are teasle brushed when completed to give a fluffy look.*

Note—*Work in g.st. throughout. All parts of mother except hooves are worked on No. 7 needles with Big Ben.*

MOTHER ZEBRA

The Body. With W cast on 40 sts. K.2 rows. Now work in stripes of 2 rows B, 4 rows W until 14 B stripes are worked.

Next row: With W k.18, (k.2 tog.) twice, k.18.

Cast off. Fold in half lengthwise. Join seam, leaving one end open for stuffing. Stuff firmly and join opening.

The Front Legs (two). With W cast on 14 sts. K.4 rows W, 2 rows B. Rep. last 6 rows once, inc. 1 st. each end of 6th row. Rep. last 12 rows twice. K.4 rows W, 2 rows B, 4 rows W, 1 row B.

Next row: With B k.2 tog., k.6, (k.2 tog.) twice, k.6, k.2 tog.

K.4 rows W.

Next row: K.2 tog., k.4, (k.2 tog.) twice, k.4, k.2 tog.

Cast off. Join side seam. Stuff firmly.

The Back Legs (two). Work 24 rows as front legs.

Next row: With W inc. in each of first 2 sts., k.7, turn. Continue on these sts. only.

Next row: With W k.2 tog., k.8 inc. in last st.

Next row: With W inc. in first st., k. to end.

K.1 row W, dec. 1 st. at beg. and inc. 1 st. at end. With B work 1 row, inc. 1 st. at beg. and dec. 1 st. at end. With B work 1 row, dec. 1 st. at beg. and inc. 1 st. at end. With W rep. last 2 rows twice.

K. (2 rows B, 4 rows W) 3 times, dec. 1 st. each end of last row. K.1 row B, dec. 1 st. each end of row. Cast off. Complete other side to match. Join short, centre seam, then join side seam. Stuff firmly.

continued overleaf

continued from previous page

The Hooves (four). With No. 11 needles and D.K. cast on 19 sts. K. 1 row. Inc. 1 st. each end of next row. Rep. last 2 rows until there are 29 sts. Cast off. Fold in half and join seam, leaving cast-off edge open. Stuff and sew to end of leg. Sew legs to body.

The Head (two pieces alike). With W cast on 19 sts. K.5 rows. Dec. 1 st. at beg. of next row. K.3 rows. Dec. 1 st. at beg. and inc. 1 st. at end of next row. Rep. last 4 rows twice.

Cast on 11 sts. at beg. of next row. Dec. 1 st. at beg. of next row. Inc. 1 st. at beg. and dec. 1 st. at end of next row. K.5 rows. Dec. 1 st. at end of next row. Rep. last 6 rows once.

K.3 rows. Dec. 1 st. each end of next row.

Now shape thus:

Next 2 rows: K.7, turn, k. back to end.

Next 2 rows: K. 8, turn, k. back to end. Continue shaping thus working 1 st. more on next and every alternate row until k.15, turn, k. back to end has been worked.

Next row: K.2 tog., k. across all sts.

Next row: Cast off 11, k. to last 2 sts., k.2 tog. Cast off.

Join pieces tog., leaving neck end open. Stuff firmly and sew to body. With B work stripes on head and neck with long straight stitches. For nose work a circle of ch.st. with B, fill in with satin st. For eyes work an oval of ch.st. with B. Work pupil in satin st. with B, with 1 W st. at inner corner.

The Ears: (2 B, 2 W). Cast on 3 sts. K.3 rows. Inc. 1 st. each end of next row. Rep. last 4 rows 3 times. K.4 rows.

Next row: K.4, k.3 tog., k.4.

Next row: K.3, k.3 tog., k.3. Cast off. Join tog. in pairs. Sew to head as shown.

The Mane. With B cast on 40 sts.

Loopstitch row: K.1, (insert needle in next st., wind wool once around first finger of left hand and right hand needle, draw loop through, place on left hand needle and p. tog. with st.) to last st., k.1. Cast off. Sew mane to head.

For tail cut 8 strands of B 15 ins. long, knot tog. in middle and sew knot to body. Tie ribbon around neck in bow.

BABY ZEBRA

With No. 11 needles and D.K. work body, legs, head, ears and mane as for Mother Zebra.

The Hooves. With B cast on 10 sts. K.1 row. Inc. 1 st. each end of next row. Rep. last 2 rows until there are 20 sts. Cast off. Make up as for Mother Zebra. For tail cut 10 strands B, 10 ins. long. Make up as for Mother Zebra. Tie ribbon around neck in bow.

FATHER LION AND CUB

Materials. *Lion:* 6 two-oz. hanks Patons Big Ben in Gold. Oddments of Brown, Rust and Black Double Knitting. 1 pair No. 8 Knitting Needles.

Cub: 5 oz. Patons Double Knitting in Gold. Oddments Double Knitting as for Lion. 1 pair No. 11 Knitting Needles.

Washable stuffing. Purple Ribbon: 1 yd., 1½ ins. wide for Lion; ½ yd., 1 in. wide for Cub.

Measurements. *Lion:* Length of body 12 inches. Height to top of head 10 inches.

Cub: Length of body 10½ inches. Height to top of head 7 inches.

Tension *Lion:* **4 stitches to 1 inch.** *Cub:* **7 stitches to 1 inch.**

Abbreviations. K. knit, st(s). stitch(es), ins. inches, g.st. garter stitch, inc. increase, dec. decrease, tog. together, beg. beginning, patt. pattern, rep. repeat, ch. chain, B Black, D.K. Double Knitting.

Note—*Toys are teasle brushed when completed to give a fluffy look.*

Note—*Work throughout in g.st.*

FATHER LION

The Body. Cast on 43 sts. K.54 rows.

Next row: K.2 tog., k.18, k.3 tog., k.18, k.2 tog.

K.17 rows.

Next row: Inc. in 1st st., k.18, inc. in next st., k.18, inc. in last st.

K.5 rows.

Next row: K.19, (k.2 tog.) twice, k.19.

K.1 row. Cast off. Fold in half lengthwise, and join seam, leaving one end open. Stuff firmly and join opening.

The Front Legs (4 pieces alike). Cast on 8 sts. K.1 row. Inc. 1 st. each end of next row. Rep. last 2 rows once. K.7 rows. Dec. 1 st. each end of next row. K.1 row.

Next row: K.4, k.2 tog., k.4.

K.5 rows.

Inc. 1 st. each end of next row.

K.9 rows. Rep. last 10 rows once.

K.11 rows.

Dec. 1 st. each end of next row. K.1 row. Rep. last 2 rows once. Dec. 1 st. each end of next row. Cast off. Join pieces tog. in pairs, leaving one end open. Stuff firmly and join opening. Sew legs to body as shown in photograph.

The Back Legs and Foot (2 pieces alike for each)

The Leg. Cast on 25 sts. K.1 row. Inc. 1 st. each end of next row. Rep. last 2 rows once. K.7 rows. Dec. 1 st. each end of next row *.

Cast off 11 sts. at beg. of next row. Dec. 1 st. each end of next row. K.5 rows. Inc. 1 st. each end of next row. K.5 rows. Dec. 1 st. each end of next row. K.1 row. Rep. last 2 rows twice. Dec. 1 st. each end of next 3 rows. Cast off. Join pieces tog., leaving an opening. Stuff firmly and join opening.

The Foot. As Leg to *. K.1 row. Dec. 1 st. at end of next row. Cast off. Join pieces, leaving opening. Stuff firmly and join opening. Mark toes with B straight stitches. Sew leg to left side of body as shown. Sew foot to body just behind left back leg.

The Head (2 pieces alike). Cast on 14 sts. K.5 rows. Inc. 1 st. at end of next row. K.1 row. Rep. last 2 rows twice. Inc. 1 st. at end of next row. Cast on 7 sts. at beg. of next row. Inc. 1 st. at end of next row. K.13 rows. Dec. 1 st. at end of next row and 1 st. at beg. of following row. Rep. last 2 rows 5 times. Dec. 1 st. each end of next 3 rows. Cast off.

The Gusset. Cast on 2 sts. K.1 row. Inc. 1 st. each end of next row. K.3 rows. Rep. last 4 rows 4 times. K.25 rows. Dec. 1 st. each end of next row. K.3 rows. Rep. last 4 rows 4 times. Cast off.

Sew gusset between head pieces with point at tip of nose.

Join front neck seam. Stuff firmly and sew to body. With B work nose and mouth in satin stitch and whiskers with long straight stitches. For eyes work a circle of ch.st. with B. Work centres in satin stitch with rust with 1 B st. in middle. Work 1 straight stitch with B over each eye for eyebrows.

The Ears (4 pieces alike). Cast on 5 sts. K.3 rows. Inc. 1 st. each end of next row. Rep. last 4 rows 3 times. K.1 row.

Next row: K.2 tog., k.3, k.3 tog., k.3, k.2 tog. Cast off.

Join pieces tog. in pairs and sew to head. For mane, knot lengths, varying from 2½ to 8 ins., all over top and back of head with lengths of rust and brown here and there.

The Tail. Cast on 3 sts. K.3 rows. Inc. 1 st. each end of next row. Rep. last 4 rows once. K.30 rows. Inc. 1 st. each end of next row. Rep. last 31 rows once. K.4 rows. Cast off. Fold in half lengthwise. Join seam, stuffing as you sew. Sew tail to body. Knot 5 in. lengths of wool as for head around end of tail.

Tie ribbon in bow around neck.

LION CUB

With D.K. and No. 11 needles work all parts except body as for Lion, working two back legs as back leg of Lion and omitting foot.

The Body. Cast on 43 sts. K.70 rows. Cast off. Make up as for Lion's body. Tie ribbon in bow around neck.

aran sweaters for boys

The heavy, chunky, style of an Aran Sweater has long been a favourite for men. Here are instructions for a design in five smaller sizes that any boy will enjoy wearing

Materials. 7 [8] [8] [9] [9] 2-oz. balls Regency Bainin Double Knitting Wool. 1 Pair each Nos. 8 and 10 Knitting Needles. 1 Set of four No. 10 Double-Pointed Needles.

Measurements. To fit chest 24 [26] [28] [30] [32] inches. Length 18 [19½] [21] [22½] [24] inches. Sleeve seam 12 [13] [14] [15] [16] inches.

Tension 5 stitches and 7 rows to 1 inch over double moss stitch on No. 8 needles.

Abbreviations. K. knit, p. purl, st(s). stitch(es), d.m.st. double moss stitch, patt. pattern, rep. repeat, beg. beginning, tog. together, sl. slip, dec. decrease, inc. increase, p.u.k. pick up loop lying between needles and knit into back of it, c.n. cable needle, ins. inches, C.4 cable 4 (sl. next 2 sts. on c.n. and leave at front of work, k.2, then knit the 2 sts. from c.n.), C.5 cable 5 (sl. next 3 sts. on c.n. and leave at front of work, p.2, then purl the 3 sts. from c.n.), Cr.3 F.P. cross 3 front purlwise (sl. next st. on c.n. and leave at front of work, p.2, then k.1 from c.n.), Cr. 3 B.P. cross 3 back purlwise (sl. next 2 sts. on c.n. and leave at back of work, k.1, then p.2 from c.n.), Cr. 3 F.K. cross 3 front knitwise (sl. next 2 sts. on c.n. and leave at front of work, p.1, then k.2 from c.n.), Cr.3 B.K. cross 3 back knitwise (sl. next st. on c.n. and leave at back of work, k.2, then p.1 from c.n.).

Note—*Instructions for the larger sizes are in brackets in size order. Where one figure only is given, this applies to all sizes.*

The Back. With No. 10 needles cast on 68 [72] [76] [80] [84] sts. Work 2 [2] [2½] [2½] [3] ins. k.1, p.1 rib.

Inc. row: Rib 8 [2] [6] [10] [4], * inc. in next st., rib 5 [6] [6] [6] [7], rep. from * to end. 78 [82] [86] [90] [94] sts. Change to No. 8 needles and proceed in patt.

1st row: (Right side) K.1, (p.1, k.1) 2 [3] [3] [4] [5] times, * k.1, k.4, p.5, k.2, p.1, k.2, p.5, k.4, p.1, * k.1, p.16 [16] [20] [20] [20], k.1. Rep. from * to *, k.1, (p.1, k.1) 2 [3] [3] [4] [5] times.

2nd row: P.1, (k.1, p.1) 2 [3] [3] [4] [5] times, * k.1, p.4, k.4, Cr.3 F.P., p.1, Cr.3 B.P., k.4, p.4, k.1, * p.1, (p.3 tog.,

k.1, p.1 and k.1 all into next st.) 4 [4] [5] [5] [5] times, p.1. Rep. from * to *, p.1, (k.1, p.1) to end.

3rd row: P.1, (k.1, p.1) 2 [3] [3] [4] [5] times, * p.1, C.4, p.4, k.2, p.1, k.1, p.1, k.2, p.4, C.4, p.1, * k.1, p.16 [16] [20] [20] [20], k.1. Rep. from * to *, p.1, (k.1, p.1) to end.

4th row: K.1, (p.1, k.1) 2 [3] [3] [4] [5] times, * k.1, p.4, k.3, Cr.3 F.P., p.1, k.1, p.1, Cr.3 B.P., k.3, p.4, k.1, * p.1, (k.1, p.1 and k.1 all into next st., p.3 tog.) 4 [4] [5] [5] [5] times, p.1. Rep. from * to *, k.1, (k.1, p.1) to end.

N.B.—The first and last 5 [7] [7] [9] [11] sts. of each of these 4 rows form d.m.st. which is repeated throughout.

5th row: D.m.st. 5 [7] [7] [9] [11], * p.1, k.4, p.3, k.2, (p.1, k.1) twice, p.1, k.2, p.3, k.4, p.1, * k.1, p.16 [16] [20] [20] [20], k.1. Rep. from * to *, d.m.st. to end.

6th row: D.m.st. 5[7][7][9][11], * k.1, p.4, k.2, Cr. 3 F.P., (p.1, k.1) twice, p.1, Cr. 3 B.P., k.2, p.4, k.1, * p.1, (p.3 tog., k.1, p.1 and k.1 all into next st.) 4 [4] [5] [5] [5] times, p.1. Rep. from * to *, d.m.st. to end.

7th row: D.m.st. 5 [7] [7] [9] [11], * p.1, C.4, p.2, k.2, (p.1, k.1) 3 times, p.1, k.2, p.2, C.4, p.1, * k.1, p.16 [16] [20] [20] [20], k.1. Rep. from * to *, d.m.st. to end.

8th row: D.m.st. 5[7][7][9][11], * k.1, p.4, k.1, Cr.3 F.P., (p.1, k.1) 3 times, p.1, Cr. 3 B.P., k.1, p.4, k.1, * p.1, (k.1, p.1 and k.1 all into next st., p.3 tog.) 4 [4] [5] [5] [5] times, p.1. Rep. from * to *, d.m.st. to end.

9th row: D.m.st. 5[7][7][9][11], * p.1, k.4, p.1, Cr. 3 F.K., (k.1, p.1) 3 times, k.1, Cr.3 B.K., p.1, k.4, p.1, * k.1, p.16 [16] [20] [20] [20], k.1. Rep. from * to *, d.m.st. to end.

10th row: D.m.st. 5 [7] [7] [9] [11], * k.1, p.4, k.2, p.2, (k.1, p.1) 3 times, k.1, p.2, k.2, p.4, k.1, * p.1, (p.3 tog., k.1, p.1 and k.1 all into next st.) 4 [4] [5] [5] [5] times, p.1. Rep. from * to *, d.m.st. to end.

11th row: D.m.st. 5 [7] [7] [9] [11], * p.1, C.4, p.2, Cr.3 F.K., (k.1, p.1) twice, k.1, Cr.3 B.K., p.2, C.4, p.1, * k.1, p.16 [16] [20] [20] [20], k.1. Rep. from * to *, d.m.st. to end.

12th row: D.m.st. 5 [7] [7] [9] [11], * k.1, p.4, k.3, p.2, (k.1, p.1) twice, k.1, p.2, k.3, p.4, k.1, * p.1, (k.1, p.1 and k.1 all into next st., p.3 tog.) 4 [4] [5] [5] [5] times, p.1. Rep. from * to *, d.m.st. to end.

13th row: D.m.st. 5 [7] [7] [9] [11], * p.1, k.4, p.3, Cr.3 F.K., k.1, p.1, k.1, Cr.3 B.K., p.3, k.4, p.1, * k.1,

p.16 [16] [20] [20] [20], k.1. Rep. from * to *, d.m.st. to end.

14th row: D.m.st. 5 [7] [7] [9] [11], * k.1, p.4, k.4, p.2, k.1, p.1, k.1, p.2, k.4, p.4, k.1, * p.1, (p.3 tog., k.1, p.1 and k.1 all into next st.) 4 [4] [5] [5] [5] times, p.1. Rep. from * to *, d.m.st. to end.

15th row: D.m.st. 5 [7] [7] [9] [11], * p.1, C.4, p.4, Cr.3 F.K., k.1, Cr.3 B.K., p.4, C.4, p.1, * k.1, p.16 [16]

[20] [20] [20], k.1. Rep. from * to *, d.m.st. to end.

16th row: D.m.st. 5 [7] [7] [9] [11], * k.1, p.4, k.5, C.5, k.5, p.4, k.1, * p.1, (k.1, p.1 and k.1 all into next st., p.3 tog.) 4 [4] [5] [5] [5] times, p.1. Rep. from * to *, d.m.st. to end.

These 16 rows form the patt. Rep. them until work measures $11\frac{1}{2}$ [$12\frac{1}{2}$] [$13\frac{1}{2}$] [$14\frac{1}{2}$] [$15\frac{1}{2}$] ins. from cast-on edge, ending with a wrong-side row.

continued overleaf

continued from previous page

Shape Raglan

Cast off 2 sts. at beg. of next 2 rows, then dec. 1 st. each end of next and every alternate row until 30 [30] [32] [32] [32] sts. remain. Cast off loosely.

The Front. Work as given for Back until 38 [38] [40] [40] [40] sts. remain when shaping raglan, ending with a wrong-side row.

Divide for Neck

Next row: K.2 tog., patt. 7, turn and leave remaining sts. on a spare needle.

Work on first set of sts. as follows:

** Dec. 1 st. each end of every alternate row until 2 sts. remain.

P.1 row. Cast off. **

Join wool to inner end of sts. on spare needle, cast off next 20 [20] [22] [22] [22] sts., patt. to last 2 sts., k.2 tog. Now work as first side from ** to **.

The Sleeves (both alike). With No. 10 needles cast on 40 [40] [40] [44] [44] sts.

Work 1½ [1½] [2] [2] [2½] ins. k.1, p.1 rib.

Inc. row: Rib 5 [5] [5] [6] [6] sts., (p.u.k., rib 2) to last 3 [3] [3] [6] [6] sts., rib to end. 56 [56] [56] [60] [60] sts.

Change to No. 8 needles and proceed in patt.:

1st row: (Right side) K.1, (p.1, k.1) 1 [1] [1] [2] [2] times. Rep. from * to * of 1st row of original patt. twice, k.1, (p.1, k.1) 1 [1] [1] [2] [2] times.

2nd to 16th rows: Work in patt. as set, beg. and ending with 3 [3] [3] [5] [5] sts. in d.m.st. as 1st row and working from * to * of corresponding original patt. rows.

Keeping patt. correct and working the extra sts. into d.m.st., inc. 1 st. each end of next and every following 14th [14th] [12th] [12th] [8th] row to 62 [66] [70] [74] [78] sts.

Work straight until sleeve measures 12 [13] [14] [15] [16] ins. from cast-on edge.

Shape Raglan

As back raglan shaping until 14 [14] [16] [16] [16] sts. remain. Cast off loosely.

The Neckband. Join raglan seams. With right-side facing, join wool to neck and using 3 of the set of No. 10 needles, as required, knit up 80 [84] [88] [92] [96] sts. all round neck. Using 4th needle, work 12 [12] [14] [14] [16] rows k.1, p.1 rib. Cast off.

To Make Up. Press work lightly on wrong side with a warm iron over a damp cloth. Join side and sleeve seams. Double neckband to wrong side and slip-stitch in position.

Press all the seams carefully.

machine knit raglan-sleeved cardigan in five sizes

The simplicity of the design pictured overleaf adds to the smartly tailored appearance of a comfortable cardigan

Materials. 14 [14] [15] [15] [16] ozs. Sirdar Majestic Wool 4-ply, or 16 [16] [17] [17] [18] ozs. Sirdar Talisman Knitting Wool 4-ply, or 16 [16] [17] [17] [18] ozs. Sirdar Fontein Crepe Wool. 6 Buttons.

Measurements. Width all round at underarm—36 [38] [40] [42] [44] inches. Length from top of shoulder—26 [26] [26] [26] [26] inches. Length of sleeve seam 20 [20] [20] [20] [20] inches.

Tension. This paragraph is most important—read it carefully before starting your garment.

To obtain the correct measurements it is essential that you work to the tension stated.

We suggest you work a small sample in the stitch before starting your garment. It is advisable to remove the sample from the machine and as most machines stretch the fabric slightly, leave for a few hours before measuring when the fabric will have returned to the normal tension.

Tension 7¼ stitches to one inch, measured over the stocking stitch. The ribbed welts are worked at a tension setting 2 settings tighter than the stocking stitch.

Abbreviations. K. knit, p. purl, beg. beginning, st(s). stitch(es). st.st. stocking stitch.

The Back. Cast on 133 [139] [145] [153] [159] sts.
Tension setting for ribbing.
1st row: Knit in k.1, p.1 rib.
Repeat the 1st row 19 times.
Change to the tension setting for st.st.
1st row: Knit.
2nd row: Knit.
Continue knitting in st.st. without shaping until the work measures 15 inches from the beginning, ending with the wool at the right hand side.
Shape Armholes
1st row: Cast off 7 [8] [9] [11] [12] sts. at the beg. of the row. Knit.
2nd row: Cast off 7 [8] [9] [11] [12] sts. at the beg. of the row. Knit.
3rd row: Decrease 1 st. at each end of the row by placing the 3rd st. on to the 4th needle from each end (2 sts. now on the 4th needle) then the 2nd st. on to the 3rd needle and the 1st st. on to the 2nd needle at each end. Knit the row.
4th row: Knit.
5th row: Knit.
Repeat from the 3rd to the 5th row (inclusive) 28 [24] [22] [18] [16] times. 61 [73] [81] [93] [101] sts.
Continue knitting in st.st. decreasing 1 st. (as before) at each end of the next and every alternate row until 33 [33] [35] [35] [37] sts. remain.
Cast off.

The Pocket Linings (both alike for all 5 sizes). Cast on 37 sts.
Tension setting for st.st.
1st row: Knit.
Repeat the 1st row 39 times.
Break off the wool. Leave these sts. on a stitch-holder.

The Right Front. Cast on 63 [67] [69] [73] [77] sts.
Tension setting for ribbing.

For the 36, 40 and 42 inch chest sizes only
1st row: Knit in k.1, p.1 rib.
Repeat the 1st row 19 times.

For the 38 and 44 inch chest sizes only
1st row: Knit in k.1, p.1 rib.
Repeat the 1st row 19 times, decreasing 1 st. at the beg. of the last row. [66] [76] sts.

For all 5 sizes, proceed as follows:
Change to the tension setting for st.st.

1st row: Knit.
Repeat the 1st row 41 times.
43rd row: Starting with the 14th st. from the left hand side, slip 37 sts. on to a separate length of wool and leave for the pocket border, then with the wrong side of the work facing, place the 37 sts. left for the pocket lining on to the same needles from which the sts. have been taken. Knit the row.
Continue knitting in st.st. without shaping until the work measures 15 inches from the beginning, ending with the wool at the right hand side.

Shape Armhole
1st row: Cast off 7 [8] [9] [11] [12] sts. at the beg. of the row. Knit.
2nd row: Knit.
3rd row: Decrease 1 st. at the armhole edge (as given for the Back). Knit.
4th row: Knit.
5th row: Knit.
Repeat from the 3rd to the 5th row (inclusive) 4 times. 51 [53] [55] [57] [59] sts.
** Continue knitting in st.st. decreasing 1 st. (as before) at the armhole edge on the next and every following 3rd row, at the same time decreasing 1 st. at the front edge on the next and every following 6th row until 16 [21] [26] [34] [39] sts. remain.

For the 36 inch chest size only
Knit 6 rows, decreasing 1 st. at the armhole edge (as before) on the 3rd and 6th rows. 14 sts.

For the 38, 40, 42 and 44 inch chest sizes only
Continue knitting in st.st. decreasing 1 st. (as before) at the armhole edge on the 2nd and every alternate row, at the same time decreasing 1 st. at the front edge on every following 6th row until [17] [14] [14] [11] sts. remain.

For all five sizes, proceed as follows:
Decrease 1 st. at the armhole edge **only** on the 2nd and every alternate row until 1 [1] [1] [1] [1] st. remains. **
Break off the wool and fasten off.

The Left Front. Cast on 63 [67] [69] [73] [77] sts.
Tension setting for ribbing.

For the 36, 40 and 42 inch chest sizes only
1st row: Knit in k.1, p.1 rib.
Repeat the 1st row 19 times.

For the 38 and 44 inch chest sizes only
1st row: Knit in k.1, p.1 rib.
Repeat the 1st row 19 times, decreasing 1 st. at the end of the last row. [66] [76] sts.

continued overleaf

continued from previous page

For all 5 sizes, proceed as follows:

Change to the tension setting for st.st.

1st row: Knit.

Repeat the 1st row 41 times.

43rd row: Starting with the 14th st. from the right hand side, slip the 37 sts. on to a separate length of wool and leave for the pocket border, then with the wrong side of the work facing, place the 37 sts. left for the pocket lining on to the same needles from which the sts. have been taken. Knit the row.

Continue knitting in st.st. without shaping until the work measures 15 inches from the beginning, ending with the wool at the left hand side.

Shape Armhole

1st row: Cast off 7 [8] [9] [11] [12] sts. at the beg. of the row. Knit.

2nd row: Decrease 1 st. at the armhole edge (as given for the Back). Knit.

3rd row: Knit.

4th row: Knit.

Repeat from the 2nd to the 4th row (inclusive) 4 times. 51 [53] [55] [57] [59] sts.

Work exactly as given for the Right Front from ** to **.

Break off the wool and fasten off.

The Pocket Borders (both alike for all 5 sizes). With the carriage at the right hand side and the wrong side of the work facing, place the 37 sts. left on the length of wool for the pocket borders on to the machine.

Rejoin the wool to the right hand edge.

Tension setting for ribbing.

1st row: Knit in k.1, p.1 rib.

Repeat the 1st row 13 times.

Cast off loosely.

The Sleeves (both alike). Cast on 59 [61] [63] [67] [69] sts.

Tension setting for ribbing.

1st row: Knit in k.1, p.1 rib.

Repeat the 1st row 41 times, increasing 1 st. at the end of the last row. 60 [62] [64] [68] [70] sts.

Change to the tension setting for st.st.

1st row: Knit.

Repeat the 1st row 4 times.

Continue knitting in st.st. increasing 1 st. at both ends of the next and every following 6th row until there are 108 [110] [112] [116] [118] sts.

Continue knitting in st.st. without shaping until the work measures 20 inches from the beginning, ending with the wool at the right hand side.

Shape Top

Cast off 7 [8] [9] [11] [12] sts. at the beg. of the next 2 rows.

Proceed as follows:

1st row: Decrease 1 st. (as given for the Back) at each end of the row. Knit.

2nd row: Knit.

3rd row: Knit.

Repeat from the 1st to the 3rd row (inclusive) 30 times. 32 [32] [32] [32] [32] sts.

Continue knitting in st.st. decreasing 1 st. (as before) on the next and every alternate row until 10 [10] [10] [10] [10] sts. remain.

Cast off.

The Front Border (for all 5 sizes). Cast on 21 sts.

Tension setting for ribbing.

1st row: Knit in k.1, p.1 rib.

Repeat the 1st row 3 times.

*** 5th row: Place a small piece of contrasting wool into the hooks of the 8th, 9th, 10th, 11th, 12th, 13th and 14th needles, working these needles by hand knit in the contrasting wool leaving the ends loose (this marks a buttonhole), then knit the row in the original colour wool.

Repeat the 1st row 34 times. ***

Repeat from *** to *** 5 times.

Continue knitting in k.1, p.1 rib until the border is of sufficient length to go up to the left front, across the back of the neck and down the right front.

Cast off.

To Make Up. Press each piece separately on the wrong side under a damp cloth with a warm iron. Sew up the side and sleeve seams. Placing seam to seam, sew the decreased edges of the sleeves to the decreased edges of the bodice. Sew the front border in position placing the top buttonhole level with the first front decreasing. Gently pull out the contrasting wool marking the buttonholes and with a needle threaded with the original colour wool, run the wool through each of the open stitches, then neatly buttonhole stitch round. Sew on the buttons to correspond with the buttonholes. Press all seams.

The comfortable fit of a raglan-sleeved cardigan makes it ideal for weekend wear. By using leather buttons, the casual smartness can be emphasised

a shift and jumper set

The contrast design of the shift is repeated effectively on the jumper sleeves

Materials. 5 [6] ozs. of Wendy Family Wool, 4-ply, in Charcoal; the same in Snow White. 1 pair each No. 9, No. 10 and No. 12 knitting needles. 1 button for Jumper.

Measurements. To fit 22 [24] inch chest. Length of Shift, 15½ [17] inches. Length of Jumper, 13 [14] inches. Sleeve seam, 8½ [10] inches.

Tension. Over pattern used for Shift, 7 stitches measure 1 inch in width, and 1 pattern (20 rows) measures 2¼ inches in depth, worked on No. 9 needles.

Over stocking stitch, 7½ stitches to 1 inch, worked on No. 10 needles.

Abbreviations. K knit, p. purl, st(s) stitch(es), st.st. stocking stitch, tog. together, t.b.l. through the back(s) of the loop(s), dec. decrease by working 2 stitches together, inc. increase by working twice into 1 stitch, sl. slip, rep. repeat, patt. pattern, beg. beginning, C Charcoal, W White.

Note—*Instructions are given for the small size. Figures in brackets are for the larger size. Where one figure only is given, this refers to both sizes.*

THE SHIFT DRESS

The Back. Cast on 104 [114] sts. with No. 10 needles and C. Work 9 rows st.st. K.1 row on wrong side to mark hemline. Change to No. 9 needles.

24 inch chest size only
Work 8 rows st.st. with C.

Both sizes
Begin patt.
1st, 2nd and 3rd rows: Knit with C. Join in W.
4th row: P.3 [4] C, * 2 W, 6 C. Rep. from * to last 5 [6] sts., 2 W, 3 [4] C.
5th row: K.3 [4] C, * 2 W, 6 C. Rep. from * to last 5 [6] sts., 2 W, 3 [4] C.
6th row: P.1 [2] C, * 6 W, 2 C. Rep. from * to last 7 [8] sts., 6 W, 1 [2] C.
7th row: K.1 [2] C, * 2 W, 2 C. Rep. from * to last 3 [4] sts., 2 W, 1 [2] C.
8th row: As 6th row.
9th row: As 5th row.
10th row: As 4th row.
11th and 12th rows: Knit with C.
13th to 20th rows: St.st. with C.

These 20 rows form the patt. Proceed in patt., decreasing at both ends of next and every 10th row following until 88 [98] sts. remain, taking care to position each motif directly over that in previous row. Finish after 11th row of 5th patt.

Break wool and leave main part of work on one side while lower armhole facings are worked.

For right back armhole facing, cast on 3 sts. with No. 10 needles and C. Work 3 rows st.st., increasing at end of both knit rows. Break wool and leave sts. on a spare needle.

For left back armhole facing, cast on 3 sts. with No. 10 needles and C. Work 3 rows st.st., increasing at beg. of both knit rows. Do not break wool.

Shape Armholes

With No. 9 needles, p. the 5 sts. of left back armhole facing, k. the 88 [98] sts. of main part, and p. the 5 sts. of right back armhole facing.
Next row: K.4, sl.1 carrying wool across wrong side of work, k.3, k.2 tog. t.b.l., k.2 tog. t.b.l., k. to last 12 sts., k.2 tog., k.2 tog., k.3, sl.1 as before, k.4.
Next row: Purl.
Rep. these 2 rows 3 times more. 82 [92] sts.

22 inch chest size only
Next row: K.4, sl.1, k.72, sl.1, k.4.

24 inch chest size only
Next row: K.4, sl.1, k.4, k.2 tog. t.b.l., k.70, k.2 tog., k.4, sl.1, k.4.

Both sizes
Next row: P.5, k.72 [80], p.5.
Proceed in patt. from 3rd row, thus:-
Next row: K.4, sl.1, knit to last 5 sts., sl.1, k.4.
Next row: P.8 C, * 2 W, 6 C. Rep. from * to last 10 sts., 2 W, 8 C.
Continue thus, working the 5 sts. at each end as set, until 2nd row of 7th patt. has been worked.

Shape Neck

Next row: K.4, sl.1, k.25 [29], k.2 tog., k.1, turn, leaving remaining sts. unworked. Cast on 5. Proceed on this set of sts. for right side of neck, working 3 motifs only to avoid breaking patt. at neck edge.
Next row: Purl.
Next row: K.4, sl.1, work to last 8 sts., k.2 tog., k.1, sl.1, k.4.
Continue to dec. thus every alternate row until 31

continued overleaf

139

continued from previous page

[33] sts. remain. Work 1 row, thus finishing after 16th [20th] row of 7th patt.

For 24 inch chest size only

K.2 rows, working facings as set.

Shape Shoulder

Proceeding in st.st., with C, and working neck facing as before, cast off 12 sts. at beg. of next row and 7 [8] sts. at beg. of next 2 alternate rows. Cast off remaining 5 sts.

Place central 16 sts. on a safety-pin. With C, cast 5 sts. on to free No. 9 needle, then proceed across remaining sts. thus: K.1, k.2 tog. t.b.l., k.25 [29], sl.1, k.4. Complete left side of neck to correspond with right, reversing shapings.

Complete Centre of Neck

With C, cast 5 sts. on to a No. 12 needle, then with right side of work facing, knit central 16 sts. on to same needle. Cast on 5. sts. Beg. with a purl row, work 5 rows st.st., decreasing at both ends of each knit row. Cast off.

The Front. Work exactly as Back.

To Make Up. Press work under a damp cloth with a warm iron. Join side and shoulder seams. Turn in neck and armhole facings along the lines of slipped sts., and catch to wrong side. Turn in centre neck and lower armhole facings to correspond. Turn up hem on lower edge. Press seams and facings.

THE JUMPER

The Back. Cast on 88 [96] sts. with W and No. 12 needles.
1st row: K.1, p.1, * k.1 t.b.l., p.1. Rep. from * to end. Rep. this row 17 times more.
Change to No. 10 needles and st.st. Proceed until work measures 8¼ [9] inches, after a purl row.

Shape Armholes

Cast off 3 sts. at beg. of next 2 rows. Dec. at both ends of next 4 [6] rows, then of following 3 alternate rows. 68 [72] sts. Proceed until 3 [3½] inches from beg. of armholes, measured on the straight after a purl row.**

Divide for Opening

Next row: K.36 [38], turn, leaving remaining sts. unworked. Work 9 more rows on these sts., knitting the 4 sts. at centre back edge in every row.

Shape Shoulder

Cast off 6 sts. at beg. of next and following alternate row, and 6 [7] at beg. of next alternate row. Leave remaining 18 [19] sts. on a spare needle.

Join wool to inner edge of remaining 32 [34] sts. Cast on 4 sts., knit to end. Complete left side of Back to correspond

with right, reversing shapings.

The Front. Work as Back as far as **.

Shape Neck

Next row: K.22 [23], turn, leaving remaining sts. unworked. Work to side edge. Proceeding on this set of sts. for left side of neck, work 8 rows, decreasing at neck edge on every alternate row. 18 [19] sts.

Shape Shoulder

Cast off 6 sts. at beg. of next and following alternate row. Work to side edge. Cast off remaining 6 [7] sts.

Place central 24 [26] sts. on a safety-pin. Join wool to inner edge of remaining 22 [23] sts. and k. to end. Complete right side of work to correspond with left, reversing shapings.

The Sleeves (both alike)

Cast on 40 [44] sts. with W and No. 12 needles. Work 20 rows twisted rib as lower edge. Change to No. 10 needles and patt.
1st, 2nd and 3rd rows: Knit. Join in C.
4th row: P.3 [5] W, * 2 C, 6 W. Rep. from * to last 5 [7] sts., 2 C, 3 [5] W.
5th row: K.3 [5] W, * 2 C, 6 W. Rep. from * to last 5 [7] sts., 2 C, 3 [5] W.
6th row: P.1 [3] W, * 6 C, 2 W. Rep. from * to last 7 [9] sts., 6 C, 1 [3] W.
7th row: K.1 [3] W, * 2 C, 2 W. Rep. from * to last 3 [5] sts., 2 C, 1 [3] W.
8th row: As 6th row.
9th row: As 5th row.
10th row: As 4th row.
11th and 12th rows: Knit with W.

This completes patt. Proceed in st.st., in W. Inc. at both ends of next and every 5th row following until there are 54 [62] sts. Proceed until 8½ [10] inches, or length required, after a purl row.

Shape Top

Cast off 3 sts. at beg. of next 2 rows and 2 sts. at beg. of next 12 [16] rows. Cast off remaining 24 sts.

The Neckband. Join shoulder seams. With right side of work facing, using No. 12 needles and W, k. sts. of left back neck, k. up 16 along left front neck, k. sts. of centre front, k. up 16 along right front neck, and k. sts. of right back. 92 [96] sts. Work 5 rows twisted rib as lower edge. In next row make buttonhole thus: Rib 2, pass wool loosely round needle, p.2 tog., rib to end. Rib 3 more rows. Cast off in rib.

To Make Up. Press work under a damp cloth, omitting ribbing. Join side, shoulder and sleeve seams. Set sleeves into armholes. Sew down underwrap at base of back opening. Press seams. Sew on button to correspond with buttonhole.

140

colourful
ski sweater

The picture in full colour on page 86 shows the attractive colour variations

Materials. 14 [15] ozs. Main Colour, 5 [5] ozs. first Contrast, 1 [1] oz. second Contrast in Sirdar Super Nylon Double Knitting, Sirdar Double Knitting Wool or Sirdar Double Crepe Wool. 1 Pair No. 8 and No. 10 Knitting Needles. 1 Circular Knitting Needle No. 8 (30 inches in length). 1 Set of four No. 8 and No. 10 Knitting Needles with points at each end.

Tension 6 stitches to one inch.

Abbreviations. K. knit, p. purl, st(s). stitch(es), sl. slip one stitch knitways, st.st. stocking stitch (1 row knit, 1 row purl), tog. together, inc. increase(ing), MC Main Colour, C Contrast.

After casting off stitches for shaping, one stitch will remain on the right hand needle which is not included in the instructions that follow.

Note—*For the small size read the instructions as given. For the large size read the figures within the brackets.*

Measurements. Width all round at underarm—to fit 34-36 [38-40] inch bust (actual measurement 36 [40] inches).
Length from top of shoulder—26 [26] inches.
Length of sleeve seam—17½ [17½] inches.

N.B. When working with two colours—the colour not in use should be stranded loosely across the back of the work to retain the elasticity of the fabric.

The Back and Front (both alike). Using the No. 8 needles and MC wool cast on 105 [119] sts.
1st row: Sl., k.1, * p.1, k.1, repeat from * to the last st., k.1.
2nd row: Sl., * p.1, k.1, repeat from * to end of row.

Repeat the 1st and 2nd rows 3 times inc. once at the end of the last row for the 34-36 inch only. 106 [119] sts.
Join in the first C and proceed as follows:-
1st row: Sl., * k.2 MC, 4 first C, 1 MC, 4 first C, 2 MC, repeat from * to the last st., 1 MC.
2nd row: Sl., * p.1 MC, 4 first C, 3 MC, 4 first C, 1 MC, repeat from * to the last st., k.1 MC.
3rd row: Sl., * k.4 first C, 2 MC, 1 first C, 2 MC, 4 first C, repeat from * to the last st., 1 MC.
4th row: Sl., * p.4 first C, 2 MC, 1 first C, 2 MC, 4 first C, repeat from * to the last st., k.1 MC.
5th row: Sl., * k.2 first C, 2 MC, (1 first C, 1 MC) twice, 1 first C, 2 MC, 2 first C, repeat from * to the last st., 1 MC.
6th row: Sl., * p.1 first C, 4 MC, 1 first C, 1 MC, 1 first C, 4 MC, 1 first C, repeat from * to the last st., k.1 MC.
7th row: Sl., * k.2 MC, 3 first C, 1 MC, 1 first C, 1 MC, 3 first C, 2 MC, repeat from * to the last st., 1 MC.

Repeat the 6th row once, the 5th row once, the 4th row once, the 3rd row once, the 2nd row once then the 1st row once.
Break off the first C.
14th row: Sl., purl to the last st., k.1.
15th row: Sl., knit to end of row.
16th row: Sl., purl to the last st., k.1.
Continue in st.st. until the work measures 16 inches from the beginning, ending on the wrong side of the work.

The Armholes. Cast off 6 sts. at the beginning of each of the next 2 rows. 94 [107] sts.
Break off the wool and leave these sts. on a thread.

The Sleeves (both alike). Using the No. 10 needles and MC wool cast on 49 [53] sts.
1st row: Sl., k.1, * p.1, k.1, repeat from * to the last st., k.1.
2nd row: Sl., * p.1, k.1, repeat from * to end of row.
Repeat the 1st and 2nd rows 10 times inc. once at the end of the last row. 50 [54] sts.
Change to No. 8 needles and proceed as follows:-
1st row: Sl., knit to end of row.
2nd row: Sl., purl to the last st., k.1.
Repeat the 1st and 2nd rows twice.
Continue in st.st., inc. once at each end of the next and every following 6th row until there are 80 [84] sts. on the needle.
Continue without shaping until the work measures 17½ inches from the beginning, ending on the wrong side of the work.

The Top. Cast off 6 sts. at the beginning of the next 2 rows. 68 [72] sts.
Break off the wool and leave these sts. on a thread.

continued overleaf

continued from previous page

The Yoke. As the sts. (may) differ for the various sizes follow the headings for the size required.

34/36 inch size only

With the right side of the work facing, using the circular needle and commencing at the Back, slip the first 47 sts. of the 94 sts. left on a thread on to the circular needle, join in the MC wool and work across the remaining 47 sts. as follows: k.46, inc. once in the next st., knit across the 68 sts. left on a thread of one sleeve, knit across the 94 sts. left on a thread of the Front, knit across the 68 sts. left on a thread of the other Sleeve, then knit the first 47 sts. which were slipped on to the circular needle. (325 sts.)

38/40 inch size only

With the right side of the work facing, using the circular needle and commencing at the Back, slip the first 54 sts. of the 107 sts. left on a thread on to the circular needle, join the MC wool and work across the remaining 53 sts. as follows: k.52, inc. once in the next st., working across the 72 sts. left on a thread of one Sleeve, inc. once in the first st., k.70, inc. once in the next st., working across the 107 sts. left on a thread of the Front, k.106, inc. once in the next st., working across the 72 sts. left on a thread of the other Sleeve, inc. once in the first st., k.70, inc. once in the next st., then knit the first 54 sts. which were slipped on to the circular needle. (364 sts.)

34/36 and 38/40 inch sizes

Working in rounds of knit, marking the beginning of each round with a coloured thread and carrying it up as each round is completed.

Join in the first C and proceed as follows:-

1st round: * K.2 MC, 4 first C, 1 MC, 4 first C, 2 MC, repeat from * to end of round.

2nd round: * K.1 MC, 4 first C, 3 MC, 4 first C, 1 MC, repeat from * to end of round.

3rd round: * K.4 first C, 2 MC, 1 first C, 2 MC, 4 first C, repeat from * to end of round.

4th round: * K.4 first C, 2 MC, 1 first C, 2 MC, 4 first C, repeat from * to end of round.

5th round: * K.2 first C, 2 MC, (1 first C, 1 MC) twice, 1 first C, 2 MC, 2 first C, repeat from * to end of round.

6th round: * K.1 first C, 4 MC, 1 first C, 1 MC, 1 first C, 4 MC, 1 first C, repeat from * to end of round.

7th round: * K.2 MC, 3 first C, 1 MC, 1 first C, 1 MC, 3 first C, 2 MC, repeat from * to end of round.

Repeat the 6th round once, the 5th round once, the 4th round once, the 3rd round once, the 2nd round once then the 1st round once.

Break off the MC wool.

14th round: Knit to end of round.

15th round: * (K.3, k.2 tog.) twice, k.3, repeat from * to end of round. 275 [308] sts.

Repeat the 14th round once.

Join in the second C.

17th round: * K.1 first C, 2 second C, 2 first C, 1 second C, 2 second C, 1 first C, repeat from * to end of round.

18th round: * K.1 second C, 2 first C, 5 second C, 2 first C, 1 second C, repeat from * to end of round.

Repeat the 17th round once.

Break off the second C.

Repeat the 14th round 3 times.

Join in the MC wool.

23rd round: * (K.3 first C, 1 MC) twice, 3 first C, repeat from * to end of round.

24th round: * K.3 first C, 2 MC, 1 first C, 2 MC, 3 first C, repeat from * to end of round.

Repeat the 24th round once.

26th round: * K.1 first C, 1 MC, 2 first C, 1 MC, 1 first C, 1 MC, 2 first C, 1 MC, 1 first C, repeat from * to end of round.

27th round: * K.3 MC, 2 first C, 1 MC, 2 first C, 3 MC, repeat from * to end of round.

Repeat the 26th round once, the 24th round twice then the 23rd round once.

Break off the MC wool.

Repeat the 14th round once.

33rd round: * K.2, k.2 tog., k.3, k.2 tog., k.2, repeat from * to end of round. 225 [252] sts.

Repeat the 14th round once.

Join in the second C.

35th round: * (K.1 second C, 1 first C) 4 times, 1 second C, repeat from * to end of round.

36th round: * K.2 second C, 1 first C, 3 second C, 1 first C, 2 second C, repeat from * to end of round.

Repeat the 35th round once.

Break off the second C.

Repeat the 14th round 3 times.

Join in the MC wool.

41st round: * K.2 first C, 2 MC, 1 first C, 2 MC, 2 first C, repeat from * to end of round.

Repeat the 41st round once.

43rd round: * (K.1 first C, 1 MC) 4 times, 1 first C, repeat from * to end of round.

44th round: * K.1 first C, 2 MC, 1 first C, 1 MC, 1 first C, 2 MC, 1 first C, repeat from * to end of round.

45th round: * K.3 first C, 3 MC, 3 first C, repeat from * to end of round.

Repeat the 44th round once, the 43rd round once then the 41st round twice.

Break off the MC wool.

Repeat the 14th round once.

51st round: * K.1, k.2 tog., k.3, k.2 tog., k.1, repeat from

* to end of round. 175 [196] sts.

Repeat the 14th round once.

Join in the second C.

53rd round: * K.1 second C, 1 first C, 3 second C, 1 first C, 1 second C, repeat from * to end of round.

54th round: * (K.1 second C, 1 first C) 3 times, 1 second C, repeat from * to end of round.

Repeat the 53rd round once.

Break off the second C.

Change to the set of four No. 8 needles.

Using one needle from the set of four k.58 [65] sts., using the second needle k.59 [66] sts. and using the third needle k.58 [65] sts.

57th round: * (K.1, k.2 tog.) twice, k.1, repeat from * to end of round. 125 [140] sts.

Repeat the 14th round once.

Join in the MC wool.

59th round: * (K.1 first C, 1 MC) twice, 1 first C, repeat from * to end of round.

60th round: * K.2 first C, 1 MC, 2 first C, repeat from * to end of round.

Repeat the 59th round once.

Break off the MC wool.

Repeat the 14th round once.

63rd round. * K.2 tog., k.1, k.2 tog., repeat from * to end of round. 75 [84] sts.

Proceed as follows for the turns for the back of the neck :

Next row: K.21, turn.

Next row: P.42, turn.

Next row: K.32 turn.

Next row: P.22, turn.

Next row: K.11.

Break off the first C, join in the MC.

Change to the set of four No. 10 needles.

As the sts. (may) differ for the various sizes follow the headings for the size required.

34/36 inch size only

Next round: K.2 tog., knit to end of round. 74 sts.

38/40 inch size only

Next round: Knit to end of round. [84] sts.

34/36 and 38/40 inch sizes

1st round: * K.1, p.1, repeat from * to end of round.

Repeat the 1st round 18 times.

Cast off loosely in rib.

To Make Up. Press carefully on the wrong side under a damp cloth with a warm iron. Sew up the side and sleeve seams. Placing seam to seam sew the cast off sts. at the armholes together. Fold the neckband in half and sew loosely in position on the wrong side of the work. Press all seams.

a warm set in fair isle

The set is pictured in colour on page 85

Materials

For Pullover. 5 [6] [7] ozs. in Main Colour of Sirdar Double Knitting Wool. 1 [1] [2] ozs. in Blue, and 1 oz. each of Rust (R), Green (G) and Orange (O).

For Beret. 1 [1] [2] ozs. in Main Colour. 1 oz. each of R G B and O.

For Mitts. 1 oz. of Main Colour. Small ball each of R G B and O.

For the Set. 7 [8] [10] ozs. of Main Colour. 1 [1] [2] ozs. of B. 1 oz. each of R G and O. 1 pair each No. 8 and No. 10 Knitting Needles. Zip fastener for Pullover.

Measurements. To fit 22 [24] [26] inch chest. Length of Pullover from shoulder—12½ [13½] [15] inches. Sleeve seam—8½ [10½] [13] inches.

Tension 6 stitches to one inch on No. 8 needles.

Abbreviations. K. knit, p. purl, st(s). stitch(es), inc. increase, dec. decrease, beg. beginning, cont. continue, foll. following, rep. repeat, patt. pattern, st.st. stocking stitch, MC Main Colour, B Blue, R Rust, O Orange, G Green, alt. alternate, rem. remain(ing).

Note—*Figures in brackets are for the two larger sizes in size order. One figure only refers to all sizes.*

Mitts: Length 6 [6¼] [6½] inches.

Beret: 14 [15½] [15¾] inches inside ribbed headband (unstretched).

THE PULLOVER

The Back. With No. 10 needles and MC cast on 69 [73] [81] sts.

1st row: K.1, * p.1, k.1, rep. from * to end.

2nd row: P.1, * k.1, p.1, rep. from * to end.

Repeat these 2 rows 4 more times.

Change to No. 8 needles and work 2 rows st.st.

Start Fair Isle pattern as follows : Join in R.

1st row: K.2 MC, * 1 R, 3 MC; rep. from * to last 3 sts.,

continued overleaf

continued from previous page

1 R, 2 MC.

2nd row: P.1 MC, * 1 R, 1 MC; rep. from * to end.

3rd row: K.1 R, * 3 MC, 1 R; rep. from * to end. Break off R.

With MC purl 1 row, knit 1 row, purl 1 row.

7th row: Join in B, K.2 MC, * 1 B, 3 MC; rep. from * to last 3 sts., 1 B, 2 MC.

8th row: P.1 MC, * 3 B, 1 MC; rep. from * to end. Break off M.C.

9th row: K.2 B, * 1 R, 3 B; rep. from * to last 3 sts., 1 R, 2 B.

10th row: P.1 B, * 3 R, 1 B; rep. from * to end.

11th row: As 9th row. Join in O.

12th row: P.1 O, * 3 B, 1 O; rep. from * to end.

13th row: K.2 O, * 1 B, 3 O; rep. from * to last 3 sts., 1 B, 2 O.

14th row: P.1 G, * 3 O, 1 G; rep. from * to end.

15th row: K.1 O, * 1 G, 1 O; rep. from * to end.

16th row: As 14th row.

17th row: K.2 O, * 1 B, 3 O; rep. from * to last 3 sts., 1 B, 2 O.

18th row: P.1 O, * 3 B, 1 O; rep. from * to end. Break off.

19th row: As 9th row.

20th row: As 10th row.

21st row: As 9th row. Break off R.

22nd row: Join in MC. As 8th row.

23rd row: As 7th row.

Break off B. With MC purl 1 row. Knit 1 row. Purl 1 row. Repeat rows 1, 2 and 3 of patt. This completes the Fair Isle pattern.

Working only with MC, purl 1 row, inc. 1 st. each end. 71 [75] [83] sts. Cont. in st.st. working straight until work measures 7 [7½] [8½] inches from beg., ending with a purl row.

Shape Raglan

Cast off 3 sts. beg. of next 2 rows.

Next row: K.2, p.2 tog., knit to last 4 sts., p.2 tog., k.2.

Next row: K.1, purl to last st., k.1. **

Rep. last 2 rows until there are 59 sts. left. Divide for back opening.

1st row: K.2, p.2 tog., knit until there are 28 sts. on right hand needle, cast off 1 st., k.24, p.2 tog., k.2. Finish this side first.

2nd row: K.1, purl to last st., k.1.

3rd row: Knit to last 4 sts., p.2 tog., k.2. Rep. last 2 rows until 8 [8] [10] sts. remain. Cast off loosely.

With wrong side of work facing, rejoin wool to rem. sts. for other side. K.1, purl to last st., k.1.

Next row: K.2, p.2 tog., knit to end. Finish this side to match the other.

The Front. Work as for Back to **, then rep. the last 2 rows until there are 37 [37] [41] sts.

Shape Neck.

Next row: K.2, p.2 tog., k.11, turn and finish this side first. Cont. to dec. at raglan armhole as before, and **at the same time** dec. 1 st. at neck edge every row until there are 7 sts. left. Dec. raglan edge only until there are 3 sts.

Next row: K.1, p.2.

Next row: K.1, p.2 tog., k.2 tog. and fasten off.

Slip 7 [7] [11] sts. from centre front on to st. holder, with wrong side facing rejoin wool to remaining 15 sts. and purl to last st., k.1.

Finish this side to match the first.

The Right Sleeve. With No. 10 needles and MC, cast on 37 [37] [41] sts., and work 12 rows in rib as for back. Change to No. 8 needles.

Next row. Knit, increasing 4 sts. evenly across row. 41 [41] [45] sts. Purl 1 row.

Work the first 3 rows of Fair Isle pattern. Break off R. Beg. with a purl row, cont. in st.st. and MC, and inc. 1 st. each end on 8th and every following 6th [6th] [8th] row until there are 53 [57] [61] sts., then cont. straight until sleeve measures 9 [11] [13½] ins. from beg., ending with a purl row.

Shape Raglan

1st row: K.2, p.2 tog., knit to last 4 sts., p.2 tog., k.2.

2nd row: K.1, purl to last st., k.1. Rep. last 2 rows until there are 9 sts. left. ***

Next row: Cast off 3 sts., knit to last 4 sts., p.2 tog., k.2.

Next row: K.1, p.4.

Next row: K.2 tog., p.2 tog., k.1, (3 sts.).

Next row: K.1, p.2 tog.

Next row: K.2 tog. and fasten off.

The Left Sleeve. Work as for Right Sleeve until ***, but omit last row, so ending with a right side row. (9 sts.)

1st row: Cast off 3, purl to last st., k.1.

2nd row: K.2, p.2 tog., k.2.

3rd row: P.2 tog., p.2, k.1.

4th row: K.2, p.2 tog.

5th row: P.2 tog., k.1. K.2 tog. and fasten off.

The Neckband. With right sides of work facing and No. 10 needles and MC, pick up and knit 8 [8] [10] sts. from left side of Back opening, 6 sts. from neck edge of Left Sleeve, 13 [14] [14] sts. down side of neck, 7 [7] [11] sts. from centre neck, 13 [14] [14] sts. up other side of front neck, 6 sts. from right sleeve, and 8 [8] [10] sts. from other side of Back neck. 61 [63] [71] sts. Work 5 rows of k.1, p.1 rib as for back. Cast off loosely in rib.

To Make Up. Press with warm iron over a damp cloth. Join last ½ in. at top of sleeve before raglan shaping to the 3 sts. cast off at underarms. Join raglan seams. Join side and sleeve seams. Sew in zip fastener to back opening. Press seams.

144

THE MITTS

Left Mitt

With No. 10 needles and MC, cast on 33 [37] [41] sts. Work 12 [16] [16] rows rib as for back of Pullover. Change to No. 8 needles, work 4 rows st.st., then **beg. with 7th row** work 6 rows Fair Isle pattern. **

Thumb

Next row: Work 18 [20] [22] of 13th row of Fair Isle pattern. Break off B and O. Turn with MC, p.5 [5] [6], turn, cast on 5 [5] [6]. Work 10 [10] [14] rows in MC. St.st. on these 10 [10] [12] sts.

Top of Thumb

Next row: K.2 tog., 5 [5] [6] times. Purl 1 row.

Next row: K.2 tog., k.1, k.2 tog., (k.2 tog., k.1, k.2 tog.) (k.2 tog. 3 times).

Break off wool, draw through remaining sts., and fasten off.

With right side facing using B and O, pick up and knit 5 [5] [6] sts. from cast on sts. at base of thumb, cont. with 13th row of patt., then work across remaining 15 [17] [19] sts. in patt.

Continue on these sts. until 23rd row of Fair Isle pattern has been worked. Break off B and O. Purl 1 row. Work 0 [0] [2] rows st.st. Cont. with MC.

Shape Top

1st row: K.2, k.2 tog., k.9 [11] [13], k.2 tog., k.3, k.2 tog., k.9 [11] [13], k.2 tog., k.2. Purl 1 row.

3rd row: K.2, k.2 tog., k.7 [9] [11], k.2 tog., k.3, k.2 tog., k.7 [9] [11], k.2 tog., k.2. Purl 1 row.

5th row: K.2, k.2 tog., k.5 [7] [9], k.2 tog., k.3, k.2 tog., k.5 [7] [9], k.2 tog., k.2. Purl 1 row.

Largest size only

7th row: K.2, k.2 tog., k.7, k.2 tog., k.3, k.2 tog., k.7, k.2 tog., k.2.

All sizes

Cast off, or graft sts. together.

Right Mitt

Work as for Left Mitt to **.

Thumb

Work 20 [22] [24] sts. of 13th row of Fair Isle patt. Break off B and O. With MC cast on 5 [5] [6] sts., turn. P.10 [10] [12] sts. Work 10 [10] [14] rows on these sts. Complete as for the left thumb.

With right side of work facing using B and O, pick up and knit 5 [5] [6] sts. in patt. from base of thumb, then cont. in patt. across rem. sts. Complete to match the Left Mitt.

To Make Up. Press with warm iron and damp cloth. Join side seam, and top if not grafted. Press seam.

THE BERET

With No. 10 needles and MC, cast on 89 [97] [99] sts. and work 6 rows in rib as for back of Pullover. Change to No. 8 needles.

Next row: * inc. in next st., k.1, rep. from * to last 1 [1] [2] sts., k.1 [k.1] (k.1, inc. in last st.). 133 [145] [149] sts. Purl 1 row.

Now work rows 1 to 23 inclusive of Fair Isle pattern as for Pullover. Break off B.

With MC purl 1 row, and work 4 rows st.st.

Smallest size only

Next row: K.2 tog., * k.4, k.2 tog., rep. from * to last 5 sts., k.3, k.2 tog. (110 sts.)

Medium size only

Next row: * K.9, k.2 tog., rep. from * to last 2 sts., k.2. (132 sts.)

Large size only

Next row: K.3 * k.2 tog., k.7, rep. from * to last 2 sts., k.2 tog. (132 sts.)

All Sizes

Purl 1 row. Now dec. for top of Beret as follows:

1st row: * K.1 MC, 1 R, 1 MC, 1 R, 3 MC, 2 R, k.3 tog. MC, 2 R, 3 MC, 1 R, 1 MC, 1 R, 1 MC, 1 R, rep. from * to end of row.

2nd row: * (p.1 MC, 1 R) 3 times, (1 MC, 3 R) twice, (1 MC, 1 R) 3 times, rep. from * to end of row.

3rd row: * (k.1 MC, 1 R) twice, 1 MC, 3 R, k.3 tog. MC, 3 R, (1 MC, 1 R) 3 times, rep. from * to end of row.

4th row: * (p.1 MC, 1 R) twice, 1 MC, 3 R, p.3 tog. MC, 3 R, (1 MC, 1 R) twice, rep. from * to end of row.

5th row: * K.1 MC, 1 R, 1 MC, 3 R, k.3 tog. MC, 3 R, (1 MC, 1 R) twice, rep. from * to end of row.

6th row: * P.1 MC, 1 R, 1 MC, 3 R, p.3 tog. MC, 3 R, 1 MC, 1 R, rep. from * to end of row.

7th row: * K.1 MC, 3 R, k.3 tog. MC, 3 R, 1 MC, 1 R, rep. from * to end of row.

8th row: * P.1 MC, 3 R, p.3 tog. MC, 3 R, rep. from * to end of row. Break off R. Join in B.

9th row: * K.2 B, k.3 tog. MC, 2 B, 1 MC, rep. from * to end of row.

10th row: * P.1 MC, 1 B, p.3 tog. MC, 1 B, rep. from * to end of row.

11th row: * K.3 tog. MC, k.1 B, rep. from * to end of row.

12th row: With B, p.2 tog. [p.3 tog.] [p.3 tog.] 5 [4] [4] times.

Break off wool, run wool through remaining sts. and fasten off.

To Make Up. Sew up back seam. Press with warm iron over a damp cloth.

tyrolean cardigan

The picture on page 85 shows the gay petal effect

Materials. 13 [15] [16] [18] ozs. Wendy D.K. Nylonised Wool in White. A pair each of Nos. 11 and 9 needles. Cable needle. 6 buttons. 1 [1] [1¼] [1¼] yards facing ribbon, 1 inch wide. Oddments of brightly coloured D.K. Wool for embroidery.

Measurements. To fit 28 [30] [32] [34] inch chest/bust sizes. Length from top of shoulders 16 [18] [20] [22] inches. Sleeve seam 13½ [15] [16½] [18] inches, or as required.

Tension 6 stitches and 8 rows to 1 inch over stocking stitch.

Abbreviations. St(s.) stitch(es), k. knit, inc. increase(ing), p. purl, rep. repeat, patt. pattern, sl.1p. slip 1 purlwise, make B. make bobble, as follows: (p.1, k.1, p.1, k.1) all into next st., turn and k.4, turn and p.4, then slip 2nd, 3rd and 4th sts. over 1st st., thus leaving 1 st. on right hand needle; cr.2 B. cross 2 back, as follows: slip next 2 sts. on to cable needle and leave at back of work, k.1, then k.2 from cable needle; cr.1 F. cross 1 front, as follows: slip next st. on to cable needle and leave at front of work, k.2, then k.1 from cable needle; tog. together, m.1 p. make 1 purlwise, as follows: pick up loop before next st. on to left hand needle and purl it through back of loop; m.1 k. make 1 knitwise, as follows: pick up loop before next st. and knit it through back of loop; beg. beginning, dec. decrease, st.st. stocking stitch, w.o. wool over.

Note—*Instructions are given for the 1st size; figures in brackets are for 2nd, 3rd and 4th sizes in size order. Where one figure only is given, this applies to all 4 sizes.*

The Left Front. With No. 11 needles cast on 47 [50] [53] [56] sts. Knit 8 rows, inc. 1 st. at end of final row.
Change to No. 9 needles.

30 and 32 inch sizes only
Next row: Knit.
Next row. K.6, purl to end.
Rep. these 2 rows 5 [3] times more.

All sizes continued. Now commence diamond patt. as follows:-
1st row: K.3 [4] [5] [5], k.2, sl.1 p., k.1, sl.1 p., k.12, make B, k.1, make B, k.12, sl.1 p., k.1, sl.1 p., k.10 [12] [14] [17].

2nd row: K.6, p.4 [6] [8] [11], sl.1 p., p.1, sl.1 p., p.27, sl.1 p., p.1, sl.1 p., p.5 [6] [7] [7].
3rd row: K.3 [4] [5] [5], cr.2 B, k.1, cr.1 F, k.9, make B, k.1, p.1, k.1, make B, k.9, cr.2 B, k.1, cr.1 F, k.8 [10] [12] [15].
4th row: K.6, p.20 [22] [24] [27], k.1, p.21 [22] [23] [23].
5th row: K.3 [4] [5] [5], k.2, sl.1 p., k.1, sl.1 p., k.9, k.2 tog., make B, k.1, m.1 p., p.1, m.1 p., k.1, make B, k.2 tog., k.9, sl.1 p., k.1, sl.1 p., k.10 [12] [14] [17].
6th row: K.6, p.4 [6] [8] [11], sl.1 p., p.1, sl.1 p., p.12, k.3, p.12, sl.1 p., p.1, sl.1 p., p.5 [6] [7] [7].
7th row: K.3 [4] [5] [5], cr.2 B, k.1, cr.1 F, k.6, k.2 tog., make B, k.1, p.1, m.1 p., p.1, m.1 p., p.1, k.1, make B, k.2 tog., k.6, cr.2 B, k.1, cr.1 F, k.8 [10] [12] [15].
8th row: K.6, p.18 [20] [22] [25], k.5, p.19 [20] [21] [21].
9th row: K.3 [4] [5] [5], k.2, sl.1 p., k.1, sl.1 p., k.7, k.2 tog., make B, k.1, p.1, m.1 p., p.3, m.1 p., p.1, k.1, make B, k.2 tog., k.7, sl.1 p., k.1, sl.1 p., k.10 [12] [14] [17].
10th row: K.6, p.4 [6] [8] [11], sl.1 p., p.1, sl.1 p., p.10, k.7, p.10, sl.1 p., p.1, sl.1 p., p.5 [6] [7] [7].
11th row: K.3 [4] [5] [5], cr.2 B, k.1, cr.1 F, k.4, k.2 tog., make B, k.1, p.1, m.1 p., p.5, m.1 p., p.1, k.1, make B, k.2 tog., k.4, cr.2 B, k.1, cr.1 F, k.8 [10] [12] [15].
12th row: K.6, p.16 [18] [20] [23], k.9, p.17 [18] [19] [19].
13th row: Patt. 13 [14] [15] [15] as before, k.2 tog., make B., k.1, p.1, m.1 p., p.7, m.1 p., p.1, k.1, make B, k.2 tog., patt. 18 [20] [22] [25].
14th row: Patt. 18 [20] [22] [25], p.3, k.11, p.3, patt. 13 [14] [15] [15].
15th row: Patt. 13 [14] [15] [15], k.1, m.1 k., make B, k.1, p.1, p.2 tog., p.5, p.2 tog., p.1, k.1, make B, m.1 k., k.1, patt. 18 [20] [22] [25].
16th row: Patt. 18 [20] [22] [25], p.4, k.9, p.4, patt. 13 [14] [15] [15].
17th row: Patt. 13 [14] [15] [15], k.2, m.1 k., make B, k.1, p.1, p.2 tog., p.3, p.2 tog., p.1, k.1, make B, m.1 k., k.2, patt. 18 [20] [22] [25].
18th row: Patt. 18 [20] [22] [25], p.5, k.7, p.5, patt. 13 [14] [15] [15].
19th row: Patt. 13 [14] [15] [15], k.3, m.1 k., make B, k.1, p.1, p.2 tog., p.1, p.2 tog., p.1, k.1, make B, m.1 k., k.3, patt. 18 [20] [22] [25].
20th row: Patt. 18 [20] [22] [25], p.6, k.5, p.6, patt. 13 [14] [15] [15].
21st row: Patt. 13 [14] [15] [15], k.4, m.1 k., make B, k.1, p.2 tog., p.1, p.2 tog., k.1, make B, m.1 k., k.4, patt. 18 [20] [22] [25].

22nd row: Patt. 18 [20] [22] [25], p.7, k.3, p.7, patt. 13 [14] [15] [15].

23rd row: Patt. 13 [14] [15] [15], k.5, m.1 k., make B, k.1, p.3 tog., k.1, make B, m.1 k., k.5, patt. 18 [20] [22] [25].

24th row: Patt. 18 [20] [22] [25], p.8, k.1, p.8, patt. 13 [14] [15] [15].

These 24 rows form the patt. Continue in patt. until 72 [84] [96] [108] rows in all have been worked above garter st. welt.

Shape Armhole

Keeping patt. correct, cast off 3 sts. at beg. of next row. Patt. 1 row. Dec. 1 st. at side edge on next 5 [5] [6] [6] rows and following 3 alternate rows. 37 [40] [42] [45] sts.

Continue straight in patt. until 38 [42] [46] [50] rows have been worked from beg. of armhole shaping.

Complete the diamond patt. at present being worked, then continue in st.st. only.

At the same time, to shape Front Neck

Next row: Patt. 24 [26] [28] [30], turn and leave remaining 13 [14] [14] [15] sts. on a holder. Dec. 1 st. at beg. (neck edge) of next row and following 3 alternate rows. 20 [22] [24] [26] sts. remain.

Shape Shoulder

Cast off 6 [6] [7] [8] sts. at beg. of next row, then take 2 tog. at beg. of following row. Rep. these 2 rows once more. Cast off remaining 6 [8] [8] [8] sts.

The Right Front. Work as for Left Front, reversing all shapings. Reverse the patt. rows by reading them backwards, from end of row to beg. Also make buttonholes as follows: Work 4 rows from beg.

Next row: K.2, cast off 2, patt. to end.

Next row: Patt. to end, casting on 2 sts. over those cast off. Work 18 [22] [26] [28] rows straight. Rep. the last 20 [24] [28] [30] rows until there are 6 buttonholes in all.

The Back. With No. 11 needles, cast on 90 [96] [102] [108] sts. K.8 rows. Change to No. 9 needles.

30 and 32 inch sizes only

Work 12 [8] rows in st.st.

All sizes continued. Now commence diamond patt. as follows:-

1st row: K.3 [4] [5] [5], k.2, sl.1 p., k.1, sl.1 p., k.12, make B, k.1, make B, k.12, sl.1 p., k.1, sl.1 p., k.14 [18] [22] [28], sl.1 p., k.1, sl.1 p., k.12, make B, k.1, make B, k.12, sl.1 p., k.1, sl.1 p., k.5 [6] [7] [7].

Continue in patt. of front as now set over the sts. Work until 72 [84] [96] [108] rows in all above garter st. welt have been completed.

★ **Shape Armholes**

Keeping patt. correct, cast off 3 sts. at beg. of next 2 rows, then dec. 1 st. at both ends of next 5 [5] [6] [6] rows and following 3 alternate rows. 68 [74] [78] [84] sts.

Complete 5 [5] [6] [7] diamond patts. in all, then continue in st.st. only, to correspond with fronts.

At the same time, work straight until armholes measure same length as fronts to beg. of shoulder shapings.

Shape Shoulders

Cast off 6 [6] [7] [8] sts. at beg. of next 4 rows and 6 [8] [8] [8] sts. at beg. of next 2 rows. Leave remaining 32 [34] [34] [36] sts. on a holder.

The Sleeves (both alike). With No. 11 needles, cast on 35 [37] [39] [41] sts. K.8 rows, inc. 1 st. at both ends of final row. 37 [39] [41] [43] sts. Change to No. 9 needles and patt. as follows:-

1st row: K.15 [16] [17] [18], k.2, sl.1 p., k.1, sl.1 p., k.2, k.15 [16] [17] [18].

Working the cross st. patt. of fronts over the centre 7 sts. only, as now set, continue in st.st. Inc. 1 st. at both ends of every 5th row until there are 65 [71] [77] [83] sts. Work straight until sleeve measures $13\frac{1}{2}$ [15] [$16\frac{1}{2}$] [18] inches from beg., or length required.

Shape Top

Keeping patt. correct, cast off 3 sts. at beg. of next 2 rows, 1 st. at beg. of following 10 rows, then 2 sts. at beg. of next 10 rows. Cast off 3 sts. at beg. of next 2 [4] [6] [8] rows. Cast off.

To Make Up. Press pieces on wrong sides with a warm iron over a damp cloth. Join shoulders, using edge-to-edge seams. Sew sleeves into armholes, then join side and sleeve seams.

The Neckband. With No. 11 needles and right side of work facing, knit up 13 [14] [14] [15] sts. from holder on right front, 7 sts. from side neck, sts. from holder at back neck, 7 sts. from left side neck and sts. from holder on left front. 72 [76] [76] [80] sts.

1st row: Knit.

2nd row: (Eyelets) K.2, (w.o., k.2 tog.) to last 6 sts., k.6. K.4 rows. Cast off.

Press all seams. Face button and buttonhole bands with facing ribbon, and press. Sew on buttons to correspond with buttonholes.

Make a twisted cord of White wool used double, and thread it through eyelets at neck, finishing each end with a small tassel.

Using Contrast wool, embroider a 4 petal lazy-daisy into each diamond; add 4 green leaves to each daisy. Press embroidery lightly on wrong side.

V-necked cardigan

The borders of cable stitch contrast attractively with the simple stocking stitch

Materials. 16 [17] [18] ozs. Robin Wonderwool Double Knitting. 1 Pair each Nos. 8 and 10 Knitting Needles. 7 Buttons.

Measurements. To fit 34 [36] [38] inch bust sizes. Length 23 [23½] [23½] inches. Sleeve seam 17 inches.

Tension 5½ stitches to 1 inch over stocking-stitch on No. 8 needles.

Abbreviations. K. knit, p. purl, tog. together, st(s). stitch(es), st.st. stocking stitch, patt. pattern, beg. beginning, cont. continue, dec. decrease, inc. increase, ins. inches, foll. following, alt. alternate, rem. remaining, rep. repeat, t.b.l. through back of loop, tw.2, twist 2 (knit into front of 2nd stitch on left-hand needle then knit 1st stitch, letting both stitches drop off needle in the usual way).

Note—*Instructions are for Size* 34. *Figures in brackets are for the 2 larger sizes in size order. One figure only refers to all 3 sizes.*

The Back. With No. 10 needles cast on 98 [104] [110] sts. and work 1½ ins. k.1, p.1 rib.

Change to No. 8 needles and st.st., working straight until work measures 16 ins. from cast-on edge.

Shape Armholes

Cast off 3 sts. at beg. of next 2 rows then dec. 1 st. each end of next and alt. rows until 80 [84] [88] sts. remain. Cont. straight until work measures 23 [23½] [23½] ins. from cast-on edge.

Shape Shoulders

Cast off 7 sts. at beg. of next 6 rows then cast off 6 [7] [8] sts. at beg. of next 2 rows. Cast off remaining 26 [28] [30] sts.

The Left Front. With No. 10 needles cast on 52 [56] [58] sts. and work 1½ ins. k.1, p.1 rib, inc. 1 st. at end of last row for smallest and largest sizes only. 53 [56] [59] sts.

Change to No. 8 needles and work thus:
** 1st row: K.35 [38] [41] sts., p.2, tw.2, p.2, k.6, p.2, tw.2, p.2.
2nd row: K.2, p.2, k.2, p.6, k.2, p.2, k.2, p.35 [38] [41].
3rd and 4th rows: As 1st and 2nd rows.
5th row: K.35 [38] [41], p.2, tw.2, p.2, slip next 3 sts. on a cable needle and leave at front of work, k.3, then k.3 from cable needle, p.2, tw.2, p.2.
6th row: As 2nd row.

7th and 8th rows: As 1st and 2nd rows.
These 8 rows are rep. Work straight until work measures 16 ins. from cast-on edge ending at side edge.

Shape Armhole and Front

Next row: Cast off 3 sts., knit to last 20 sts., k.2 tog. t.b.l., patt. 18.

Dec. 1 st. at armhole edge at beg. of 6 [7] [8] foll. alt. rows then keep this edge straight, at the same time dec. 1 st. at inside edge of patt. as before at end of every 4th row, working thus until 31 [32] [33] sts. rem. Cont. straight until armhole matches Back armhole ending at side edge.

Shape Shoulder

Cast off 7 sts. at beg. of next and 2 foll. alt. rows. Work 1 row. Cast off rem. 10 [11] [12] sts.

The Right Front. Work as for Left Front to ** but smallest and largest sizes inc. at beg. of last row instead of at end.
1st row: P.2, tw.2, p.2, k.6, p.2, tw.2, p.2, k.35 [38] [41]. Cont. to match the Left Front, reversing shapings and when shaping the front edge k.2 tog. in the usual way and not t.b.l.

The Sleeves (both alike). With No. 10 needles cast on 44 [46] [48] sts. and work 3 ins. k.1, p.1 rib. Change to No. 8 needles and st.st., inc. 1 st. each end of 3rd row and every foll. 6th row until there are 74 [78] [78] sts. Cont. straight until work is 17 ins. from cast-on edge.

Shape Top

Cast off 3 sts. at beg. of next 2 rows then dec. 1 st. each end of next and alt. rows until 56 sts. rem., then each end of every row to 26 sts. Cast off.

The Front Band. With No. 10 needles cast on 12 sts. Work ½ in. in k.1, p.1 rib.

Make Buttonhole

Next row: Rib 5, cast off 2, rib 5.
Next row: Rib 5, cast on 2, rib 5. Cont. in rib making 6 more buttonholes with 2¼ ins. between, measured from the base of each one, then cont. straight until long enough when slightly stretched to fit all round front edge. Cast off.

To Make Up. Press with a warm iron over a damp cloth. Join shoulder, side and sleeve seams. Set in sleeves. Sew on front band. Press seams and sew on the buttons.

149

christening robe in 2-ply

Materials. 4 ozs. of Patons Beehive Fingering, 2-ply. A pair each of Nos. 8, 9, 11, 12 and 13 needles. 3 buttons. 1½ yards ribbon.

Measurements. To fit 18-19 inch chest. Length from back neck 21½ inches. Length of sleeve seam 1¼ inches.

Tension 9 stitches and 11 rows to 1 inch over stocking stitch on No. 12 needles.

Abbreviations. St(s.) stitch(es), p. purl, k. knit, rep. repeat, w.f. wool forward, tog. together, beg. beginning, patt. pattern, sl. slip, p.s.s.o. pass slipped stitch over, st.st. stocking stitch (1 row knit, 1 row purl alternately), dec. decrease, inc. increase.

The Back. ** With No. 9 needles, cast on 141 sts.
1st row: Purl.
2nd row: Knit.
Rep. these 2 rows once.
5th row: (Wrong side facing, picot holes.) P.1, (w.f., p.2 tog.) to end. Inc. 1 st. at beg. of next row, work 2 rows all knit.

Change to No. 8 needles and work 2 more rows all knit. 142 sts.

Now commence Shetland lace patt. as follows:

1st row: K.1, * k.5, k.2 tog., w.f., k.1, w.f., k.2 tog., k.9, k.2 tog., w.f., k.1, w.f., k.2 tog., k.4; rep. from * to last st., k.1.

2nd row: K.1, * k.3, k.2 tog., w.f., k.3, w.f., k.2 tog., k.7, k.2 tog., w.f., k.3, w.f., k.2 tog., k.4; rep. from * to last st., k.1.

3rd row: K.1, * k.3, (k.2 tog., w.f.) twice, k.1, (w.f., k.2 tog.) twice, k.5, (k.2 tog., w.f.) twice, k.1, (w.f., k.2 tog.) twice, k.2; rep. from * to last st., k.1.

4th row: K.1, * k.1, k.2 tog., w.f., k.7, w.f., k.2 tog., k.3, (k.2 tog., w.f.) twice, k.3, (w.f., k.2 tog.) twice, k.2; rep. from * to last st., k.1.

5th row: K.1, * k.1, (k.2 tog., w.f., k.2, w.f., k.2 tog., k.1) twice, (k.2 tog., w.f.) twice, k.1, w.f., sl.1, k.2 tog., p.s.s.o., w.f., k.1, (w.f., k.2 tog.) twice; rep. from * to last st., k.1.

6th row: K.1, * w.f., k.2 tog., k.9, k.2 tog., w.f., k.1, w.f., k.2 tog., k.3, w.f., sl.1, k.2 tog., p.s.s.o., w.f., k.3, k.2 tog., w.f., k.1; rep. from * to last st., k.1.

7th row: K.1, * (k.1, w.f., k.2 tog., k.2, k.2 tog., w.f.) twice, k.1, w.f., k.2 tog., (k.1, w.f., sl.1, k.2 tog., p.s.s.o., w.f.) twice, k.1, k.2 tog., w.f.; rep. from * to last st., k.1.

8th row: K.1, * w.f., k.2 tog., k.9, k.2 tog., w.f., k.1, w.f., k.2 tog., k.1, k.2 tog., w.f., k.3, w.f., k.2 tog., k.1, k.2 tog., w.f., k.1; rep. from * to last st., k.1.

9th row: K.1, * k.1, w.f., k.2 tog., k.2, w.f., k.2 tog., k.1, k.2 tog., w.f., k.2, k.2 tog., w.f., k.1, w.f., (k.2 tog.) twice, w.f., k.1, w.f., sl.1, k.2 tog., p.s.s.o., w.f., k.1, w.f., (k.2 tog.) twice, w.f.; rep. from * to last st., k.1.

10th row: K.1, * w.f., k.2 tog., k.9, k.2 tog., w.f., k.1, w.f., k.2 tog., k.3, w.f., sl.1, k.2 tog., p.s.s.o., w.f., k.3, k.2 tog., w.f., k.1; rep. from * to last st., k1.

11th row: K.1, * k.1, w.f., k.2 tog., (k.2, k.2 tog., w.f., k.1, w.f., k.2 tog.) twice, (k.1, w.f., sl.1, k.2 tog., p.s.s.o., w.f.) twice, k.1, k.2 tog., w.f.; rep. from * to last st., k.1.

12th row: K.1, * w.f., k.2 tog., k.9, k.2 tog., w.f., k.1, w.f., k.2 tog., k.1, k.2 tog., w.f., k.3, w.f., k.2 tog., k.1, k.2 tog., w.f., k.1; rep. from * to last st., k.1.

13th row: K.1, * k.2, (w.f., k.2 tog., k.1) twice, (k.2 tog., w.f., k.1) twice, k.2, w.f., k.2 tog., k.2, w.f., sl.1, k.2 tog., p.s.s.o., w.f., k.2, k.2 tog., w.f., k.1; rep. from * to last st., k.1.

14th row: K.1, * k.2, w.f., k.2 tog., k.5, k.2 tog., w.f., k.5, w.f., k.2 tog., k.1, w.f., sl.1, k.2 tog., p.s.s.o., w.f., k.1, k.2 tog., w.f., k.3; rep. from * to last st., k.1.

15th row: K.1, * k.4, w.f., k.2 tog., k.3, k.2 tog., w.f., k.7, w.f., k.2 tog., k.3, k.2 tog., w.f., k.3; rep. from * to last st., k.1.

16th row: K.1, * w.f., k.2 tog., k.2, w.f., k.2 tog., k.1, k.2 tog., w.f., k.3, k.2 tog., (w.f.) twice, k.2 tog., k.2, w.f., k.2 tog., k.1, k.2 tog., w.f., k.3, k.2 tog., w.f.; rep. from * to last st., k.1.

17th row: K.1, * k.6, w.f., sl.1, k.2 tog., p.s.s.o., w.f., k.11 (knitting into front of the 1st w.f. of previous row, and knitting into back of 2nd w.f.), w.f., sl.1, k.2 tog., p.s.s.o., w.f., k.5; rep. from * to last st., k.1.

18th row: K.1, * k.2 tog., (w.f.) twice, k.2 tog., k.6, k.2 tog., (w.f.) twice, k.2 tog.; rep. from * to last st., k.1.

19th row: Knit to end, knitting into front of 1st w.f. and back of 2nd w.f. each time a double w.f. appears.

20th row: K.1, * w.f., (k.2 tog.) twice, (w.f.) twice, k.2 tog., k.2, (k.2 tog., w.f., w.f., k.2 tog.) 3 times, k.2, k.2 tog., (w.f.) twice, (k.2 tog.) twice, w.f.; rep. from * to last st., k.1.

21st row: As 19th row.

22nd row: As 18th row.

23rd row: As 19th row.

24th row: K.1, * w.f., k.2 tog., k.2, k.2 tog., w.f., k.1, w.f., k.2 tog., k.3, k.2 tog., (w.f.) twice, k.2 tog., k.2, k.2 tog., w.f., k.1, w.f., k.2 tog., k.3, k.2 tog., w.f.; rep. from * to last st., k.1.

25th row: K.1, * k.4, k.2 tog., w.f., k.3, w.f., k.2 tog., k.7 (knitting into front of 1st w.f., and back of 2nd w.f.), k.2 tog., w.f., k.3, w.f., k.2 tog., k.3; rep. from * to last st., k.1.

26th row: K.1, * k.2, (k.2 tog., w.f.) twice, k.1, (w.f., k.2 tog.) twice, k.5, (k.2 tog., w.f.) twice, k.1, (w.f., k.2 tog.) twice, k.3; rep. from * to last st., k.1.

27th row: K.1, * k.2, k.2 tog., w.f., k.7, w.f., k.2 tog., k.3, (k.2 tog., w.f.) twice, k.3 (w.f., k.2 tog.) twice, k.1; rep. from * to last st., k.1.

28th row: K.1, * k.2 tog., w.f., k.2, w.f., k.2 tog., k.1, k.2 tog., w.f., k.2, k.2 tog., w.f., k.1, (k.2 tog., w.f.) twice, k.1, w.f., sl.1, k.2 tog., p.s.s.o., w.f., k.1, (w.f., k.2 tog.) twice, k.1; rep. from * to last st., k.1.

29th row: K.1, * k.1, w.f., k.2 tog., k.9, k.2 tog., w.f., k.1, w.f., k.2 tog., k.3, w.f., sl.1, k.2 tog., p.s.s.o., w.f., k.3, k.2 tog., w.f.; rep. from * to last st., k.1.

30th row: K.1, * w.f., k.2 tog., (k.2, k.2 tog., w.f., k.1, w.f., k.2 tog.) twice, (k.1, w.f., sl.1, k.2 tog., p.s.s.o., w.f.) twice, k.1, k.2 tog., w.f., k.1; rep. from * to last st., k.1.

31st row: K.1, * k.1, w.f., k.2 tog., k.9, k.2 tog., w.f., k.1, w.f., k.2 tog., k.1, k.2 tog., w.f., k.3, w.f., k.2 tog., k.1, k.2 tog., w.f.; rep. from * to last st., k.1.

32nd row: K.1, * w.f., k.2 tog., k.2, w.f., k.2 tog., k.1, k.2 tog., w.f., k.2, k.2 tog., w.f., k.1, w.f., (k.2 tog.) twice, w.f., k.1, w.f., sl.1, k.2 tog., p.s.s.o., w.f., k.1, w.f., (k.2 tog.) twice, w.f., k.1; rep. from * to last st., k.1.

33rd row: K.1, * k.1, w.f., k.2 tog., k.9, k.2 tog., w.f., k.1, w.f., k.2 tog., k.3, w.f., sl.1, k.2 tog., p.s.s.o., w.f., k.3, k.2 tog., w.f.; rep. from * to last st., k.1.

34th row: K.1, * w.f., k.2 tog., k.2, w.f., k.2 tog., k.1, w.f., k.2 tog., k.2, k.2 tog., w.f., k.1, w.f., k.2 tog., (k.1, w.f., sl.1, k.2 tog., p.s.s.o., w.f.) twice, k.1, k.2 tog., w.f., k.1; rep. from * to last st., k.1.

35th row: K.1, * w.f., k.2 tog., k.1, k.2 tog., w.f., k.3, w.f., k.2 tog., k.1, k.2 tog., w.f., k.1, w.f., k.2 tog., k.9, k.2 tog., w.f., k.1; rep. from * to last st., k.1.

36th row: K.1, * (k.1, w.f., k.2 tog.) twice, (k.1, k.2 tog., w.f.) twice, k.3, w.f., k.2 tog., k.2, w.f., sl.1, k.2 tog., p.s.s.o., w.f., k.2, k.2 tog., w.f., k.2; rep. from * to last st., k.1.

37th row: K.1, * k.3, w.f., k.2 tog., k.5, k.2 tog., w.f., k.5, w.f., k.2 tog., k.1, w.f., sl.1, k.2 tog., p.s.s.o., w.f., k.1, k.2 tog., w.f., k.2; rep. from * to last st., k.1.

38th row: K.1, * k.3, w.f., k.2 tog., k.3, k.2 tog., w.f., k.7, w.f., k.2 tog., k.3, k.2 tog., w.f., k.4; rep. from * to last st., k.1.

39th row: K.1, * k.5, w.f., k.2 tog., k.1, k.2 tog., w.f., k.9, w.f., k.2 tog., k.1, k.2 tog., w.f., k.4; rep. from * to last st., k.1.

40th row: K.1, * k.5, w.f., sl.1, k.2 tog., p.s.s.o., w.f., k.11, w.f., sl.1, k.2 tog., p.s.s.o., w.f., k.6; rep. from * to last st., k.1.

41st and 42nd rows: Knit to end.

Rep. this 42 row patt. twice more, then rep. 1st to 23rd rows inclusive.

continued overleaf

continued from previous page

Next row: Knit to end.
Next row: (Right side facing) K.1, * (k.2 tog.) 3 times, k.1; rep. from * to last st., k.1. 82 sts.
Change to No. 12 needles. Purl one row.
Next row: (Ribbon holes) K.2, (w.f., k.2 tog.) to end. **
Beg. with a purl row, continue in st.st. to end. Work 11 more rows.

Shape Raglan Armholes

Cast off 3 sts. at beg. of next 2 rows.
Next row: K.2, sl.1 knitwise, k.1, p.s.s.o., knit to last 4, k.2 tog., k.2. Rep. this row every following right side row until 62 sts. remain. P.1 row.

Divide for Button Opening

Next row: K.2, sl.1 knitwise, k.1, p.s.s.o., k.29, turn and leave remaining 29 sts. on a holder.
Complete right side as follows: Keeping 4 k. sts. at inner edge on every row, continue to dec. at armhole edge on every right side row. Work thus until 29 sts. remain, ending at finish of a wrong side row.
Next row: (Buttonhole) K.2, sl.1 knitwise, k.1, p.s.s.o., knit to last 4, k.2 tog., (w.f.) twice, k.2.
Next row: K.2, k.1 into double w.f. of previous row letting 2nd loop fall, k.1, purl to end.
Continuing to shape as already set, rep. this buttonhole row twice more on following 12th rows: 16 sts. remain.
Purl 1 row. Cast off.
Transfer sts. from holder to No. 12 needle and join wool to inner end.
Next row: Cast on 4 sts. (for underwrap), then knit to last 4 sts., k.2 tog., k.2.
Omitting the buttonholes, complete to match right side.

The Front. Work as given for Back from ** to **.
Purl 1 row. Now change to st.st. with central panel of Shetland lace, as follows:-
Next row: K.27, (k.5, k.2 tog., w.f., k.1, w.f., k.2 tog., k.9, k.2 tog., w.f., k.1, w.f., k.2 tog., k.4), k.27.
Continue to keep the central 28 sts. in Shetland lace patt. of back, next row being 2nd row of the patt. and the 28 sts. those given in brackets in preceding row.
At the same time, shape as follows: Work 9 more rows straight.

Shape Raglan Armholes

Cast off 3 sts. at beg. of next 2 rows.
Next row: K.2, sl.1 knitwise, k.1, p.s.s.o., patt. to last 4 sts., k.2 tog., k.2.
Continue to dec. as set every right side row until 48 sts. remain. Work 1 wrong side row (40 rows of Shetland lace patt. completed).

Shape Neck

Next row: K.2, sl.1 knitwise, k.1, p.s.s.o., k.13, turn and leave remaining 31 sts. on a holder.
Next row: Purl to end.
Next row: K.2, sl.1 knitwise, k.1, p.s.s.o., knit to last 4 sts., k.2 tog., k.2.
Next row: Purl.
Next row: K.2, sl.1 knitwise, k.1, p.s.s.o., knit to end.
Next row: Purl.
Rep. the last 4 rows until 2 sts. remain. Sl. first st. over 2nd st. and fasten off.
Leaving centre 14 sts. on a holder, transfer remaining sts. to No. 12 needle and work as follows: Knit to last 4 sts., k.2 tog., k.2. Purl 1 row.
Next row: K.2, sl.1 knitwise, k.1, p.s.s.o., knit to last 4 sts., k.2 tog., k.2. Purl 1 row.
Next row: Knit to last 4 sts., k.2 tog., k.2. Purl 1 row.
Rep. the last 4 rows until 2 sts. remain. Slip first st. over 2nd st., and fasten off.

The Sleeves (both alike). With No. 11 needles, cast on 53 sts. Change to No. 12 needles.
1st row: Knit.
2nd row: Purl.
Rep. these 2 rows once.
5th row: K.1, (w.f., k.2 tog.) to end.
6th row: Inc. into first st., purl to end, 54 sts.
Complete the sleeve in st.st. Inc. 1 st. at each end of following 5th row and 2 following 4th rows. 60 sts. Purl 1 row.

Shape Top

Cast off 3 sts. at beg. of next 2 rows.
Next row: K.2, sl.1 knitwise, k.1, p.s.s.o., knit to last 4 sts., k.2 tog., k.2.
Rep. this row every following alternate row until 6 sts. remain. Purl 1 row. Cast off.

To Make Up. Pin out pieces on wrong sides and press with a warm iron over a damp cloth. Sew raglan sleeves into armholes. Join side and sleeve seams. Fold picot hem to wrong side, in line with holes, then catch stitch neatly. Repeat for each sleeve.

The Neckband. With No. 13 needles and right side facing, evenly knit up 85 sts. all round neck edge. Beg. with a purl row, work 3 rows st.st.
Next row: K.1, (w.f., k.2 tog.) to end. Work 3 more rows st.st. Cast off.
Fold neckband to wrong side at line of holes to form picot hem, then catch stitch neatly on wrong side.
Neaten lower end of underwrap and sew on buttons to correspond with buttonholes. Give robe a final press. Thread ribbon through holes at yoke and tie in a bow at centre front.

red coat with cravat and cuffs

The brass buttons and white cravat and cuffs give a military smartness to the garment, pictured overleaf

Materials: 34 [36] [38] ozs. of Wendy Family Wool, 4-ply, 1 pair each No. 8 and No. 10 knitting needles. 9 buttons. 2 press studs. 1 yard of white fabric, 36 inches wide.

Measurements. To fit 34 [36] [38] inch bust. Length 28 [29] [30] inches. Sleeve seam 16 inches.

Tension 6 stitches to 1 inch over pattern on No. 8 needles, using wool double.

Abbreviations. K. knit, p. purl, st(s). stitch(es), st.st. stocking stitch, tog. together, t.b.l. through the backs of the loops, w.f. wool forward, w.b. wool back, sl. slip, rep. repeat, patt. pattern, beg. beginning, dec. decrease by working 2 sts. together, inc. increase by working twice into 1 stitch.

Note—*Instructions are given for 34 inch bust size. Figures in brackets are for the two larger sizes in size order. Where one figure only is given this refers to all sizes.*

The Back. With No. 10 needles and wool used single, cast on 101 [107] [113] sts. Work 9 rows st.st., inc. at both ends of every purl row. 109 [115] [121] sts. K.1 row on wrong side, to form hemline.

Join on another strand of wool, and using wool double, change to No. 8 needles and patt. thus:

1st row: Knit.
2nd row: Purl.
3rd row: Knit.
4th row: K.1, * keeping wool at back, sl.1, k.1, rep. from * to end.
5th row: K.1, * w.f., sl.1, w.b., k.1, rep. from * to end.
6th row: Purl.
These 6 rows form the patt. Proceed until work measures

19½ [20] [20½] ins. from hemline, finishing after a wrong side row.

Shape Armholes
Cast off 2 sts. at beg. of next 2 rows. 105 [111] [117] sts. Proceed thus:
1st row: K.4, k.2 tog. t.b.l., patt. to last 6 sts., k.2 tog., k.4.
2nd row: K.1, p.4, patt. to last 5 sts., p.4, k.1.
3rd row: K.5, patt. to last 5 sts., k.5.
4th row: K.1, p.3, p.2 tog., patt. to last 6 sts., p.2 tog. t.b.l., p.3, k.1.
5th row: As 3rd row.
6th row: As 2nd row.
Rep. these 6 rows twice [3] [3] times more. For 34 and 38 inch bust sizes work 1st 2 rows of armhole shaping again. 91 [95] [99] sts.
Proceed thus:-
1st row: K.5, patt. to last 5 sts., k.5.
2nd row: K.1, p.4, patt. to last 5 sts., p.4, k.1.
Continue thus until work is 8 [8½] [9] inches from beg. of armholes, measured on the straight, after a wrong side row.

Shape Shoulders
Cast off 8 [9] [10] sts. at beg. of next 2 rows and 8 sts. at beg. of next 4 rows. Cast off remaining 43 [45] [47] sts. for back neck.

The Left Front. With No. 10 needles and single wool cast on 67 [71] [75] sts. Work 9 rows st.st., inc. at both ends of every purl row. 75 [79] [83] sts. K.1 row to form hemline.
Join in another strand of wool and change to No. 8 needles and patt. Proceed until work matches Back to armholes, finishing at side edge.

Shape Armhole
Cast off 2 sts. at beg. of next row. Work back.
Proceed thus:-
1st row: K.4, k.2 tog. t.b.l., patt. to end.
2nd row: Patt. to last 5 sts., p.4, k.1.
3rd row: K.5, patt. to end.
4th row: Patt. to last 6 sts., p.2 tog. t.b.l., p.3, k.1.
5th row: As 3rd row.
6th row: As 2nd row.
Proceed thus until 66 [69] [72] sts. remain.
Working border at armhole edge as for Back, proceed until 6 [6½] [7] inches from beg. of armhole, measured on the straight, finishing at side edge.

Shape Neck
Next row: Patt. 33 [34] [35], cast off next 23 [25] [27] sts.,

continued overleaf

153

continued from previous page

1 st. now on right hand needle after casting off. Patt. remaining 9 sts.

Proceeding on last set of 10 sts., dec. at neck edge (i.e., edge at which sts. were cast off) on next 6 rows, then on every alternate row until all sts. are worked off.

Join wool to inner edge of remaining 33 [34] [35] sts. Dec. at neck edge of next 6 rows, then of every alternate row until 24 [25] [26] sts. remain. Continue until work matches Back to outer shoulder.

Shape Shoulder

Cast off 8 [9] [10] sts. at beg. of next side-edge row and 8 on next 2 alternate rows.

The Right Front. Work as Left until 8 [9] [10] inches from hemline, after a wrong side row.

Make 1st pair of buttonholes thus: Patt. 5, cast off 5, patt. 22 [24] [26], making 23 [25] [27] sts. on right hand needle after 1st buttonhole, cast off 5, patt. to end. On next row cast on 5 sts. over each group cast off.

Complete to correspond with Left Front, reversing shapings and making 3 more evenly spaced pairs of buttonholes, the last $\frac{3}{4}$ inch below beg. of neck shaping.

The Sleeves (both alike). With No. 10 needles and single wool cast on 59 [63] [67] sts. Work 9 rows st.st. K.1 row to form hemline. Join in another strand of wool and change to No. 8 needles and patt. Inc. at both ends of the 7th and every 6th row following until there are 79 [83] [87] sts., then of every 12th row until 87 [91] [95] sts. Proceed until 16 inches from hemline, after a wrong side row.

Shape Top

Cast off 2 sts. at beg. of next 2 rows. Proceed thus:-

1st row: K.4, k.2 tog. t.b.l., patt. to last 6 sts., k.2 tog., k.4.

2nd row: K.1, p.4, patt. to last 5 sts., p.4, k.1.

Rep. these 2 rows until 63 [65] [67] sts. remain. Cast off.

The Collar. With No. 10 needles and double wool cast on 99 [103] [107] sts.

1st row: K.2, * p.1, k.1. Rep. from * to last st., k.1.

2nd row: K.1, * p.1, k.1. Rep. from * to end.

Rep. these 2 rows until work measures $1\frac{1}{2}$ inches. Change to No. 8 needles and patt.

Work 27 rows, inc. at both ends of the 3rd and every 6th row following. 109 [113] [117] sts. Cut 1 strand of wool. Change to No. 10 needles. K.1 row on wrong side for hemline. Beg. again with a knit row, work 8 rows st.st., dec. at both ends of 1st, 2nd, 4th, 5th, 7th and 8th rows. Cast off.

The Belt (make 2 pieces alike). With No. 8 needles and double wool, cast on 15 sts. Work 9 [9½] [10] inches patt. Dec. at both ends of next 4 right-side rows, then dec. at both ends of every row until 3 sts. remain. K.3 tog.

The Facings. Press all parts under a damp cloth.

With right side of work facing, using No. 10 needles and single wool, knit up 166 [172] [178] sts. along right front edge from hemline to neck. K.1 row for hemline. Beg. again with a knit row, work 6 rows st.st., dec. at lower edge on every alternate row and at neck edge on every row. Cast off. Complete left front facing to correspond.

Measure up 4 inches from hemline on right side seam of back. With right side facing, using No. 10 needles and single wool, knit up 26 sts. along these 4 inches. K.1 row. Beg. again with a knit row, work 8 rows st.st., dec. at lower edge on every alternate row. Cast off. Complete left side of back and both sides of fronts to correspond.

With right side of collar facing, using No. 10 needles and single wool, leaving edge of ribbing free, knit up 20 sts. along 1 side of collar. K.1 row. Beg. again with a knit row, work 8 rows st.st., dec. at upper edge on 1st, 2nd, 4th, 5th, 7th and 8th rows. Cast off. Complete 2nd side of collar to correspond.

With right side of 1 belt section facing, using No. 10 needles and single wool, knit up 58 [61] [64] sts. along straight edge of belt. K.1 row. Beg. again with a knit row, work 8 rows st.st. Cast off. Complete 2nd side of belt section and both sides of 2nd belt section to correspond.

To Make Up. Turn in and hem belt and collar facings, and press.

Join side seams, inserting short straight edges of belt in seams. Join shoulder and sleeve seams. Set sleeves into armholes. Turn in and hem facings on fronts, sleeves, side slits and lower edge, mitring corners neatly where necessary. Sew cast-on edge of collar to neck edge, end of collar above top buttonhole on right hand side, and at corresponding point on left. Neaten remainder of front neck edges with buttonhole stitching. Neaten buttonholes. Press seams. Sew on buttons to match buttonholes. Fasten neck edges with press studs. Overlap ends of belt at back and secure with a button.

To make cravat, press any creases out of fabric, fold diagonally with right side inside, and mark a line parallel with fold and 6 inches from it. Cut the double fabric along this line. Leaving 4 inches open at centre, stitch just inside this line and diagonal ends. Turn inside out and close remaining 4 inches.

Make cuffs in same way from remaining fabric, diagonally folded, about 3 inches wide and 9½ [10] [10½] inches long, with straight ends.

Press cravat and cuffs. Stitch cuffs inside coat sleeves, allowing about 1½ inches to project.

a lady's bed jacket in double knitting

The variation of stitch across the yoke adds interest to this delicate but warm jacket with a ribbon-tie neck

Materials. 18 ozs. of Robin Bri-Nylon Double Knitting. 1 pair each knitting needles No. 6 and No. 10. Set of 4 No. 8 needles, points both ends. 1½ yds. ribbon. 1 press stud. 3 stitch holders.

Measurements. To fit up to 40 inch bust. Length from back neck—20 inches. Sleeve seam—18 inches.

Tension 6 sts. and 8 rows to 1 inch on No. 8 needles over stocking stitch. 5 sts. and 7 rows to 1 inch on No. 6 needles over pattern.

Abbreviations. K. knit, p. purl, st(s). stitch(es), ins. inches, sl. slip, beg. beginning, tog. together, dec. decrease, rep. repeat, inc. increase, patt. pattern, m.1 make a stitch by winding wool over needle, p.s.s.o. pass slipped stitch over.

Back. With No. 10 needles cast on 107 sts.
1st row: * K.1, p.1; rep. from * to last st., k.1.
Rep. the last row 5 times more.
7th row: Moss st. 4, * inc. in next st., moss st. 6; rep. from * to last 5 sts., inc. in next st., moss st. 4. 122 sts.
Change to No. 6 needles and work patt. thus:
1st row: Right side * P.2, m.1 (see abbreviations). sl.1, k.1, p.s.s.o.; rep. from * to last 2 sts., p.2.
2nd row: * K.2, p.2; rep. from * to last 2 sts., k.2.
3rd row: * P.2, k.2 tog., m.1; rep. from * to last 2 sts., p.2.
4th row: As 2nd row.
These 4 rows form the patt. Continue in patt. until work measures 12½ ins. from beg., ending with a 2nd row of patt.

Shape Armholes
Keeping the patt. correct, cast off 4 sts. at beg. of next 2 rows, then dec. 1 st. at both ends of next and every alternate row until 96 sts. remain.
Sl. sts. on to a holder.

Left Front. With No. 10 needles cast on 55 sts.
1st row: * K.1, p.1; rep. from * to last st., k.1.
Rep. this row 5 times more.
7th row: (K.1, p.1) twice, k.1, inc. in next st., (moss st. 8, inc. in next st.) 5 times, moss st. 4: 61 sts.
Change to No. 6 needles and patt. as follows:
1st row: Right side * P.2, m.1, sl.1, k.1, p.s.s.o.; rep. from * to last 5 sts., (k.1, p.1) twice, k.1.
2nd row: (K.1, p.1) twice, k.1, * p.2, k.2; rep. from * to end.
3rd row: * P.2, k.2 tog., m.1; rep. from * to last 5 sts., (k.1, p.1) twice, k.1.
4th row: As 2nd row.
Rep. these 4 rows of patt. until work measures 12½ ins. from beg., ending with a 2nd row of patt.

Shape Armhole
Next row: Cast off 4 sts., patt. to end. Work 1 row. Dec. 1 st. at the armhole edge on the next and every alternate row until 48 sts. remain. Sl. these sts. on to a holder.

Right Front. Cast on and work the first 7 rows as for left front. 61 sts.
Change to No. 6 needles and patt. thus:
1st row: Right side (k.1, p.1) twice, k.1, * m.1, sl.1, k.1, p.s.s.o., p.2; rep. from * to end.
2nd row: * K.2, p.2; rep. from * to last 5 sts., (k.1, p.1) twice, k.1.
3rd row: (K.1, p.1) twice, k.1, * k.2 tog., m.1, p.2; rep. from * to end.
4th row: As 2nd row.
Rep. these 4 rows of patt. until work measures 12½ ins. from beg., ending with a 3rd row of patt.

Shape Armhole
Work as left front reversing all shapings.

Sleeves (alike). With No. 10 needles cast on 54 sts. and work 22 rows k.1, p.1 rib.
23rd row: Rib 7, * inc. in next st.; rep. from * to last 7 sts., rib 7. 94 sts.
Change to No. 6 needles and work in patt. as given for back until work measures 18 ins. from beg. ending with a 2nd row of patt.

continued overleaf

continued from previous page

Shape Top

Cast off 4 sts. at beg. of next 2 rows, then dec. 1 st. at each end of next and every alternate row until 68 sts. remain. Sl. these sts. on to a holder.

Yoke. Arrange the 48 sts. from right front, 68 sts. from first sleeve, 96 sts. from back, 68 sts. from the 2nd sleeve and 48 sts. from left front evenly on to the set of No. 8 needles. 328 sts.

Next row: Wrong side (k.1, p.1) twice, k.1, p.13, (p.2 tog., p.15) 17 times, p.2 tog., p.14, (k.1, p.1) twice, k.1. 310 sts.

1st row: (K.1, p.1) twice, k.1, p.2 tog., * k.1, p.1; rep. from * to last st., k.1. 309 sts.

2nd row: * K.1, p.1; rep. from * to last st., k.1. Rep this row 5 times more.

8th row: (K.1, p.1) twice, k.1, * p.2, p.2 tog.; rep. from * to last 8 sts., p.3, (k.1, p.1) twice, k.1. 235 sts.

9th row: (K.1, p.1) twice, k. to last 4 sts., (p.1, k.1) twice.

10th row: (K.1, p.1) twice, k.1, p. to last 5 sts., (k.1, p.1) twice, k.1.

11th and 12th rows: As 9th and 10th rows.
Rep. last 2 rows once.

15th to 21st rows: As 2nd row.

22nd row: (K.1, p.1) twice, k.1, * p.2 tog., p.1; rep. from * to last 8 sts., p.3 tog., (k.1, p.1) twice, k.1: 159 sts.

23rd and 24th rows: As 9th and 10th rows.
Rep. last 2 rows twice more.

29th to 35th rows: As 2nd row.

36th row: (K.1, p.1) twice, k.1, (p.2 tog.) 74 times, p.1, (k.1, p.1) twice, k.1. 85 sts.

37th and 38th rows: As 9th and 10th rows.
Rep. last 2 rows twice more.

Neckband

1st row: Cast off 5 sts., * k.1, p.1; rep. from * to end.

2nd row: As 1st row.

3rd row: * P.1, k.1; rep. from * to last st., p.1.
Rep. last row 4 times more.

8th row: P.1, k.1, * m.1, k.2 tog.; rep. from * to last st, p.1.
Rep. 3rd row 7 times more.
Cast off loosely in patt.

To Make Up. With wrong side facing press lightly with a warm iron over a damp cloth if required. Join raglan, side and sleeve seams. Fold neckband in half on to wrong side and slip stitch, leaving sides open to take ribbon. Sew press stud to top of front border. Press all seams. Thread ribbon through neckband.

matching

The full colour picture on page 33 illustrates the charm of matching patterns knitted in different colours

Materials. 15 [17] ozs. of Wendy Double Knitting Nylonised—in Main colour—3 [3] ozs. of 1st contrasting colour, 2 [3] ozs. of 2nd contrasting colour, 2 [3] ozs. of 3rd contrasting colour. 1 pair each Nos. 8, 9 and 10 Knitting Needles.
Length 26 [27½] inches. Sleeve seam 16 [18] inches.

Tension 6½ stitches to one inch in pattern on No. 8 needles.

Abbreviations. K. knit, p. purl, st(s). stitch(es), rep. repeat, sl.1 slip one stitch knitways, inc. increase, M Main Colour—Contrasting Colours are numbered C1, C2, C3. St.st. stocking stitch, beg. begin(ning).

Note—*Instructions are given for size 36. Figures in brackets are for size 40. Where one set of figures only is given, this refers to both sizes.*

Measurements. To fit Bust 36 inches (chest 40 inches).

Front and Back (both alike). With No. 10 needles and M wool cast on 124 [144] sts.
Work 2 inches in k.2 p.2 rib, inc. 3 [1] sts. evenly along last row. 127 [145] sts. Join in C1.
Change to No. 8 needles and pattern as follows:

1st row: (K.1 C1, k.2 M, k.3 C1, k.3 M, k.1 C1, k.3 M, k.3 C1, k.2 M) rep. to last st., k.1 C1.

2nd row: (P.2 M, p.3 C1, (p.3 M, p.3 C1) twice, p.1 M) rep. to last st., p.1 M.

3rd row: (K.1 M, k.3 C1, k.3 M, k.5 C1, k.3 M, k.3 C1) rep. to last st., k.1 M.

4th row: (P.3 C1, p.3 M, p.3 C1, p.1 M, p.3 C1, p.3 M, p.2 C1) rep. to last st., p.1 C1.

5th row: (K.2 C1, k.3 M, k.2 C1, k.2 M, k.1 C1, k.2 M, k.2 C1, k.3 M, k.1 C1) rep. to last st., k.1 C1.

6th row: (P.1 C1, p.3 M, p.1 C1, p.1 M, p.1 C1, p.5 M, p.1 C1, p.1 M, p.1 C1, p.3 M) rep. to last st., p.1 C1.

7th row: (K.3 M, k.4 C1, k.5 M, k.4 C1, k.2 M) rep. to last st., k.1 M.

8th row: (P.2 M, p.2 C1, p.3 M, (p.1 C1, p.3 M) twice, p.2 C1, p.1 M) rep. to last st., p.1 M.

air isle sweaters

9th row: (K.1 M, k.3 Cl, k.4 M, k.1 Cl, k.1 M, k.1 Cl, k.4 M, k.3 Cl) rep. to last st., k.1 M.

10th row: (P.3 Cl, p.1 M, (p.1 Cl, p.4 M) twice, p.1 Cl, p.1 M, p.2 Cl) rep. to last st., p.1 Cl.

11th row: As 9th row.

12th row: As 8th row.

13th row: As 7th row.

14th row: As 6th row.

15th row: As 5th row.

16th row: As 4th row.

17th row: As 3rd row.

18th row: As 2nd row.

19th row: As 1st row.

Rows 20 to 38: Join in C2. Repeat rows 1 to 19, reading p. for k., and k. for p., and C2 for Cl.

Rows 39 to 57: Join in C3. Repeat rows 1 to 19, reading C3 for Cl.

Rows 58 to 76: Repeat rows 1 to 19, reading p. for k., and k. for p., and reading Cl as given.

Rows 77 to 95: Repeat rows 1 to 19, reading C2 for Cl.

Rows 96 to 114: Repeat rows 1 to 19, reading p. for k., and k. for p., and C3 for Cl.

Man's Size only: Repeat 1st to 19th rows once more.

Both Sizes: Continue in pattern beg. with 1st row—for Woman's Sweater use Cl, beg. with a k. row, and for Man's, use C2, beg. with a p. row.

Now shape neck (and on each of the following turns, sl.1, pass wool round sl. st., and replace on left hand needle).

Continuing in pattern (with rows 2 and 3) work to last 3 sts., turn and work back to last 3 sts., turn.

Work to last 6 sts., turn and work back to last 6 sts., turn.

Continue to work 3 sts. less in every row than in previous row, before turning and working back, until 21 sts. are left unworked each end, turn.

Work to last 31 [35] sts., turn and work back to last 31 [35] sts., turn.

Work to last 39 [45] sts., turn and work back to last 39 [45] sts. Slip these last sts. on to right hand needle. Break off C wool.

With M wool, knit across all sts., decreasing 3 [1] sts. evenly across this row. 124 [144] sts.

Next row: P.1 * k.2, p.2, rep. from * to last 3 sts., k.2, p.1.

Next row: K.1 * p.2, k.2, rep. from * to last 3 sts., p.2, k.1.

Repeat last 2 rows for 2 inches.

Cast off in rib.

The Sleeves (both alike). With No. 10 needles and M wool, cast on 52 [56] sts. Work 2 inches in k.2, p.2 rib.

Change to No. 9 needles and st.st. inc. 1 st. each end on the 3rd and every following 6th row until there are 84 [92] sts. Work until sleeve measures 16 [18] inches from beg.

Cast off 4 sts. beg. of every row until 12 sts. remain. Cast off.

(N.B. When casting off slip the first st. in every row.)

To Make Up. Press with a warm iron and damp cloth. Sew shoulder seams for 6 [7½] inches on either side. Measure 8 [9] inches from shoulder seams down side of work, pin, and sew sleeves in along this line. Sew up side and sleeve seams. Press seams.

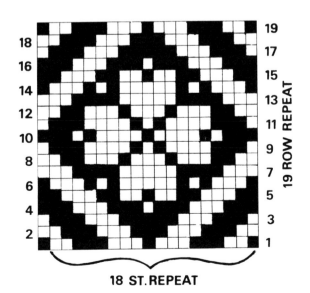

18 · 16 · 14 · 12 · 10 · 8 · 6 · 4 · 2

19 · 17 · 15 · 13 · 11 · 9 · 7 · 5 · 3 · 1

19 ROW REPEAT

18 ST. REPEAT

A pair of gloves always make a welcome present

Materials, Children's gloves 2 (2) ozs., **Ladies' gloves** 3 ozs., **Men's gloves** 3 ozs., Robin Crepe, Service or Colorama Double Knitting, 1 pair No. 10 knitting needles. Stitch holders.

Measurements (all round hand). Children's gloves—5 (5¾) inches. Ladies' gloves—7 inches. Men's gloves—8 inches.

Tension 7 stitches and 9 rows to 1 inch stocking stitch on No. 10 needles.

Abbreviations. K. knit, p. purl, st(s). stitch(es), tog. together, ins. inches, inc. increasing, dec. decrease, rep. repeat, st.st. stocking stitch (1 row k., 1 row p.), m.1 make one stitch by picking up loop before next st. and knitting into back of it.

CHILDREN'S GLOVES

Note. Instructions for the larger size are in brackets. Where only one figure is given, this applies to both sizes.

With No. 10 needles cast on 34 [38] sts.
Work 1¾ [2¼] ins. k.1, p.1 rib.
Work 2 rows st.st.

Shape Thumb
1st row: K.16 [18], m.1 (see abbreviations), k.2, m.1, k.16 [18].
Work 3 rows st.st.
5th row: K.16 [18], m.1, k.4, m.1, k.16 [18].
Work 3 rows st.st.
Continue in this way inc. 2 sts. every 4th row to 42 [46] sts.
Work 1 [3] rows st.st.

Thumb
Next row: K.26 [28], turn, cast on 1 [2] sts., leave remaining sts. on a holder.
Next row: P.11 [12], turn, cast on 1 [2] sts., leave remaining sts. on a holder.
Work 1½ [1¾] ins. st.st. on these 12 [14] sts., ending with a p. row.

Shape Top
★ **1st row:** * K.1, k.2 tog.; rep. from * to end (last 2 sts., k.2).
2nd row: P.

3rd row: * K.2 tog.; rep. from * to end.
Break wool, draw through sts. and fasten tightly. Join seam ★.
With right side facing rejoin wool to base of thumb; k. up 2 [4] sts. from base, k. across 16 [18] sts. from first holder.
Next row: P. to end including sts. from second holder: 34 [40] sts.
Work 1¼ [1½] ins. st.st., ending with a p. row.

First Finger
Next row: K.22 [26] turn, cast on 1 st.
Next row: P.11 [13] turn, cast on 1 st.
Work 2 [2¼] ins. st.st. on these 12 [14] sts., ending with a p. row.

Shape Top
Work as thumb from ★ to ★.

Second Finger
With right side facing rejoin wool to base of finger, k. up 2 sts. from base, k.4 [5] sts. from left hand needle, turn and cast on 1 st.
Next row: P.11 [13] sts., turn and cast on 1 st. Work 2½ [2¾] ins., ending on a p. row.

Shape Top
Work as thumb from ★ to ★.

Third Finger
Work as second finger but working 2 [2¼] ins. st.st. before shaping top.

Fourth Finger
With right side facing rejoin wool to base of 3rd finger, k. up 2 [3] sts. from base of finger, k. across remaining sts. from left hand needle, turn.
Next row: P. to end.
Work 1¼ [1½] ins. on these 10 [11] sts. ending on a p. row.

Shape Top
Next row: * K.1, k.2 tog.; rep. from * twice more, k.1 [2].
Next row: P.
Next row: * K.2 tog.; rep. from * twice more, k.1 [k.2 tog.].
Break wool, draw through sts. and fasten tightly. Join finger and side seam.

the family

and can be knitted in attractive colours

Work a second glove in the same way. Press each glove lightly using a warm iron over a damp cloth.

LADIES' GLOVES

With No. 10 needles cast on 44 sts. Work $2\frac{1}{2}$ ins. k.1, p.1 rib.
Work 2 rows st.st.

Shape Thumb

1st row: K.21, m.1 (see abbreviations), k.2, m.1, k.21.
Work 3 rows st.st.
5th row: K.21, m.1, k.4, m.1, k.21.
Work 3 rows st.st.
Continue in this way inc. 2 sts. every 4th row to 54 sts.
Work 1 row.

Thumb

Next row: K.33, turn, cast on 2 sts., leave remaining sts. on a holder.
Next row: P.14, turn, cast on 2 sts., leave remaining sts. on a holder.
Work $2\frac{1}{4}$ ins. on these 16 sts.

Shape Top

★ **Next row:** * K.1, k.2 tog.; rep. from * to last st., k.1.
Next row: P.
Next row: K.2 tog. 5 times, k.1.
Break wool, draw through remaining sts. and fasten tightly.
Join seam ★.
With right side facing rejoin wool at base of thumb and k. up 4 sts. from cast on sts. at base, k. across the sts. from first holder.
Next row: P. to end, including sts. from second holder: 46 sts.
Work $1\frac{3}{4}$ ins. st.st. ending on a p. row.

First Finger

Next row: K.29, turn, cast on 1 st.
Next row: P.13, turn, cast on 1 st.
Work $2\frac{3}{4}$ ins. on these 14 sts., ending on a p. row.

Shape Top

★ ★ **Next row:** * K.1, k.2 tog.; rep. from * to last 2 sts., k.2.
Next row: P.

continued overleaf

continued from previous page

Next row: K.2 tog. 5 times.
Break wool, draw through remaining sts. and fasten tightly.
Join seam ★★.

Second Finger

With right side facing rejoin wool to base of first finger, k. up 2 sts. from cast on sts., k.6 sts., turn and cast on 1 st.
Next row: P.15, turn and cast on 1 st.
Work 3¼ ins. on these 16 sts., ending on a p. row.

Shape Top

Work as thumb from ★ to ★.

Third Finger

With right side facing rejoin wool to base of second finger and k. up 2 sts. from cast on sts., k.5 sts. from left hand needle, turn and cast on 1 st.
Next row: P.13, turn and cast on 1 st.
Work 2¾ ins. on these 14 sts.

Shape Top

Work as first finger from ★★ to ★★.

Fourth Finger

With right side facing rejoin wool to base of third finger, k. up 2 sts. from cast on sts., k. across sts. from left hand needle, turn and p. to end.
Work 2 ins. on these 14 sts., ending on a p. row.

Shape Top

Work as first finger from ★★ to ★★.
Work a second glove in the same way. Press each glove lightly using a warm iron over a damp cloth.

MEN'S GLOVES

With No. 10 needles cast on 50 sts. Work 3 ins. k.1, p.1 rib.
Work 2 rows st.st.

Shape Thumb

1st row: K.24, m.1 (see abbreviations), k.2, m.1, k.24.
Work 3 rows st.st.
5th row: K.24, m.1, k.4, m.1, k.24.
Work 3 rows st.st.
Continue in this way inc. 2 sts. every 4th row to 62 sts.
Work 1 row.

Thumb

Next row: K.38, turn, cast on 2 sts., leave remaining sts. on a holder.
Next row: P.16, turn, cast on 2 sts., leave remaining sts. on a holder.
Work 2½ ins. on these 18 sts., ending with a p. row.

Shape Top

★ **Next row:** * K.1, k.2 tog.; rep. from * to end.
Next row: P.
Next row: K.2 tog. 6 times.
Break wool, draw through remaining sts. and fasten tightly. Join seam ★.
With right side facing rejoin wool at base of thumb and k. up 6 sts. from base, k. across sts. from first holder.
Next row: P. to end, including sts. from second holder: 54 sts.
Work 1¾ ins. st.st., ending on a p. row.

Shape Top

★★ **Next row:** * K.1, k.2 tog.; rep. from * to last st., k.1.
Next row: P.
Next row: K.2 tog. 5 times, k.1.
Break wool, draw through remaining sts. and fasten off tightly.
Join seam ★★.

First Finger

Next row: K.34, turn and cast on 1 st.
Next row: P.15, turn and cast on 1 st.
Work 3 ins. on these 16 sts., ending with a p. row.

Second Finger

With right side facing, rejoin wool to base of first finger, k. up 2 sts. from cast on sts., k.7 from left hand needle, turn, cast on 1 st.
Next row: P.17, turn and cast on 1 st.
Work 3½ ins. on these 18 sts., ending with a p. row.

Shape Top

Work as thumb from ★ to ★.

Third Finger

With right side facing rejoin wool to base of second finger and k. up 2 sts. from cast on sts., k.6 sts. from left hand needle, turn and cast on 1 st.
Next row: P.15, turn and cast on 1 st.
Work 3 ins. on these 16 sts., ending on a p. row.

Shape Top

Work as first finger from ★★ to ★★.

Fourth Finger

With right side facing rejoin wool to base of third finger and k. up 2 sts. from cast on sts. K. remaining 7 sts. from left hand needle.
Next row: P.16.
Work 2¼ ins., ending on a p. row.

Shape Top

Work as first finger from ★★ to ★★.
Work a second glove in the same way. Press each glove lightly using a warm iron over a damp cloth.

child's mittens

For younger children, mittens are some-times more suitable than gloves, and, of course, they are more simple to knit

Materials. 2 ozs. Double Knitting Wool. A pair each of No. 10 and No. 8 needles.

Measurements. Length from top of ribbing at wrist to fingertip 5 [5½] [6] inches (adaptable).

Tension 5½ stitches and 7½ rows to 1 inch on No. 8 needles over stocking-stitch.

Abbreviations: See page 100.

Start at Wrist
Using No. 10 needles cast on 36 [38] [40] sts.
1st row: (K.1, p.1) to end. Rep. this row 25 times more, increase 1 st. at end of final row. (37 [39] [41] sts.) Change to No. 8 needles.
1st row: Knit.
2nd row: Purl.
For the 2nd and 3rd sizes, rep. these last 2 rows once more.

Shape for Thumb
1st row: K.18 [19] [20], make 1 by lifting yarn between stitches on previous row and knitting it t.b.l., k.1, make 1, k.18 [19] [20].

2nd and alternate rows: Purl.
3rd row: K.18 [19] [20], make 1, k.3, make 1, k.18 [19] [20].
5th row: K.18 [19] [20], make 1, k.5, make 1, k.18 [19] [20].
Continue to increase in same fashion every knit row until you have 47 [49] [53] sts., ending after a purl row.

Work Thumb
1st row: K.29 [30] [33], turn.
2nd row: P.11 [11] [13], cast on 2 sts., turn.
3rd row: K.13 [13] [15].
4th row: P.13 [13] [15].
Rep. these last 2 rows 1 [2] [2] times more.
Next row: K.1, k.2 tog., knit until 3 sts. rem., k.2 tog. t.b.l., k.1.
Next row: Purl.

Rep. these last 2 rows 1 [1] [2] times more.
Thread rem. sts. on to double yarn, pull tight and knot on inside.

Work Hand
Returning to sts. still on needle, with right side facing join in the wool in front of sts. on left-hand needle and knit these 18 [19] [20] sts.
Next row: P.18 [19] [20], cast on 2 sts., purl across the rem. set of 18 [19] [20] sts.
Cont. in st.st. on these 38 [40] [42] sts. to complete 4½ [5] [5½] ins., (or ½ in. less than required length) from completion of ribbing at Wrist, ending after a purl row.

Top of Hand
1st row: (K.1, k.2 tog., k.13 [14] [15], k.2 tog. t.b.l., k.1) twice.
2nd row: Purl.
3rd row: (K.1, k.2 tog., k.11 [12] [13], k.2 tog. t.b.l., k.1) twice.
4th row: (P.1, p.2 tog. t.b.l., p.9 [10] [11], p.2 tog., p.1) twice.
Cast off.
Work another identical Mitten.

To Make Up. Press st.st. sections. Sew seam round Hand, and sew Thumb seam. Press seams.

a complete doll's outfit

A dress, coat, vest and pants, bootees and bonnet that will delight any little girl with a doll to dress. The pattern is designed for a 14/16" and 18/20" doll

Materials. The Dress, Coat, Bonnet & Bootees can be worked from: 3 [5] ozs. Sirdar Baby-Nylon 3-ply, or 3 [5] ozs. Sirdar Majestic Wool 3-ply.

The Vest and Pants can be worked from 1 [2] ozs. in any of the above qualities.

1 Pair each of Nos. 10 and 12 Knitting Needles. 3 small Buttons for the Dress. 3 medium sized Buttons for the Coat. 2 Buttons for the Vest. 16 [20] inches Ribbon for the Bonnet. 20 [25] inches narrow Ribbon for the Bootees. 10 [12] inches Elastic for the Pants. 1 No. 12 Crochet Hook.

Tension 7½ stitches to one inch.

Abbreviations. K. knit, p. purl, st(s), stitch(es), tog. together, sl. slip one stitch knitways, st.st. stocking stitch (1 row knit, 1 row purl), w.f. wool forward, p.s.s.o. pass the slipped stitch over, w.r.n. wool round needle, dec. decreasing, inc. increasing.

After casting off stitches for shaping, one stitch will remain on the right-hand needle which is not included in the instructions that follow.

Note—*For the small size read the instructions as given.
For the large size read the figures within the brackets.*

THE DRESS

Measurements. Width all round at underarm—to fit 12 [14] inches. Length from top of shoulder—8 [11] inches. Length of sleeve seam—1¼ [1½] inches.

The Back. Using the No. 10 needles cast on 86 [100] sts.
1st row: Sl., knit to end of row.

continued overleaf

165

continued from previous page

Repeat the 1st row 3 times.
Proceed as follows:
**

1st row: Sl., k.1, * w.f., sl., k.1, p.s.s.o., k.1, k.2 tog., w.f., k.2; repeat from * to end of row.

2nd row: Sl., purl to the last st., k.1.

3rd row: Sl., k.1, * k.1, w.f., sl., k.2 tog., p.s.s.o., w.f., k.3; repeat from * to end of row.

4th row: Sl., purl to the last st., k.1.

Repeat from the 1st to the 3rd row (inclusive) once.

8th row: Sl., knit to end of row.

Repeat the 8th row twice. **

Continue in st.st. until the work measure 4 [6½] inches from the beginning, ending on the wrong side of the work.

1st row: Sl., k.3, (k.2 tog., k.2) twice, (k.2 tog) 31 [38] times, (k.2, k.2 tog.) twice, k.4. 51 [58] sts.

2nd row: Sl., knit to end of row.

Repeat the 2nd row twice.

Repeat from ** to ** once. ***

Shape Armholes and Divide for Back Opening

Next row: Cast off 4 sts., k.23 [27], turn.

Working on these 24 [28] sts. only proceed as follows:

Next row: Sl., k.4 [5], purl to the last st., k.1.

As the buttonholes (may) differ for the various sizes follow the headings for the size required.

14/16 inch size only

1st row: K.2 tog., knit to end of row.

2nd row: Sl., k.4, purl to the last 2 sts., k.2 tog.

3rd row: K.2 tog., knit to the last 4 sts., w.f., k.2 tog., k.2.

4th row: Sl., k.4, purl to the last 2 sts., k.2 tog.

18/20 inch size only

1st row: K.2 tog., knit to the last 4 sts., w.f., k.2 tog., k.2.

2nd row: Sl., k.5, purl to the last 2 sts., k.2 tog.

3rd row: K.2 tog., knit to end of row.

4th row: Sl., k.5, purl to the last 2 sts., k.2 tog.

14/16 and 18/20 inch sizes

Keeping the continuity of the st.st. and garter st. border (throughout) work 4 rows dec. once at the armhole edge in every row. 16 [20] sts.

Work 20 [26] rows without shaping, working a buttonhole (as before) in the 11th [13th] row.

Shape Right Shoulder

1st row: Cast off 3 [4] sts., knit to end of row.

2nd row: Sl., k.4 [5], purl to end of row.

Repeat the 1st and 2nd rows once.

Break off the wool, slip the remaining 10 [12] sts. on to a safety pin.

Cast on 5 [6] sts., using the same needle and with the right side of the work facing work across the remaining 23 [26] sts. as follows: knit to end of row. 28 [32] sts.

Next row: Cast off 4 sts. purlways, purl to the last 5 [6] sts., k.5 [6]. 24 [28] sts.

Keeping the continuity of the st.st. and garter st. border (throughout) work 8 [8] rows dec. once at the armhole edge in every row. 16 [20] sts.

Work 21 [27] rows without shaping.

Shape Left Shoulder

1st row: Cast off 3 [4] sts. purlways, purl to the last 5 [6] sts., k.5 [6].

2nd row: Sl., knit to end of row.

Repeat the 1st row once.

Do not break off the wool, slip the remaining 10 [12] sts. on to a safety pin.

The Front. Using the No. 10 needles cast on 86 [100] sts.

Work exactly as given for the Back until *** is reached.

Shape Armholes

Cast off 4 sts. at the beginning of each of the next 2 rows.

Work 8 [8] rows dec. once at each end of every row. 27 [34] sts.

Work 6 [10] rows without shaping.

Shape Neck

Next row: Sl., k.10 [13], cast off 5 [6] sts., k.10 [13], turn.

Working on the first 11 [14] sts. only proceed as follows:

Work 5 [6] rows dec. once at the neck edge in every row. 6 [8] sts.

Work 9 [10] rows without shaping.

Shape Left Front Shoulder

1st row: Cast off 3 [4] sts. purlways, purl to the last st., k.1.

2nd row: Sl., knit to end of row.

Cast off the remaining 3 [4] sts. purlways.

With the wrong side of the work facing, rejoin the wool to the remaining 11 [14] sts. and proceed as follows:

Next row: K.2 tog., purl to the last st., k.1.

Work 4 [5] rows dec. once at the neck edge in every row. 6 [8] sts.

Work 8 [9] rows without shaping.

Shape Right Front Shoulder

1st row: Cast off 3 [4] sts., knit to end of row.

2nd row: Sl., purl to end of row.

Cast off the remaining 3 [4] sts.

Sew up the shoulder seams.

The Neckband. With the right side of the work facing and using the No. 10 needles, work across the 10 [12] sts. left on a safety-pin at the left side of the back of the neck as follows: Sl., k.9 [11], pick up and knit 12 [14] sts. evenly along the left side of the neck, 5 [6] sts. from the

5 [6] cast off sts. at the front of the neck, 12 [14] sts. evenly along the right side of the neck, work across the 10 [12] sts. left on a safety-pin at the right side of the back of the neck as follows: k.10 [12]. 49 [58] sts.

1st row: Sl, knit to end of row.
2nd row: Sl., knit to the last 4 sts., w.f., k.2 tog., k.2.
Repeat the 1st row twice.
Cast off.

The Sleeves (both alike). Using the No. 10 needles cast on 40 [48] sts.
1st row: Sl., knit to end of row.
Repeat the 1st row 3 times.
Proceed as follows:
1st row: Sl., knit to end of row.
2nd row: Sl., purl to the last st., k.1.
Continue in st.st. until the work measures 1¼ [1½] inches from the beginning, ending on the wrong side of the work.

Shape Top
Cast off 3 sts. at the beginning of each of the next 2 rows.
Cast off 1 st. at the beginning of each of the next 12 [14] rows.
Cast off 2 sts. at the beginning of each of the next 6 [8] rows. 10 [12] sts.
Cast off.

To Make Up. Press each piece separately on the wrong side under a damp cloth with a warm iron. Sew up the side and sleeve seams. Sew in the sleeves placing seam to seam. Sew the underlay in position on the wrong side. Sew on buttons to correspond with the buttonholes.
Press all seams.

THE COAT
Measurements. Width all round at underarm—to fit 13 [15] inches. Length from top of shoulder—7 [10] inches. Length of sleeve seam—3¾ [4] inches.

The Back. Using the No. 10 needles cast on 72 [79] sts.
1st row: Sl. knit to end of row.
Repeat the 1st row 3 times.
5th row: Sl., knit to end of row.
6th row: Sl., purl to the last st., k.1.
Continue in st.st. until the work measures 3 [5½] inches from the beginning, ending on the wrong side of the work.
As the shapings (may) differ for the various sizes follow the headings for the size required.

14/16 inch size only
Next row: Sl., (k.2 tog., k.3) 6 times, k.2 tog., k.6, (k.2 tog., k.3) 6 times, k.2 tog., k.1. 58 sts.

18/20 inch size only
Next row: Sl., (k.2 tog., k.4) 6 times, k.2 tog., k.1, (k.2 tog., k.4) 6 times, k.2 tog., k.1. [65] sts.

14/16 and 18/20 inch sizes
1st row: Sl., knit to end of row.
Repeat the 1st row twice.
Work 6 [6] rows in st.st.

Shape Armholes
Cast off 4 sts. at the beginning of each of the next 2 rows.
Work 8 [8] rows, dec. once at each end of every row. 34 [41] sts.
Work 24 [30] rows without shaping.

Shape Shoulders
1st row: Cast off 3 [4] sts. at the beginning of each of the next 4 rows.
Cast off the remaining 22 [25] sts.

The Left Front. Using the No. 10 needles cast on 41 [47] sts.
1st row: Sl., knit to end of row.
Repeat the 1st row 3 times.
5th row: Sl., knit to end of row.
6th row: Sl., k.3, purl to the last st., k.1.
Keeping the continuity of the garter st. border and st.st. (throughout) continue until the work measures 3 [5½] inches from the beginning, ending on the wrong side of the work.
As the shapings (may) differ for the various sizes follow the headings for the size required.

14/16 inch size only
Next row: (K.2 tog., k.1) 4 times, (k.2 tog.) 3 times, k.1, (k.2 tog.) 3 times, (k.1, k.2 tog.) 4 times, k.4. 27 sts.

18/20 inch size only
Next row: (K.2 tog., k.2) twice, (k.2 tog., k.1) 7 times. (k.2 tog., k.2) 3 times, k.2 tog., k.4. 34 sts.

14/16 and 18/20 inch sizes
1st row: Sl., knit to end of row.
Repeat the 1st row twice.
Keeping the continuity of the garter st. border work 6 [6] rows in st.st.

Shape Armhole
1st row: Cast off 4 sts., knit to end of row.
2nd row: Sl., k.3, purl to the last st., k.1.
Work 8 [8] rows dec. once at the armhole edge in every row. 15 [22] sts.
Work 15 [17] rows without shaping.

continued overleaf

continued from previous page

Shape Neck

1st row: Sl., k.3, p.1 [3], slip these 5 [7] sts. on to a safety-pin, purl to the last st., k.1.

Work 4 [7] rows dec. once at the neck edge in every row. 6 [8] sts.

Work 4 [5] rows without shaping.

Shape Shoulder

1st row: Cast off 3 [4] sts., knit to end of row.

2nd row: Sl., purl to end of row.

Cast off the remaining 3 [4] sts.

The Right Front. Using the No. 10 needles cast on 41 [47] sts.

1st row: Sl., knit to end of row.

Repeat the 1st row 3 times.

5th row: Sl., knit to end of row.

6th row: Sl., purl to the last 4 sts., k.4.

Keeping the continuity of the garter st. border and st.st. (throughout) continue until the work measures 3 [5½] inches from the beginning, ending on the wrong side of the work.

As the shapings (may) differ for the various sizes follow the headings for the size required.

14/16 inch size only

Next row: Sl., k.3, (k.2 tog. k.1) 4 times, (k.2 tog.) 3 times, k.1, (k.2 tog.) 3 times, (k.1, k.2 tog.) 4 times. 27 sts.

18/20 inch size only

Next row: Sl., k.3, (k.2 tog., k.2) 3 times, (k.2 tog., k.1) 7 times, (k.2, k.2 tog.) twice, k.2 tog. 34 sts.

14/16 and 18/20 inch sizes

1st row: Sl., knit to end of row.

2nd row: Sl., k.1, w.f., k.2 tog., knit to end of row.

Repeat the 1st row once.

Keeping the continuity of the garter st. border work 7 [7] rows in st.st.

Shape Armhole

1st row: Cast off 4 sts. purlways, purl to the last 4 sts., k.4.

Work 8 [8] rows, dec. once at the armhole edge in every row. 15 [22] sts.

As the buttonholes (may) differ for the various sizes follow the headings for the size required.

14/16 inch size only

Next row: Sl., k.1, w.f., k.2 tog., knit to end of row.

18/20 inch size only

Next row: Sl., knit to end of row.

Next row: Sl., purl to the last 4 sts., k.2 tog., w.f., k.2.

14/16 and 18/20 inch sizes

Work 15 [16] rows without shaping.

Do not break off the wool.

Shape Neck

Slip the first 5 [7] sts. on to a safety-pin, rejoin a second ball of wool to the remaining 10 [15] sts. and proceed as follows:

Work 4 [7] rows dec. once at the neck edge in every row. 6 [8] sts.

Work 5 [6] rows without shaping.

Shape Shoulder

1st row: Cast off 3 [4] sts. purlways, purl to the last st., k.1.

2nd row: Sl., knit to end of row.

Cast off the remaining 3 [4] sts. purlways.

Sew up the shoulder seams.

The Neckband. With the right side of the work facing and using the No. 10 needles work across the 5 [7] sts. left on a safety-pin on the right front as follows: Sl., k.4 [6], pick up and knit 12 [14] sts. evenly along the right side of the neck, 22 [25] sts. from the 22 [25] cast off sts. at the back of the neck, 12 [14] sts. evenly along the left side of the neck, working across the 5 [7] sts. left on a safety-pin on the left front as follows: k.5 [7]. 56 [67] sts.

1st row: Sl., knit to end of row.

2nd row: Sl., k.1, w.f., k.2 tog., knit to end of row.

Repeat the 1st row twice.

Cast off.

The Sleeves (both alike). Using the No. 10 needles cast on 30 [38] sts.

1st row: Sl., knit to end of row.

Repeat the 1st row 3 times.

5th row: Sl., knit to end of row.

6th row: Sl., purl to the last st., k.1.

Repeat the 5th and 6th rows once.

Continue in st.st. inc. once at each end of the next and every following 4th row until there are 42 [50] sts. on the needle.

Continue without shaping until the work measures 3¾ [4] inches from the beginning, ending on the wrong side of the work.

Shape Top

Cast off 4 sts. at the beginning of each of the next 2 rows.

Cast off 1 st. at the beginning of each of the next 14 [16] rows.

Cast off 2 sts. at the beginning of each of the next 6 [8] rows. 8 [10] sts.

Cast off.

To Make Up. Press each piece separately on the wrong side under a damp cloth with a warm iron. Sew up the side

and sleeve seams. Sew in the sleeves placing seam to seam.
Sew on buttons to correspond with the buttonholes.

Press all seams.

THE VEST

Measurements. Width all round at underarm—10 [12] inches. Length from top of shoulder—5½ [7] inches. Length of sleeve seam—1 [1] inch.

The Back. Using the No. 10 needles cast on 39 [45] sts.

1st row: Sl., * p.1, k.1, repeat from * to end of row.

Repeat the 1st row 3 times, inc. once at the end of the last row. 40 [46] sts.

5th row: Sl., * k.2, p.1, repeat from * to the last 3 sts., k.3.

6th row: Sl., purl to the last st., k.1.

These last 2 rows form the pattern.

Keeping the continuity of the pattern (throughout) continue until the work measures 2½ [2¾] inches from the beginning, ending on the wrong side of the work. ***

Shape Armholes

Cast off 2 [2] sts. in pattern at the beginning of each of the next 2 rows.

Work 4 [4] rows dec. once at each end of every row. 28 [34] sts.

Work 22 [26] rows without shaping.

Shape Shoulders

Cast off 4 [4] sts. in pattern at the beginning of each of the next 4 rows.

Cast off the remaining 12 [18] sts. in pattern.

The Front. Using the No. 10 needles cast on 39 [45] sts.

Work exactly as given for the Back until *** is reached.

Shape Armholes and Divide for the Front Opening

Next row: Cast off 2 [2] sts., (p.1, k.2) 5 [6] times, cast on 4 [4] sts., turn.

Working on these 20 [23] sts. only proceed as follows:

1st row: K.1, p.1, k.1, purl to the last st., k.1.

2nd row: K.2 tog., (k.2, p.1) 5 [6] times, k.1, p.1, k.1.

3rd row: Sl., p.1, k.1, purl to the last 2 sts., k.2 tog.

4th row: K.2 tog., (p.1, k.2) 4 [5] times, (p.1, k.1) twice.

5th row: Sl., p.1, k.1, purl to the last 2 sts., k.2 tog. 16 [19] sts.

6th row: Sl., (k.2, p.1) 4 [5] times, k.1, p.1, k.1.

7th row: Sl., p.1, k.1, purl to the last st., k.1.

Repeat the 6th and 7th rows 4 times then the 6th row once.

Shape Neck

1st row: Cast off 4 [5] sts. in pattern, purl to the last st., k.1.

Work 4 [6] rows dec. once at the neck edge in every row. 8 [8] sts.

Work 6 [8] rows without shaping.

Shape Shoulder

1st row: Cast off 4 [4] sts. in pattern, work in pattern to the last st., k.1.

2nd row: Sl., purl to end of row.

Cast off the remaining 4 [4] sts. in pattern.

With the right side of the work facing, rejoin the wool to the remaining 22 [25] sts. and proceed as follows:

1st row: K.1, p.1, k.1, (p.1, k.2) 6 [7] times, k.1.

2nd row: Cast off 2 [2] sts. purlways, purl to the last 3 sts., k.1, p.1, k.1.

3rd row: Sl., p.1, k.1, (p.1, k.2) 5 [6] times, k.2 tog.

4th row: K.2 tog., purl to the last 3 sts., k.1, p.1, k.1.

5th row: Sl., p.1, w.r.n., p.2 tog., (k.2, p.1) 4 [5] times, k.2 tog.

6th row: K.2 tog., purl to the last 3 sts., k.1, p.1, k.1. 16 [19] sts.

7th row: Sl., p.1, k.1, (p.1, k.2) 4 [5] times, k.1.

8th row: Sl., purl to the last 3 sts., k.1, p.1, k.1.

Repeat the 7th and 8th rows 3 times.

Proceed as follows:

1st row: Sl., p.1, w.r.n., p.2 tog., (k.2, p.1) 3 [4] times, k.3.

2nd row: Sl., purl to the last 3 sts., k.1, p.1, k.1.

Shape Neck

1st row: Cast off 4 [5] sts. in pattern, work in pattern to the last st., k.1.

2nd row: Sl., purl to the last st., k.1.

Work 4 [6] rows, dec. once at the neck edge in every row. 8 [8] sts.

Work 7 [9] rows without shaping.

Shape Shoulder

1st row: Cast off 4 [4] sts. purlways, purl to the last st., k.1.

2nd row: Sl., work in pattern to end of row.

Cast off the remaining 4 [4] sts. purlways.

The Sleeves (both alike). Using the No. 10 needles cast on 31 [37] sts.

1st row: Sl., * p.1, k.1, repeat from * to end of row.

Repeat the 1st row 3 times.

Proceed as follows:

5th row: Sl., * k.2, p.1, repeat from * to the last 3 sts., k.3.

6th row: Sl., purl to the last st., k.1.

These last 2 rows form the pattern.

Repeat the 5th and 6th rows twice.

Shape Top

Cast off 1 st. in pattern at the beginning of each of the next 12 [10] rows.

Cast off 2 sts. in pattern at the beginning of each of the next 4 [8] rows. 11 [11] sts.

Cast off in pattern.

continued overleaf

continued from previous page

To Make Up. Press each piece separately on the wrong side under a damp cloth with a warm iron. Sew up the side, shoulder and sleeve seams. Sew in the sleeves placing seam to seam. Sew the 4 cast on sts. in position on the wrong side to form an underlay. Using a No. 12 crochet hook work 1 row of double crochet round the neck. Sew on buttons to correspond with the buttonholes.

Press all seams.

THE BONNET

Measurements. Width round face—8 [10] inches.

The Bonnet. Using the No. 10 needles cast on 62 [90] sts.
1st row: Sl., knit to end of row.
Repeat the 1st row 3 times.
Proceed as follows:
1st row: Sl., k.3, * w.f., sl., k.1, p.s.s.o., k.1, k.2 tog., w.f., k.2, repeat from * to the last 2 sts., k.2.
2nd row: Sl., k.2, purl to the last 3 sts., k.3.
3rd row: Sl., k.4, * w.f., sl., k.2 tog., p.s.s.o., w.f., k.4, repeat from * to the last st., k.1.
4th row: Sl., k.2, purl to the last 3 sts., k.3.
Repeat from the 1st to the 3rd row (inclusive) once.
8th row: Sl., knit to end of row.
Repeat the 8th row twice.
11th row: Sl., knit to end of row.
12th row: Sl., k.2, purl to the last 3 sts., k.3.
Repeat the 11th and 12th rows 10 [15] times.

Shape Crown
As the shapings (may) differ for the various sizes follow the headings for the size required.

14/16 inch size only
1st row: K.2 tog., * k.2 tog., k.4, repeat from * to end of row.
2nd and every alternate row: Sl., knit to end of row.
3rd row: Sl., * k.2 tog., k.3, repeat from * to end of row.
5th row: Sl., * k.2 tog., k.2, repeat from * to end of row.
7th row: Sl., * k.2 tog., k.1, repeat from * to end of row.
9th row: Sl., * k.2 tog., repeat from * to end of row. 11 sts.
10th row: Sl., knit to end of row.
Break off the wool. Run the wool through the remaining sts., draw up and fasten off.

18/20 inch size only
1st row: K.2 tog., * k.2 tog., k.6, repeat from * to end of row.
2nd and every alternate row: Sl., knit to end of row.
3rd row: Sl., * k.2 tog., k.5, repeat from * to end of row.
5th row: Sl., * k.2 tog., k.4, repeat from * to end of row.

7th row: Sl., * k.2 tog., k.3, repeat from * to end of row.
9th row: Sl., * k.2 tog., k.2, repeat from * to end of row.
11th row: Sl., * k.2 tog., k.1, repeat from * to end of row.
13th row: Sl., * k.2 tog., repeat from * to end of row. 12 sts.
14th row: Sl., knit to end of row.
Break off the wool. Run the wool through the remaining sts., draw up and fasten off.

To Make Up. Press carefully on the wrong side under a damp cloth with a warm iron. Commencing at the crown sew up the crown seam. Cut the ribbon in half and sew in position to each side of the bonnet.
Press the seam.

THE PANTS

Measurements. Width all round at widest part—11 [13½] inches. Length from waist to gusset—3½ [4] inches.

The Back and Front (both alike). Using the No. 10 needles cast on 9 [9] sts.
1st row: Sl., (p.1, k.2) twice, p.1, k.1.
2nd row: K.1, purl to end of row, cast on 3 sts.
3rd row: K.1, (p.1, k.2) 3 times, p.1, k.1, cast on 3 sts.
4th row: K.1, purl to end of row, cast on 3 sts.
Keeping the continuity of the pattern (throughout) cast on 3 sts. at the end of every row until there are 45 [57] sts. on the needle.
Next row: K.1, purl to the last st., k.1.
Work 22 [24] rows, dec. once at each end of the next and every following 4th row. 33 [45] sts.
Change to No. 12 needles and proceed as follows:
1st row: Sl., k.1, * p.1, k.1, repeat from * to the last st., k.1.
Repeat this row 3 times.
5th row: Sl., k.1, * w.f., k.2 tog., repeat from * to the last st., k.1.
Repeat this row 3 times.
Cast off loosely in moss st.
Sew up the gusset seam.

The Leg Borders (both alike). With the right side of the work facing and using the No. 12 needles, pick up and knit 35 [43] sts. evenly round the leg edge.
1st row: Sl., k.1, * p.1, k.1, repeat from * to the last st., k.1.
Repeat the 1st row 4 times.
Cast off loosely in moss st.

To Make Up. Press carefully on the wrong side under a damp cloth with a warm iron. Sew up the side seams. Thread the elastic through the holes at the waist.
Press all seams.

THE BOOTEES

Measurements. Length of leg to base of heel—$1\frac{1}{2}$ [$2\frac{1}{2}$] inches. Length of foot—$1\frac{1}{2}$ [$2\frac{1}{2}$] inches.

The Bootees (both alike). Using the No. 10 needles cast on 23 [30] sts.

1st row: Sl., knit to end of row.
Repeat the 1st row 3 times.
Repeat from ** to ** as given for the Dress Back once.
As the shapings (may) differ for the various sizes follow the headings for the size required.

14/16 inch size only

Next row: Sl., * w.f., k.2 tog., repeat from * to end of row.

18/20 inch size only

Next row: Sl., * w.f., k.2 tog., repeat from * to the last st., k.1.

14/16 and 18/20 inch sizes

Work 1 [3] rows in garter st. inc. once at the end of the 1st row for the 14/16 inch size only. 24 [30] sts.

Shape Instep

1st row: Sl., k.15 [19], turn.
2nd row: Sl., k.7 [9], turn.
Working on these 8 [10] sts. only proceed as follows:
Work 8 [10] rows in garter st.
Break off the wool.
With the right side of the work facing, rejoin the wool to the instep end of the first 8 [10] sts. which were left and pick up and knit 3 [5] sts. evenly along the right side of the instep, knit across the 8 [10] instep sts., pick up and knit 3 [5] sts. evenly along the left side of the instep, knit across the remaining 8 [10] sts. 30 [40] sts.
Work 3 [5] rows in garter st.

Shape Foot

1st row: Sl., k.2 tog., k.8 [12], k.2 tog., k.4 [6], k.2 tog., k.8 [12], k.2 tog., k.1.
2nd and 4th rows: Sl., knit to end of row.
3rd row: Sl., k.2 tog., k.7 [11], k.2 tog., k.2 [4], k.2 tog., k.7 [11], k.2 tog., k.1.
5th row: Sl., k.2 tog., k.6 [10], k.2 tog., k.0 [2], k.2 tog., k.6 [10], k.2 tog., k.1. 18 [28] sts.
6th row: Sl., knit to end of row.
Cast off.

To Make Up. Press carefully on the wrong side under a damp cloth with a warm iron. Sew up the foot and leg seams. Cut the ribbon in half and thread through the holes at the ankle.
Press all seams.

long line jacket

Pictured overleaf is the smart, casual two colour jacket. The full length zip and neat little pockets are in line with fashion and it is the perfect garment to take on holiday to slip over a simple dress

Materials. 14 [15] [16] ozs. of Robin Casino Crepe. 4-ply, in Main Colour, and 2 [2] [3] ozs. in Contrast. 1 pair each No. 9, No. 10 and No. 13 knitting needles. 2 stitch holders. A 22 inch zip fastener with open ends.

Measurements. To fit 34 [36] [38] inch bust. Actual measurement underarms, 38 [40] [42] inches. Length, $26\frac{1}{2}$ [27] [$27\frac{1}{2}$] inches. Sleeve seam, 16 [$16\frac{1}{4}$] [$16\frac{1}{2}$] inches.

Tension $7\frac{1}{2}$ stitches to 1 inch over stocking stitch on No. 10 needles.

Abbreviations. K. knit, p. purl, st(s) stitch(es), st.st. stocking stitch, m.st. moss stitch, tog. together, sl. slip, p.s.s.o. pass slipped stitch over, dec. decrease by working 2 stitches together, inc. increase by working twice into 1 stitch, rep. repeat, beg. beginning, patt. pattern, tw.2, twist 2, thus: knit the 2nd stitch on left-hand needle, then knit the 1st stitch, and drop both stitches from needle together, M Main Colour, C Contrast.

Note—*Instructions are given for 34 inch bust size. Figures in brackets are for the two larger sizes in size order. Where one figure only is given, this refers to all sizes.*

The Back. Using No. 10 needles and C, cast on 165 [173] [181] sts. Change to No. 13 needles. Work 12 rows m.st., increasing at end of last row. Change to No. 10 needles and M.
Next row: K.56 [60] [64]. * k.1, tw.2. ** Rep. from * 5 times more, k.17. Rep. from * to ** 6 times, k.57 [61] [65].
Next row: P.56 [60] [64], * k.1, p.2, ** Rep. from * 5 times more, k.1, p.16. Rep. from * to ** 6 times, k.1, p.56 [60] [64].
Next row: K.56 [60] [64], * p.1, tw.2, ** Rep. from *

continued overleaf

continued from previous page

5 times more, p.1, k.16. Rep. from * to ** 6 times, p.1, k.56 [60] [64].

The last 2 rows form the patt. Proceed until work measures 3 [3½] [4] inches in all, finishing after a wrong side row.

1st dec. row: K.22, sl.1, k.1, p.s.s.o., k.2 tog., work to last 26 sts., sl.1, k.1, p.s.s.o., k.2 tog., k.22.

Keeping patt. correct, proceed until work measures 6 [6½] [7] inches in all, finishing after a wrong side row.

2nd dec. row: K.21, sl.1, k.1, p.s.s.o., k.2 tog., work to last 25 sts., sl.1, k.1, p.s.s.o., k.2 tog., k.21.

Proceed until work measures 9 [9½] [10] inches in all, after a wrong side row.

3rd dec. row: K.20, sl.1, k.1, p.s.s.o., k.2 tog., work to last 24 sts., sl.1, k.1, p.s.s.o., k.2 tog., k.20.

Keeping continuity of shapings correct by working 1 st. less at each side of decreasings, continue to dec. thus at 3 inch intervals until 5th dec. row has been worked, when 146 [154] [162] sts. will remain, and work measures 15 [15½] [16] inches.

Proceed until 17 [17½] [18] inches, then work 6th dec. row.

Continue with 142 [150] [158] sts. until work measures 18 [18½] [19] inches, after a wrong side row.

Shape Armholes

Cast off 8 [10] [12] sts. at beg. of next 2 rows, then dec. at both ends of every alternate row until 110 [114] [118] sts. remain.

Continue until work measures 25½ [26] [26½] inches, after a wrong side row.

Shape Shoulders

Cast off 6 sts. at beg. of next 8 rows and 4 [6] [8] at beg. of next 2 rows. Cast off remaining 54 sts.

Pocket Backs. Work 2 large pocket backs thus: Using No. 10 needles and M, cast on 30 sts. Work 30 rows st.st. Break wool and leave sts. on a spare needle.

Work 2 small pocket backs thus: Using No. 10 needles and M, cast on 22 sts. Work 20 rows st.st. Break wool and leave sts. on a spare needle.

The Left Front. Using No. 10 needles and C, cast on 83 [87] [91] sts. Change to No. 13 needles. Work 12 rows m.st. Change to No. 10 needles and M.

Next row: K.56 [60] [64], * k.1, tw.2. Rep. from * 5 times more, k.1, and slip remaining 8 sts. on to a safety-pin. Turn.

Next row: Inc. in 1st st., p.2, * k.1, p.2. Rep. from * 4 times more, k.1, p.56 [60] [64]. 76 [80] [84] sts.

Next row: K.56 [60] [64], * p.1, tw.2. Rep. from * 5 times more, p.1, k.1.

Next row: K.1, * k.1, p.2. Rep. from * 5 times more, k.1, p.56 [60] [64].

The last 2 rows form the patt. Proceed until work measures 3 [3½] [4] inches, after a wrong side row.

1st dec. row: K.22, sl.1, k.1, p.s.s.o., k.2 tog., work to end.

Proceed until 30 rows of patt. have been worked, excluding m.st. border.

Join Pocket

Next row: K.24 [28] [32], place next 30 sts. on a stitch holder and k. across sts. of large pocket back in place of them. Work to end.

Proceed until work measures 6 [6½] [7] inches in all, after a wrong side row.

2nd dec. row: K.21, sl.1, k.1, p.s.s.o., k.2 tog., work to end.

Continue to dec. thus at 3 inch intervals until 5th dec. row has been worked, when 66 [70] [74] sts. will remain, and work measures 15 [15½] [16] inches. Proceed until 17 [17½] [18] inches, then work 6th dec. row.

Proceed on 64 [68] [72] sts. until 18 [18½] [19] inches, finishing at side edge.

Shape Armhole

Cast off 8 [10] [12] sts. at beg. of next row, then dec. at side edge of every alternate row until 48 [50] [52] sts. remain.

Continue until work measures 20 [20½] [21] inches in all, after a wrong side row.

Join 2nd Pocket

Next row: K.6 [8] [10], place next 22 sts. on a stitch holder and k. sts. of small pocket back in place of them. Work to end.

Proceed until 23½ [24] [24½] inches.

Shape Neck

Cast off 5 sts. at beg. of next neck-edge row, then dec. at this edge of every row until 28 [30] [32] sts. remain.

Proceed until 25½ [26] [26½] inches.

Shape Shoulder

Cast off 6 sts. at beg. of every side-edge row until 4 [6] [8] sts. remain. Work to side edge. Cast off.

Complete Pocket Tops

Using No. 13 needles and C, with right side of work facing, k. across sts. left on holder. Change to m.st. Work 11 rows. Cast off in m.st., using a No. 10 needle. Complete 2nd pocket top in same way.

The Right Front. Using No. 10 needles and C, cast on 83 [87] [91] sts. Change to No. 13 needles. Work 12 rows m.st.

Next row: M.st. 8 sts. and slip them on a safety-pin.
Change to No. 10 needles and M. * K.1, tw.2. Rep. from *
5 times more, k.57 [61] [65].

Next row: P.56 [60] [64], * k.1, p.2. Rep. from * 5 times
more, inc. in last st. 76 [80] [84] sts.

Next row: K.1, * p.1, tw.2. Rep. from * 5 times more,
p.1, k.56 [60] [64].

Next row: P.56 [60] [64], * k.1, p.2. Rep. from * 5 times
more, k.2.

The last 2 rows form the patt. Working patt. as set,
and reversing shapings and position of pockets, complete
to correspond with Left Front.

The Sleeves (both alike). Using No. 10 needles and C,
cast on 67 [71] [75] sts. Change to No. 13 needles. Work 12
rows m.st., increasing at end of last row. Change to No. 10
needles and M. Proceed in st.st. Inc. at both ends of the
11th and every 12th row following until there are 88 [92]
[96] sts. Proceed until 16 [16¼] [16½] inches in all, or length
required. Mark edge of work with a coloured thread.

Shape Top

Proceed straight for a further 1 [1¼] [1½] inches, ending
after a wrong side row. Dec. at both ends of next and every
alternate row until 58 [62] [66] sts. remain. Cast off 4 sts.
at beg. of next 10 rows. Cast off remaining 18 [22] [26] sts.

The Collar. Using No. 9 needles and M, cast on 181 sts.
1st row: P.1, * tw.2, p.1. Rep. from * to end.
2nd row: K.1, * p.2, k.1. Rep. from * to end.
These 2 rows form patt. Proceed until work measures
2 inches. Change to No. 10 needles. Work 1 inch. Cast off.

To Make Up. Press parts under a damp cloth. Join side
and shoulder seams. Join sleeve seams as far as markers.
Remove markers and set sleeves into armholes. Stitch
pocket backs and side edges of pocket tops in position.
Sew cast-off edge of collar to neck edge.

Complete Borders and Collar Edge

With wrong side facing, place the 8 sts. left on safety-pin
on left front on a No. 13 needle. Join in C. Inc. in 1st st.,
m.st. to end. Proceed in m.st. until band is long enough to
fit front edge and edge of collar when slightly stretched,
ending after a row on right side of garment. Break wool
and leave sts. on a spare needle.

Beg. with a row on right side, and increasing at beg. of
1st row, complete right front border to correspond. Do
not break wool.

Now work sts. of right front band, k. up 179 sts. across
collar, then work sts. of left front band. Work 11 rows
m.st. Cast off in m.st., using a No. 10 needle.

Sew on borders. Press seams and borders. Sew in zip.

beaded evening jacket

The simple elegance of this evening jacket will help to highlight any dress over which you wear it. The additional touch of a single piece of jewellery adds to the overall effect and charm

Materials. 9 [10] [10] [11] [11] ozs. Sirdar Majestic Wool 3-ply, or Sirdar Gaiety Nylon 3-ply. 3 [3] [3] [3] [3] ozs. beads size 8/0. 1 Pair No. 10 and No. 12 Knitting Needles.

Measurements. Width all round at underarm—to fit 34 [36] [38] [40] [42] inch bust (actual measurement 36½ [38½] [40¾] [42¾] [45] inches).

Length from top of shoulder—22 [22] [22] [23] [23] inches.
Length of sleeve seam—16½ inches.

Tension 7½ stitches to one inch on No. 10 needles.

Abbreviations. K. knit, p. purl, sts. stitches, sl. slip one stitch knitways, tog. together, p.s.s.o. pass the slipped stitch over, wl.fwd. wool forward, wl.frt. wool to front, wl.bk. wool to back, inc. increase, dec. decreasing.

After casting off stitches for shaping, one stitch will remain on the right hand needle which is not included in the instructions that follow.

Note—*For the smallest size read the instructions as given. For the larger sizes read the figures within the brackets in size order.*

Before Starting to Knit. Approximately 2 ozs. of wool will be required for the Jacket ribbings and front borders.
Thread approximately 250 beads on to each of the remainins ozs. and use for the beaded pattern.

Back and Fronts together
Using the No. 12 needles and unbeaded wool, cast on 309 [325] [341] [357] [373] sts.

1st row: Sl., k.1, * p.1, k.1; repeat from * to the last st., k.1.

2nd row: Sl., * p.1, k.1; repeat from * to end of row.
Repeat the 1st and 2nd rows 7 times then the 1st row once.

18th row: Sl., (p.1, k.1) 12 times, slip these 25 sts. on to a safety-pin and leave for the front border, * p.1., k.1, repeat from * to the last 26 sts., p.1, slip the remaining 25 sts. on to a safety-pin and leave for the front border. 259 [275] [291] [307] [323] sts.

Break off the wool.

Change to No. 10 needles and using the beaded wool for the pattern proceed as follows:

1st row: Sl., k.3, * k.2 tog., wl.fwd., k.6; repeat from * to the last 7 sts., k.2 tog., wl.fwd., k.5.

2nd and every alternate row: Sl., purl to the last st., k.1.

3rd row: Sl., wl.frt., slip the next st. purlways, pass a bead as close as possible to the front of the work, wl.bk. (this will now be termed 'sl. B'), k.1, * k.2 tog., wl.fwd., k.1, wl.fwd., sl., k.1, p.s.s.o., k.1, sl. B, k.1; repeat from * to end of row.

5th row: Sl., k.1, * k.2 tog., wl.fwd., k.1, wl.fwd., k.2 tog., wl.fwd., sl., k.1, p.s.s.o., k.1; repeat from * to the last st., k.1.

7th row: * K.2 tog., wl.fwd., k.6; repeat from * to the last 3 sts., k.2 tog., wl.fwd., k.1.

9th row: Sl., k.1., * wl.fwd., sl., k.1, p.s.s.o., k.1, sl. B, k.1, k.2 tog., wl.fwd., k.1; repeat from * to the last st., k.1.

11th row: Sl., * wl.fwd., k.2 tog., wl.fwd., sl., k.1, p.s.s.o., k.1, k.2 tog., wl.fwd., k.1; repeat from * to the last 2 sts., wl.fwd., k.2 tog.

12th row: Sl., purl to the last st., k.1.
These 12 rows form the pattern.
Keeping the continuity of the pattern (throughout) continue until the work measures 12 [12] [12] [13] [13] ins. from the beginning, ending on the wrong side of the work.

Divide for the Back and Fronts
Next row: Pattern 55 [59] [63] [67] [71] sts., cast off 12 sts. knitways, pattern 124 [132] [140] [148] [156] sts., cast off 12 sts. knitways, pattern 54 [58] [62] [66] [70] sts., turn.

Working on the first 55 [59] [63] [67] [71] sts. only, proceed as follows:

Left Front
Next row: Sl., purl to the last st., k.1.
As the shaping (may) differ for the various sizes, follow the headings for the size required.

34 inch size only
Work 8 rows dec. once at the armhole edge in the next and the following 4th row. 53 sts.

34, 36, 38, 40 and 42 inch sizes
Work 70 [78] [78] [78] [74] rows dec. once at the armhole
continued overleaf

continued from previous page

edge in the next and every alternate row. 18 [20] [24] [28] [34] sts.

42 inch size only
Work 4 rows dec. once at the armhole edge in every row. [30] sts.

34, 36, 38, 40 and 42 inch sizes
Next row: K.2 tog., work in pattern to end of row. 17 [19] [23] [27] [29] sts.

Shape the Neck
34, 36, 38 and 40 inch sizes only
Next row: Cast off 2 [2] [2] [3] sts. purlways, purl to the last st., k.1.

42 inch size only
Next row: Cast off 3 sts. purlways, purl to the last 2 sts., k.2 tog.

34, 36, 38 and 40 inch sizes only
Work 8 [8] [4] [2] rows, dec. once at the armhole edge in the next and every alternate row at the same time dec. once at the neck edge in the next and every alternate row. 7 [9] [17] [22] sts.

34 and 36 inch sizes only
Work 8 [4] rows, dec. once at the armhole edge only in the next and every alternate rows. 3 [7] sts.

36 inch size only
Work 4 rows, dec. once at the armhole edge only in every row. [3] sts.

38, 40 and 42 inch sizes only
Work [4] [10] [12] rows, dec. once at the armhole edge in every row at the same time dec. once at the neck edge in the next and every alternate row. [11] [7] [7] sts.
Work [8] [4] [4] rows dec. once at the armhole edge only in every row. [3] [3] [3] sts.

34, 36, 38, 40 and 42 inch sizes
1st row: K.2 tog., k.1.
2nd row: K.2 tog.
Break off the wool and fasten off.

The Back. With the wrong side of the work facing, rejoin the wool to the first 125 [133] [141] [149] [157] sts. and proceed as follows:
Next row: K.1, purl to the last st., k.1.
As the shapings (may) differ for the various sizes follow the headings for the size required.

34 inch size only
Work 8 rows, dec. once at each end of the next and the following 4th row. 121 sts.

34, 36, 38, 40 and 42 inch sizes
Work 84 [92] [84] [82] [74] rows dec. once at each end of the next and every alternate row. 37 [41] [57] [67] [83] sts.

38, 40 and 42 inch sizes only
Work [8] [10] [18] rows dec. once at each end of every row. [41] [47] [47] sts.

34, 36, 38, 40 and 42 inch sizes
Next row: K.2 tog., pattern 5 [7] [7] [7] [7] sts., cast off 23 [23] [23] [29] [29] sts. knitways, pattern 4 [6] [6] [6] [6] sts., k.2 tog., turn.
Working on the first 6 [8] [8] [8] [8] sts. only proceed as follows:

34 inch size only
1st row: Sl., p.4, k.1.
2nd row: K.2 tog., pattern 2 sts., k.2 tog.
3rd row: Sl., p.2, k.1.
4th row: (K.2 tog.) twice.
5th row: K.2 tog.
Break off the wool and fasten off.

36, 38, 40 and 42 inch sizes only
1st row: K.2 tog., p.5, k.1.
2nd row: K.2 tog., pattern 3 sts., k.2 tog.
3rd row: K.2 tog., p.2, k.1.
4th row: (K.2 tog.) twice.
5th row: K.2 tog.
Break off the wool and fasten off.

34, 36, 38, 40 and 42 inch sizes
With the wrong side of the work facing, rejoin the wool to the remaining 6 [8] [8] [8] [8] sts. and proceed as follows:

34 inch size only
1st row: K.1, p.4, k.1.
2nd row: K.2 tog., pattern 2 sts., k.2 tog.
3rd row: Sl., p.2, k.1.
4th row: (K.2 tog.) twice.
5th row: K.2 tog.
Break off the wool and fasten off.

36, 38, 40 and 42 inch sizes only
1st row: K.1, p.5, k.2 tog.
2nd row: K.2 tog., pattern 3 sts., k.2 tog.
3rd row: Sl., p.2, k.2 tog.
4th row: (K.2 tog.) twice.
5th row: K.2 tog.
Break off the wool and fasten off.
The Right Front. With the wrong side of the work facing, rejoin the wool to the remaining 55 [59] [63] [67] [71] sts. and proceed as follows:

Next row: K.1, purl to the last st., k.1.

As the shapings (may) differ for the various sizes follow the headings for the size required.

34 inch size only
Work 8 rows, dec. once at the armhole edge in the next and the following 4th row. 53 sts.

34, 36, 38, 40 and 42 inch sizes
Work 70 [78] [78] [78] [74] rows, dec. once at the armhole edge in the next and every alternate row. 18 [20] [24] [28] [34] sts.

42 inch size only
Work 4 rows, dec. once at the armhole edge in every row [30] sts.

Shape the Neck
34, 36, 38 and 40 inch sizes only
Next row: Cast off 2 [2] [2] [3] sts. knitways, work in pattern to the last 2 sts., k.2 tog.
Next row: Sl., purl to the last st., k.1.

42 inch size only
Next row: Cast off 3 sts. knitways, work in pattern to the last 2 sts., k.2 tog.
Next row: K.2 tog., purl to the last st., k.1.

34, 36, 38 and 40 inch sizes only
Work 8 [8] [4] [2] rows, dec. once at the neck edge in the next and every alternate row at the same time dec. once at the armhole edge in the next and every alternate row. 7 [9] [17] [22] sts.

34 and 36 inch sizes only
Work 8 [4] rows, dec. once at the armhole edge only in the next and every alternate row. 3 [7] sts.

36 inch size only
Work 4 rows, dec. once at the armhole edge only in every row. [3] sts.

38, 40 and 42 inch sizes only
Work [4] [10] [12] rows dec. once at the neck edge in the next and every alternate row at the same time dec. once at the armhole edge in every row. [11] [7] [7] sts.
Work [8] [4] [4] rows dec. once at the armhole edge only in every row. [3] [3] [3] sts.

34, 36, 38, 40 and 42 inch sizes
1st row: Sl., k.2 tog.
2nd row: K.2 tog.
Break off the wool and fasten off.
The Sleeves (both alike). Using the No. 12 needles and unbeaded wool, cast on 59 [59] [59] [67] [67] sts.
1st row: Sl., k.1, * p.1, k.1, repeat from * to the last st., k.1.
2nd row: Sl., * p.1, k.1, repeat from * to end of row.
Repeat the 1st and 2nd rows 16 times then the 1st row once.
As the sts. (may) differ for the various sizes follow the headings for the size required.

34, 36 and 38 inch sizes only
36th row: Sl., * inc. once in the next st. purlways, (k.1, p.1) 3 times, k.1, * repeat from * to * 6 times, inc. once in the next st. purlways, k.1. 67 [67] [67] sts.

40 and 42 inch sizes only
36th row: Sl., p.1, * inc. once in the next st., (p.1, k.1) 4 times, inc. once in the next st. purlways, (k.1, p.1) 4 times, * repeat from * to * twice, inc. once in the next st., (p.1, k.1) 4 times, inc. once in the next st. purlways, k.1. [75] [75] sts.

34, 36, 38, 40 and 42 inch sizes
Break off the wool.
Change to No. 10 needles and using the beaded wool for the pattern proceed as follows:
1st row: Sl., k.3, * k.2 tog., wl.fwd., k.6; repeat from * to the last 7 sts., k.2 tog., wl.fwd., k.5.
2nd and every alternate row: Sl., purl to the last st., k.1.
3rd row: Sl., sl. B, k.1, * k.2 tog., wl.fwd., k.1, wl.fwd., sl., k.1, p.s.s.o., k.1, sl. B, k.1; repeat from * to end of row.
5th row: Sl., k.1, * k.2 tog., wl.fwd., k.1, wl.fwd., k.2 tog., wl.fwd., sl., k.1, p.s.s.o., k.1; repeat from * to the last st., k.1.
7th row: * K.2 tog., wl.fwd., k.6; repeat from * to the last 3 sts., k.2 tog., wl.fwd., k.1.
9th row: Sl., k.1, * wl.fwd., sl., k.1, p.s.s.o., k.1, sl. B, k.1, k.2 tog., wl.fwd., k.1; repeat from * to the last st., k.1.
11th row: Sl., * wl.fwd., k.2 tog., wl.fwd., sl., k.1, p.s.s.o., k.1, k.2 tog., wl.fwd., k.1; repeat from * to the last 2 sts., wl.fwd., k.2 tog.
12th row: Sl., purl to the last st., k.1.
These 12 rows form the pattern.
Keeping the continuity of the pattern (throughout) inc. once at each end of the next and every following 8th row until there are 99 [99] [99] [107] [107] sts. on the needle.
Continue without shaping until the work measures $16\frac{1}{2}$ ins. from the beginning, ending on the wrong side of the work.

Shape for the Top
1st row: Cast off 6 sts. knitways, work in pattern to end of row.
2nd row: Cast off 6 sts. purlways, purl to the last st., k.1. 87 [87] [87] [95] [95] sts.
Work 44 [44] [44] [28] [28] rows dec. once at each end of the next and every following 4th row. 65 [65] [65] [81] [81] sts.
Work 54 [54] [54] [70] [70] rows dec. once at each end of the next and every alternate row. 11 [11] [11] [11] [11] sts.
Cast off knitways.
To Make Up. Press each piece separately on the wrong

continued overleaf

continued from previous page

side under a damp cloth with a warm iron. Sew up the sleeve seams. Placing the sleeve seams to the centre of the cast off sts. at the armholes sew the decreased edges of the sleeves to the decreased edges of the bodice.

The Right Front Border. Using the No. 12 needles and with the wrong side of the work facing, rejoin the unbeaded wool to the 25 [25] [25] [25] [25] sts. left on a safety-pin and proceed as follows:

1st row: K.1, (p.1, k.1) 12 times.
2nd row: Sl., (k.1, p.1) 11 times, k.2.
3rd row: Sl., (p.1, k.1) 12 times.

Repeat the 2nd and 3rd rows until the border is of sufficient length to go up the right front to the commencement of the neck shaping, ending with the 3rd row.

Proceed as follows:

1st row: Sl., (k.1, p.1) 10 times, k.1, turn.
2nd row: (P.1, k.1) 11 times.
3rd row: Sl., (k.1, p.1) 9 times, k.1, turn.
4th row: (P.1, k.1) 10 times.

Work 10 rows turning in this manner working 2 sts. less between each turn in the next and every alternate row.

Proceed as follows:

1st row: Sl., (k.1, p.1) 11 times, k.2.
2nd row: Sl., (p.1, k.1) 12 times.

Repeat the 1st and 2nd rows 27 [27] [27] [29] [29] times. Cast off in rib.

The Left Front Border. Using the No. 12 needles and with the right side of the work facing, rejoin the unbeaded wool to the 25 [25] [25] [25] [25] sts. left on another safety-pin and proceed as follows:

1st row: Sl., (k.1, p.1) 11 times, k.2.
2nd row: Sl., (p.1, k.1) 12 times.

Repeat the 1st and 2nd rows until the border is of sufficient length to go up the left front to the commencement of the neck shaping, ending with the 1st row.

Proceed as follows:

1st row: Sl., (p.1, k.1) 10 times, p.1, turn.
2nd row: (K.1, p.1) 10 times, k.2.
3rd row: Sl., (p.1, k.1) 9 times, p.1, turn.
4th row: (K.1, p.1) 9 times, k.2.

Work 10 rows turning in this manner working 2 sts. less between each turn in the next and every alternate row.

Next row: Sl., (p.1, k.1) 12 times.

Proceed as follows:

1st row: Sl., (k.1, p.1) 11 times, k.2.
2nd row: Sl., (p.1, k.1) 12 times.

Repeat the 1st and 2nd rows 27 [27] [27] [29] [29] times. Cast off in rib.

To complete. Sew the ends of the borders together and placing the seam to the centre back of neck, sew the borders in position.

Press the borders and all seams.

a complete

The layette is pictured in colour on page 52

Materials. 28 ozs. of Hayfield Beaulon Baby Quick-knit for the Set, or if knitted separately
4 ozs. each for Dress and Jacket.
2 ozs. each for Bonnet and Hat.
1 oz. each for Bootees and Mitts.
16 ozs. for Shawl.
1 pair long No. 8 (for shawl) and 1 pair each No. 8 and No. 9 Knitting Needles. 3 yds. baby ribbon. 2½ yds. small daisy braid. 6 small buttons. 1 yd. of 1 inch wide ribbon for bonnet ties.

Tension 7 stitches to one inch over lace pattern on No. 8 needles.

Abbreviations. K. knit, p. purl, st(s). stitch(es), m.st. moss stitch, tog. together, wl.fwd. wool forward, patt. pattern, ins. inches, cont. continue, beg. beginning, rep. repeat, dec. decreasing, foll. following, inc. increasing, rem. remain(ing).

Measurements. To fit an 18 inch chest. (Birth to six months). Shawl 42½ inches by 44 inches (measured across centre).

THE SHAWL

Using long No. 8 needles cast on 286 sts. and work in m.st.

1st row: M.st. (k.1, p.1) to end.
2nd row: M.st. (p.1, k.1) to end. Repeat these 2 rows for 7½ ins.

Now work in fancy st. as follows:

1st row: M.st. 41, (k.2 tog.) twice, * (k.1, wl.fwd.) 4 times, (k.2 tog.) 4 times; rep. from * to last 49 sts., (k.1, wl.fwd.) 4 times, (k.2 tog.) twice, m.st. 41.
2nd row: M.st. 41, knit until 41 sts. remain, m.st. 41.

Repeat last 2 rows until work measures 35 ins. Then work in m.st. across all sts. for 7½ ins. Cast off in m.st.

To Make Up. Press with cool iron and damp cloth. Sew single daisies all round shawl about 2 ins. from each edge (optional).

THE DRESS

The Back. With No. 8 needles cast on 108 sts. and work in m.st. for 1 in. Change to foll. patt.

1st row: (K.2 tog.) twice, * (k.1, wl.fwd.) 4 times, (k.2 tog.) 4 times; rep. from * to last 8 sts., (k.1, wl.fwd.) 4 times, (k.2 tog.) twice.

ayette

2nd row: Knit.

These 2 rows form patt. Cont. in patt. When work measures 10½ ins. ending after a 1st patt. row, decrease as follows:

Next row: K.2; (k.2 tog.) to last 2 sts., k.2. 56 sts. Change to No. 9 needles, and divide for back opening.

Next row: M.st. to end.

Next row: M.st. 26, turn and cast on 4 sts. Finish this side first.

Continue straight in m.st. until work measures 11½ ins. ending at side edge.

Shape Armhole

Cast off 3 sts. beg. of next row, then dec. 1 st. at armhole edge on next 2 rows. Cont. straight until work measures 14½ ins. Cast off.

Rejoin wool to other sts. and work in m.st. for 1 inch, ending at front edge. Make buttonhole.

Next row: M.st. 3, wl.fwd., k.2 tog., patt. to end. Make another buttonhole after 14 rows in the same way. and when work measures 14½ ins. cast off.

The Front. Work as for Back until 56 sts. rem., then cont. straight in m.st. across all sts. until work measures 11½ ins., ending after a wrong side row.

Shape Armhole

Cast off 3 sts. beg. of next 2 rows, then dec. 1 st. each end of next 2 rows. Work straight until armhole measures 1¾ ins., ending after a wrong side row.

Shape Neck

Next row: M.st. 19, cast off 8, m.st. to end.

Work on last 19 sts., dec. 1 st. at neck edge on next 6 rows. When armhole measures the same as Back to shoulder, cast off. Rejoin wool to rem. sts. and work to match.

The Sleeves (both alike). With No. 9 needles cast on 37 sts. and work in m.st., inc. 1 st. each end of every 3rd row until there are 43 sts.

Shape Top

Cast off 3 sts. beg. of next 2 rows, then dec. 1 st. each end of every row until there are 15 sts. left. Cast off.

The Neckband. Join shoulders. With No. 9 needles and right side of work facing, pick up and knit 59 sts. round neck, and work in k.1, p.1 rib for 3 rows, making a buttonhole in last row. Cast off in rib.

To Make Up. Press with warm iron and damp cloth. Sew in sleeves. Sew sleeve and side seams. Stitch down under placket at back. Sew on buttons to correspond with buttonholes. Thread baby ribbon through holes at waist formed by fancy patt. and tie in bow at front. Sew braid round neck and sleeve edges.

THE JACKET

The Back. Work exactly as for Dress Back until work measures 6½ ins. ending after a right side row.

Next row: K.3, * (k.2 tog.) twice, k.1, rep. from * to end. 66 sts. Change to No. 9 needles and work in m.st. for 1 inch.

Shape Armholes

Cast off 3 sts. beg. of next 2 rows, then dec. 1 st. each end of next 4 rows. 52 sts. Cont. straight until work measures 10½ ins. Cast off.

The Left Front. With No. 8 needles cast on 66 sts. and work 1 inch in m.st. Change to patt. as follows:

1st row: (K.2 tog.) twice, * (k.1, wl.fwd.) 4 times, (k.2 tog.) 4 times; rep. from * to last 14 sts., (k.1, wl.fwd.) 4 times, (k.2 tog.) twice, m.st. 6.

2nd row: M.st. 6, knit to end. Rep. these 2 rows until work measures 6½ ins., ending after a right side row.

Next row: M.st. 6, * (k.2 tog.) twice, k.1; rep. from * to end. 42 sts. Change to No. 9 needles and cont. in m.st. for 1 inch, ending at side edge.

Shape Armholes

Cast off 3 sts. beg. of next row, then dec. 1 st. at armhole edge of next 4 rows. Cont. in m.st. until armhole measures 2 ins., ending at front edge.

Shape Neck

Cast off 10 sts. beg. of next row, then dec. 1 st. at neck

continued overleaf

continued from previous page

edge every row until 15 sts. rem. Cont. straight until work measures same as Back to shoulders. Cast off.

Place pins on border to mark for buttons, 1st one at beg. of all-over m.st. patt. at waist, and 2nd 1 inch from neck and 3rd one equally between these two.

The Right Front. Work to match Left Front, reversing shapings and making buttonholes as for dress, at pin positions.

Sleeves (both alike). With No. 9 needles cast on 39 sts. and work in m.st. inc. 1 st. each end every 6th row until there are 47 sts. Cont. straight until work measures 6 ins.

Shape Top

Cast off 3 sts. beg. of next 2 rows, then dec. 1 st. each end of every row until 23 sts. rem., then cast off 3 sts. at beg. of next 4 rows. Cast off.

Neckband. Join shoulders tog.

With No. 9 needles and right side of work facing, pick up and knit 67 sts. round neck, and work in k.1, p.1 rib for 3 rows, working buttonhole in last row. Cast off in rib.

To Make Up. Pin out and press all pieces with damp cloth and warm iron. Sew in sleeves. Sew up side and sleeve seams, allowing 1½ ins. for turning back cuffs. Sew back cuff. Sew on buttons to correspond to buttonholes. Sew braid round each cuff. Make posies of 3 daisies and stitch in position at waist edge as shown in photograph.

THE BONNET

With No. 8 needles cast on 84 sts. and work in m.st. for 3 rows. Work in fancy patt. as for Dress in 1 in. Change to No. 9 needles and cont. straight until work measures 5½ ins., ending after a right side row.

Cast off 28 sts. at beg. of next 2 rows, then cont. in m.st. on rem. sts., dec. 1 st. each end of every 5th row until 16 sts. rem. Work straight until panel measures 3¾ ins. from cast off side edge. Cast off in m.st.

To Make Up. Sew side edge of panel to cast off side edges. Turn back border for 1½ ins. Cut wider ribbon in half and stitch to each side of bonnet to form ties.

THE HAT

With No. 8 needles cast on 96 sts. and work in m.st. for 3 rows. Change to fancy patt. as for Dress for 1 inch. Change to No. 9 needles and work in m.st. until work measures 5½ ins.

Shape Crown

1st row: * M.st. 4, work 3 tog., m.st. 5; rep. from * to end. Work 2 rows in m.st.

4th row: * M.st. 3, work 3 tog., m.st. 4; rep. from * to end. Work 2 rows in m.st.

7th row: * M.st. 2, work 3 tog., m.st. 3; rep. from * to end. Work 1 row in m.st.

9th row: * M.st. 1, work 3 tog., m.st. 2; rep. from * to end. Work 1 row in m.st. Break wool, thread end in needle and draw through rem. sts. Pull up tightly and fasten off.

To Make Up. Join back seam. Make a small pompom and sew to top of crown. Turn back brim for 1½ ins.

THE MITTENS

With No. 9 needles cast on 36 sts. and work in m.st. for 3 rows. Change to No. 8 needles and work in fancy patt. as for Dress for 1 inch. Change to No. 9 needles.

Next row: K.1, (wl.fwd., k.2 tog.) to last st., k.1. Cont. in m.st. until work measures 3½ ins.

Next row: Work 2 tog., m.st. 14, (work 2 tog.) twice, m.st. 14, work 2 tog.

Next row: Work in m.st.

Next row: Work 2 tog., m.st. 12, (work 2 tog.) twice, m.st. 12, work 2 tog.

Next row: Work in m.st.

Next row: Work 2 tog., m.st. 10, (work 2 tog.) twice, m.st. 10, work 2 tog.

Cast off in m.st.

To Make Up. Sew up side seams. Thread baby ribbon through holes.

THE BOOTEES

With No. 9 needles cast on 36 sts. and work in m.st. for 3 rows. Change to No. 8 needles and work in fancy patt. as for Dress for 12 rows. Change back to No. 9 needles.

Next row: K.1, (wl.fwd., k.2 tog.) to last st., k.1.

Divide for Instep

Next row: M.st. 24, turn and leave rem. 12 sts. on safety pin.

Next row: M.st. 12, turn and leave other 12 sts. on safety pin. Cont. on these 12 sts. for 1½ ins., ending after a wrong side row. Pick up and purl 11 sts. down side of instep, then m.st. across the 12 sts. on safety pin.

Next row: M.st. across all sts., then pick up and knit 11 sts. down side of instep and m.st. across rem. 12 sts. on other safety pin. M.st. for 12 rows.

Next row: Work 2 tog., m.st. to last 2 sts. work 2 tog.

Next row: In m.st.

Next row: Work 2 tog., m.st. 24, (work 2 tog.) twice, m.st. 24, work 2 tog. Cast off in m.st.

To Make Up. Sew up foot and leg seam. Thread baby ribbon through holes.

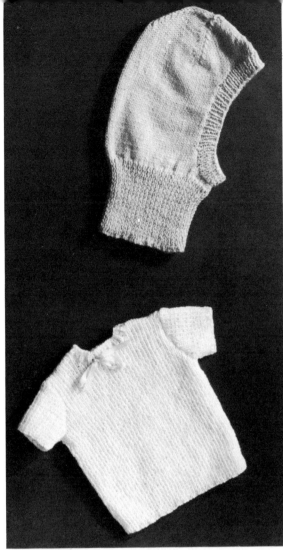

more patterns from odd ounces

A practical way of using up those odd balls of wool that are invariably collected over a period of time

Materials. 3 [3] [4] ozs. Double Knitting Wool. A pair each of No. 10 and No. 8 needles.

Measurements. Size of Face Opening 18 [20] [23] inches (slightly stretched). From crown of head to top of neck ribbing $8\frac{1}{2}$ [9] [$10\frac{1}{2}$] inches.

Tension $5\frac{1}{2}$ stitches and $7\frac{1}{2}$ rows to 1 inch on No. 8 needles over stocking-stitch.

Abbreviations. See page 100.

a warm balaclava

Start at lower edge of Neckband. Using No. 10 needles cast on 78 [88] [98] sts.

Neck Ribbing
1st row: Sl.1, k.1 (p.1, k.1) to end. Rep. this row to complete $3\frac{1}{2}$ [4] [$4\frac{1}{2}$] ins. from beg., ending after a wrong-side row.
Change to No. 8 needles.

Work Head
1st row: Sl.1, knit to end.
2nd row: Sl.1, purl until 1 st. rem., k.1.

Largest Size only
Rep. these last 2 rows once.

Shape Face Opening
Cast off 8 [9] [10] sts. at beg. of each of next 2 rows.
continued overleaf

181

continued from previous page

(62 [70] [78] sts.) Work 6 [8] [10] rows in st.st., dec. 1 st. at both ends of next and foll. alt. rows. (56 [62] [68] sts.)

Slipping the 1st st. in every row as above, cont. str. in st.st. to complete 38 [42] [50] rows from completion of Neck Ribbing.

Work 8 rows in st.st., inc. 1 st. at both ends of next and every foll. alt. row. (64 [70] [76] sts.) Cast on 9 [10] [11] sts. at beg. of each of next 2 rows.

Shape Top of Head

1st row: K.1, k.2 tog., k.15 [17] [19], k.2 tog. t.b.l., k.1, k.2 tog., k.15 [17] [19], k.2 tog. t.b.l., (k.2 tog.) twice, k.15, [17] [19], k.2 tog. t.b.l., k.1, k.2 tog., k.15 [17] [19], k.2 tog. t.b.l., k.1.

2nd and alternate rows: Sl.1, purl until 1 st. rem., k.1.

3rd row: Sl.1, k.2 tog., (k.13 [15] [17], k.2 tog. t.b.l., k.1, k.2 tog.) 3 times, k.13 [15] [17], k.2 tog. t.b.l., k.1.

5th row: Sl.1, k.2 tog., (k.11 [13] [15], k.2 tog. t.b.l., k.1, k.2 tog.) 3 times, k.11 [13] [15], k.2 tog., k.1. (57 [65] [73] sts.)

Cont. to dec. by 8 sts. in same fashion every right-side row until 17 sts. rem.

Next row: Sl.1, (p.3 tog., p.1) 4 times. Break wool. Thread rem. 9 sts. on to double yarn, pull tight and knot on inside.

Face Ribbing

Sew seam at top of head. With right side facing and using No. 10 needles, pick up and knit the 8 [9] [10] cast off sts. at top of neck ribbing, 28 [31] [35] sts. along right side of Face Opening, 19 [21] [23] sts. from cast on sts. at top, 28 [31] [35] sts. along left side of Face Opening, and 8 [9] [10] sts., cast off at top of neck ribbing. (91 [101] [113] sts.)

1st row: Sl.1, (k.1, p.1) to end.

2nd row: Sl.1, (p.1, k.1) to end.

Rep. these last 2 rows twice more and then work 1st row once again. Cast off in rib.

To Make Up. Press st.st. sections. Sew seam at front of neck.

baby's ribbed vest

Materials. 3 ozs. 4-ply wool. A pair each of No. 12 and No. 10 needles. ¾ yd. Baby Ribbon.

Measurements. To fit a 16 [18] [20] inch chest. Length 10 [11] [12] inches (adaptable).

Tension 10 stitches and 9 rows to 1 inch on No. 10 needles over Pattern.

Abbreviations: See page 100.

The Front. Using No. 12 needles cast on 74 [84] [94] sts. and work 12 rows in k.1, p.1 rib.

Change to No. 10 needles and cont. in k.1, p.1 rib to complete 6½ [7] [7½] ins. from cast on edge, ending after a wrong-side row.

N.B. If necessary, adjust length of Vest at this point.

Shape Armholes

Keeping ribbing correct, cast off 2 sts. at beg. of next 2 rows., dec. 1 st. at both ends of next 4 [6] [7] rows and of following 2 [2] [3] alt. rows. (58 [64] [70] sts.) Work str. in rib to complete 2 [2½] [3] ins. from beg. of Armholes, ending after a wrong-side row.

Shape Front Neck

Next row: Rib 21 [23] [25], turn. Work in all another 5 rows as for Left Shoulder, dec. 1 st. at beg. of next and of 2 foll. alt. rows. (18 [20] [22] sts.)

Shape Shoulder

Next row: Cast off 5 [6] [6] sts., rib to end.

Next row: K.2 tog., rib to end.

Rep. these last 2 rows once.

Cast off rem. 6 [6] [8] sts.

Returning to sts. still on needle, slip 1st 16 [18] [20] sts. on to a pin and complete 2nd Front Shoulder to match with 1st, reversing shapings.

The Back. Exactly as Front.

The Sleeves (both alike). Using No. 12 needles cast on 44 [54] [64] sts. and work 6 rows in k.1, p.1 rib.

Change to No. 10 needles and work 6 rows in k.1, p.1 rib.

Top of Sleeve. Cast off 2 sts. at beg. of next 8 [10] [12] rows and 3 sts. at beg. of foll. 2 [4] [6] rows. Cast off.

The Neckband. Do not press. Sew right shoulder seam, pulling sewing-wool so that ribbing remains closed.

With right side facing and using No. 12 needles, start at Left Front Shoulder and pick up 10 sts. along side of neck, 16 [18] [20] sts. from pin, 10 sts. from right side of front neck as far as shoulder seam, 11 sts. from side of back of neck, 16 [18] [20] sts. from pin, and 11 sts. along rem. side. (74 [78] [82] sts.)

1st row: (K.1, p.1) to end.

2nd row (Ribbon Eyelets): K.1 (wool over, k.2 tog.) until 1 st. rem., p.1.

Rep. 1st row 3 times more. Cast off loosely in rib.

To Make Up. Do not press. Sew left shoulder seam as right, joining sides of Neckband. Set in sleeves. Using edge-to-edge seam, sew side- and sleeve-seams. Press very lightly, being careful not to open ribbing. Thread ribbon through Ribbon Eyelets at neck, and tie in a bow.

comfy bed socks

Materials. 4 ozs. Double Knitting Wool. A pair each of No. 10 and No. 8 needles.

Measurements. Length of Leg to top of ankle ribbing 5 inches. Length of Foot from back of heel to toe 9 inches (adaptable).

Tension $5\frac{1}{2}$ **stitches and** $7\frac{1}{2}$ **rows to 1 inch on No. 8 needles over stocking-stitch.**

Abbreviations. See page 100.

Special Abbreviation. Up 1: lift running thread between stitches on row below and knit it.

Using No. 10 needles cast on 49 sts.

1st row: P.1, (k.1, p.1) to end.
2nd row: K.1, (up 1, p.1, k.2 tog. t.b.l., k.1, k.2 tog., p.1, up 1, k.1) to end.
Rep. these last 2 rows once and then work 1st of them once again.
Change to No. 8 needles.

Pattern
1st row: P.1, (k.7, p.1) to end.
2nd row: K.1, (p.7, k.1) to end.
Rep. these last 2 rows twice more.
7th row: P.1, (k.1, [k.2 tog.] 3 times, p.1) to end.
8th row: K.1, (p.1, [up 1, k.1] twice, up 1, p.1, k.1) to end.
These 8 rows form Patt. for Leg. Rep. them twice more. Change to No. 10 needles and work 8-row Patt. once and then work 1st 6 rows of Patt. once again.
This completes Leg.

Ankle Ribbing
1st row: P.1, (k.1, p.1) to end.
2nd row: K.1, (p.1, k.1) to end.
Rep. these last 2 rows 3 times more. Change to No. 8 needles.

Work Foot
Work 1st 4 rows of the 8 patt. rows once.

Turn Heel
1st row: K.11, turn.
2nd row: Sl.1, p.10.
Rep. these last 2 rows 7 times more.
Next row: K.3, k.2 tog. t.b.l., k.1, turn.
Next row: Sl.1, purl to end.
Next row: K.4, k.2 tog. t.b.l., k.1, turn.
Next row: Sl.1, purl to end.
Next row: K.5, k.2 tog. t.b.l., k.1, turn.
Next row: Sl.1, purl to end.
Next row: K.6, k.2 tog. t.b.l., pick up and knit the 9 slip-st. loops along side of heel, k.5 (p.1, k.7) until 1 st. rem., p.1.
Next row: P.11, turn.
Next row: Sl.1, knit to end.
Rep. these last 2 rows 7 times more.
Next row: P.3, p.2 tog., p.1, turn.
Cont. as for 1st side of heel until 8 sts. rem., ending after a knit row.
Next row: P.6, p.2 tog., pick up and purl the 9 slip-st. loops along side of heel, p.5, (k.1, p.7) until 1 st. rem., k.1. (59 sts.) This completes Heel.

Work Instep
1st row: K.15, k.2 tog., k.4, (p.1, k.1, [k.2 tog.] 3 times) twice, p.1, k.4, k.2 tog. t.b.l., k.15.
2nd row: P.20, (k.1, k.1, [up 1, k.1] twice, up 1, p.1) twice, k.1, p.20.
3rd row: K.14, k.2 tog., k.4, patt. 17, k.4, k.2 tog. t.b.l., k.14.
4th row: P.19, patt. 17, patt. 19.
Keeping the patt. correct on centre 17 sts., cont. to dec. in same fashion every right-side row until 49 sts. rem., and then cont. str. to complete 7 ins. from back of heel, ending after a wrong-side row.
N.B. If necessary, adjust length of Foot at this point.

Shape Toe
Change to No. 10 needles.
1st row: K.10, k.2 tog. t.b.l., k.2 tog., k.21, k.2 tog. t.b.l., k.2 tog., k.10.
2nd and alternate rows: Purl.
3rd row: K.9, k.2 tog. t.b.l., k.2 tog., k.19, k.2 tog. t.b.l., k.2 tog., k.9.
Cont. to dec. in same fashion every right-side row until 25 sts. rem. Cast off.

To Make Up. Press st.st. and patterned sections. Using edge-to-edge seam, join back of leg and seam under sole. Fold so that seam is in correct position and, using edge-to-edge seam, close toe. Press seams.

183

holiday casuals

Holiday tops for the children, a beach tunic for him and a cardigan for her

BEACH TUNIC

Materials. 3 [4] [5] [5] ozs. Emu Super Crimp Bri-Nylon 4-ply in White (W), 1 oz. each in Red (R), Blue (B) and Navy (N); 1 pair No. 10 knitting needles; 2 open-ended zip fasteners, 10 [12] [12] [14] inches in length.

Measurements. To fit chest 24 [26] [28] [30] inches; length, 15 [17½] [18½] [20] inches.

Tension 7 stitches to 1 inch.

Abbreviations. K. knit, p. purl, st(s). stitch(es), ins. inches, inc. increase(ing), dec. decrease(ing), rep. repeat, rem. remain(ing), alt. alternate, cont. continue, st.st. stocking stitch, patt. pattern, tog. together, foll. following, k.1, b. knit into row below on next st., sl. slip, g.st. garter stitch.

Note—*Figures in brackets refer to larger sizes in size order, where only one figure is given, this refers to all sizes.*

The Back and Front (worked alike). With W, cast on 92 [98] [106] [112] sts.
Work 7 rows st.st.
Next row: K. for hemline.
Beg. with k. row, work 6 rows st.st.
Next row (make hem): K. tog. st. on needle, with loop of cast-on all along row.
Beg. with p. row, work 3 [6] [7] [10] rows st.st.
Join in B. Beg. with B, cont. in st.st. in stripes of 1 row B, 1 row W for 15 [19] [21] [23] rows.
Cont. in W for 10 [13] [14] [17] rows.
Join in R and rep. stripe patt. as before.
Work in W for 10 [13] [14] [17] rows.
Join in N and work stripe patt. as before.
Break off N and cont. in W until work measures 9½ [11½] [12] [13½] ins. from lower edge, ending after p. row.

Shape Armholes
Cast off 7 [8] [8] [9] sts. at beg. of next 2 rows; dec. 1 st. at both ends of next and alt. rows to 66 [70] [74] [78] sts. Cont. straight until work measures 13 [14½] [15] [16½] ins. from lower edge, ending after p. row.

Shape Neck
Work 23 [24] [26] [27] sts., turn; leave rem. sts. on spare needle. Working on 1st set of sts., dec. 1 st. at neck edge every row to 11 [12] [14] [14] sts. Cont. straight until work

measures 15 [17½] [18½] [20] ins. from lower edge. Cast off. Return to rem. sts., sl.20 [22] [22] [24] sts. on to needle and leave for neck, join yarn to rem. sts. and complete to match other side.

The Neckband. Join right shoulder seam; with right side facing and W, pick up and k.104 [112] [120] [126] sts. round neck, including sts. on spare needles. Work 4 [4] [6] [6] rows g.st. Cast off.

The Armbands. Join left shoulder seam. With right side facing and W, pick up and k.72 [80] [88] [96] sts. evenly round armhole edge. Work 4 [4] [6] [6] rows g.st. Cast off. Work other armhole to match.

To Make Up. Sew zips into sides of tunic, closed ends to armhole edges. Thread tassels through tags at end of zips. Press very lightly with cool iron.

COSY CARDIGAN

Materials. 5 [6] [7] ozs. Emu Bri-Nylon Double Knitting in Main Colour (M), 4 [5] [6] ozs. in Contrast (C); 1 pair No. 8 knitting needles; 5 buttons.

Measurements. To fit 25 [27] [29] inch chest; length, 16 [17] [18½] inches; sleeve seam, 10½ [12½] [14] inches.

Tension 4 stitches and 10 rows to 1 square inch over pattern.

Abbreviations. K. knit, p. purl, st(s). stitch(es), ins. inches, inc. increase(ing), dec. decrease(ing), rep. repeat, rem. remain(ing), alt. alternate, cont. continue, st.st. stocking stitch, patt. pattern, tog. together, foll. following, k.1 b. knit into row below on next st., sl. slip, g.st. garter stitch.

Note—*Figures in brackets refer to larger sizes in size order, where only one figure is given, this refers to all sizes.*

The Back. With M, cast on 56 [60] [64] sts. Work in k.1, p.1 rib for 2½ ins.
Cont. in patt. thus:
1st row: Join in C, * with C k.1, k.1 b; rep. from * to last 2 sts., k.2.
2nd row: With C, k. to end.
3rd row: With M, k.2, * k.1 b., k.1; rep. from * to end.
4th row: With M, k. to end.

Rep. last 4 rows until work measures 10 [10½] [11¼] ins. from beg., ending after wrong side row.

Shape Raglan

Keeping patt. correct, cast off 2 sts. at beg. of next 2 rows. Work 2 rows straight. Dec. 1 st. at both ends of next and every foll. 4th row to 28 [32] [36] sts.; then at both ends of alt. rows to 18 sts. Cast off.

The Left Front. With M, cast on 26 [28] [30] sts. Work 2½ ins. k.1, p.1 rib.

Cont. in patt. as Back, until work matches Back to armhole, ending after wrong side row.

Shape Raglan and Front

Cast off 2 sts. at beg. of next row. Work 3 rows straight. Dec. 1 st. at beg. of next and every foll. 4th row, *at the same time* dec. 1 st. at front edge on 10th row from beg. of armhole shaping, then every foll. 7th row until 3 sts. rem. Work 2 rows. Cast off.

The Right Front. As Left Front, reversing shapings.

The Sleeves (both alike). With M, cast on 32 [34] [34] sts. Work 2 ins. k.1, p.1 rib.

Cont. in patt. as Back, inc. 1 st. at both ends of 9th then every foll. 20th row to 40 [42] [44] sts.

Cont. straight until sleeve measures 10½ [12½] [14] ins., ending after same row as Back before start of raglan shaping.

Shape Raglan

Cast off 2 sts. at beg. of next 2 rows. Work 2 rows straight. Dec. 1 st. at both ends of next and every foll. 4th row to 8 sts. Work 3 rows straight. Cast off.

The Front Band. With M, cast on 8 sts. Work ½ [¾] [¾] ins. in k.1, p.1 rib.

Next row (buttonhole): Rib 3, cast off 2, rib to end.

On next row, cast on sts. over those cast off.

Cont. in rib, making 4 more buttonholes at intervals of 2½ [2½] [2¾] ins., measured from base of previous buttonhole. Cont. in rib until band will fit all around fronts, sleeve tops and neck. Cast off in rib.

To Make Up. Press lightly with cool iron over dry cloth. Sew in raglan sleeves. Sew on front band. Sew on buttons. Press seams very lightly.

patchwork blanket

Made of strips in four colours with bobbles at the centre of each motif

Materials. 22 balls each of Red, White, Jade and Pale Green Lister Bel Air Courtelle Double Crepe; pair No. 11 knitting needles.

Size. 6 ft. 6 ins. by 4 ft. 4 ins.

Tension 7 stitches and 13 rows to 1 inch.

Abbreviations. K. knit, p. purl, st(s). stitch(es), g.st. garter stitch, inc. increase, dec. decrease, beg. beginning, rep. repeat, patt. pattern, bobble one, work (k.1, p.1, k.1 p.1, k.1) all in next st., turn, k.5, turn, p.5, turn, k.5, turn, p.5, turn, slip 1, k.2 together, pass slip st. over, k.2 together, turn, k.2 together.

Strip A. With Jade yarn cast on 23 sts.

*Work in g.st., inc. 1 st. each end of every 3rd row until there are 41 sts. K.1 row.

Now patt. thus:

1st row (right side): K.20, bobble one, k.20.

K.3 rows, inc. 1 st. each end of 1st row.

5th row: Inc. in first st., k.20, bobble one, k.20, inc. in last st.

K.3 rows, inc. 1 st. each end of 3rd row.

9th row: K.20, bobble one, k.5, bobble one, k.20.

K.3 rows, inc. 1 st. each end of 2nd row. (49 sts.).

13th row: K.18, bobble one (k.5, bobble one) twice, k.18.

K.3 rows, dec. 1 st. each end of 2nd row.

Rep. 9th row.

K.3 rows, dec. 1 st. each end of 1st row.

Rep. 5th row but dec. each end of row instead of inc.

K.3 rows, dec. 1 st. each end of 3rd row.

Rep. 1st row.

Continue in g.st., dec. 1 st. each end of 2nd and every following 3rd row until 23 sts. remain. K.1 row ***.

Break of Jade and join Pale Green. Rep. from * to ***. Continue thus, working motifs alternately in Jade and Pale Green until there are four motifs in each colour.

Cast off in Pale Green.

Work 7 more strips to match.

Strip B. With Red yarn cast on 49 sts. Work from ** to *** as Strip A.

Break off Red and join White. Work from * to *** as Strip A. Break off White and join Red.

Continue working from * to *** as Strip A, using Red and White alternately until 4 whole White motifs are completed.

Break off White and join Red. Work from * to ** as Strip A. Rep. 13th patt. row.

Cast off.

Work 2 more strips to match.

Strip C. As Strip B, but working White for Red and vice versa. Work 3 more strips to match.

Side Strip. With Red yarn cast on 26 sts.

1st row: K.1, bobble one, k.5, bobble one, k.18.

K.3 rows, dec. 1 st. at end of 2nd row.

5th row: K. 4, bobble one, k.20.

K.3 rows, dec. 1 st. at beg. of 1st row.

9th row: K.1, bobble one, k.20, k.2 tog.

K.3 rows, dec. 1 st. at beg. of 3rd row.

13th row: K.1, bobble one, k.20.

Continue in g.st. dec. 1 st. at end of 2nd row and at this edge on every following 3rd row, until 13 sts. remain.

K.1 row ****.

Break off Red and join White. Continue in g.st., inc. 1 st. at end of 3rd row and at this edge on every 3rd row until there are 22 sts. K.1 row.

Next row: As 13th. K.3 rows, inc. 1 st. at beg. of 1st row.

Next row: As 9th but inc. at end of row instead of dec.

K.3 rows, inc. 1 st. at beg. of 3rd row.

Next row: As 5th.

K.3 rows, inc. 1 st. at end of 2nd row. (26 sts.).

Now rep. from 1st row to ****. Break off White and join Red. Work as for White motif and continue working motifs of White and Red alternately until 4 White motifs in all are completed. Work another Red half motif until there are 26 sts. Rep. 1st row.

Cast off.

Work 1 more side strip.

To Make Up. Do not press. Place 4 of Strips A with Jade motif at lower edge and 4 with Pale Green motif at lower edge and arrange alternately. Place Side Strips on ends and place Strips B and C between the A Strips, beg. and ending with a C Strip. Pin together, tack on wrong side matching shapes exactly, then oversew seams.

fancy-stitch girl's cardigan

This garment is photographed on page 8, where the stitch can be seen in detail

Materials. 12 balls (½-oz. each) Lister Listrada Terylene/Bri-Nylon Double Knitting. 1 pair each Nos. 10 and 8 needles. 7 buttons. 2 stitch holders.

Measurements. To fit 32 inch chest. Length from shoulder 18½ inches. Length of sleeve seam 15 inches.

Tension 6 stitches and 8 rows equal one inch on No. 8 needles.

Abbreviations. K. knit, p. purl, st(s) stitch(es), ins. inches, tog. together, st.st. stocking stitch, s.k.p.o. slip 1, knit 1, pass slip stitch over, sl. slip, s.k.2 tog. p.o. sl.1 knit 2 together, pass slip stitch over, m. make a stitch by bringing yarn to front of work before a knit stitch, and by wrapping yarn round needle before a purl stitch, t.b.s. through back of stitch, cont. continue, inc. increase, dec. decrease, rep. repeat, rem. remaining, moss st. alternating rows of knit 1, purl 1, p.s.s.o.b.s. pass slip stitch over both stitches.

The Back. With No. 10 needles cast on 90 sts. and work in k.1 p.1 rib for 2 ins., inc. into last st. at end of last row. (91 sts.)

Change to No. 8 needles and cont. in st.st. (1st row knit) until work measures 11 ins. from beg., ending with a purl row.

Shape Raglan
Cast off 3 sts. at beg. of next 2 rows.
1st row: K.1, s.k.p.o., knit to last 3 sts., k.2 tog., k.1.
2nd row: K.1, purl to last st., k.1.
Rep. last 2 rows until 25 sts. rem. Cast off.

The Sleeves. With No. 10 needles cast on 48 sts., and work in k.1, p.1 rib for 2 ins., inc. in last st. on last row.

(49 sts.) Change to No. 8 needles.
1st row: K.12, p.1, k.3, p.1, k.5, k.2 tog., m.1, k.1, m.1, k.2 tog. t.b.s., k.5, p.1, k.3, p.1, k.12.
2nd row: K.1, p.11, k.1, p.3, k.1, p.15, k.1, p.3, k.1, p.11, k.1.
3rd row: K.12, p.1, sl.1, k.2, p.s.s.o. b.s., p.1, k.4, k.2 tog., m.1, k.3, m.1, k.2 tog. t.b.s., k.4, p.1, sl.1, k.2, p.s.s.o. b.s., p.1, k.12.
4th row: K.1, p.11, k.1, p.1, m.1, p.1, k.1, p.15, k.1, p.1, m.1, p.1, k.1, p.11, k.1.
5th row: K.12, p.1, k.3, p.1, k.3, (k.2 tog., m.1) twice, k.1, (m.1, k.2 tog. t.b.s.) twice, k.3, p.1, k.3, p.1, k.12.
6th row: As 2nd row.
7th row: Inc. in 1st st., k.11, p.1, sl.1, k.2, p.s.s.o. b.s., p.1, k.2, (k.2 tog., m.1) twice, k.3, (m.1, k.2 tog. t.b.s.) twice, k.2, p.1, sl.1, k.2, p.s.s.o. b.s., p.1, knit to last st., inc. in last st.
8th row: K.1, p.12, k.1, p.1, m.1, p.1, k.1, p.15, k.1, p.1, m.1, p.1, k.1, p.12, k.1.
9th row: K.13, p.1, k.3, p.1, k.1, (k.2 tog., m.1) twice, k.5, (m.1, k.2 tog. t.b.s.) twice, k.1, p.1, k.3, p.1, k.13.
10th row: As 2nd row, working extra sts. into pattern.
11th row: K.13, p.1, sl.1, k.2, p.s.s.o. b.s., p.1, (k.2 tog., m.1) twice, k.7, (m.1, k.2 tog. t.b.s.) twice, p.1, sl.1, k.2, p.s.s.o. b.s., p.1, k.13.
12th row: As 4th row, working extra sts. each end into pattern.
13th row: K.13, p.1, k.3, p.1, k.2, (m.1, k.2 tog. t.b.s.) twice, k.3, (k.2 tog., m.1.) twice, k.2, p.1, k.3, p.1, k.13.
14th row: As 2nd row working extra sts. into pattern.
15th row: Inc. in 1st st., k.12, p.1, sl.1, k.2, p.s.s.o. b.s., p.1, k.3 (m.1, k.2 tog. t.b.s.) twice, k.1 (k.2 tog., m.1) twice, k.3, p.1, sl.1, k.2, p.s.s.o. b.s., p.1, k.12, inc. in last st.
16th row: As 4th row, working extra sts. into pattern.
17th row: K.14, p.1, k.3, p.1, k.4, m.1, k.2 tog. t.b.s., m.1, s.k.2 tog. p.o., m.1, k.2 tog., m.1, k.4, p.1, k.3, p.1, k.14.
18th row: As 2nd row, working extra sts. into pattern.
19th row: K.14, p.1, sl.1, k.2, p.s.s.o. b.s., p.1, k.5, m.1, k.2 tog. t.b.s., k.1, k.2 tog., m.1, k.5, p.1, sl.1, k.2, p.s.s.o. b.s., p.1, k.14.
20th row: As 4th row, working extra sts. into pattern.
21st row: K.14, p.1, k.3, p.1, k.6, m.1, s.k.2 tog. p.o., m.1, k.6, p.1, k.3, p.1, k.14.
22nd row: As 2nd row, working extra sts. into pattern.
23rd row: As 3rd row, inc. in 1st and last st., working extra sts. into patt. Cont. in this way, keeping patt. correct, and increasing at each end of every 8th row until there are 71 sts. on needle.

Cont. without further incs. until work measures 15 ins. from beg.

Shape Raglan
Cast off 3 sts. at beg. of next 2 rows.

1st row: K.1, k.2 tog. t.b.s., patt. to last 3 sts., k.2 tog. k.1.

2nd row: K.1, patt. to last st., k.1.

Rep. last 2 rows until 5 sts. rem. Cast off.

The Left Front

With No. 10 needles cast on 56 sts.

1st row: (K.1, p.1) rep. to last 10 sts., k.2, (p.1, k.1) 4 times.

These last 9 sts. form moss st. border.

2nd row: (K.1, p.1) to end.

Rep. these 2 rows until work measures 2 ins. inc. in last st. of last row. 57 sts. Change to No. 8 needles.

1st row: K.23, p.1, k.3, p.1, k.5, k.2 tog., m.1, k.1, m.1, k.2 tog. t.b.s., k.5, p.1, k.3, p.1, (k.1, p.1) to last st., k.1.

2nd row: (K.1, p.1) 4 times, k.2, p.3, k.1, p.15, k.1, p.3, k.1, purl to last st., k.1.

Keeping pattern correct, cont. until work measures the same as Back to armholes, ending with a purl row.

Shape Raglan

Next row: Cast off 3 sts., patt. to end. Pattern next row.

1st row: K.1, k.2 tog. t.b.s., patt. to last 36 sts., k.2 tog., patt. to end.

2nd row: Patt. to last st., k.1.

Keeping to pattern, cont. dec. at sleeve edge every alternate row, and outside fancy panel every 4th row until decs. meet.

Now cont. dec. at sleeve edge only every other row until there are 27 sts. left., then dec. every row until 9 moss sts. left.

Work in moss. st. on these 9 sts. until sufficient has been worked to be sewn across top of sleeve, and to centre of back neck without stretching. Cast off.

The Right Front. With No. 10 needles cast on 56 sts.

1st row: (K.1, p.1) to end.

2nd row: (K.1, p.1) rep. to last 10 sts., k.2, (p.1, k.1) to end.

Rep. these 2 rows for 2 ins. working a buttonhole on 5th row thus: (K.1, p.1) twice, m.1, p.2 tog., (k.1, p.1) to end of row.

Inc. once in 1st st. of last row of rib. 57 sts.

Change to No. 8 needles.

1st row: (K.1, p.1) 5 times, sl.1 purlwise, k.2, p.s.s.o. b.s., p.1, k.5, k.2 tog., m.1, k.1, m.1, k.2 tog. t.b.s., k.5, p.1, sl.1 purlwise, k.2, p.s.s.o. b.s., p.1, knit to end.

Keeping patt. correct, make a buttonhole on every 14th row from first buttonhole, until 7 made altogether, and work this Front to match the Left, reversing all shapings.

To Make Up. Sew sleeves to raglan armholes of front and back. Sew side and sleeve seams. Sew end of moss st. border tog., and sew to back neck. Sew on buttons to correspond to buttonholes.

a simple day dress in blue

The very flattering line of this dress and the fashionable tie are shown in the picture on the following page

THE DRESS

Materials. 18 [19] [20] ozs. of Robin Casino Crepe, 4-ply, in Main Colour. 1 oz. in White. 1 pair each No. 11 and No. 12 knitting needles. 1 button.

Measurements. To fit 34 [36] [38] inch bust. Length 34 [34½] [35] inches, or as required.

Tension 7½ stitches and 9½ rows to 1 inch over stocking stitch.

Abbreviations. K. knit, p. purl, st(s). stitch(es), st.st. stocking stitch, dec. decrease by working 2 stitches together, inc. increase by working twice into 1 stitch, rep. repeat, patt. pattern, beg. beginning, M. Main Shade, W. White.

Note—*Instructions are given for 34 inch bust size. Figures in brackets are for the two larger sizes. Where one figure only is given, this refers to all sizes.*

The Back. Cast on 150 [158] [166] sts. with No. 12 needles and M. Work 11 rows st.st. K.1 row on wrong side to mark hemline. Change to No. 11 needles. Proceed in st.st., beg. with a k. row. Work 4 inches. Dec. at both ends of next and every 16th row following until 136 [144] [152] sts. remain, then of every 6th row until 126 [134] [142] sts. remain. Proceed until work measures 18 inches from hemline.

Mark edge of work with a coloured thread, to denote waistline. Adjust length if required at this point.

Work 10 rows. Inc. at both ends of next and every 6th row following until there are 132 [140] [148] sts. Proceed until 7½ inches from marker, after a p. row.

continued overleaf

continued from previous page

Shape Sleeves, while changing to Yoke Pattern

Inc. at both ends of every row, while working the following patt:

1st row: Knit.

2nd row: Purl.

3rd row: Purl.

4th row: Knit.

These 4 rows form yoke patt., and are repeated throughout remainder of work.

Continue to inc. at both ends of every row for a further 8 rows, then cast on 5 sts. at beg. of next 4 rows. 176 [184] [192] sts. **

Work 12 [8] [4] rows without shaping.

Next row: K.1, inc. in next st., k. to last 2 sts., inc. in next st., k.1. Inc. in this manner at both ends of every 8th row until there are 188 [198] [208] sts. Work 11 rows.

Shape Shoulders

Cast off 5 [6] [7] sts. at beg. of next 8 rows, 8 at beg. of next 8 rows and 11 at beg. of next 4 rows. Cast off remaining 40 [42] [44] sts.

The Front. Work exactly as Back as far as **.

Divide for Opening

K.86 [90] [94], turn, leaving remaining sts. unworked. Proceed on this set of sts. for left side. Cast on 4 sts. for underwrap, work to end. *** Work 10 [6] [2] rows. Inc. at side edge, working shaping as for corresponding edge of Back, on next and every 8th row following until there are 96 [101] [106] sts. Work 11 rows.

Shape Neck and Shoulder

1st row: Cast off 5 [6] [7] sts., work to end.

2nd row: Cast off 8 [9] [10] sts., work to end.

Now work 6 rows, casting off 5 [6] [7] sts. at beg. of every side-edge row and decreasing at neck edge on every row. 62 sts. Work 8 rows, continuing to dec. at neck edge on every row, and casting off 8 sts. at beg. of every side-edge row. 22 sts.

Working neck edge straight, cast off 11 sts. at beg. of next 2 side-edge rows.

Join wool to inner edge of remaining 90 [94] [98] sts. Work 2 rows. Complete right side to correspond with left from ***, reversing neck and shoulder shapings.

The Collar. Cast on 36 sts. with No. 11 needles and M. Work 4 rows yoke patt. Proceeding in yoke patt., shape collar edge thus:

Work 30, turn, work back, Work 24, turn, work back. Work 18, turn, work back. Work 12, turn, work back. Proceed on all sts. until work measures 15 inches along shorter edge, finishing after a 2nd patt. row. Shape 2nd edge thus:

Work 12, turn, work back. Work 18, turn, work back. Work 24, turn, work back. Work 30, turn, work back. Work 4 rows. Cast off.

To Make Up. Press work with a warm iron under a damp cloth, omitting collar and yoke. Join side and shoulder seams. Turn up hem on lower edge. Sew down underwrap at base of opening. Sew collar to neck edge, beg. 2 sts. from front edge each side. Press seams. Sew button to left side of opening and work a button-loop on right side by buttonhole-stitching over loop made from 3 strands of wool.

THE TIE

Note. To avoid leaving a hole in the work when turning within the row, k. the required number of sts., bring wool forward between needles, slip next st., take wool back, turn, slip same st. and take wool back ready to knit.

1st Section

Cast on 148 sts. with No. 11 needles and W. K.2 rows.

3rd row: Cast off 1 st. (1 st. is now on right hand needle), k.98 more, making 99 on right hand needle, turn, leaving 48 unworked.

4th, 6th and 8th rows: K. to end.

5th row: Cast off 1 st., k. to end.

7th row: Cast off 1 st., k.96 more, turn, leaving 48 unworked.

9th row: Cast off 1 st., k. to last 48 sts. as before, turn.

10th row: Drop W wool and leave it hanging, join in M and k. to end with M.

11th row: With M, cast off 1 st., k. to last 48 sts., drop M wool and k. to end with W.

12th row: K.48 with W, then k. to end with M.

13th row: With M, cast off 1 st., k. to last 48 sts., turn.

14th row: K. to end with M.

15th and 16th rows: as 11th and 12th rows.

17th row: With M, cast off 1 st., k. to last 48 sts., turn.

18th row: K. to end with W.

19th to 24th rows: As 3rd to 8th rows.

25th and 26th rows: As 5th and 6th rows.

Rep. 9th to 26th rows.

Cast off with W.

2nd Section

Cast on 164 sts. with No. 11 needles and W. K.2 rows.

3rd row: Cast off 1 st., k.114 more, turn, leaving 48 unworked.

4th, 6th and 8th rows: K. to end.

5th row: Cast off 1 st., k. to end.

7th row: Cast off 1 st., k.112 more, turn, leaving 48 unworked.

Continue as 1st section, noting that there are 16 sts. more throughout.

To Make Up. Join short ends. Press under a damp cloth.

191

a perfect pram set

Any mother will be proud to take out her baby dressed in this sweet set made in easy-to-wash Bri-Nylon

Materials. 8 [9] ozs. of Ladybird Baby Quick Knit Super Bri-Nylon. 1 pair each No. 7 and No. 10 knitting needles. 3 buttons for the Coat. Ribbon for the Bonnet.

Measurements. Coat: To fit 16 [18] inch chest. Length 9½ [10] inches. Sleeve seam 4½ [5] inches.
Bonnet: Round face 13 [14½] inches.
Leggings: Front length from waist to ankle 16 [17½] inches.

Tension 11 stitches measure 2 inches in width, and 15 rows measure 2 inches in depth, over stocking stitch on No. 7 needles.

Abbreviations. K. knit, p. purl, st(s). stitch(es), st.st. stocking stitch, g.st. garter stitch, tog. together, dec. decrease by working 2 stitches together, inc. increase by working twice into 1 stitch, sl. slip, p.s.s.o. pass slipped stitch over, t.b.l. through the back of the loop, rep. repeat, beg. beginning, patt. pattern, y.r.n. yarn round needle, y.o.n. yarn over needle, y.f. yarn forward.

Note—*Instructions are given for the small size. Figures in brackets are for the larger size. Where one figure only is given, this refers to both sizes.*

THE COAT

The Back. Using No. 7 needles cast on 88 [96] sts. Work 8 rows g.st.
Beg. with a p. row, proceed in st.st. until work measures 5 [5½] inches, ending with a p. row.

Shape Raglan
** Cast off 1 st. at beg. of next 2 rows.
Next row: K.1, sl.1, k.1, p.s.s.o., k. to last 3 sts., k.2 tog., k.1.
Next row: Purl.
Rep. last 2 rows 4 times more. *** 76 [84] sts.

Decrease for Yoke
Next row: K.2 tog. to end. 38 [42] sts. Break yarn and leave sts. on a spare needle.

The Sleeves (alike). Using No. 10 needles cast on 30 [34] sts. Work 10 rows k.1 p.1 rib.
Change to No. 7 needles.
Next row: K.1 [3], * inc. in next st., k.2. Rep. from * to last 2 [4] sts., inc. in next st., k.1 [3]. 40 [44] sts.
Beg. with a p. row, continue in st.st. until work measures 4½ [5] inches, ending with a p. row.

Shape Top
Work as given for Back from ** to ***. 28 [32] sts.

Decrease for Yoke
Next row: K.4 [6], * k.2 tog., k.4. Rep. from * to last 6 [8] sts., k.2 tog., k.4 [6]. 24 [28] sts. Break yarn and leave sts. on a spare needle.

The Right Front. Using No. 7 needles cast on 47 [51] sts. Work 8 rows g.st.
Next row: P. to last 5 sts., k.5.
Keeping 5 sts. at front edge in g.st. and working remaining sts. in st.st., proceed until work measures same as Back to beg. of raglan, ending with a wrong side row. K. to side edge.

Shape Raglan
Cast off 1 st. at beg. of next row, p. to last 5 sts., k.5.
Next row: K. to last 3 sts., k.2 tog., k.1.
Next row: P. to last 5 sts., k.5.
Rep. last 2 rows 4 times more. 41 [45] sts.

Decrease for Yoke
Next row: K.5, then k.2 tog. to end. 23 [25] sts.
Break yarn and leave sts. on a spare needle.

The Left Front
Using No. 7 needles cast on 47 [51] sts. Work 8 rows g.st.
Next row: K.5, p. to end.
Keeping 5 sts. at front edge in g.st., and working remaining sts., in st.st., proceed until work measures same as Back to beg. of raglan, after a wrong side row.

Shape Raglan
Cast off 1 st. at beg. of next row, k. to end. Work 1 row.
Next row: K.1, sl.1, k.1, p.s.s.o., k. to end.
Next row: K.5, p. to end.
Rep. last 2 rows 4 times more. 41 [45] sts.

continued overleaf

continued from previous page

Decrease for Yoke

Next row: K.2 tog. until 5 sts. remain, k.5. 23 [25] sts.

The Yoke. Using No. 7 needles, continuing with yarn at left front, with wrong side of work facing, k. sts. of left front, sleeve, back, 2nd sleeve and right front. 132 [148] sts.

In next row make buttonhole thus: K.2, pass yarn loosely round needle, k.2 tog., k. to end.

K.1 row.

Begin patt.

1st row: k.5, p.4, k.2, * p.6, k.2. Rep. from * to last 9 sts., p.4, k.5.

2nd row: K.9, p.2, * k.6, p.2. Rep. from * to last 9 sts., k.9.

3rd row: K.5, p.3, * k.2 tog., y.f., sl.1, k.1, p.s.s.o., p.4. Rep. from * to last 12 sts., k.2 tog., y.f., sl.1, k.1, p.s.s.o., p.3, k.5.

4th row: K.8, * p.1, k. into back then into front of next st. (this will now be termed inc. 1), p.1, k.4. Rep. from * to last 11 sts., p.1, inc. 1, p.1, k.8.

5th row: K.5, p.2, * k.2 tog., y.f., k.2, y.f., sl.1, k.1, p.s.s.o., p.2. Rep. from * to last 5 sts., k.5.

6th row: K.7, * p.6, k.2. Rep. from * to last 5 sts., k.5.

7th row: K.5, p.1, * k.2 tog., y.f., k.2 tog., y.f., sl.1, k.1, p.s.s.o., y.f., sl.1, k.1, p.s.s.o. Rep. from * to last 6 sts., p.1, k.5.

8th row: K.6, p.3, * inc. 1, p.6. Rep. from * to last 10 sts., inc. 1, p.3, k.6. Change to No. 10 needles.

9th row: K.5, p.1, y.o.n., * sl.1, k.1, p.s.s.o., y.f., sl.1, k.1, p.s.s.o., k.2 tog., y.f., k.2 tog., y.f. Rep. from * to last 6 sts., y.r.n., p.1, k.5.

10th row: K.6, k.1 t.b.l., p.6, * inc. 1, p.6. Rep. from * to last 7 sts., k.1 t.b.l., k.6.

11th row: K.2, y.r.n. loosely (for 2nd buttonhole), k.2 tog., k.1, p.2, * y.o.n., sl.1, k.2 tog., p.s.s.o., y.f., k.3 tog., y.r.n., p.2.

Rep. from * to last 5 sts., k.5.

12th row: K.7, * k.1 t.b.l., p.1, inc. 1, p.1, k.1 t.b.l., k.2. Rep. from * to last 5 sts., k.5.

13th row: K.5, p.3, * y.o.n., sl.1, k.1, p.s.s.o., k.2 tog., y.r.n., p.4. Rep. from * to last 12 sts., y.o.n., sl.1, k.1, p.s.s.o., k.2 tog., y.r.n., p.3, k.5.

14th row: K.8, * k.1 t.b.l., p.2, k.1 t.b.l., k.4. Rep. from * to last 12 sts., k.1 t.b.l., p.2, k.1 t.b.l., k.8.

Now shape yoke thus:

1st row: K.5, p.2, * p.2, k.2 tog., p.2, p.2 tog. Rep. from * to last 13 sts., p.2, k.2 tog., p.4, k.5. 103 [115] sts.

2nd and every alternate row: Knit.

3rd row: K.5, * p.4, p.2 tog. Rep. from * 6 [7] times more, p.9, p.2 tog., * p.4, p.2 tog. Rep. from * to last 9 sts., p.4, k.5. 89 [99] sts.

5th row: K.5, p.4, p.2 tog., * p.3, p.2 tog. Rep. from *

5 [6] times more, p.7, p.2 tog., * p.3, p.2 tog. Rep. from * to last 9 sts., p.4, k.5. 75 [83] sts.

7th row: K.5, p.4, p.2 tog., * p.2, p.2 tog. Rep. from * 5 [6] times more, p.5, p.2 tog., * p.2, p.2 tog. Rep. from * to last 9 sts., p.4, k.5. 61 [67] sts.

9th row: K.5, p.4, p.2 tog., * p.1, p.2 tog. Rep. from * 5 [6] times, more, p.3, p.2 tog., * p.1, p.2 tog. Rep. from * to last 9 sts., p.4, k.5. 47 [51] sts.

10th row: Knit.

Work Neckband

K.2 rows. In next row make buttonhole as before. K.3 rows. Cast off.

To Make Up. Press lightly, using a cool iron and dry cloth. Join raglan seams, side and sleeve seams. Press seams. Sew on buttons.

THE BONNET

Beg. at front edge, cast on 72 [80] sts., using No. 7 needles. Work 5 rows g.st. Begin patt:

1st row: K.3, p.4, k.2, * p.6, k.2. Rep. from * to last 7 sts., p.4, k.3.

2nd row: K.7, p.2, * k.6, p.2. Rep. from * to last 7 sts., k.7.

3rd row: K.3, p.3, * k.2 tog., y.f., sl.1, k.1, p.s.s.o., p.4. Rep. from * to last 10 sts., k.2 tog., y.f., sl.1, k.1, p.s.s.o., p.3, k.3.

4th row: K.6, * p.1, k. into back then into front of next st. (this will now be termed inc. 1), p.1, k.4. Rep. from * to last 9 sts., p.1, inc.1, p.1, k.6.

5th row: K.3, p.2, * k.2 tog., y.f., k.2, y.f., sl.1, k.1, p.s.s.o., p.2. Rep. from * to last 3 sts., k.3.

6th row: K.5, * p.6, k.2. Rep. from * to last 3 sts., k.3.

7th row: K.3, p.1, * k.2 tog., y.f., k.2 tog., y.f., sl.1, k.1, p.s.s.o., y.f., sl.1, k.1, p.s.s.o. Rep. from * to last 4 sts., p.1, k.3.

8th row: K.4, p.3, * inc.1, p.6. Rep. from * to last 8 sts., inc. 1, p.3, k.4.

9th row: K.3, p.1, y.o.n., * sl.1, k.1, p.s.s.o., y.f., sl.1, k.1, p.s.s.o., k.2 tog., y.f., k.2 tog., y.f. Rep. from * to last 4 sts., y.r.n., p.1, k.3.

10th row: K.4, k.1 t.b.l., p.6, * inc.1, p.6. Rep. from * to last 5 sts., k.1 t.b.l., k.4.

11th row: K.3, p.2, * y.o.n., sl.1, k.2 tog., p.s.s.o., y.f., k.3 tog., y.r.n., p.2. Rep. from * to last 3 sts., k.3.

12th row: K.5, * k.1 t.b.l., p.1, inc.1, p.1, k.1 t.b.l., k.2. Rep. from * to last 3 sts., k.3.

13th row: K.3, p.3, * y.o.n., sl.1, k.1, p.s.s.o., k.2 tog., y.r.n., p.4. Rep. from * to last 10 sts., y.o.n., sl.1, k.1, p.s.s.o., k.2 tog., y.r.n., p.3, k.3.

14th row: K.6, * k.1 t.b.l., p.2, k.1 t.b.l., k.4. Rep. from * to last 10 sts., k.1 t.b.l., p.2, k.1 t.b.l., k.6.

Next row: K.3, p.4, y.o.n., k.2 tog., * p.6, y.o.n., k.2 tog. Rep. from * to last 7 sts., p.4, k.3.

Now work 6 rows g.st., ending with a row on the right side.

Next row: K.3, p. to last 3 sts., k.3.

Continue in st.st. with border of 3 sts. at each end in g.st., until work measures $4\frac{1}{4}$ [$4\frac{1}{2}$] inches from beg.

Cast off the 3 border sts. at beg. of next 2 rows. 66 [74] sts. Continue in st.st. until work measures $4\frac{3}{4}$ [$5\frac{1}{4}$] inches, ending with a p. row.

Shape Top

1st row: K.4, k.2 tog., * k.6, k.2 tog. Rep. from * to last 4 sts., k.4. 58 [65] sts.

2nd and every alternate row: Knit.

3rd row: K.4, k.2 tog., * k.5, k.2 tog. Rep. from * to last 3 sts., k.3. 50 [56] sts.

5th row: K.3, k.2 tog., * k.4, k.2 tog. Rep. from * to last 3 sts., k.3. 42 [47] sts.

7th row: * K.3, k.2 tog. Rep. from * to last 2 sts., k.2. 34 [38] sts.

9th row: * K.2, k.2 tog. Rep. from * to last 2 sts., k.2. 26 [29] sts.

11th row: K.2, k.2 tog., * k.1, k.2 tog. Rep. from * to last st., k.1. 18 [20] sts.

K.2 tog. all across next row. 9 [10] sts. now remain.

Cut yarn, thread through sts., draw up and fasten off.

To Make Up. Join back seam to point where g.st. borders were cast off. Sew cast-off sts. of borders tog. Press lightly. Sew on ribbons.

THE LEGGINGS

The Right Leg. Using No. 10 needles cast on 53 [59] sts.

1st row: * K.1, p.1. Rep. from * to last st., k.1.

2nd row: K.2, * p.1, k.1. Rep. from * to last st., k.1.

Rep. these 2 rows. In next row make eyelet holes thus: Rib 1 [3], * y.f., k.2 tog., rib 2. Rep. from * to end. Rib 5 more rows.

Change to No. 7 needles and st.st.

Shape Back

1st row: K.5 [11], turn.

2nd and every alternate row: Sl.1, p. to end.

3rd row: K.13 [19], turn.

5th row: Inc. in 1st st., k.20 [26], turn.

Continue in this way, working 8 sts. more at every turn, and increasing at beg. of every 6th row (back edge), until all sts. are worked on to 1 needle.

Proceed on all sts., continuing to inc. at beg. of every 6th row until there are 62 [68] sts. Continue without shaping until shorter (front) edge measures 7 [$7\frac{1}{2}$] inches from eyelet holes, ending with a p. row.

Shape Crutch

1st row: Inc. in 1st st., k. to end.

2nd row: Inc. in 1st st., p. to last 2 sts., inc. in next st., p.1. Rep. last 2 rows until there are 71 [77] sts., then work 1st row again. 72 [78] sts. P.1 row.

** Shape Leg

Cast off 1 st. at beg. of next 2 rows. Dec. at both ends of next and every alternate row until 52 [58] sts. remain, then dec. at both ends of every 3rd row until 31 [35] sts. remain.

Continue without shaping until work is 8 [9] inches from beg. of leg shaping, measured on the straight, ending with a p. row.

Shape Ankle

Change to No. 10 needles. Work 4 rows k.1 p.1 rib, as given for waist ribbing. In next row make eyelet holes as before. Rib 3 more rows, decreasing at end of last row. 30 [34] sts.

Change to No. 7 needles. ***

Shape Instep

K.25 [28], turn. P.10, turn.

Work 12 [14] rows st.st. on these 10 sts., then dec. at beg. of next 6 rows. Break yarn.

With right side of work facing, k. up 12 [14] sts. along 1st side of instep, k. across the 4 toe sts., and k. up 12 [14] along 2nd side of instep, then k. remaining 5 [6] sts.

Next row: K. across all 48 [56] sts.

Change to No. 10 needles. Work 6 rows g.st.

Shape Sole

1st row: K.3 [4], k.2 tog. twice, k.6 [8], k.2 tog. twice, k.24 [28], k.2 tog. twice, k.3 [4].

2nd row: Knit.

3rd row: K.2 [3], k.2 tog. twice, k.4 [6], k.2 tog. twice, k.22 [26], k.2 tog. twice, k.2 [3].

4th row: Knit.

5th row: K.1 [2], k.2 tog. twice, k.2 [4], k.2 tog. twice, k.20 [24], k.2 tog. twice, k.1 [2].

Cast off remaining 30 [38] sts.

The Left Leg. Using No. 10 needles cast on 53 [59] sts. Work ribbing and eyelet holes as for Right Leg. Change to No. 7 needles and st.st.

Shape Back

1st row: Knit.

2nd row: P.5 [11], turn.

3rd row: Sl.1, k. to end.

4th row: P.13 [19], turn.

5th row: Sl.1, k. to last st., inc. in last st.

continued overleaf

continued from previous page

6th row: P.22 [28], turn.

Continue to work 8 sts. more at every turn, and inc. at end of every 6th row, until all sts. are worked on to 1 needle, there are 62 [68] sts., and shorter edge measures 7 [7½] inches from eyelet holes, ending with a p. row.

Shape Crutch

1st row: K. to last 2 sts., inc. in next st., k.1.

2nd row: Inc. in 1st st., p. to last 2 sts., inc. in next st., p.1. Rep. last 2 rows until there are 71 [77] sts., then work 1st row again. P.1 row.

Work as Right Leg from ** to ***.

Shape Instep

K.15 [16], turn. P.10, turn. Work 12 [14] rows st.st. on these 10 sts., then dec. at beg. of next 6 rows. Break yarn.

With right side of work facing, k. up 12 [14] sts. along 1st side of instep, k. across the 4 toe sts., and k. up 12 [14] along 2nd side of instep, then k. remaining 15 [18] sts.

Next row: K. across all 48 [56] sts.

Change to No. 10 needles. Work 6 rows g.st.

Shape Sole

1st row: K.3 [4], k.2 tog. twice, k.24 [28], k.2 tog. twice, k.6 [8], k.2 tog. twice, k.3 [4].

2nd row: Knit.

3rd row: K.2 [3], k.2 tog. twice, k.22 [26], k.2 tog. twice, k.4 [6], k.2 tog. twice, k.2 [3].

4th row: Knit.

5th row: K.1 [2], k.2 tog. twice, k.20 [24], k.2 tog. twice, k.2 [4], k.2 tog. twice, k.1 [2].

Cast off.

To Make Up. Join front, back and leg seams. Join foot seams from centre of toe to centre of heel. Press lightly. Make twisted cords and thread through eyelet holes at waist and ankles.

HOODED JACKET AND BOOTEES

Materials. 7 [8] ozs. of Ladybird Baby Quick-Knit Super Bri-Nylon. 3 No. 8 knitting needles. 3 buttons.

Measurements. Jacket: To fit 17 [19] inch chest. Length from shoulder, 10½ [11] inches. Sleeve seam, 5½ [6] inches.

Hood: Round face, 14 [15] inches.

Bootees: Foot length, 3½ [4] inches.

Tension 6 stitches to 1 inch.

Abbreviations. K. knit, p. purl, st(s) stitch(es), st.st. stocking stitch, tog. together, dec. decrease by working 2 stitches together, inc. increase by working twice into 1 stitch, y.f. yarn forward, rep. repeat, patt. pattern, beg. beginning.

Note—*Instructions are given for the small size. Figures in brackets are for the larger size. Where one figure only is given, this refers to both sizes.*

THE JACKET

The Back and Front (Worked in one piece to underarm). Cast on 122 [134] sts. K.2 rows. Begin pattern:-

1st row: K.1, * y.f., k.3, slip the 1st of these 3 sts. over remaining 2, rep. from * to last st., k.1.

2nd row: K.1, purl to last st., k.1.

3rd row: * K.3, slip the 1st of these 3 sts. over remaining 2, y.f., rep. from * to last 2 sts., k.2.

4th row: As 2nd row.

5th to 8th rows: As 1st to 4th rows.

9th and 10th rows: As 2nd row.

11th to 16th rows: Work in st.st., beg. and ending wrong side rows with k.1.

17th and 18th rows: As 2nd row.

These 18 rows form the patt. Rep. them twice more, then work 1st 9 rows again.

Divide Stitches

Next row: (Wrong side), k.1, p.25 [28]. These sts. are for Left Front. Cast off 8 sts., 1 st. being on right hand needle after casting off. P.53 [59] more, making 54 [60] sts. for Back. Cast off 8 sts., 1 st. now being on right hand needle, p.24 [27], k.1. Leave sts. on a spare needle.

The Sleeves (both alike). Cast on 33 [36] sts. Work 8 [12] rows st.st., increasing at both ends of last row.

* Work the 18 patt. rows, increasing at both ends of 9th, 13th and 17th rows. Rep. from *, 47 [50] sts. Work 1st 8 patt. rows. Now p.2 rows, casting off 3 sts. at beg. of each row. Leave remaining 41 [44] sts. on a spare needle.

The Yoke. With right side of work facing, rejoin yarn at right front edge and knit across sts. of Right Front, Sleeve, Back, 2nd Sleeve and Left Front. 18 [206] sts.

Beg. with a purl row, work 4 rows st.st.

Next row: P.13 [6], * p.2 tog., p.3 [4]. Rep. from * until 10 [2] sts. remain, p.10 [2]. 155 [173] sts.

Work 17th and 18th patt. rows, then 1st to 9th rows.

Next row: P.13 [6], * p.2 tog., p.2 [3]. Rep. from * until 10 [2] sts. remain, p.10 [2]. 122 [140] sts.

Work 11th to 15th patt. rows.

Next row: P.8 [6], * p.2 tog., p.2 [4]. Rep. from * until 6 [2] sts. remain, p.6 [2]. 95 [118] sts.

Work 17th and 18th patt. rows, then 1st to 9th rows.

Next row: P.8 [6], * p.2 tog., p.1 [3]. Rep. from * until

6 [2] sts. remain, p.6 [2]. 68 [96] sts.

Larger size only

Work 3 rows st.st., then dec. on next row thus: p.5, * p.2 tog., p.2. Rep. from * until 3 sts. remain, p.3. 74 sts.

Both sizes

Work 2 rows st.st.

Proceed for Hood

Continue on 68 [74] sts. Rep. the 1st 4 patt. rows for 6 [6½] inches. Cast off 24 [27] sts. at beg. of next 2 rows. Work 4 [4½] inches on remaining 20 sts. Cast off.

The Front Border. Join side edges of centre piece of hood to cast-off sts. each side. Using 3 needles for easy working, with right side of work facing, knit up 63 [66] sts. along right front edge as far as neck, 92 [98] sts. round face edge of Hood and 63 [66] sts. along left front edge. K.1 row. Work 1st 10 patt. rows as given for main part of Jacket. Cast off purlwise.

To Make Up. Join sleeve seams. Set sleeves into armholes below yoke. Turn 4 rows on lower edges of sleeves to wrong side, and hem. Press work lightly with a cool iron.

Make twisted cord about 30 inches long with wool (see *Cord,* page 29), and thread through holes in patt. ½ inch above base of Hood. Sew 3 evenly-spaced buttons to left front border, using holes in patt. as buttonholes.

THE BOOTEES
(Work both alike)

Cast on 32 [38] sts. K.2 rows. Work the 1st 4 patt. rows as given for Jacket, then work 1st and 2nd rows again. P.2 rows. Work 4 rows st.st. P.2 rows. Work 1st 4 patt. rows, then 1st and 2nd rows again.

Shape Instep

P.12 [14], k.8 [10], turn, leaving 12 [14] sts. unworked. Beg. with a purl row, work 15 rows st.st. on central 8 [10] sts. Break yarn.

With 12 [14] sts. on right hand needle, pick up and p.12 sts. from 1st side of instep, purl central 8 [10] sts., pick up and p.12 sts. from 2nd side of instep and purl remaining 12 [14] sts. 56 [62] sts. P.1 row.

Now rep. 1st to 4th patt. rows twice. P.2 rows, casting off 24 [26] sts. at beg. of each row.

Work Sole

Work 28 [32] rows st.st. on remaining 8 [10] sts. Cast off.

To Make Up. Join back seam. Join edges of sole to cast-off sts. each side. Press. Make twisted cords, each 15 inches long, and thread through holes in patt. at ankles.

girl's machine-knit cardigan in 3 sizes

The cardigan is photographed in colour on page 51 and is ideal for school during the colder weather

Materials. 10 [11] [12] ozs. Sirdar Double Crepe Wool, or 11 [12] [13] ozs. Sirdar Double Knitting Wool, or 10 [11] [12] ozs. Sirdar Super Nylon Double Knitting. 5 [5] [5] Buttons.

Measurements. Width all round at underarm—29 [31] [33] inches. Length from top of shoulder—17½ [18] [18½] inches. Length of sleeve seam—16½ [17] [17½] inches.

Tension. This paragraph is most important—read it carefully before starting your garment.

To obtain the correct measurements it is essential that you work to the correct tension.

We suggest you work a small sample in the stitch before
continued overleaf

continued from previous page

starting your garments. It is advisable to remove the sample from the machine and as most machines stretch the fabric slightly, leave for a few hours before measuring when the fabric will have returned to the normal tension.

Tension 6 stitches to one inch measured over the stocking stitch worked on every alternate needle. The ribbed welts are worked at 2 tension settings tighter than the stocking stitch.

Abbreviations. K. knit, p. purl, beg. beginning, st(s) stitch(es), st.st. stocking stitch, w.p. working position.

Note—*This pattern is only suitable for machines with* 174 *needles or more.*

Note—*For the 9 year size read the instructions as given. For larger sizes read the figures within the brackets, in size order.*

The Back. Cast on 87 [93] [99] sts. on every alternate needle.
Tension setting for ribbing.
1st row: Knit in k.1, p.1 rib.
Repeat the 1st row 23 times.
Change to tension setting for st.st.
1st row: Knit.
2nd row: Knit.
Continue knitting in st.st. without shaping until the work measures 9½ [10] [10½] inches from the beginning, ending with the wool at the right hand side.

Shape Armholes
Cast off 6 [6] [6] sts. at the beg. of each of the next 2 rows.

For the 9 and 11 year sizes only
1st row: Decrease 1 st. at each end of the row, by placing the 3rd st. on to the 4th needle at each end (2 sts. now on the 4th needle), then the 2nd st. on to the 3rd needle and the 1st st. on to the 2nd needle. Knit the row. (All the decreasings worked at the armhole shapings should be worked in this manner).
2nd row: Knit.
3rd row: Knit.
4th row: Knit.
Repeat from the 1st to the 4th row (inclusive) 3 [1] times.

For all 3 sizes
Repeat the 1st and 2nd rows 24 [28] [32] times then the 1st row once.
Cast off the remaining 17 [19] [21] sts.

The Left Front. Cast on 39 [43] [45] sts. on every alternate needle.
Tension setting for ribbing.
1st row: Knit in k.1, p.1 rib.
Repeat the 1st row 23 times, increasing 1 st. at the beg. of the last row for the 9 and 13 year sizes **only.** 40 [43] [46] sts.
Change to tension setting for st.st.
1st row: Knit.
2nd row: Knit.
Continue knitting in st.st. without shaping until the work measures 9½ [10] [10½] inches from the beginning, ending with the wool at the left hand side.

Shape Armhole
1st row: Cast off 6 [6] [6] sts. at the beg. of the row. Knit.

For the 9 and 11 year sizes only
2nd row: Decrease 1 st. (as given for the Back) at the armhole edge. Knit.
3rd row: Knit.
4th row: Knit.
5th row: Knit.
Knit 12 [4] rows decreasing 1 st. (as before) at the armhole edge on the next and every following 4th row, at the same time decreasing 1 st. at the front edge on the next and every following 4th row. 27 [34] sts.

For the 13 year size only
2nd row: Decrease 1 st. (as given for the Back) at the armhole edge. Knit.
3rd row: Knit.
Repeat the 2nd and 3rd rows once.

For all 3 sizes
Knit 13 [25] [33] rows decreasing 1 st. (as before) at the armhole edge on the next and every alternate row, at the same time decreasing 1 st. at the front edge on the next and every following 4th row. 16 [14] [12] sts.
Continue knitting, decreasing 1 st. (as before) on the 2nd and every alternate row until 1 st. remains.
Break off the wool and fasten off.

The Right Front. Cast-on 39 [43] [45] sts. on every alternate needle.
Tension setting for ribbing.
1st row: Knit in k.1, p.1 rib.
Repeat the 1st row 23 times, increasing 1 st. at the end of the last row for the 9 and 13 year sizes **only.** 40 [43] [46] sts.
Change to tension setting for st.st.
1st row: Knit.
2nd row: Knit.
Continue knitting in st.st. without shaping until the work measures 9½ [10] [10½] inches from the beginning, ending with the wool at the right hand side.

198

Shape Armhole

1st row: Cast off 6 [6] [6] sts. at the beg. of the row. Knit.

2nd row: Knit.

For the 9 and 11 year sizes only

3rd row: Decrease 1 st. (as given for the Back) at the armhole edge. Knit.

4th row: Knit.

5th row: Knit.

6th row: Knit.

Knit 12 [4] rows decreasing 1 st. (as before) at the armhole edge on the next and every following 4th row, at the same time decreasing 1 st. at the front edge on the next and every following 4th row. 27 [34] sts.

For the 13 year size only

3rd row: Decrease 1 st. (as given for the Back) at the armhole edge. Knit.

4th row: Knit.

Repeat the 3rd and 4th rows once.

For all 3 sizes

Knit 13 [25] [33] rows decreasing 1 st. (as before) at the armhole edge on the next and every alternate row, at the same time decreasing 1 st. at the front edge on the next and every following 4th row. 16 [14] [12] sts.

Continue knitting decreasing 1 st. (as before) on the 2nd and every alternate row until 1 st. remains.

Break off the wool and fasten off.

The Sleeves.

The Left Sleeve. Cast on 39 [41] [43] sts. on every alternate needle.

Tension setting for ribbing.

1st row: Knit in k.1, p.1 rib.

Repeat the 1st row 23 times, increasing 1 st. at the end of the last row. 40 [42] [44] sts.

Change to tension setting for st.st.

1st row: Knit.

2nd row: Knit.

Repeat the 1st and 2nd rows twice.

Continue knitting, increasing 1 st. at each end of the next and every following 6th row until there are 66 [68] [70] sts.

Continue knitting without shaping until the work measures 16½ [17] [17½] inches from the beginning, ending with the wool at the right hand side.

Shape Top

Cast off 6 [6] [6] sts. at the beg. of each of the next 2 rows.

Proceed as follows:

1st row: Decrease 1 st. (as given for the Back) at each end of the row. Knit.

2nd row: Knit.

3rd row: Knit.

4th row: Knit.

Repeat from the 1st to the 4th row (inclusive) 6 [5] [4]

times, the 1st and 2nd rows 14 [16] [18] times, then the 1st row once. 10 [10] [10] sts. ***

Proceed as follows:

1st row: Knit.

2nd row: Cast off 5 sts. at the beg. of the row, decrease 1 st. (as before) at the left hand edge. Knit.

3rd row: Knit.

4th row: Decrease 1 st. at the neck edge. Knit.

Repeat the 3rd and 4th rows twice.

Break off the wool and fasten off.

The Right Sleeve. Cast on 39 [41] [43] sts. on every alternate needle.

Work exactly as given for the Left Sleeve until *** is reached.

Proceed as follows:

1st row: Cast off 5 sts. at the beg. of the row. Knit.

2nd row: Decrease 1 st. (as above) at the right hand edge. Knit.

3rd row: Knit.

4th row: Decrease 1 st. at the neck edge. Knit.

Repeat the 3rd and 4th rows twice.

Break off the wool and fasten off.

The Front Border. Cast on 11 sts. on every alternate needle.

Tension setting for ribbing.

1st row: Knit in k.1, p.1 rib.

Repeat the 1st row 3 times.

** **5th row:** Place a small piece of contrasting wool into the hooks of the 5th, 6th and 7th needles, working these needles by hand, knit in the contrasting wool (this marks the buttonhole); then using the original colour wool knit the row in k.1, p.1 rib.

Repeat the 1st row 17 [18] [19] times. **

Repeat from ** to ** 3 [3] [3] times, then the 5th row once.

Continue knitting in k.1, p.1 rib until the border is of sufficient length to go up the right front, across the back of the neck and down the left front.

Cast off.

To Make Up. Press each piece separately on the wrong side under a damp cloth with a warm iron. Sew up the side and sleeve seams. Placing seam to seam, sew the decreased edges of the sleeves to the decreased edges of the bodice.

Sew the pocket linings in position on the wrong side of the work, sew the pocket borders in position on the right side. Sew the front border in position, placing the top buttonhole level with the first front decreasing.

Gently pull out the contrasting wool marking the buttonhole and with a needle threaded with the main colour wool, run the wool through each of the open stitches then neatly buttonhole stitch round.

Sew on the buttons to correspond with the buttonholes.

Press all seams.

socks and stockings

These designs are intended to give a lot of hard wear and yet be comfortable and attractive. The ladies' stockings are particularly suitable for country wear

Materials. Robin Sportswear, Colorama or Service 4-ply.

Boys' Stockings. 4 [5] [5] ozs. Main Shade and oddment of Contrast Shade for stripes.

Men's Socks. 5 ozs.

Ladies' Stockings. 8 ozs.

1 pair No. 12 needles for Boys' Stockings.
1 set of 4 No. 13 needles for Men's Socks.
1 set of 4 No. 11 needles for Ladies' Stockings.
Stitch holders.
Cable needle for Men's Socks.

Measurements

Boys'. Length—15½ [16½] [17] inches, including turn over top. Foot—8 [9] [10] inches.

Men's. Length—12 inches. Foot—11 inches.

Ladies'. Length—27 inches (or required length). Foot—9 [9½] [10] inches.

Tension

Boys'. 17 stitches to 2 inches on No. 12 needles.

Men's. 9 stitches to 1 inch on No. 13 needles.

Ladies'. 17 stitches to 2 inches over pattern on No. 11 needles.

Abbreviations. K. knit, p. purl, st(s). stitch(es), ins. inches, tog. together, rep. repeat, inc. increasing, dec. decrease, sl. slip, beg. beginning, patt. pattern, M. Main shade, C. Contrast, t.b.l. through back of loop, p.s.s.o. pass slipped stitch over, tw.2 twist 2 (k.2 tog. but leave sts. on needle, k. into first st. again, then sl. both sts. off needle tog.), c.6 cable 6, slip the next 3 sts. on to a cable needle and leave at back of work, k. the next 3 sts., then k. sts. from cable needle.

Note—*Instructions for the larger sizes are in brackets in size order; where only one figure is given this applies to all sizes.*

BOYS' STOCKINGS

With No. 12 needles and M. cast on 72 sts. Work 6 rows k.1, p.1 rib.

★ Join in C., k. 1 row. Work 5 rows k.1, p.1 rib, leave C. With M. k. 1 row.

Work 5 rows k.1, p.1 rib.

Rep. from ★ once more. Break off C.

Work 15 rows k.1, p.1 rib.

Change to wide rib patt. as follows; work is now reversed.

1st row: (Right side) K.3, p.1, * k.4, p.1; rep. from * to last 3 sts., k.3.

2nd row: P.3, k.1, * p.4, k.1; rep. from * to last 3 sts., p.3.

These 2 rows form wide rib patt., rep. them until work measures 9 ins. from beg., ending with a wrong side row.

Begin Leg Shaping

Next row: K.1, k.2 tog. t.b.l., patt. to last 3 sts., k.2 tog., k.1.

Keeping rib correct and allowing for dec. sts., work 5 rows.

Rep. last 6 rows until 58 sts. remain.

Work straight until leg measures 15½ [16½] [17] ins. from beg., ending on a wrong side row.

Next row: Patt. 44, turn and leave remaining sts. on a holder.

Next row: Patt. 30, turn and leave remaining sts. on a holder.

Continue in patt. on remaining sts. until instep measures 5 [5½] [6] ins., ending on a wrong side row.

Shape Toe

Work in st.st. thus:

Next row: K.1, sl.1, k.1, p.s.s.o., k. to last 3 sts., k.2 tog., k.1.

Next row: P.

Rep. last 2 rows until 12 sts. remain. Leave sts. on holder.

Shape Heel

Place the 28 sts. from holders on to one needle with back edges of sock in centre of needle. Rejoin wool and work 26 rows st.st.

Turn Heel

1st row: K.18, k.2 tog., turn.

2nd row: P.9, p.2 tog., turn.

3rd row: K.9, k.2 tog., turn.

Continue dec. in this manner until all sts. are worked. 10 sts.

Next row: K.10, k. up 15 sts. from side of heel.

Next row: P.25, p. up 15 sts. from second side of heel.

Next row: K.1, sl.1, k.1, p.s.s.o., k. to last 3 sts., k.2 tog., k.1.

Next row: P.

Rep. last 2 rows until 28 sts. remain.

Continue in st.st. until foot measures same as instep to beg. of toe shaping, ending on a p. row.

Shape Toe

Work as instep toe shaping. Graft or cast off both sets of sts. tog.

Make a second stocking to match.

To Complete. Press lightly on wrong side, join leg and foot seams. Press all seams.

LADIES' STOCKINGS

With set of 4 No. 11 needles cast on 136 sts. loosely: 48 [40] [48] sts. on needles.

Work ¾ in. k.2, p.2 rib.

Next round : * Rib 6, rib 2 tog., rep. from * to end of round: 42 [35] [42] sts.

Begin Pattern

1st round: * K.3, p.1, k.2, p.1; rep. from * to end of round.

2nd round: * K.3, p.1, tw.2, p.1; rep. from * to end of round. Rep. last 2 rounds until leg measures 4 ins. from beg., ending on a 2nd round.

Next round: K.1, k.2 tog., p.1, k.2, p.1; rep. from * to end of round: 36 [30] [36] sts. on needles.

Next round: * K.2, p.1, tw.2, p.1; rep. from * to end of round.

Next round: * K.2, p.1; rep. from * to end of round.

Rep. the last 2 rounds until leg measures 13½ ins. from beg., ending on a twist patt. round.

Next round: K.2 tog., patt. to last 3 sts., k.2 tog. t.b.l., k.1.

Work 3 rounds.

Rep. the last 4 rounds until 60 sts. remain.

Work without further dec. until leg measures 27 ins. or required length to heel.

Divide for Heel

K.15, sl. the 15 sts. from 3rd needle on to end of these sts.: 30 sts.

Divide the remaining sts. on to 2 needles and leave for instep.

Heel

Working in rows, work 2¼ ins. st.st., beg. and ending on a p. row.

Turn Heel

Next row: K.18, sl.1, k.1, p.s.s.o., turn, p.7, p.2 tog., turn.

continued overleaf

continued from previous page

Next row: K.8, sl.1, k.1, p.s.s.o., turn, p.9, p.2 tog., turn.

Continue in this manner until all sts. are worked on to one needle again: 18 sts.

Sl. all instep sts. on to one needle.

Next round: K.9, using the spare needle k. the remaining 9 sts. from heel, then k. up 18 sts. from side of heel, using 2nd needle patt. across 30 instep sts., using 3rd needle k. up 18 sts. from 2nd side of heel, then k.9 heel sts.: 84 sts.

Shape Instep
1st round
1st needle: K.
2nd needle: Patt.
3rd needle: K.
2nd round
1st needle: K. to last 3 sts., k.2 tog., k.1.
2nd needle: Work in patt.
3rd needle: K.1, k.2 tog. t.b.l., k. to end.
Rep the last 2 rounds until 60 sts. remain.
Continue without further dec. until foot measures 6¾ [7¼] [7¾] ins. from heel.

Shape Toe
Worked in st.st. throughout.
1st round
1st needle: K. to last 3 sts., k.2 tog., k.1.
2nd needle: K.1, k.2 tog. t.b.l., k. to last 3 sts., k.2 tog., k.1.
3rd needle: K.1, k.2 tog. t.b.l., k. to end.
2nd round: K.
Rep. the last 2 rounds until 24 sts. remain.
K. sts. from first needle on to end of third needle.
Graft or cast off sts. from both needles together.
Work another stocking in the same manner.
Press very lightly on wrong side.

MEN'S SOCKS
With the set of 4 No. 13 needles cast on 84 sts. (28 sts. on each of 3 needles).
Work 3½ ins., k.2, p.2 rib.
Change to st.st. with cable panels as follows:-

1st round
1st needle: K.18, p.2, k.6, p.2.
2nd needle: K.26, p.2.
3rd needle: K.6, p.2, k.20.
Rep. this round twice more.
4th round: K.18, p.2, c.6, p.2, k.26, p.2, c.6, p.2, k.20.

Rep. 1st round 4 times more.
Rep. these 8 rounds until leg measures 7 ins. from beg.

Shape Leg
Next round: K.1, k.2 tog., work to last 3 sts. of 3rd needle, sl.1, k.1, p.s.s.o., k.1.
Keeping cable panels correct work 4 rounds.
Rep. the last 5 rounds 3 times more: 76 sts.
Continue without further shaping until leg measures 12 ins., cable panels are now complete.

Divide for Heel
Sl. last 20 sts. from 3rd needle on to 4th needle and on to same needle k. first 18 sts. from first needle.
Arrange the remaining 38 sts. on 2 needles and leave for instep.

The Heel
1st row: * Sl.1, p.1, rep. from * to end.
2nd row: K.
Rep. these 2 rows 14 times.

Turn Heel
Next row: P.21, p.2 tog., p.1, turn, k.6, k.2 tog, k.1, turn.
Next row: P.7, p.2 tog., p.1, turn, k.8, k.2 tog, k.1, turn.
Next row: P.9, p.2 tog., p.1, turn, k.10, k.2 tog, k.1, turn.
Continue in this manner until all sts. are worked: 22 sts.
Now k. up 16 sts. from side of heel, k. the 38 sts. for instep on to one needle, k. up 16 sts. from second side of heel on to this needle, k.11 sts. from heel: 27, 38, 27, sts. on needles, k.27.

Shape Instep
1st round: K.
2nd round
1st needle: K.38.
2nd needle: K.1, sl.1, k.1, p.s.s.o., k. to end.
3rd needle: K. to last 3 sts., k.2 tog., k.1.
Rep. last 2 rounds until 72 sts. remain.
Work straight until foot measures 9½ ins. from back of heel.
Sl.1 st. from each end of 1st needle on to 2nd and 3rd needles: 36 [18] [18] sts. on needle.

Shape Toe
1st needle: K.1, k.2 tog., k. to last 3 sts., sl.1, k.1, p.s.s.o., k.1.
2nd needle: K.1, k.2 tog., k. to end.
3rd needle: K. to last 3 sts., sl.1, k.1, p.s.s.o., k.1.
Next round: K.
Rep. these 2 rounds until 24 sts. remain, graft or cast off sts. tog.
Work a second sock to match. Press lightly on wrong side.

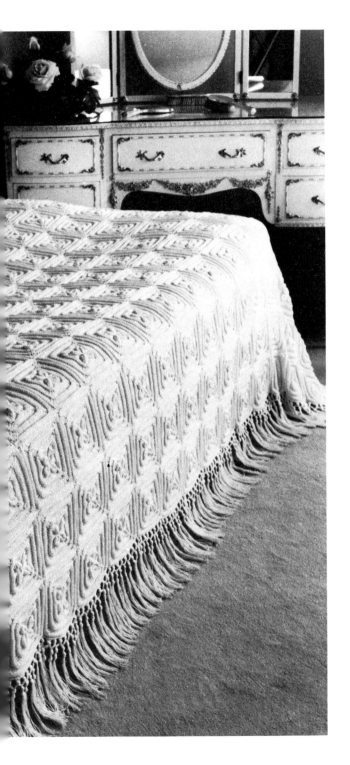

knit a cotton bedspread

A beautiful bedspread knitted in squares then the cast off edge is drawn up to form a flower effect. It can be made to fit any size of bed

Materials. Coats Mercer Crochet No. 5. 1 ball will make 1 square (the small quantity remaining can be used for the optional fringe). 5 No. 12 double pointed needles. A medium size Crochet Hook (for fringe).

Measurement. Each square measures $4\frac{1}{2}$ inches.

Tension 7 stitches to 1 inch.

Abbreviations. K. knit, p. purl, st(s). stitch(es), patt. pattern, sl. slip, p.s.s.o. pass slipped stitch over, tog. together, rep. repeat, ins. inches.

To Make a Square

Cast on 32 sts. on to each of 4 needles.

1st round: Knit taking care not to twist sts.

2nd round: Knit.

3rd round: (K.1, sl.1, k.1, p.s.s.o., k. to last 3 sts. on needle, k.2 tog., k.1) 4 times.

* 4th to 7th rounds: Purl.

Rep. 2nd and 3rd rounds 3 times. Rep. from * twice.

P. 4 rounds. Cast off, leaving approx. 10 in. of cotton. Thread needle and draw centre of each "side" to middle of square, forming a flower patt. Join squares.

The Fringe (optional): Cut 20 in. strands. Using crochet hook, knot 2 strands through every st. along edge. Knot 4 groups tog. $\frac{1}{2}$ in. below. Now take $\frac{1}{2}$ of one group tog. with half of next group and knot tog. $\frac{1}{2}$ in. below, then knot same groups tog. again, $\frac{1}{2}$ in. below.

203

Index